An IMAAG Publication
First Edition

Maritime Anti-Piracy

The Captain's Guidebook

Peter King

Former UK Maritime Special Forces - SBS

Published by IMAAG Publishing

First printed 2012 ISBN 978-0-9583028-0-7

MARITIME

ANTI-PIRACY

THE CAPTAIN'S GUIDEBOOK

FIRST EDITION 2012

A Captain's guide to help protect a vessel and crew, from the smallest of sailing yachts to the largest of commercial ships, against common thieves and organised pirates, both underway and at anchor in all parts of the world.

PUBLISHED BY IMAAG

First printed 2012   ISBN 978-0-9583028-0-7

WITH RESPECT TO THE IMO, ICC-IMB, UKMTO, OCIMF AND MSCHOA, FOR ALL THEIR EFFORTS TO COMBAT PIRACY AND ROBBERY AT SEA

This book is dedicated to:

Joanne Armstrong **A loving sister**

Anton Turner **A man amongst men**

Richard Van der Horst OBE **A friend and former CO SBS**

Orlando Rogers **Friend, Co-Founder and Director of Solace Global Maritime Services**

PREFACE

ABOUT THIS GUIDEBOOK

The author, Peter King was a specialist in maritime counter terrorism within the UK's Special Forces: The Special Boat Service. After leaving he worked for many on the UK's leading security companies and a security consultant specialising in the maritime field and worked internationally both on and off the seas for companies such as Saudi Aramco: the world's largest oil and gas company.

From 2007 onwards, Peter found himself being asked more frequently to help deliver sailing yachts though hostile waters including South America, West Africa and the Gulf of Aden. Being a qualified skipper he took to the job well, but was shocked when he realised the complete lack of a decent handbook for sailors to turn to. After buying the guide "Pirates & armed robbers" for a sum of £20 and realising it was not sufficient, had the idea of creating a simple A5 booklet, (similar to the excellent RYA booklets) to help sailing vessels when transiting or on vacation in high-risk areas of the world.

During his time off watches, he started to write "Maritime Anti-piracy, A Captain's Guidebook" that was back in 2008. This version of the book you are reading now is the 8th edition. The first seven were never made publically available; in hindsight he should have done so, and created a new edition each year. Working alongside fellow maritime security personnel, Captains of sailing and super yachts, as well as commercial ships, material, feedback and suggestions have all helped in making this book as professional as possible.

Not all of the material is the author's, and where possible extreme gratitude has been expressed to those who contributed, an example of which is the information given by Captain P Mukundan of the ICC IMB and PRC. Many photographs have been taken by Peter, others given and some from public source websites. Every effort has been made to ensure that these photographs and other information are not copyrighted and where it is, permission has been granted to reproduce it. This book is aimed at helping seamen and mariners of all creeds, sex and colour when at sea, if any profit is made, a percentage will be donated to Help for Heroes and the Special Boat Service charities.

For a former member of the UK Special Forces, one has to gain permission to print from the UKSF Disclosure Office, London. This was approved in 2011 after certain photographs and information were removed. The author has deliberately removed sensitive material too, that would indeed help thieves and pirates if and when they read this book. The maritime industry has since released BMP 3 & 4, both excellent, free guides to help commercial shipping in the Somali pirate high-risk area. This guide is not to replace or compete with that booklet, but unlike the booklet covers **all** vessels, for **all** areas of the world, **at anchor and underway**. It covers products and counter-measures that do work and advice on armed security of which many still disagree with.

Hopefully this will become a default book on private yachts and commercial ships in the years to come, with updated and better editions being available in the future as circumstances, laws and tactics change. It will not be available electronically. It is recommended that a copy is available of the bridge and another kept in the ship's citadel. Any feedback, comments, and suggestions will be warmly welcomed; a product can only be improved upon if feedback is given and acted upon.

Peter King
Director IMAAG
International Maritime
Anti-Piracy Advisory
Group

The International Maritime Anti-Piracy Advisory Group

IMAAG

Who we are: Directed by Peter King with a group of consultants specialising in maritime security, whether it be in the hydro-carbon industry, littoral asset protection, offshore asset protection, anti-piracy, training and advisory services.

Where: Currently the company headquarters are located in Gibraltar.

Primary services: IMAAG is not a security company; it's an advisory company that can give the best advice from security experts first hand. The company can offer advice, consultation, and training to the largest of shipping companies or to a small family planning to sail on their beloved yacht around the Maldives.

Why IMAAG? At present there are so-called maritime security companies appearing each week across the world; some are good, others average and a few are just out to make quick profits from the window of opportunity that has arisen with the problem caused exclusively by the Somali pirates. Anyone can put on a suit and have a handful of eye-catching business cards and quote directly from the handbook BMP4 giving the impression of professionalism.
We assure the client the very best consultation. Each of our hand picked consultants can deliver advice with personal knowledge in their own field, recommending the best products available, how to save money in a time of global financial crisis and to ensure quality control. If we are given a problem or subject in an area that we do not cover, we do not pursue the contract but recommend to the client which company may be able to assist them.

Languages: At IMAAG we speak English, Spanish and German.

Shipping companies: The Company Security Officer may have a large fleet of commercial ships to protect when they transport their goods through the high-risk areas of the world. It is never easy to know which anti-boarding products to buy; which are the safest passage plans to use; whether to sail through the IRTC with the 18kt convoy, or steam solo at full speed 22kts? There are a hundred new private maritime security companies (PMSCs) to choose from, but which are the better ones and which should be avoided? IMAAG can give you honest unaffiliated advice when it comes to deciding.

Privately Contracted Armed Security Personnel: IMAAG can give you recommendations of which qualifications you need, where to train and which PMSC companies are worth approaching. The difference in contracts is enormous; some companies have bad reputations and some very good.

Oil and Gas Industry: Having worked for the largest oil & gas companies in the world, IMAAG can give clear, concise consultation of how to best protect your facilities both onshore and offshore as well as vulnerable assets including the safekeeping of the staff and their families.

Super yacht management: Most aspects of BMP4 cannot be applied to superyachts, therefore careful planning, training and preparation needs to be done before the vessels makes its voyage from one hemisphere to the other, usually via the Gulf of Aden. IMAAG have been working very closely with the superyacht industry and understand the Captain and Owner's needs regarding to the safe delivery of safe vacation with hazardous waters.

Fishing Industry: Some national fishing fleets are prone to hijacking during their long periods at sea. The Spanish Tuna fleet operating in the Indian Ocean would be a well-known example of such. IMAAG can give consultation to such fleet managers on the best and most cost effective way to protect the vessel, crew, and cargo from such risks.

Television, filmmakers, and media: Whether it be information on how a Somali pirate boards a vessel, or actually physically climbing from a small speedboat on to a ship underway at full speed, IMAAG can offer this. IMAAG's consultants each have a background in maritime Special Forces and have a plethora of such skills. The media quite often get misinformed about certain subjects; IMAAG can give clear guidance on the modus operandi of thieves and pirates around the globe.

Equipment specialists: Before buying the wrong item or the wrong quantity, IMAAG can give you the correct advice on what you really need for you vessel type. Shipping agents add large profit margins onto the real value of products. By contacting us first and pre-arranging the delivery you could save the company money.

Private Maritime Security Companies: IMAAG can offer advice on how to set up your new company: which equipment to buy, from where, at the best price. Which training facilities to use and the production of documentation. The staff at IMAAG are extremely well vetted, all having UK CRB, Disclosure and in some cases DV clearances. We are extremely discreet with information fro our clients and any information we give out will come from us, not 'copy and pasted' from another company. Quality control: IMAAG can offer quality control to the Vessel Protection Team or group briefings to the Team Leaders. Training, there are market-leading companies out there that can offer packages to the team members and to the team leaders. This will probably become compulsory in the future; IMAAG knows which are the best training providers.

Associated companies: Having worked for and with other leading companies in the past, IMAAG can recommend whom to consider when wanting specialist services. For example, when your superyacht arrives in St. Tropez, they can pre-book the VIP suite in Cave de Roi and covertly bodyguard the guests to and from the venue.

Feedback

Products can only be improved by feedback and IMAAG will strive to make this publication as perfect as possible. As time moves on the book must be updated with a new edition. If the reader has any feedback please email us; we will address your comments as soon as we can.

Similarly any queries such as bulk orders, change of language or advertisement of products, services or otherwise please contact the office on the below email address.

Website: www.imaag.co.uk

Email: info@imaag.co.uk

IMAAG

INTERNATIONAL MARITIME ANTI-PIRACY ADVISORY GROUP

MARITIME ACRONYMS & ABBREVIATIONS

- **AIS**- Automated Identification System
- **ASAP**-As Soon As Possible
- **BeM or BaM**-Bab el Mandeb (the choke point at the southernmost part of the Red Sea)
- **BMPs**-Best Management Practices
- **CG**- Contracting Government, includes reference to the Designated Authority
- **CSO**-Company Security Officer
- **CSR**-Continuous Synopsis Record
- **DA**-Designated Authority. Organisation or administrations identified within CG responsible for ensuring the implementation of the provisions of Chap X1-2 pertaining to PF security and ship/port interface from the point of view of the port.
- **DOS**- Declaration of Security. An agreement between port and ship or another ship, specifying the security measures each will implement.
- **DRA**-Designated Restricted Area
- **ETA**-Expected Time of Arrival
- **ERV**-Emergency Rendezvous Point
- **Flag State**-County of which the ship is registered
- **GoA** Gulf of Aden
- **GMDSS**-Global Maritime Distress and Safety System
- **HRA**-High Risk Area (the area of operations as used by Somali pirates)
- **IMB**-International Maritime Bureau
- **IMO**-International Maritime Organisation
- **IRTC**- Internationally Recommended Transit Corridor
- **ISM**-International Safety Management Code 2002
- **ISPS**-International Ship and Port Facility Code and SOLAS amendments 2002
- **ISSC**-International Ship Security Certificate
- **MCA**-Maritime Coastguard Agency
- **MTSA**-(American) Maritime Transport Security Act
- **PAG**-Pirate Attack Group (Normally small mothership and skiffs)
- **PF**-Port Facility Engaged in International Trade
- **PFSO**-Port Facility Security Officer
- **PFSA**-Port Facility Security Assessment

- **PFSP**-Port Facility Security Plan
- **POA**-Point of Aim (weapons)
- **Port State**-Country where ships call
- **PSC**-Port State Control
- **RSO**-Recognized Security Organisation
- **RV**-Rendezvous Point
- **SCEG**- The Security in Complex Environments Group
- **SSA**-Security Assessment Audit
- **SOPs**-Standard Operating Procedures
- **STCW-95**-Standards of Training, Certification and Watchkeeping for seafarers
- **Security level 1**-The level of which the minimum appropriate protective security measures shall be maintained at all times.
- **Security level 2**- The level of which appropriate additional protective security measures shall be maintained at all times.
- **Security Level 3**-The level for which further specific protective security measures shall be maintained for a limited period of time when a security incident is probable or imminent, although it may not be possible to identify the specific target.
- **SOLAS**-Safety of Life at Sea Convention
- **SoC**-Statement of Compliance (ports)
- **SSO**-Ship's Security Officer
- **SSA**-Ship's Security Assessment
- **SSP**-Ship's Security Plan
- **SSAS**-Ships Security Alert System
- **TRANSEC**- The Transport Security and Contingency Directorate of the Department of transport

Acknowledgements

The author would like to express his gratitude to the following that have helped in the making of this book, among them:

Admiral The Lord Boyce GCB OBE DL	**Member of the Houses of Parliament**
Capt. Pottengal Mukundan	**Director ICC- IMB London**
Keith Simpson MBE	**Ironside Associates**
Capt. Ben Marshall and crew	**SY Red Dragon**
Rachel Hagan & Joel Dowling	**Editors**
Jamie Courtenay Grimwood	**Upstanding Englishman**
Ian Drury	**Sheil Land Associates**
George Whitmarsh MBE	**Security Expert & Good Friend**
Pete & Celine Murphy	**Air Partner**
Russell Corn	**Fulcrum Chambers LLP**
John Lowe	**ESP Group**
Carl Sykes	**Neptune Maritime Security**
Dave Buston	**Trident Operations**
Angela Sargent	**EuropeAxess Media**
Michael Rossmeier	**Trickionary**
Susi, Sol and Luna	**For all their support & patience.**
All at	**International Maritime Anti-piracy Advisory Group (IMAAG)**

Foreword by

Admiral The Lord Boyce GCB OBE DL

As is well known and described in this guidebook, piracy is on the increase - not just off Somalia but in other oceans of the world. The oft-given official response to this problem is that it must be addressed by tackling the root of the cause, which invariably lies ashore in the failed or failing state spawning and harbouring the pirates.

However, correct though this may be, the pace at which the UN will bring this about will be extremely slow and it may take years rather than months for any tangible progress to be made; and meanwhile ships and vessels will continue to be attacked. It thus behoves ship owners and mariners who have to pass through choke points and similar areas where potential danger lies to take sensible precautions.

There is a wealth of information to guide them through this, but where to start - beginning with a sound understanding of the problem – is a challenge; and it is here that this guidebook will prove its worth. Written in an easy-to-read style- reminiscent of a mariners' 'Pilot' – it provides useful background on the piracy situation and methodology, and many practical, tried and tested ideas and solutions for protection as well as pointers for those who want to develop deeper understanding of the subject or who want third party support.

The guidebook is written by a subject-matter expert who has serious practical knowledge and experience of global maritime security and it should be a required read for anyone holding responsibility for the safe passage, working operations or vacations in high-risk areas and troubled waters.

For Judith, Roger, Susi, Sol & Luna.

Thank you for everything.

CONTENTS

Introduction

This up-to-date book is designed to give clear practical guidelines as how to prevent unauthorised boarding of all types of vessels both at anchor and underway. It is a thorough guide to help shipping companies, Captains and crew, from the smallest of private sailing yachts to the largest of ships from being hijacked, raided or boarded. It deals in the main with the Somali pirates and waters they operate in, but applies to all other high-risk areas of the world. This guide was started in 2008 and has expanded and been updated over the last four years, it is not to compete with, copied from, or to replace the excellent Best Management Practices 4 (BMP4), but gives very detailed information as how to best defend one's self when at sea, including the controversial use of private armed security guards.

Piracy is on the increase. The International Maritime Bureau (IMB) had only two reported incidents of piracy in the Gulf of Aden (GoA) in 2004, whereas in 2009 the total number of incidents attributed to the Somali pirates was 217, with 47 vessels hijacked and 867 crewmembers taken hostage. During 2010 there were 445 global attacks, a 10% increase from 2009; Somali pirates captured a record 49 ships and this dropped to 31 ships in 2011 but with a huge number of failed attempts.

The level of violence towards the crew has increased, along with the number of crew injuries, torture and mock executions. With huge ransoms being paid to release crews and vessels, this lucrative kidnap and ransom business may well tempt criminals to do the same in other lawless areas such as the Gulf of Guinea and the West African coastline.

The information given in this book derives mainly from first-hand, personal, practical experiences of the author, who has been working in a military and private maritime security environment since 1986. Additional information has been gleaned from working with international leaders of this maritime field. Statistical information is derived with thanks to the ICC IMB PRC and other public information sources of which the author is extremely grateful for.

Personal experience, agency guidelines, recommendations, and post-attack reports have all been taken into consideration when producing this Captain's guidebook. Some products have been recommended not because of financial gain or affiliation, but to help the reader to buy the best equipment rather than spending hours and days researching various items or, worse still, buying the wrong item.

Having served a career in maritime special forces (SBS), and the last seven years protecting yachts and commercial ships (unarmed and armed) the author is well-practised in techniques as used by waterborne criminals; the counter measures that do work and knows intimately how to prevent and deny both simple and complex boarding methods, and is therefore highly qualified to convey how to make a situation, crew and vessel as safe as possible against such incidents.

It is presumed that this book will at some point fall into the wrong hands, therefore not all of the information available is published, as this would make the lives of thieves and pirates far too easy and make the passages of vessels all the more hazardous and susceptible to illegal boarding. It is recommended that the author be contacted via the International Maritime Anti-piracy Advisory Group (IMAAG) so that, all sensitive information can be passed over, with the reassuring knowledge that the shipping company, Captain and crew will have the best advice, training and updates available for the area of transit or vacation. To arrange a pre-deployment package, contact: info@imaag.co.uk .

1. A Brief History Of Modern Piracy

Definition

Maritime piracy, according to the United Nations Convention on the Law of the Sea (UNCLOS) of 1982, consists of any criminal act of violence, detention or depredation committed for private ends by the crew or the passengers of a private ship or aircraft that is directed on the high seas against another ship, aircraft, or against persons or property on board a ship or aircraft. Piracy can also be committed against a ship, aircraft, persons, or property in a place outside the jurisdiction of any state. Despite the fact that piracy was the first example of universal jurisdiction, the international community is still facing many problems in bringing pirates to justice.

Piracy dates back beyond the 13th Century BC; throughout history there have been references to different types of pirate: Suetonius relates that Julius Caesar spent months as a prisoner aboard a Corsair Ship in the Mediterranean. Privateers or corsairs used similar methods to a pirate, but acted while in possession of a commission or letter of marque from a government or monarch that authorised the capture of merchant ships belonging to an enemy nation. Perhaps Britain's most famous mariner Sir Francis Drake was just such a glorified pirate. These days, pirates, and thieves are after financial gain; if they have to impose violence to gain it then they will, especially in lawless states.

Indonesian pirates with an array of modern weapons

Maritime piracy against commercial vessels remains a significant issue (with estimated worldwide losses of US $13 to $16 billion per year), particularly in the waters between the Red Sea and the Indian Ocean off the Somali coast, and also in the Strait of Malacca and Singapore, which are used by over 50,000 commercial ships a year. A recent surge in piracy off the Somali coast spurred a multi-national effort led by the United States to patrol the waters near the Horn of Africa (CTF 150/151). While ships off the coasts of North Africa, Iran and the Mediterranean are still assailed by pirates, the US Navy and the US Coastguard have almost eradicated piracy in US waters and in the Caribbean.

Modern pirates favour small fast boats (skiffs) and take advantage of the small number of crewmembers on modern cargo vessels. They also use mother craft to launch smaller attack or boarding vessels.

Modern pirates can be successful because a large amount of international commerce occurs via shipping. Major shipping routes take cargo ships through narrow bodies of water (such as the GoA and the Strait of Malacca), making them vulnerable to be overtaken and boarded by small skiffs. Other active areas include the South China Sea and West Africa. As usage increases, many of these ships have to lower cruising speeds to allow for navigation and traffic control, making them prime targets for piracy. Small ships are also capable of disguising themselves as fishing vessels or cargo vessels when not carrying out piracy in order to avoid or deceive inspection.

This older ploy has now been almost replaced by using the recently pirated ship to capture other vessels prior to sailing it to Somalia, making detection difficult for all sea going traffic, unless immediately informed.

During the next few pages the diagrams show the increase and distribution of modern piracy, in particularly around Somalia.[1]

Piracy watchdog IMB records an unprecedented jump in global sea attacks in 2009

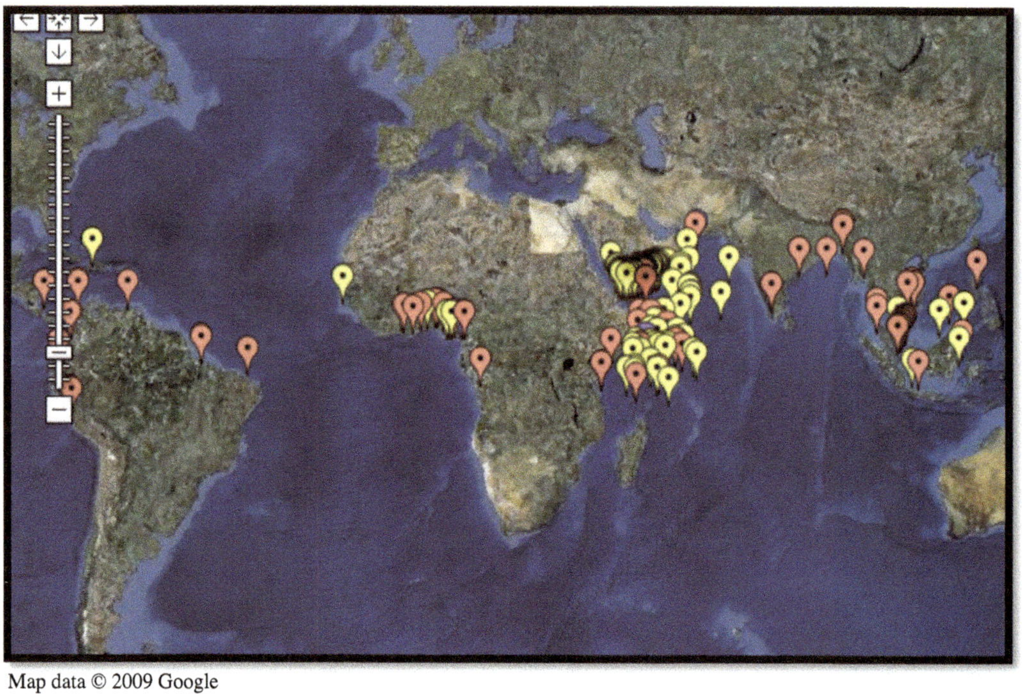

Map data © 2009 Google

The ICC International Maritime Bureau's Piracy Reporting Centre (IMB PRC)

Based in London, UK, and directed by Captain Mukundan, the IMB also has the PRC, based in Kuala Lumpur and run solely on a voluntary basis.

---

[1] The following images are courtesy of the IMB

More people were taken hostage at sea in 2010 than in any year on record. The number of pirate attacks against ships has risen every year for the last four years, IMB revealed. Ships reported 445 attacks in 2010, up 10% from 2009. According to IMB, hijackings off the coast of Somalia accounted for 92% of all ship seizures in 2010 with 49 vessels hijacked and 1,016 crewmembers taken hostage.

2011

In 2011, the capture success rate fell due to the military presence in the High Risk Area (HRA), ships complying with BMP4 recommendations and also the increase in shipping companies using privately contracted security guards (armed). Placing armed guards on ships is controversial and has those for and against; but whilst people argue, no armed ship has ever been taken. The 2011worldwide incidents are shown on page 11.
Somalia has not had an effective government since 1991 when the overthrow of a dictatorship plunged the country into chaos. Besides frequent land battles, the power vacuum has also allowed pirates to operate freely around Somalia's 1,900-mile (3,060-kilometre) coastline. The Somali attacks peaked in 2009 between March and April, with no attacks recorded in June. The decline was largely because of monsoon-related poor weather that can extend through to August. International naval patrols in the gulf have also helped to thwart pirate activity, though military vessels are hard-pressed to cover the vast expanse of ocean along Somalia's coastline. This effectiveness has pushed the pirates further into the two million square miles of Indian Ocean, making the jobs of navies around the world so much harder.

Somali pirates in their fast and manoeuvrable skiff. Earlier models used a single 40HP engine capable of 20-25 kts on a flat sea, newer longer skiffs have 2x 40HP engines that can exceed 30 kts depending upon weight and sea state.

Pie charts showing how piracy has increased and decreased around the globe, 2004-07 [1]

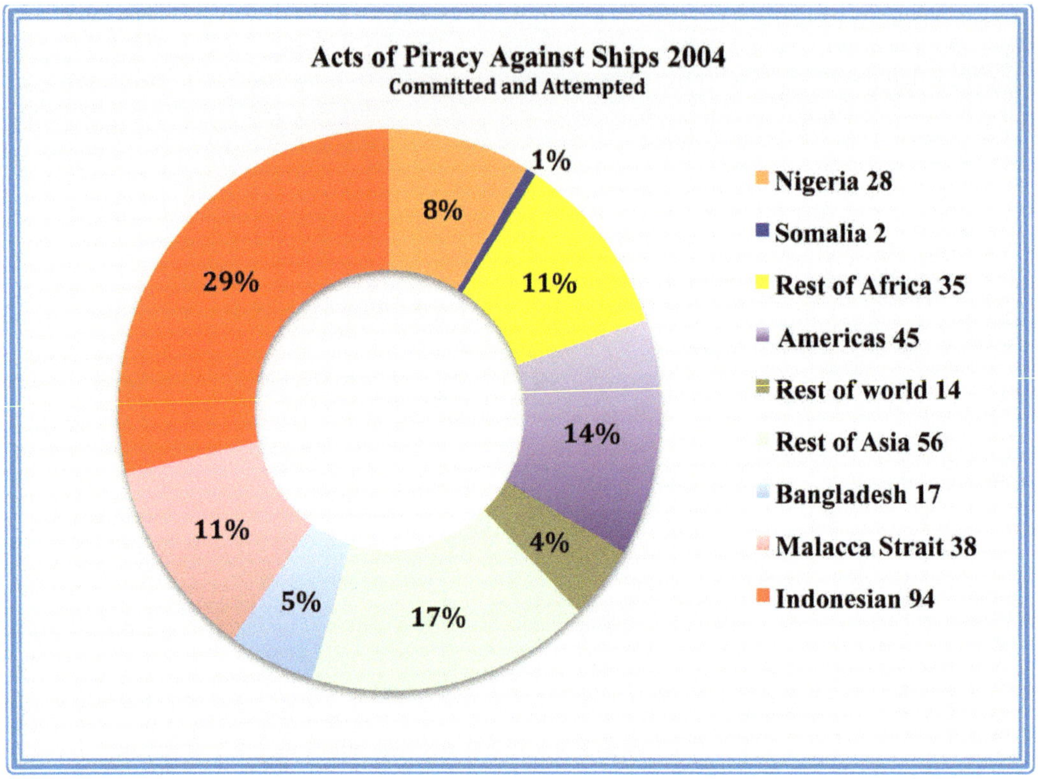

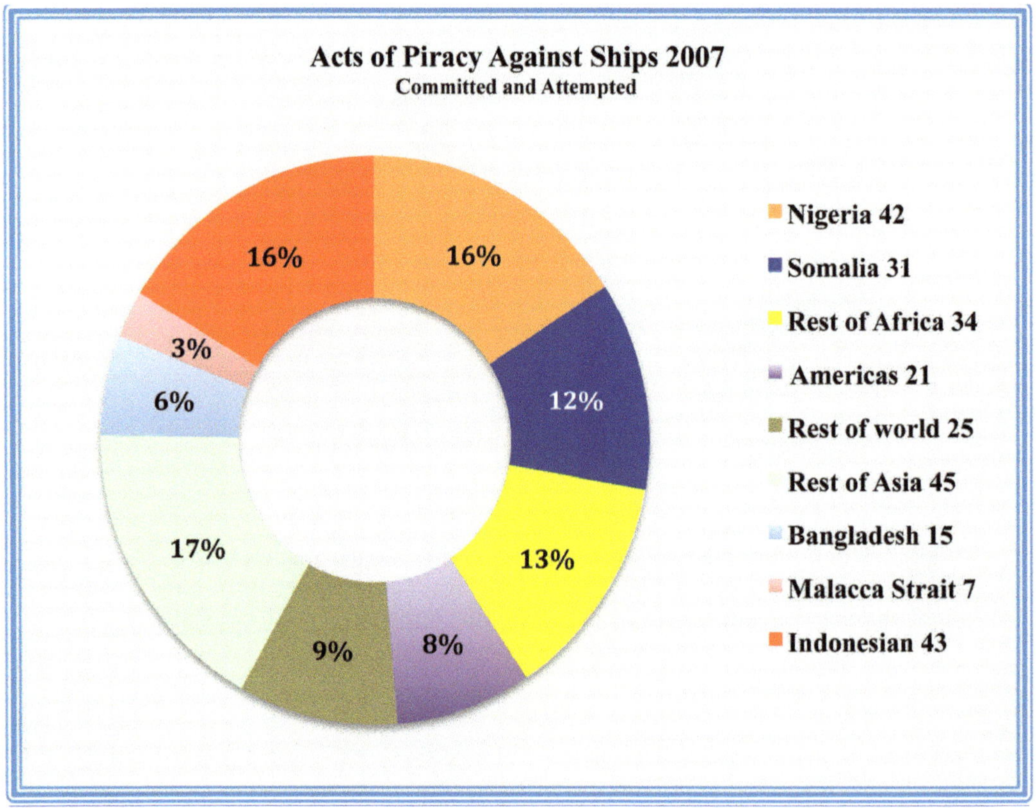

[1] Source IMB

The IMB urges governments to heighten security patrols in their waters and ships to remain vigilant against attacks. Unfortunately for the operating navies, their hands are tied: under the current rules of engagement they can only engage if they are fired upon – pirates have soon become aware of this law, or flaw as seen by frustrated naval forces and seaman alike.

The following illustrations are to show how the scourge of piracy, both from Somalia and globally has spread over the last 5 years. These IMB images paint a clear picture of piracy increases and hotspots

The following information is courtesy of Capt. P Mukundan and the ICC IMB/PRC.

Below: Gulf of Aden, 2007

Map data © 2007 Google

As seen here, there are very few attacks and well spread out, all within reach of the Somali coast

In 2008 Naval pressure in the GoA starts to push pirates further into the Indian Ocean

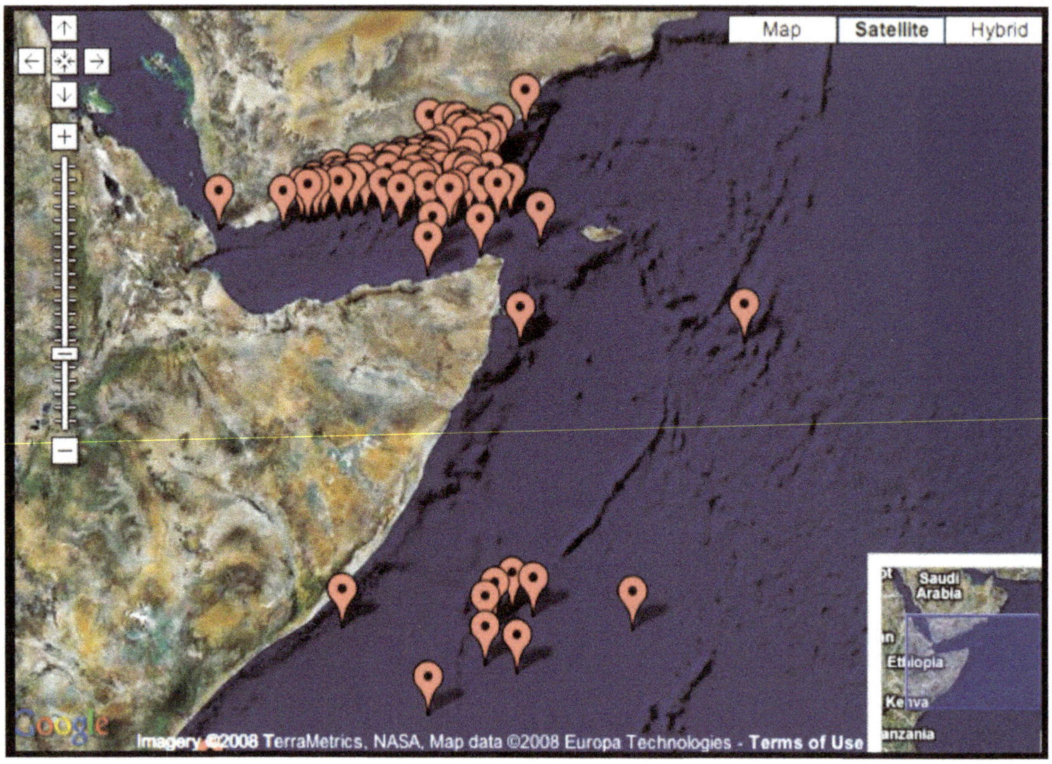

In 2009 Somali pirates concentrated some of their efforts in the Indian Ocean using motherships.

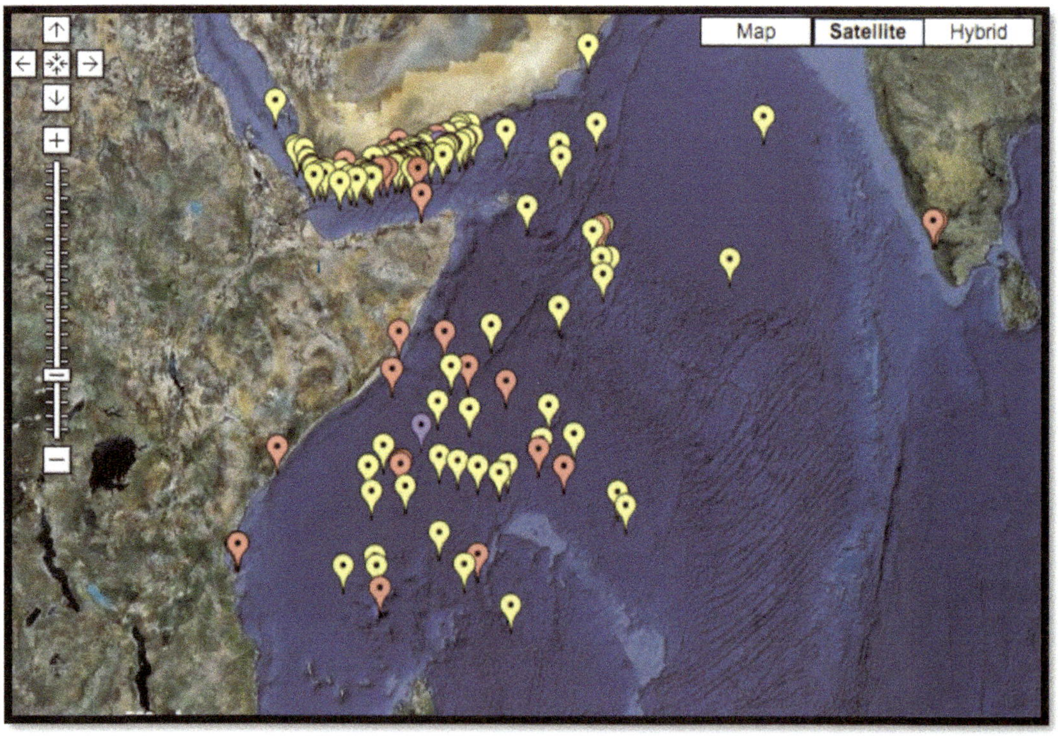

Map data © 2009 Google

Below: In 2009 worldwide piracy figures surpassed 400 attacks

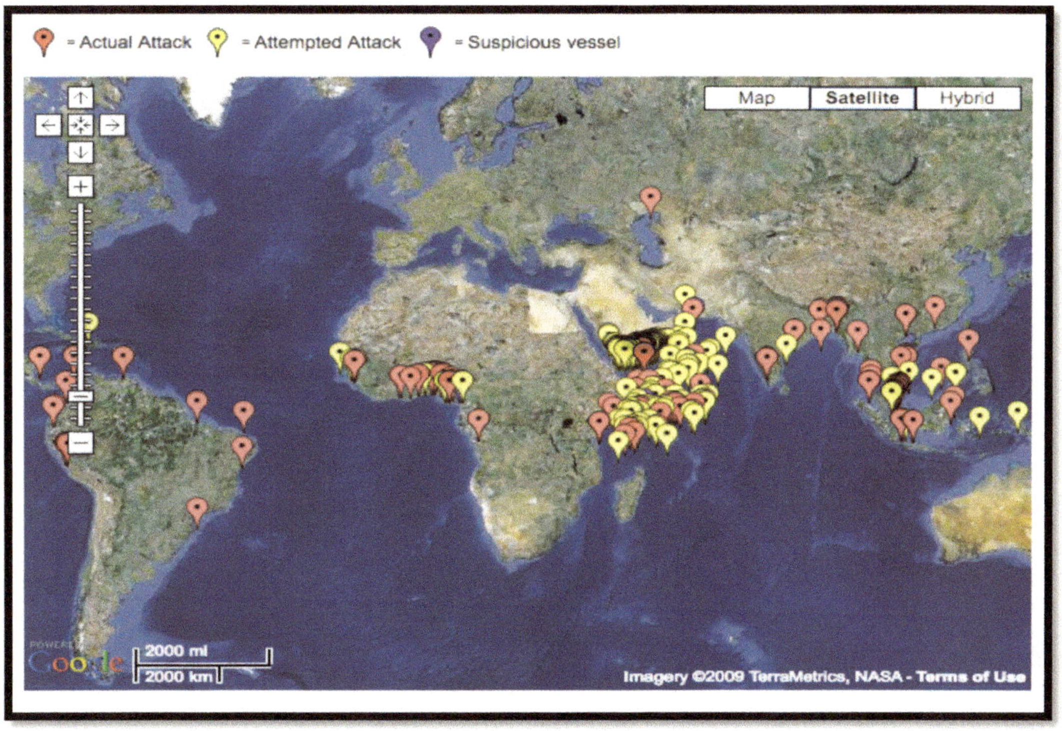

Below: Note the distances that Somali pirates were pushing south and east across the Indian Ocean 2010

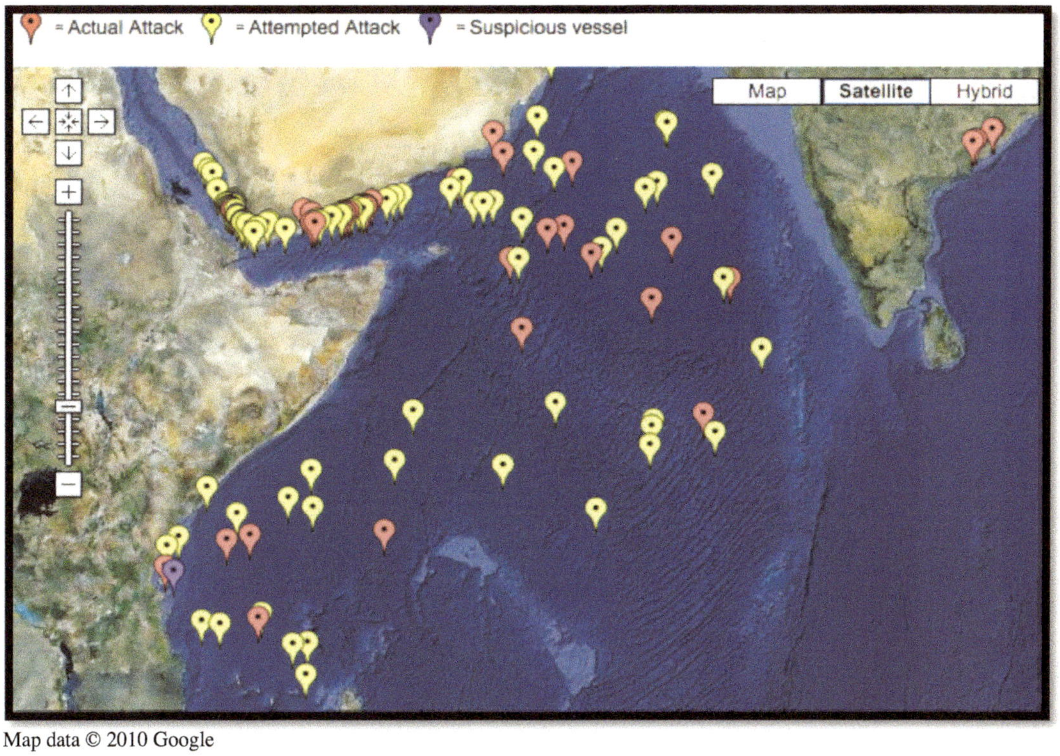

Map data © 2010 Google

2010: this image shows the big increase in attacks from the Southern Red Sea through Bab al Mandeb to Aden (easy attack points especially during the Monsoon)

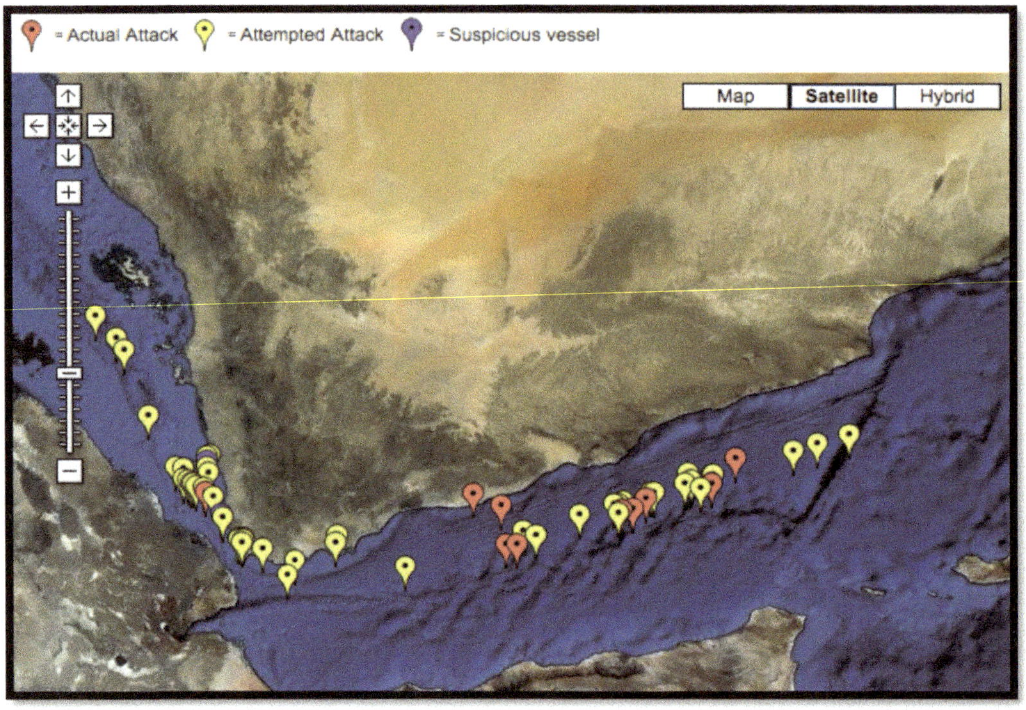

Map data © 2010 Google

The below image shows the global total amount of attacks in 2010

Map data © 2010 Google

In 2008, 111 vessels were targeted by Somali pirates resulting in 42 hijackings. Whilst the number of incidents in 2009 almost doubled, the number of successful hijackings is proportionately less. This can be directly attributed to the increased presence and co-ordination of the international navies along with heightened awareness and robust action by the Masters in transitting these waters 'The international navies play a critical role in the prevention of piracy in Somalia and it is vital that they remain.' In 2009 there was a significant shift in the area of attacks off Somalia. While the 2008 attacks were predominantly focused in the Gulf of Aden, 2009 witnessed more vessels being targeted along the east coast of Somalia. Since October 2009, increased activity has been observed in the Indian Ocean, with 33 incidents reported, including 13 hijackings. Thirteen of these last-quarter incidents occurred east of the recommended east of 60° east – including four hijacked vessels. Many of these attacks occurred at distances of approximately 1000 nautical miles off Mogadishu. Motherships have traditionally posed as fishing vessels or dhows to avoid detection. Reports of such crafts so far from the coast should be questioned and investigated.'

IMB Piracy & Armed Robbery Map 2011

The Piracy & Armed Robbery Map below follows the definition of Piracy as laid down in Article 101 of the 1982 United Nations Convention on the Law of the Sea (UNCLOS) and Armed Robbery as laid down in Resolution A.1025 (26) adopted on 2 December 2009 at the 26th Assembly Session of the International Maritime Organisation (IMO).

Below, figures for piracy and armed robbery incidents as reported to the IMB PRC in 2011	
Worldwide Incidents:	**Incidents Reported for Somalia:**
Total Attacks Worldwide: 439	Total Incidents: 237
Total Hijackings Worldwide: 42	Total Hijackings: 28
Total Hostages: 802	
Total crewmembers killed: 8	

This map shows all the piracy and armed robbery incidents reported to the IMB Piracy Reporting Centre during 2011. If exact coordinates are not provided, estimated positions are shown based on information provided. Pointers may be superimposed on each other.

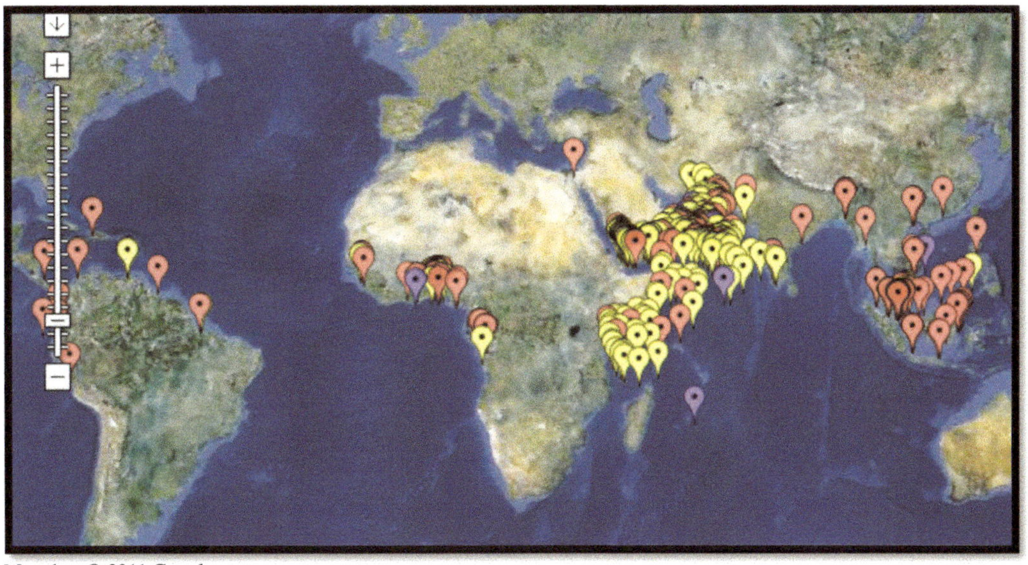

Map data © 2011 Google

Global attacks in 2012 as of October 2012

Map data © 2012 Google

Worldwide Incidents: updated on 27 Oct 2012
Total Attacks Worldwide: 252
Total Hijackings Worldwide: 26

Incidents Reported for Somalia:
Total Incidents: 71
Total Hijackings:13
Total Hostages: 212

Current vessels held by Somali pirates:
Vessels: 9 Hostages: 154.

IMAAG graph showing global pirate attacks over a six-year period, 2006-11

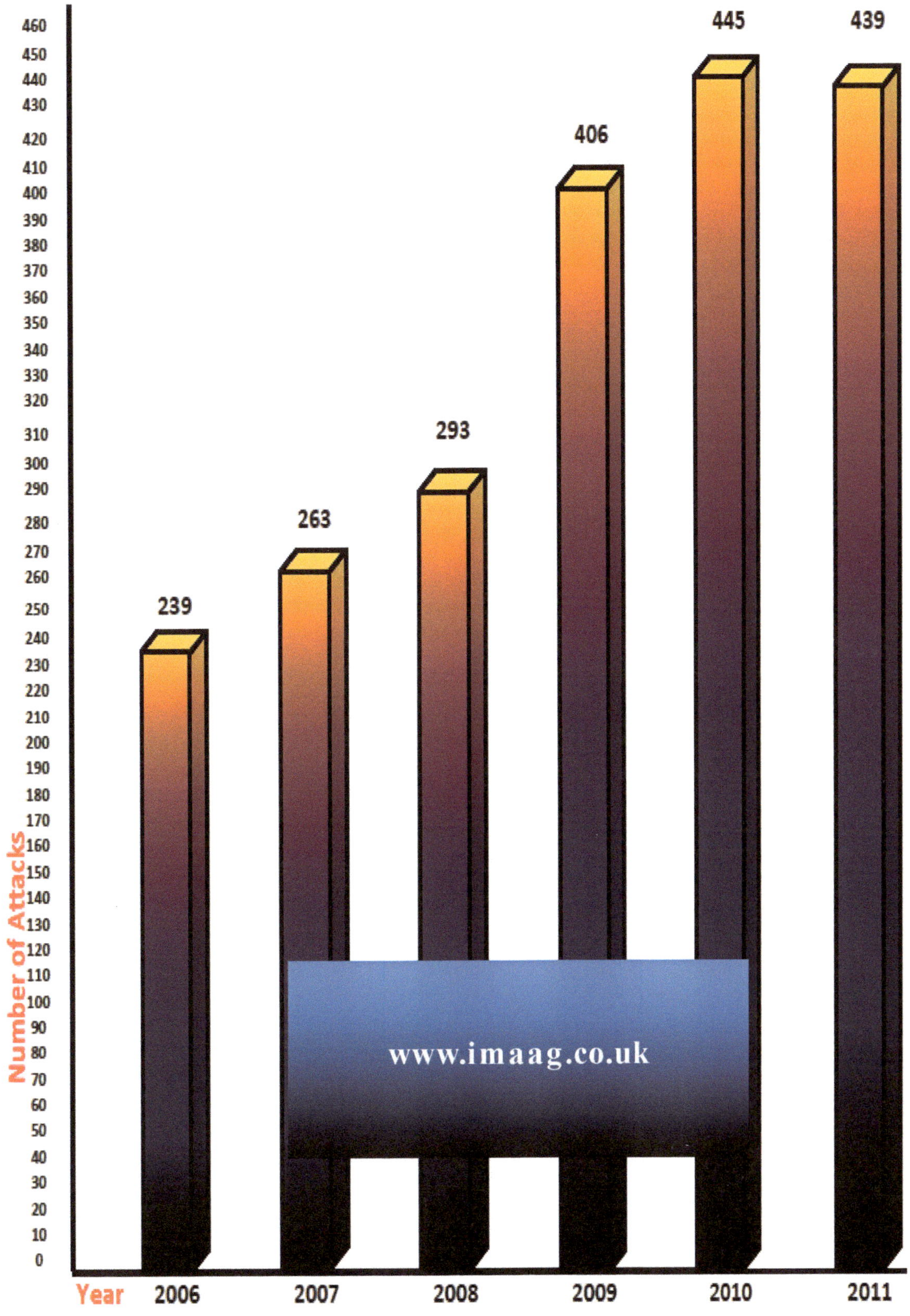

Hostage-taking at sea rises to record levels, says IMB 17th January 2011

In 2010, more people were taken hostage at sea than in any year on record, the International Chamber of Commerce (ICC) International Maritime Bureau's (IMB) global piracy report disclosed in January 2011. Pirates captured 1,181 seafarers and killed eight. A total of 53 ships were hijacked. The number of pirate attacks against ships has risen every year for the last four years, IMB revealed. Ships reported 445 attacks in 2010, up 10% from 2009. While 188 crewmembers were taken hostage in 2006, 1,050 were taken in 2009 and 1,181 in 2010.

"These figures for the number of hostages and vessels taken are the highest we have ever seen," said Captain Pottengal Mukundan, Director of the IMB's Piracy Reporting Centre, which has monitored piracy worldwide since 1991. "The continued increase in these numbers is alarming. " As a percentage of global incidents, piracy on the high seas has increased dramatically over armed robbery in territorial waters," "On the high seas off Somalia, heavily armed pirates are overpowering ocean-going fishing or merchant vessels to use as a base for further attacks. They capture the crew and force them to sail to within attacking distance of other unsuspecting vessels."

According to IMB, hijackings off the coast of Somalia accounted for 92% of all ship seizures in 2010 with 49 vessels hijacked and 1,016 crewmembers taken hostage. A total of 28 vessels and 638 hostages were still being held for ransom by Somali pirates as of 31 December 2010.

While attacks off the coast of Somalia remain high, the number of incidents in the Gulf of Aden more than halved last year, with 53 attacks in 2010 down from 117 in 2009. IMB attributes this reduction to the deterrence work of naval forces from around the world that have been patrolling the area since 2008 and to ships' application of self-protection measures recommended in Best Management Practices, version 4 (BMP 4), a booklet published by the shipping industry.

"The naval units in the seas off the Horn of Africa should be applauded for preventing a huge number of piracy attacks in the region," said Captain Mukundan. "The continued presence of international navies is vital in protecting merchant ships along these important trade routes."

Somali pirates are travelling further afield. In December 2010, they reached as far south as the Mozambique Channel and as far east as 72° East longitude in the Indian Ocean, an operating is unprecedented. What can be done to stop the surge of piracy on the high seas? The answer lies primarily onshore in South Central Somalia. "There is a desperate need for a stable infrastructure in this area, it is vital that governments and the United Nations devote resources to developing workable administrative infrastructures to prevent criminals from exploiting the vacuum left from years of failed local government. All measures taken at sea to limit the activities of the pirates are undermined because of a lack of responsible authority back in Somalia from where the pirates begin their voyages and return with hijacked vessels."

Elsewhere, violent attacks continued around Nigeria, with incidents concentrated near the port of Lagos. Overall, 13 vessels were boarded; four vessels fired upon and there were two attempted attacks. In Bangladesh, the number of armed robbery incidents rose for the second successive year. Mainly attackers armed with knives boarded twenty-one vessels. Almost all were anchored in the port of Chittagong. Indonesia saw its highest levels of armed robbery against ships since 2007. Thirty vessels were boarded, nine attacks were thwarted, and one vessel was hijacked. Vessels were underway in 15 of the attacks. The South China Seas recorded 31 incidents, more than double the previous year. Twenty-one vessels were boarded, seven attacks attempted, two vessels were fired upon and one was hijacked.

Twenty-eight incidents were reported for Nigeria in 2009. Of these, 21 vessels were boarded, three vessels were fired upon, one vessel was hijacked, and three masters reported an attempted attack on their vessel. One crewmember was killed as robbers tried to escape after looting the vessel. Vessels attacked included: general cargo, bulk carriers, reefers, and all types of tankers. The majority of incidents related to the oil industry and fishing vessels have gone unreported. Information from external sources would suggest at least a further 30 unreported attacks occurred in Nigeria in 2009.

Captain Mukundan adds, 'The Nigerian attacks are however much more violent in nature than Somalia, localised but with the capacity to attack vessels and installations further from the coast. The incidence of violent attacks against ships has also spilled over into neighbouring states.'
Indonesia is applauded for its tireless efforts in curbing piracy and armed robbery in its waters. There continues to be a year-on-year decline in the number of incidents, with 15 incidents for 2009, the majority opportunistic in nature. Only two incidents were reported in the Malacca Strait – the same number as in 2008. This is the second year in a row where incidents in the Singapore Straits have increased. Nine incidents were reported in 2009, compared with six in 2008. Of these, six vessels were boarded and three reported attempted attacks.

Thirteen incidents were reported by ships steaming in the South China Seas. This is the highest number of incidents in the previous five years. Of these, eleven were boarded, one vessel was hijacked and one reported an attempted attack. In some attacks the bridge crew were physically removed from the bridge for a short period of time – leaving the vessel effectively not under command. Even though there has been significant improvement in the safety and security of the South East Asian and Far East waters, there still remains an underlying potential for incidents to increase without any prior warning. The pressure on pirates and robbers has to be maintained by the littoral states through their constant physical presence in these waters.

Bangladesh (Chittagong) has shown a slight increase in the number of attacks compared with 2008. Most of these have been opportunistic. Of the 17 vessels attacked, 14 were boarded and ship's stores stolen. Most of the incidents have taken place within the Chittagong anchorage.
Thirty-seven incidents have been reported from countries in the South American continent, compared with 14 in 2008. Twelve incidents have occurred in the anchorage of Callao in Peru in 2009, compared with five the previous year. Other countries affected are Brazil, Colombia, Costa Rica, Ecuador, Haiti and Venezuela. Most of these attacks were successful and were carried out while the vessels were berthed in port or while at anchor. This is a similar trend to 2008.

The IMB strongly urges all shipmasters and owners to report all incidents of actual and attempted piracy and armed robbery to the IMB PRC. This is the first step in the response chain and vital in ensuring that adequate resources are allocated by governments to deal with the problem. A set of transparent statistics, from an independent, non-political, international organisation such as the IMB PRC, acts as an effective catalyst to achieve this goal.

IMB Director:

Capt. Pottengal Mukundan

This diagram depicts the distances that Somali pirates have travelled from 2005 to 2010 (image courtesy of the BBC)

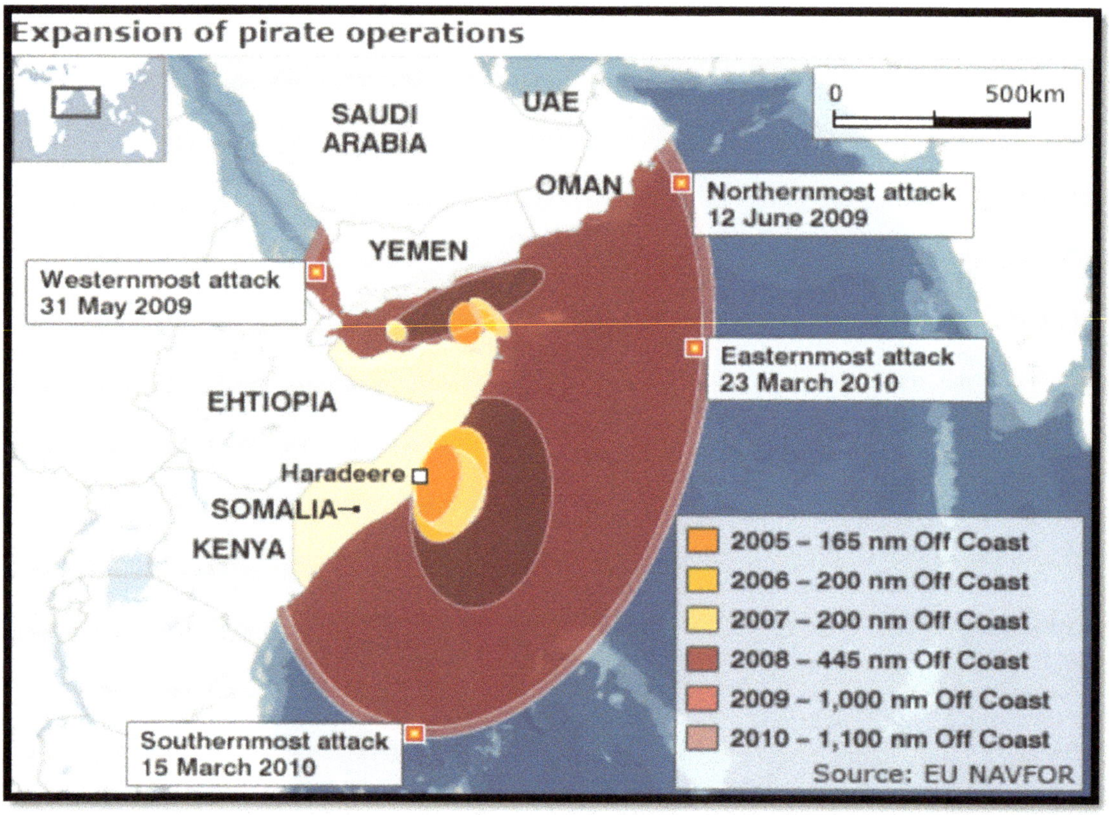

Below: the distances that Somali pirates have travelled with the aid of their mother craft in 2009

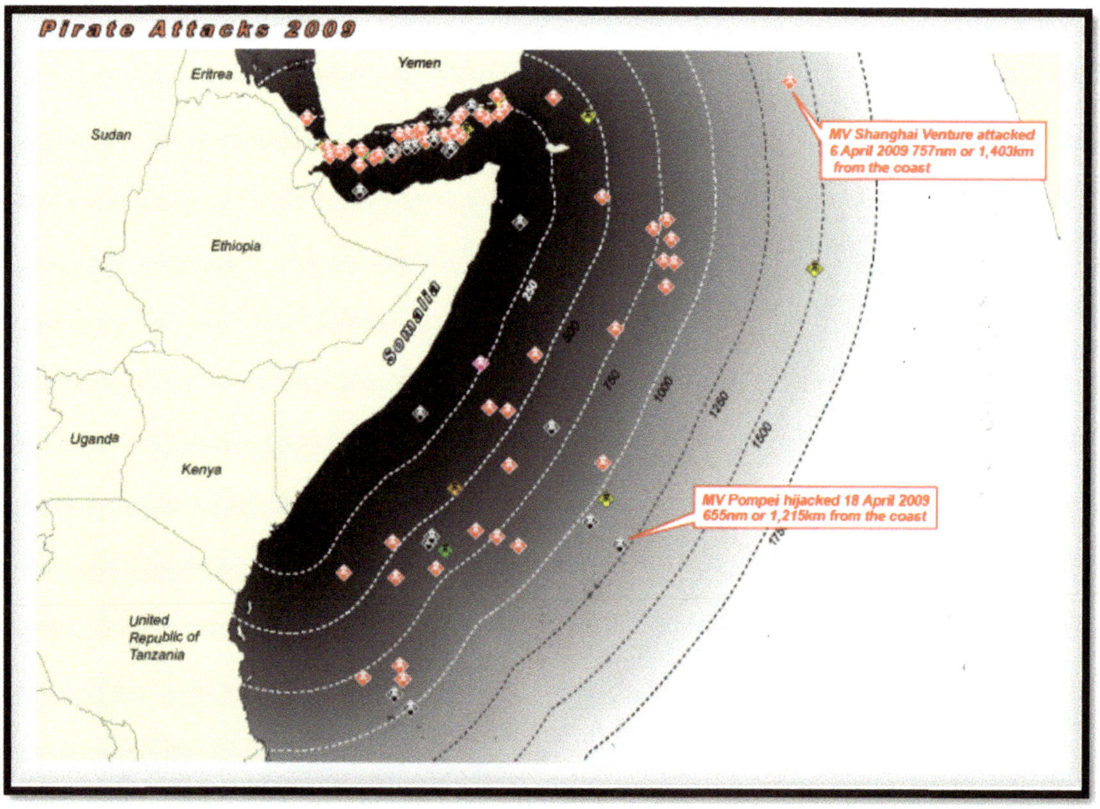

In 2011, those distances were pushed further and further afield, see below.

One Month, One Map[3]

The map shows Somali pirate activity for about a 35-day period.

Bright yellow pins are successful hijackings.
Dull yellow pins are unsuccessful hijackings.
Red pins are attacks.
Green pins are suspected mothership sightings.

53 attacks, hijackings, and attempted hijackings. In just over one month.

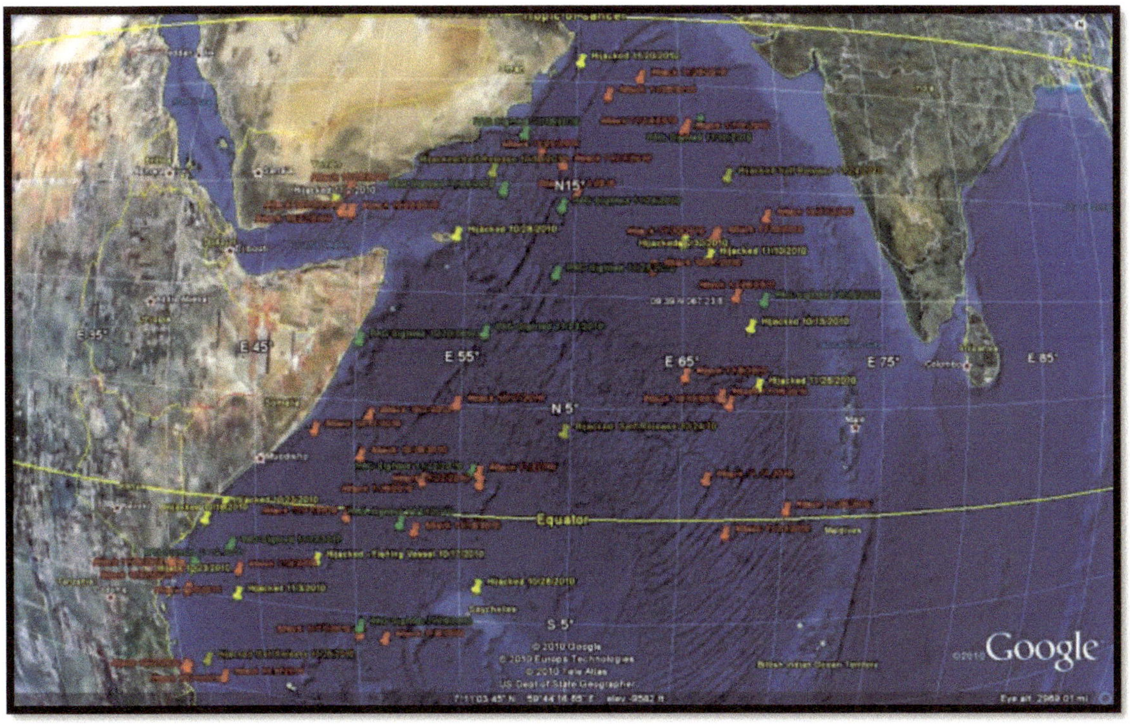

The above image is to show the reader, not the details of the vessels attacked, but to consider how far out the Somali pirates will travel to attack vessels. Originally hugging their coastline, the pirates now are using motherships to transport them to far reaches such as the Indian coast, Maldives, Seychelles, Madagascar and as far south as Mozambique. This is an enormous area for coalition warships to cover, hence the need for onboard or nearby security (escorting vessel).

---

[3] Information courtesy of Eagle Speak,

Pirate Activity in the High Risk Area

Courtesy of the NATO Shipping Centre, Northwood.

Last updated: 01 August 2012

Not added to the list are yachts, dhows and local fishing vessels

For comments or suggestions send an Email to info@shipping.nato.int

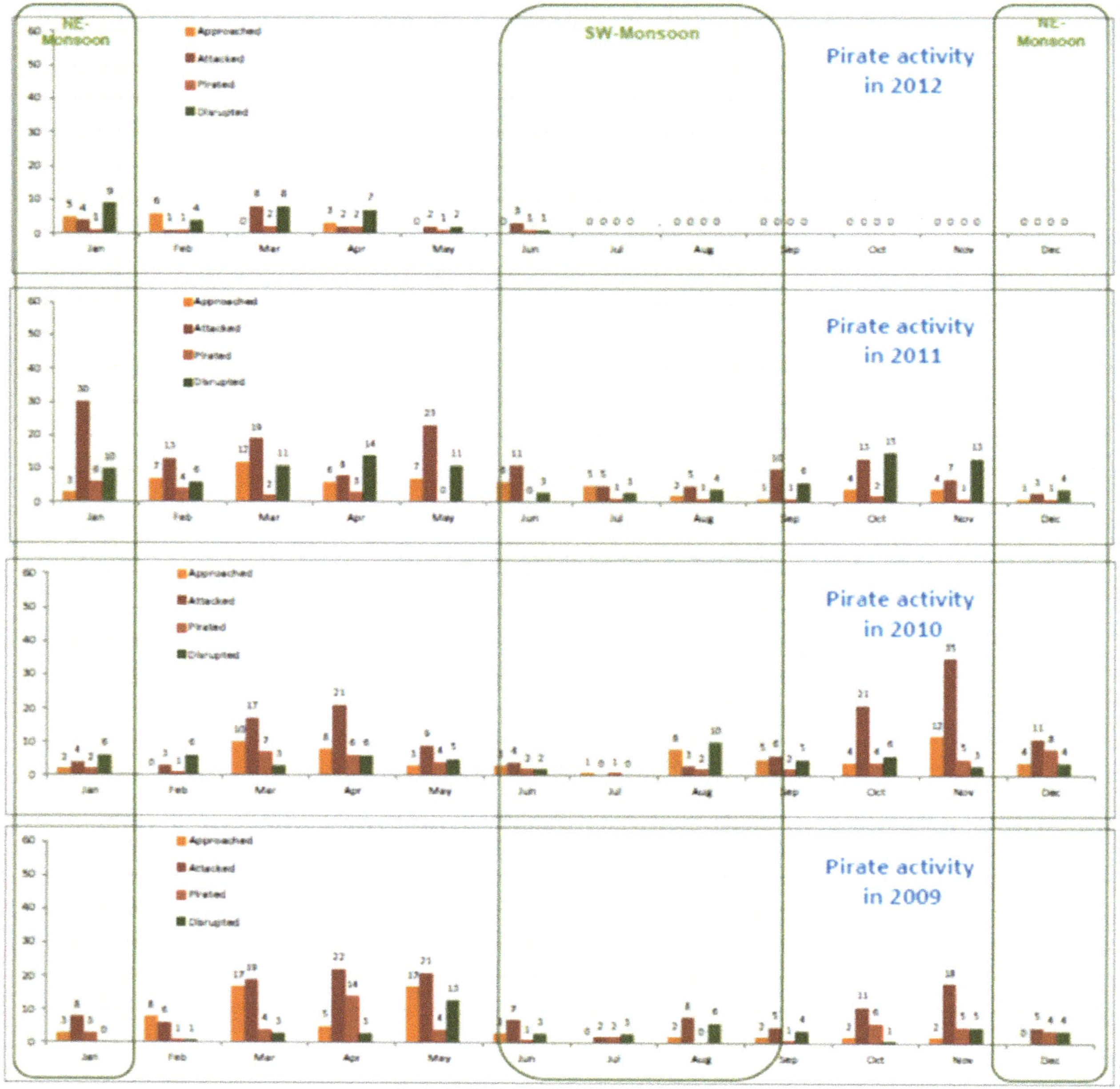

Somaly Piracy Activity in total

2012	Approach	Attacked	Pirated	Disrupted
Jan	5	4	1	9
Feb	6	1	1	4
Mar	0	8	2	8
Apr	3	2	2	7
May	0	2	1	2
Jun	0	3	1	1
Jul	0	0	0	0
Aug				
Sep				
Oct				
Nov				
Dec				
Total 2012	14	20	8	31

2011	Approach	Attacked	Pirated	Disrupted
Jan	3	30	6	10
Feb	7	13	4	6
Mar	12	19	2	11
Apr	6	8	3	14
May	7	23	0	11
Jun	6	11	0	3
Jul	5	5	1	3
Aug	2	5	1	4
Sep	1	10	1	6
Oct	4	13	2	15
Nov	4	7	1	13
Dec	1	3	1	4
Total 2011	58	147	22	100

2010	Approach	Attacked	Pirated	Disrupted
Jan	2	4	2	6
Feb	0	3	1	6
Mar	10	17	7	3
Apr	8	21	6	6
May	3	9	4	5
Jun	3	4	2	2
Jul	1	0	1	0
Aug	8	3	2	10
Sep	5	6	2	5
Oct	4	21	4	6
Nov	12	35	5	3
Dec	4	11	8	4
Total 2010	60	134	44	56

2009	Approach	Attacked	Pirated	Disrupted
Jan	3	8	3	0
Feb	8	6	1	1
Mar	17	19	4	3
Apr	5	22	14	3
May	17	21	4	13
Jun	3	7	1	3
Jul	0	2	2	3
Aug	2	8	0	6
Sep	2	5	1	4
Oct	2	11	6	1
Nov	2	18	5	5
Dec	0	5	4	4
Total 2009	61	132	45	46

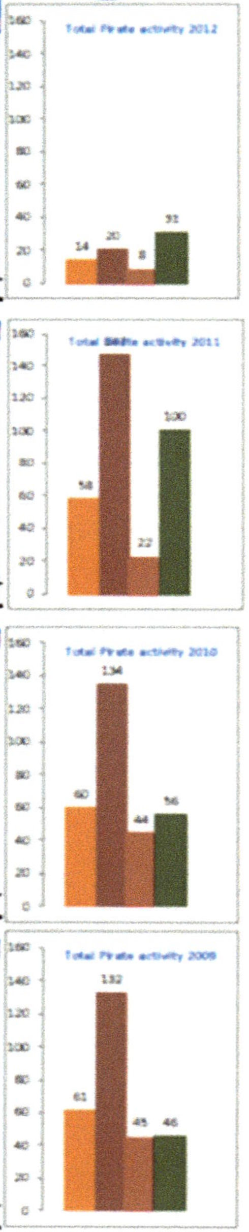

2. GLOBAL HIGH-RISK AREAS

For up-to-date information refer to the IMB website, as areas do change, for better or for worse.

A. Somalia, the Gulf of Aden (GoA) and the Indian Ocean

The Gulf of Aden (GoA) used to be a hotbed for pirate attacks launched from Somalia; however, due to the heavy naval presence there pirates have now ventured further afield into the Indian Ocean and attacks have taken place off the East African coastlines (as far as Mozambique) and the outer islands such as the Seychelles, Maldives and Madagascar. Somali pirates are dangerous and will fire their automatic weapons and RPG 7 (rocket-propelled grenade launchers) at ships in order to stop them. Pirates are known to be using motherships to launch attacks further away from the coast. These motherships are able to operate far out to sea and launch smaller boats (skiffs) to attack and hijack passing ships. Some of these attacks have taken place beyond 1000 nautical miles from the coast.

The IMB, in co-operation with the MSCHOA, advises that vessels not making scheduled calls to ports in Somalia should keep as far away as possible from the Somali coast when sailing to and from. Sea goers should not be fooled into thinking that pirates will only come from mothercraft or from Somalia itself. It has not yet been proven, but it is thought that Somali pirates are also operating from the south coast of Yemen. There are many inaccessible places from land that can support a small community with the basics such as water and covert shelter.

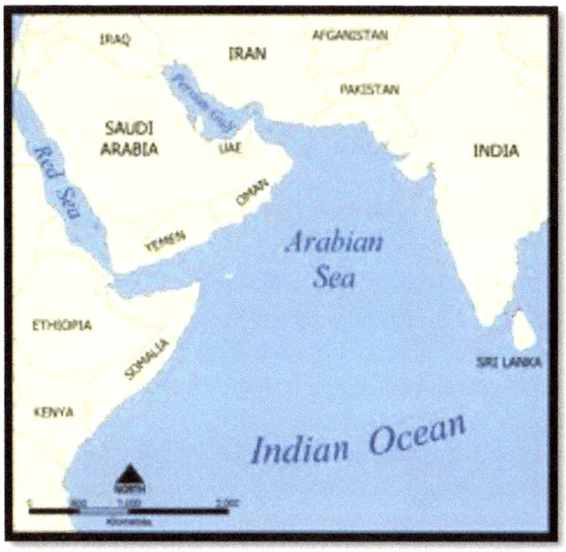

Map data © 2007 - 2021

Since coalition forces increased in numbers in the GoA, Somali pirates have changed their tactics to compensate. Various sized vessels are being seized by pirates and are being used as motherships. These give the pirates longevity at sea, as they are able to sail for hundreds of miles to hunt down their prey. Trawlers, dhows, and tugboats are just some of the types of vessels that have been used in the past; currently pirates are capturing larger ships to venture further out away from coalition forces. Pirates have shown us that they are prepared to sail beyond the Seychelles, towards India, to Madagascar and parallel to the African coast to the Mozambique Channel.

As of February 2011, Somali pirates continue to attack vessels in the northern Somali coast in the Gulf of Aden and southern Red Sea in the Bab el Mandeb (BeM/BaM) TSS despite increased presence of warships.

The pirates are firing automatic weapons and RPGs in an attempt to board and hijack vessels. Once the attack is successful and the vessel hijacked, they would sail the vessel towards the Somali coast (unless it is used as a mothership for a while) and thereafter demand a ransom for the release of the vessel and crew. You should remember to report any incident, even if it is a fishing dhow with following skiffs that are clearly fishing. If information is not passed on, every vessel that sees this activity panics and tells the IMB that there are hostile pirates in the vicinity. This 'calling wolf' can lead to coalition forces being directed in completely the wrong direction, leaving real pirates to attack unhindered.

There is usually a lull in Somali pirate attacks from the end of June until August, when the southwesterly monsoon season makes it hard for pirate skiffs to operate on rough seas. During the monsoon, pirates will move to areas where the seas are more sheltered, such as the southern Red Sea or handrailing the Omani coastline. In 2011, many ships were attacked in Bab el Mandeb and near to the Hanish Islands, blending in with the many fishing skiffs located there. However, as the weather starts improving, attacks will increase, Somali pirates continue aggressively to attack and will kill if necessary, as happened to the American sailors aboard SY Quest. Masters are cautioned that attacks have taken place as far east as 72°E and as far south as 22°S and as far north as 21.5°N Mariners are advised to report any attacks and suspicious boats to the IMB PRC.A 24 hour visual and radar watch must be maintained at all times while transiting these waters as early sightings / detection and accurate assessment will allow Masters to take evasive actions, increase speed and at the same time request for assistance and escape. Monitor and keep clear of all small boats if possible. Adhere to the latest BMP recommendations.

Arabian Sea / Off Oman:

Sightings and calls from suspect small boats. In some cases, ships were chased with unknown intent. Attacks reported off Oman and Arabian Sea where a number of vessels were attacked and hijacked. Pirates believed to be Somali pirates extending their attack areas such as the ship hijacked only 30nm from Salalah Port 2011 and the failed attack on January 16th 2012, where both Omani Coastguard and warships are berthed, pirates will also hug the Omani coast during the SW monsoon period. In summary, this is an extremely dangerous part of the world, vessels should be on full alert with all sentries, and hardening in situ, the same applies to the next paragraph.

Indian Ocean / Off Seychelles / Off Madagascar / Off west Maldives / Off Mozambique:

Suspected Somali pirates attacking and hijacking vessels in these areas. Attacks also extend to west coast of Maldives, India, and Minicoy Island. Pirates also using hijacked ocean going fishing vessels and hijacked merchant vessels to conduct piracy operations. Mothervessels sail far from Somali coast to attack and hijack passing vessels. Smaller skiffs are launched from the pirate mother vessel to attack the vessels. Pirates are heavily armed with automatic weapons and RPGs and use the kidnapped crew as human shields. Heavy military presence in the GoA force pirates further offshore, vigilance should be as important if not more so than in the GoA.

Iraq: Be very alert in and around Umm Qasr

A. Red Sea

The Red Sea is used to be a peaceful area and a great place to pre-plan and prepare for southbound vessels heading for 'pirate alley'. A few attacks have taken place in 2010, but more so in 2011 during the monsoon season, so Masters need to be aware, especially further south. Captains should be prepared for the high-risk passage from 18 ° north when sailing south, and can relax once passed latitude 18 ° north, when heading north. When heading towards the narrow bottleneck of the Hanish Islands and Bab el Mandeb, crews should be on full alert. This area is generally buzzing with small skiffs chasing the masses of tuna and bonito that are found around there. In 2010 through to late 2012, the pirates started to push north through Bab el Mandeb and attack vessels in the southern end of the Red Sea; the pirates mix with local fishermen, making identification difficult. It is essential to use very good optics, such as image-stabilised binoculars as made by Canon, is a must.

Captains must be extra vigilant when in the waters around the Hanish Islands and Bab al Mandeb, especially during the SW Monsoon period.

Note the group of attacks recorded in 2010/11 around the Hanish Islands

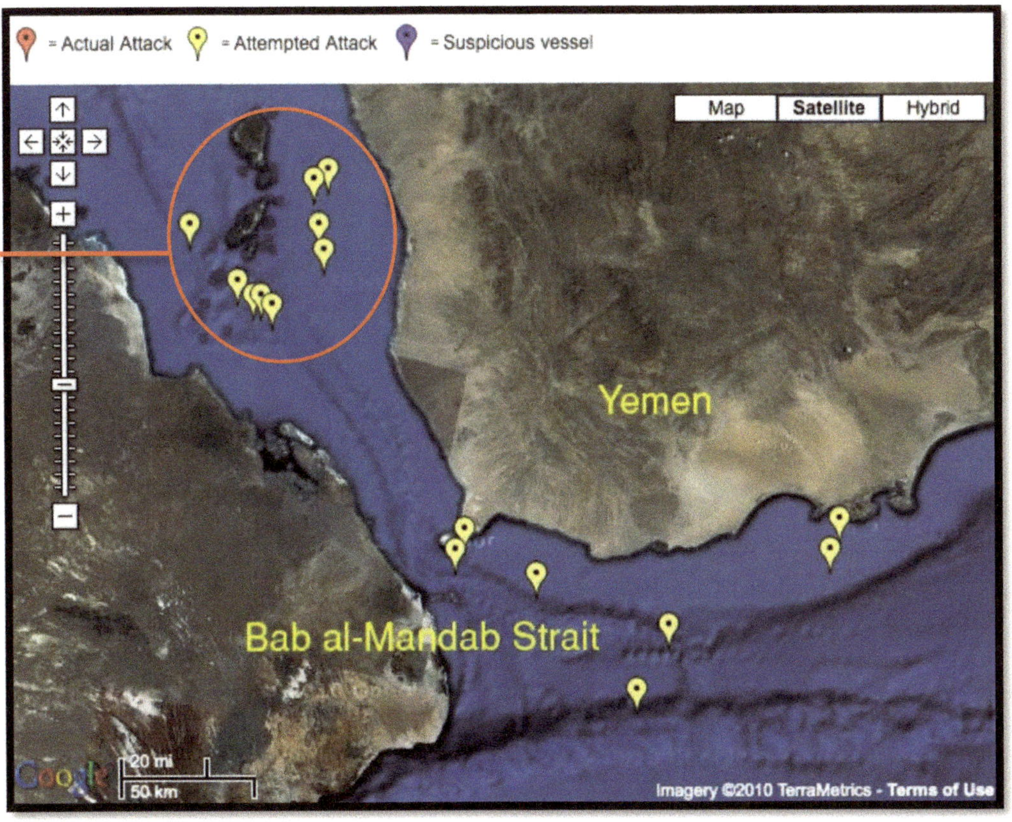

Image courtesy of EagleSpeak/Google

Onboard security must be calm and <u>professional</u> in these waters.

In this area, at night, there are dozens of brightly illuminated squid boats moored just north of the NE shipping lane. On many a passage, vessels have 'stood to' because of one or multiple skiffs that have charged at the boat. Often, they are simply curious fishermen having a look or trying to sell fish or beg food, water, or cigarettes. Such occasions provide the perfect opportunity for crew to execute the relevant drills and give feedback after the threat has passed.

It certainly gets the adrenaline going for all involved; if armed security guards are on board; a very high standard of discipline is needed. As seen in Iraq, it is all too easy for a frightened, inexperienced armed guard to shoot an innocent civilian thinking he is a potential threat*.

*This has taken place in recent global conflicts, it has been brought to our attention via the media where upon private security companies operating in high-risk areas such as Baghdad have been approached by innocent civilian cars, the armed security team, panicked and shot the occupants of the vehicle, thinking that the occupants were suicide bombers or a 'hit-squad'. The occupants were killed or injured due to the unprofessional conduct of those unprofessional security men. This sort of behavior in completely unacceptable and these companies need to have regulations to stop this manslaughter from taking place. A similar incident happened where the Italian Marines shot two Indian fishermen, thinking they were Somali pirates.

B. West Africa:

Nigeria

Nigeria is famous for being a hotspot for violence, corruption, and piracy. It still can be an extremely dangerous place if a vessel is in the wrong area at the wrong time. On land, most places around Lagos and Port Harcourt are out of bounds at night to visitors. In 2001, there were 10 deaths, in 2003, there were 21 deaths, and in the first six months of 2004, there were already 30 deaths due to the armed gangs that operate in and around that area. As Somali piracy decreases; West African piracy is increasing.

Analysts blame the proliferation of weapons in the oil-rich Niger Delta region, where armed gangs trade stolen crude oil. Around Lagos and Bonny River, pirates are violent and have attacked and robbed vessels, and kidnapped crews along the coast and rivers, at anchorages and ports. Vessels are advised to be vigilant in other areas of Nigeria. Vessels have been attacked in the anchorage around the fairway marker buoy. In the area of the Lagos anchorage in 2009, the author was providing security for a vulnerable survey vessel, the ship remained underway throughout the night, however, on a nearby ship three men climbed a vessel's anchor chain and entered the bridge with machetes. Three persons were very seriously injured and were lucky to live. Even if there are hundreds of ships around a vessel, it does not mean it is safe.

There are many different pirate gangs in and around the delta area; probably the most notorious are MEND- The Movement for the Emancipation of the Niger Delta. Many violent attacks, kidnappings, and deaths have been blamed on this heavily armed group.
There are a great many other areas that are dangerous around the African coast; the African map from the IMB, showing attacks that have taken place, almost circumnavigates the entire continent.

Movement for the Emancipation of the Niger Delta

The Movement for the Emancipation of the Niger Delta ("MEND") is one of the largest militant groups in the Niger Delta region of Nigeria. The organization claims to expose exploitation and oppression of the people of the Niger Delta and devastation of the natural environment by public-private partnerships between the Federal Government of Nigeria and corporations involved in the extraction of oil in the Niger Delta. The Economist has described the organization as one that "portrays itself as political organisation that wants a greater share of Nigeria's oil revenues to go to the impoverished region that sits atop the oil. In fact, it is more of an umbrella organisation for several armed groups, which it sometimes pays in cash or guns to launch attacks."

M.E.N.D

MEND has been linked to attacks on petroleum operations in Nigeria as part of the Conflict in the Niger Delta, engaging in actions including sabotage, theft, property destruction, guerrilla warfare, and kidnapping.

MEND's stated goals are to localize control of Nigeria's oil and to secure reparations from the federal government for pollution caused by the oil industry.

In an interview with one of the group's leaders, who used the alias Major-General Godswill Tamuno, the BBC reported that MEND was fighting for "total control" of the Niger Delta's oil wealth, saying local people had not gained from the riches under the ground and the region's creeks and swamps."

In a January 2006 email, MEND warned the oil industry, "It must be clear that the Nigerian government cannot protect your workers or assets. Leave our land while you can or die in it. Our aim is to totally destroy the capacity of the Nigerian government to export oil." Additionally MEND called upon then President Olusegun Obasanjo to free two jailed Ijaw leaders — Mujahid Dokubo-Asari, who was jailed and charged with treason, and Diepreye Alamieyeseigha, a former governor of Bayelsa State convicted of corruption. Obasanjo's successor, President Umaru Musa Yar'Adua authorised the release of Dokubo-Asari and Alamieyeseigha in 2007.

Origins and context

For the roughly fifty years since Nigeria declared independence from British colonial rule, oil has been produced in Nigeria. Throughout this period, corporate politics has intersected with successive dictatorships. Under these dictatorships the Nigerian government has signed laws that appropriated oil resources and placed these under the control of multinational oil companies, such as Chevron Corporation and most notoriously, Royal Dutch Shell.

From the point of view of MEND, and its supporters, the people of the Niger Delta have suffered an unprecedented degradation of their environment due to unchecked pollution produced by the oil industry. As a result of this policy of dispossessing people from their lands in favour of foreign oil interests, within a single generation, many now have no ability to fish or farm. People living in the Niger Delta have found themselves in a situation where their government and the international oil companies own all the oil under their feet, the revenues of which are rarely seen by the people who are suffering from the consequences of it.

Kenneth Roth, Executive Director of Human Rights Watch, has said of the situation, "The oil companies can't pretend they don't know what's happening all around them. The Nigerian government obviously has the primary responsibility to stop human rights abuse. But the oil companies are directly benefiting from these crude attempts to suppress dissent, and that means they have a duty to try and stop it." Eghare W.O. Ojhogar, chief of the Ugborodo community, said: "It is like paradise and hell. They have everything. We have nothing... If we protest, they send soldiers." Over the last twenty years, various political movements and activists have emerged in opposition to the perceived injustices perpetrated upon the people of the Niger Delta by the government and the oil companies. These were usually non-violent. Perhaps the most famous of these activists was, an Ogoni poet-turned-activist who was executed by the Nigerian government in 1995 on what many believe to be deliberately false charges with the aim of silencing his vocal opposition to the oil interests in Nigeria.

In Saro-Wiwa's footsteps came others who, having seen the government's reaction to nonviolent activism, advocated violence as resistance to what they regarded as the enslavement of their people.

Militants in the delta enjoy widespread support among the region's approximately 20 million people, most of whom live in poverty despite the enormous wealth generated in the oil-rich region.

Constituency and organization

MEND is closely connected with Asari's Niger Delta People's Volunteer Force, a rebel group with similar aims. MEND reportedly seeks "a union of all relevant militant groups in the Niger Delta." However, the identity of MEND is somewhat obscure since its leaders like to remain faceless and its cause has been taken up by completely unrelated groups inspired by the original MEND, one of which is claiming responsibility for some of the violence that has occurred. However, the original members of MEND (recognized as MEND by the United States government and Chevron security) have claimed that impostors are causing some of the violence that is now occurring. MEND's evolving approach to conducting warfare has been described as "open source", so called because it is analogous to the decentralized communal development process now prevalent in the software industry, making it extremely quick to innovate and move new technologies and tactics rapidly from cell to cell without the direction of a vulnerable leadership hierarchy. Former United States Air Force "counter-terrorism" officer, technology analyst, and software entrepreneur, John Robb, in a Wired Magazine interview about the emergence of "open source guerrillas", alleged that MEND "doesn't even field its own guerillas. They hire their experts and fighters mostly from criminal gangs and tribal warrior cults to do their operations."

Tactics

MEND's attacks involve substantially more sophisticated tactics than those of previous militant groups in the Niger Delta. MEND's recent tactics have included:

- Swarm-based manoeuvres: guerrillas are using speed boats in the Niger Delta's swamps to quickly attack targets in succession. Multiple, highly manoeuvrable units have kept the government and Shell's defensive systems off-balance defending their sprawling networks.

- Radically improved firepower and combat training: allowing guerrillas to overpower a combination of Shell's Western-trained private military guards and elite Nigerian units in several engagements. (One of Shell's private military operators was captured as a hostage.)

- Effective use of system disruption: targets have been systematically and accurately selected to completely shut down production and delay and/or halt repairs, and the guerrillas are making effective use of Shell's hostages to coerce both the government and the multinational.

The militants have repeatedly bombed pipelines, triggering an international increase in the cost of oil. They have also kidnapped foreign oil workers. The IMB said piracy in Africa's Gulf of Guinea, ranging from Benin to Togo, was becoming increasingly dangerous, with 34 cases in the first nine months of 2012. It said the attacks were often violent, planned and aimed at stealing refined oil products.
Captain Mukundan said 21 attacks were recorded in Nigeria alone, but he praised the country's navy for helping to rescue vessels. He said many navies in the vast gulf don't have resources to fight piracy far out at sea, allowing gangs to shift their operations to other areas.

In 2007 MEND captured workers from Chevron's facilities

Other high-risk areas of West Africa:

Gulf of Guinea area:

Conakry (Guinea):

Pirates armed with automatic weapons are violent and aggressive in the attacks. In some attacks, pirates dressed in military uniforms.

Douala Outer Anchorage (Cameroon):

Two attacks with kidnapping of crews occurred at Douala. Generally, things are becoming worse in this area.

Benin: Cotonou:

Attacks are increasing. Armed pirates are violent and in some incidents, pirates fired at ships. A number of ships particularly tankers were attacked and hijacked. Pirates forced Masters to sail to unknown location where ship's properties at sometimes part cargo stolen. A number of crewmembers were injured in the past. Also in 2011, a probable extension of Nigerian piracy into neighbouring Benin included 20 incidents against tankers, eight of which were hijacked and had cargoes partly stolen. Although the average length of captivity for ships taken off the coasts of Nigeria and Benin tends to be roughly 10 days, compared to six months in Somali hijackings, IMB warns that these attacks can be more violent.

Recent African hotspots

Nigeria and Benin continued to be piracy hotspots. While 10 attacks were reported in Nigeria, including two hijackings, IMB warns that this number is not representative of the real threat of Nigeria piracy. Underreporting of attacks in Nigeria continues to be a cause for concern, and IMB states that it is aware of at least another 34 unreported incidents in Nigerian waters.

Across the continent on West Africa's oil-rich Gulf of Guinea, criminal gangs are stepping up their attacks. The perpetrators, often steeped in Nigeria's violent and organized criminal culture, are quick to kill. In mid-February 2012, pirates boarded the Fourseas, a Taiwanese-owned bulk cargo ship, 126 miles off the coast of Nigeria. They killed the ship's captain and chief engineer in a barrage of gunfire unleashed from their speedboat, according to local news reports.

The attack took place in the heart of the busy trade routes. It is just the latest example of an escalation that has governments and shippers worried.

Piracy attacks in East and West Africa dominate world report

Pirate attacks against vessels in East and West Africa accounted for the majority of world attacks in 2011, signaling a rising trend, the International Chamber of Commerce (ICC) International Maritime Bureau's Global piracy report revealed. Of the 439 attacks reported to the IMB in 2011, 275 attacks took place off Somalia on the east coast and in the Gulf of Guinea on the west coast of Africa. The report showed a slight drop in the total number of recorded incidents of piracy and armed robbery worldwide, comparing the 439 recorded incidents of piracy and armed robbery in 2011 to 445 in 2010. The falling numbers come after four consecutive years of increased piracy and armed robbery worldwide. The 802 crewmembers taken hostage in 2011 also marks a decrease from the four-year high of 1,181 in 2010. Overall, in 2011, there were 45 vessels hijacked, 176 vessels boarded, 113 vessels fired upon, and 105 reported attempted attacks. A total of eight crewmembers were killed throughout the year, the same number as 2010.

Somali pirates remain greatest threat

Somali pirates continue to account for the majority of attacks – approximately 54%. Nevertheless, while the overall number of Somali incidents increased from 219 in 2010 to 237 in 2011, the number of successful hijackings decreased from 49 to 28. The overall figures for Somali piracy could have been much higher if it were not for the continued efforts of international naval forces, IMB reports. In the last quarter of 2011 alone, pre-emptive strikes by international navies disrupted at least 20 Pirate Action Groups (PAGs) before they could become a threat to commercial fleets. The last quarter of 2010 saw 90 incidents and 19 vessels hijacked; in 2011, those numbers fell to 31 and four, respectively.

"These pre-emptive naval strikes, the hardening of vessels in line with the Best Management Practices and the deterrent effect of Privately Contracted Armed Security Personnel (PCASP), have all contributed to this decrease," said Pottengal Mukundan, Director of the IMB Piracy Reporting Centre (IMB PRC), which has been monitoring piracy worldwide since 1991. "The role of the navies is critical to the anti-piracy efforts in this area''. Although the number of vessels employing and reporting the carriage of PCASP increased in 2011, the regulation and vetting of PCASP still needs to be adequately addressed, Pottengal Mukundan warned. Until a comprehensive legal framework is in place, owners and Masters should follow the International Maritime Organization and industry guidelines on the carriage of PCASP. The IMB report shows that Somali pirate attacks were predominantly concentrated within the cross roads of the Arabian Sea and the Gulf of Aden. However, 2011 marked the first hijacking by Somali pirates of an anchored vessel from within the territorial waters of a foreign State – namely, Oman – highlighting the need for ports and vessels at anchorages in the region to be vigilant.

In 2011, August, the waters off the coast of Nigeria and Benin were — for the first time — judged to be as risky as those off Somalia by Lloyd's Market Association, a group of London-based maritime insurers.

The number of recorded pirate strikes in West Africa rose from 45 in 2010 to 64 in 2011, but it is widely believed that sea hits in this region are underreported. There were at least 10 assaults in January and February this year, according to the UN's International Maritime Organization.

A recent British parliament report noted the "copycat" nature of West African pirate gangs, but added, "while lessons should be learned from the experience with Somali piracy, such as the importance of swift intervention, piracy in the Gulf of Guinea has on the whole followed a different model to that of Somali piracy."

An important difference, and one that works against the pirates, is that while Nigeria is dysfunctional and highly corrupt, it is a state with a government and security forces, unlike Somalia. Another key distinction is that while Somali piracy is essentially an exercise in kidnap for ransom, Gulf of Guinea bandits target the cargo rather than the crew. Sailors on vessels hijacked off West Africa are unlikely to spend long months as hostages because the pirates may well kill them instead.

The economic effects of maritime crime[5]

Oil tankers are particularly prized by West Africa's pirates. Once seized, they are moored to other tankers. Their crude is transferred then sold on the black market, according to a recent UN report. These largely unprotected shipments are attractive — and easy — targets. Of all the attacks off West Africa last year, at least 20 were oil tankers, according to the IMB. Experts warn that piracy could disrupt oil supplies from the Gulf of Guinea, which produces an estimated 3 million barrels per day, most of which comes from Nigeria, the world's 8th largest oil exporter, according to the US Energy Information Administration.

Approximately 95 percent of Nigeria's exports are petroleum and petroleum-based products. In 2010, the country exported about $70 billion worth of petroleum products, at least 15 percent of which went to the US, according to One Earth Future's annual 'Economic ' report. "The United States believes that piracy in the Gulf of Guinea requires the strongest possible regional response, with international help," said US Ambassador to the UN Susan Rice at a UN Security Council meeting that was convened in New York at the end of February to discuss piracy in the Gulf of Guinea. Rice estimated that the gangsters on the sea are costing impoverished West Africa $2 billion a year. "There can be no doubt that the situation has become more grave. The impact of maritime crime on local economies is staggering," she said. The UN called for a joint international effort to halt piracy in the Gulf of Guinea.

"The threat not only persists but appears to be gaining ground in a region where the high-value assets the pirates target are abundant," said Under-Secretary General Lynn Pascoe. The United States values security along the West African coast because that allows oil ships to travel freely across the Atlantic. The US has been at the forefront of helping the mostly poor and ill-equipped West African countries to better confront the threat of maritime insecurity through the military Africa Command (AFRCIOM) and its annual Africa Partnership Station training exercises. The navy vessel USS Simpson arrived in Lagos, Nigeria, to begin this year's deployment in mid-February. The US spent $35 million over the last five years on training regional coastguards and navies, upgrading radar and other facilities, and refurbishing equipment, Rice said. Nevertheless, as in Somalia, it is likely that the solution to West African piracy is more effective governments that can maintain order both on land and at sea.

04 January 2012 IMB warns over Nigerian oil scams

The ICC International Maritime Bureau is warning members over ongoing scams involving the fraudulent sale of Nigerian petroleum products. The Bureau is regularly referred cases where vessels belonging to members are caught in the middle of a dispute. Most cases involve small companies based in either Nigeria or Ghana and poor quality documents that IMB analyses quickly proved as fake. The documents purportedly show the ownership of cargoes carried on board certain vessels and the scam centres on these spurious documents being sold on to unwitting buyers, often at a heavy discount or for a hefty advance fee. The IMB recently investigated a case on behalf of a German buyer which, involved much better quality documentation, including one apparently confirming that the Nigerian National Petroleum Company (NNPC) had indeed supplied the seller with the goods.

---

[5] **Courtesy of GlobalPost:**

Furthermore, the details of the cargo appeared to match that of a genuine shipment, which had taken place. More detailed checks, however, confirmed that the deal was nothing more than an advance-fee fraud. IMB Deputy Director Michael Howlett commented: "These scams often rest on the fact that the victim is not well-versed in commodity trading. An experienced oil trader would recognise these scams for what they are. However, someone less experienced may well be tempted by the low price and apparent authenticity of the documents." The NNPC has a select clientele of major oil traders, as such it is only those who normally sell the product to other established companies. Often, the sellers suggest to victims that they contact the vessels themselves and verify that the cargo is on board. It is possible, with relatively, minimal effort to confirm the cargo that a vessel is carrying. Confirming the ownership of such cargo, however, is more problematic.

IMB has recently seen cases where vessels have been detained at West African ports on the basis of false documentation regarding the ownership of cargo. Whilst innocence is quickly proved, there is still an impact in time and resources that could have been avoided were it not for these spurious transactions. Stringent due diligence checks on all parties involved in any major transaction are strongly recommended by IMB, even on parties with established trading records. Furthermore, the Bureau advises that all details of the shipment appearing on the documents are verified independently to prevent losses.

A. South and Central America and the Caribbean waters

Attacks have been reported in various ports in South America including Colombia, Venezuela, Peru, Ecuador and the Caribbean. However, the Brazilian ports of Rio de Janeiro and Santos remain by far the most affected areas, accounting for more than 80% of all the cases reported in the region. Some 20 incidents were reported in Brazil back in 1996, the largest number of attacks for a single country worldwide in that year. Attacks usually occur in ports or anchorages and occasionally extreme violence has been reported. The usual pattern in these places is that opportunist thieves will approach an anchored boat at random, climb aboard – armed with knives, machetes and guns – and demand cash and high-value goods.
Although the number of reported attacks has dropped in Santos, ships are advised to remain vigilant.

Brazil: Vila do Conde: Attacks have increased. Most attacks occurred at anchorage area.
Although the number of reported attacks has dropped in Santos, ships are advised to remain vigilant.

Peru: Callao: most attacks occurred at anchor despite vessel employing security watchmen.

Venezuela: Puerto La Cruz: Most attack occurred at anchorage.

Haiti: Port Au Prince: Attacks have increased especially in anchorage areas.

B. South East Asia and the Indian Sub-Continent

Bangladesh:

The area is still listed as high risk. Pirates are seen targeting ships preparing to anchor. Most attacks reported at Chittagong anchorages and approaches. In South East Asia and the Indian Subcontinent, 2011, vessels in Bangladesh reported 10 incidents of armed robbery in the approaches to Chittagong.

This is a significant reduction from the 23 incidents reported in 2010 and reflects the initiatives taken by the Bangladesh Coast Guard to curb piracy in their waters. Nonetheless, anchorages in the approaches to Chittagong remain an area of concern.

India:

Kandla. Most ships were attacked while at anchor. However, with Somali motherships being used as standard, the western seaboard of India should brace itself against further attacks. The Maltese-flagged Melina 1 came under attack by armed men in skiffs on 11 March 2010, about 200 nautical miles west of India's Lakshadweep Islands.
India's navy dispatched a coastguard ship and helicopter to the area, and the attackers fled.
The modus operandi of the attackers shows that they were most likely to be Somali gunmen.

Malacca Strait:

The situation in the Malacca Strait gives particular cause for concern. It is one of the busiest waterways in the world. The strait, in some stretches, is shallow and narrow and requires precise navigation.

Most attacks in the region have been on ships underway. The pattern used by the pirates is to board a steaming ship at night, undetected, and make their way to the ship's bridge. Once there, they overpower the officer of the navigational watch and either tie him up or handcuff him to the rail while the rest of the gang make for the master's and crew's cabins to demand money and valuables. Apart from the danger to the crew of the ship under attack, there is the horrifying hazard posed by a ship, often carrying dangerous cargoes, steaming at full speed, unattended, in confined waters.

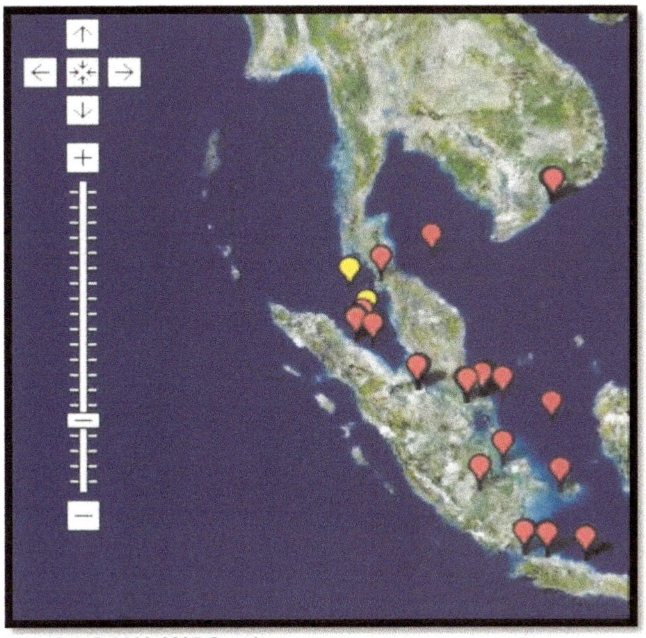

Map data © 2002-2007 Google

From 2002–2007, the IMB has recorded 258 pirate attacks in the Malacca Strait and surrounding waters, including more than 200 sailors held hostage and eight killed.

Only 2 incidents were reported in the Malacca Strait in 2009 – the same as in 2008. The insurance arm of Lloyd's classified the strait as a war zone in June 2005. Malaysia, Singapore, and Indonesia responded by bolstering security in their respective waters, and Lloyd's suspended the rating in August 2006. Therefore, the strait has been downgraded from a high-risk zone.

However, although the number of attacks has dropped due to the increase and aggressive patrols by the littoral states authorities since July 2005, ships are advised to continue maintaining a strict anti-piracy watch when transiting the straits. Currently, there are no indications as to how long these patrols will continue or reduce.

Indonesia:

Anambas/Natuna/Mangkai/SubiBesar islands area. Pirates normally armed with guns/knives and/or machetes. Generally, be vigilant in other areas. Many attacks may have gone unreported. Pirates normally attack vessel at night. When spotted, pirates usually abort the attempted boarding. Indonesia has seen a rise in armed robbery for the second straight year. The incidents continue to be local and opportunistic, according to IMB, and usually against anchored vessels.

The 46 reported incidents – up from 40 in 2010 – include 41 vessels boarded, two attempted attacks, and three cases of tugs and barges being hijacked whilst underway.

Malaysia:

Off Tioman/PulauAur/South China Sea. Although no reported attacks recently, vessels are advised to remain vigilant. In the past, pirates armed with guns and knives attack vessels during the hour of darkness. A number of tugs / barges were also hijacked in the area.

South China Sea:

This used to be one of the most treacherous areas of water in the world, with regular acts of violent piracy and murders taking place. This should be borne in mind if a vessel is planning to go there. A number of reports described persons attempting to stop and board the ships in the guise of officials or wearing uniforms. It has not been possible to confirm whether those involved were officials acting within their jurisdiction, officials acting outside their normal duties or private individuals dressed as officials.

Be careful in the vicinity off Anambas/Natuna /Mangkai slands/SubiBesar area. Attacks in the South China Sea fell from 31 in 2010 to 13 in 2011. This included nine boarded vessels, three attempted attacks, and the hijacking of one tug and its barge.

Philippines: Manila – Pirates tend to target ships at anchor.

Singapore Straits:

Vessels are advised to continue maintaining adequate anti-piracy watch and measures despite the reduction in attacks. Pirates attack ships while underway or while anchored at Eastern OPL.

Vietnam: In the vicinity off Vung Tau

E. Rest of the World

Europe: Recently attacks have taken place off Italy, Sardinia, Corsica and, in July–August 2009, the cargo vessel Baltic Sea off the Swedish coast.

That chapter and the following are to show how far and wide the scourge of piracy and robbery spreads across the globe.

Not all pirates follow a code of conduct and will kill if challenged or resisted.

SOME EXAMPLES OF GLOBAL PIRACY AND THEFT:

This list is to show examples of areas where they took place.

SY Seamaster, Brazil, December 2001:

The New Zealand yachting legend Sir Peter Blake was murdered by armed attackers in Amazonia while acting as a United Nations Environment Program Ambassador. He was 53. His yacht, Seamaster, was attacked at night and he is reported to have died instantly from gunshot wounds. Sir Peter Blake will be remembered not only as the man who won the America's Cup for New Zealand, but also for his devotion to environmental work.

SY Tiara, Corsica, August 2008:

Four armed men commandeered the Tiara, a 55-metre luxury yacht, near the French island of Corsica, looting the vessel's safe. Arriving on a dinghy, the men seized the vessel overnight as it was lying at anchor off the southern Corsican town of Porto Vecchio, overcoming the ship's 10-man crew and nine passengers before fleeing. This attack is thought to have been spurred by corrupt officials who knew the amount of cash and people on board; however that has never been proven.

SY Mr Bean, Thailand, March 2009:
A British couple's trip of a lifetime, sailing around the world on their yacht Mr Bean, ended in horror after 3 Burmese pirates tied up his wife and then killed the husband, and tossed his body overboard. The attack occurred close to the Buntang Islands off Thailand in the NE area of the Malacca Strait, the body of water notorious for piracy that runs between mainland South East Asia and Indonesia.

Motor boat, Italy, June 2009:

Naple's Bay, near Posillipo
At 2100 hours, three people aboard a fast launch rammed a 42-foot motorboat with two people on board. They boarded the boat and robbed the owner and his friend, then made them put on life jackets before throwing them overboard and stealing the boat and disappearing into the dusk. The two victims were rescued, suffering from mild hypothermia.

The Baltic Sea, Sweden, July 2009:

Russian seafarers on board. It was en route from Finland to the Algerian port of Bejaia with a cargo of sawn timber. The ship was reportedly hijacked in Swedish waters after being boarded by a group of armed men claiming to be anti-drugs police. Later reports say the vessel was recaptured by Russian forces in the area of the Cape Verde Islands.

The Sirius Star , Indian Ocean, 2008:

The $3,000,000+ ransom being dropped by parachute

On 17 November 2008, the US navy announced that the Sirius Star, a Saudi-owned super tanker loaded with crude oil, had been hijacked by Somali pirates. The hijacking of the Sirius Star marks the first pirate attack on a very large crude carrier, and was reportedly the furthest ship from land to be hijacked at that time. The attack occurred on Saturday 15 November, approximately 450 miles off the coast of Kenya. Twenty-five crewmembers were aboard the ship, which was sailing under a Liberian flag. This famous hijacking was a major turning point in the fight against piracy. The world realised how vulnerable their vessels were, despite distance from Somalia, despite the speed and size of the vessel. The pirates realised how easy it was to take such as ship and reap the rewards of such a large profit.

On 9 January 2009, the ship and its crew were released after the pirates were paid a reported $3 million+ ransom. All crewmembers were reportedly accounted for and unharmed. Shortly after they left the Sirius Star, the pirates' ship capsized due to rough weather. According to a local journalist, four of the pirates drowned and one survived. The surviving pirate reported that some of the ransom money was also lost at sea.

SY Lynn Rival: Gulf of Aden 23 Oct 2009

SY Lynn Rival

Paul and Rachel Chandler

Photos courtesy of 'Yachtpals'

The 100-strong crew of the RFA Wave Knight were under orders not to open fire as Paul and Rachel Chandler, of Tunbridge Wells, Kent, were taken from their yacht, for fear that the couple could be executed by the pirates. With the nearest warship, HMS Cumberland, two hours away, the lightly armed Royal Fleet Auxiliary ship, which was carrying a helicopter crew and 75 merchant seamen, was forced to play a high-stakes waiting game, the Royal Navy said. However, there were fears that the presence of the British ship may even have rushed the pirates into taking the couple off their 38-foot yacht, the Lynn Rival, more quickly.

This picture taken from the Wave Knight shows the Chandlers' empty yacht drifting - and HMS Cumberland, which arrived too late

The gang that kidnapped the Chandlers from their yacht had demanded a $7 million ransom and had threatened to shoot the couple if they don't get the money. Sailors of small vessels often and incorrectly assume that the pirates will not target them as their small vessel is worth much less than a larger commercial vessel. The Somali pirates don't care about the vessel, as they well know that the ransom will be paid for the safe release of the people. After 12 gruelling months the Chandlers were safely released in October 2010. [6]

Le Ponant , GoA, 11 April 2008

The 87-metre, Le Ponant

The three-masted, 32-cabin vessel, which is operated by CMA CGM cruise subsidiary, Compagnie des Iles du Ponant, was taken over by pirates off the northern Somali coast in the GoA on 4 April 2008. It was taken under the pirates' control to Garacad, south of the port of Eyl, where it spent one week whilst negotiations were under way between representatives of the pirates and CMA CGM and the French authorities. There were no passengers on board the 87-metre (288-foot), yacht when it was hijacked with 30 crewmembers on board. Six of the pirates who took over Le Ponant were arrested by French forces following the liberation of the vessel's 30 crewmembers.

---

[6] Details of their ordeal can be read in their excellent book "Hostage" ISBN 978-1-84596-795-6.

The head of the French army, Général Jean-Louis Georgelin, said that the pirates were arrested after having gone ashore about one hour after the freeing of the crew of the Le Ponant. 'We were able to track the pirates, which made it possible to intercept about half the commando through a helicopter action,' he said.

Armed Somali pirates on board the Le Ponant

The operation was carried out with the authorisation of the Somali authorities, according to Général Georgelin, who indicated that warning and interception shots were fired but said that there had been no direct firing on the pirates themselves. The arrested pirates were being held off the Somali coast on the helicopter carrier Jeanne d'Arc, according to a senior French navy spokesman.

French military leaders, who were speaking in a press conference at the headquarters of the French presidency, the Elysées Palace, indicated that no state funds had been paid to the pirates to obtain the liberation of the crew of the Le Ponant but did not rule out the possibility that a ransom had been paid by Le Ponant's owner, the CMA CGM shipping group.

The French presidency announced that the Le Ponant's 30-strong crew – 22 French nationals, six Filipinos, a Ukrainian and a Cameroonian – had been liberated after The French presidency announced that the Le Ponant's 30-strong crew – 22 French nationals, six Filipinos, a Ukrainian and a Cameroonian – had been liberated after talks with representatives of the pirates.

Maersk Alabama, Indian Ocean 2009

On 8 April 2009, four Somali pirates boarded the Maersk Alabama when it was located 240 nautical miles southeast of the Somali port city of Eyl. With a crew of 20, the ship was en route to Mombasa, Kenya. Maersk Line Limited is one of the US Defence's primary shipping contractors, although the vessel was not under military contract at the time. The ship was carrying 17,000 metric tonnes of cargo, of which 5,000 metric tonnes were relief supplies bound for Somalia, Uganda and Kenya.

According to Chief Engineer Mike Perry, the engineers sank the pirate speedboat shortly after the boarding by continuously swinging the rudder of the Maersk Alabama, thus scuttling the smaller boat.

As the pirates were boarding the ship, the crewmembers locked themselves in the engine room while the captain, Richard Phillips, and two other crewmembers remained on the bridge.
The engineers then took away control of the ship from down below, rendering the bridge controls useless. The pirates were thus unable to control the ship.
The crew later used brute force to overpower one of the pirates, and freed one of the hostages. Frustrated, the pirates decided to leave the ship, and took the captain with them to a lifeboat as their bargaining tool. The crew attempted to exchange a captured pirate, whom they had kept tied up for twelve hours, for Captain Phillips. The captured pirate was released but the pirates refused to release Phillips. After running out of fuel in the ship's man overboard boat, they transferred and left in the ship's covered lifeboat, taking Phillips with them. The lifeboat carried ten days of food rations, water, and basic survival supplies.

On the same day, the destroyer USS Bainbridge was dispatched to the Gulf of Aden in response to a hostage situation, and reached the Maersk Alabama early on 9 April. Maersk Alabama then departed from the area, with an armed escort, towards its original destination in Mombasa, Kenya, with the vessel's chief mate, S Murphy, in charge. On 9 April, a standoff began between USS Bainbridge and the pirates in the Maersk Alabama's lifeboat, where they continued to hold Captain Phillips hostage.

On Saturday 11April, Maersk Alabama arrived in the port of Mombasa, still under US military escort, where Captain Aasheim, who had previously been captain of the Maersk Alabama until Phillips had relieved him eight days prior to the pirate attack, relieved Murphy. An 18-man marine security team was on board. The FBI secured the ship as a crime scene. On Sunday 12 April, Phillips was rescued in good condition. Acting under prior authorisation from US president Barack Obama, the captain of USS Bainbridge ordered the action upon determining that life was in immediate danger, as provided by US navy SEAL reports that an AK-47 assault rifle was being pointed at him. The US Navy SEAL snipers on Bainbridge's fantail opened fire, killing the three pirates remaining in the lifeboat. A fourth, injured pirate surrendered and was taken into custody.

Second pirate attack on Maersk Alabama, November 2009

At 6.30am on 18 November 2009, the Maersk Alabama was reportedly sailing some 350 nautical miles east of Somalia when four pirates wielding automatic weapons and travelling in a skiff fired upon it. The assault failed after guards on the ship responded with small-arms fire and acoustical weapons. Afterwards, a Djibouti-based patrol plane flew to the scene and an EU ship searched the area.

"There is an obvious lesson to be learned from this; until a non-lethal system is available and works, to ensure the safety of your vessel, use professional, armed guards." PK

Two and a half years later, the nautical hero ends up in court because he sailed too close to the Somali coast. The following newspaper article explains.

Capt. Phillips' crew sues Maersk following Somali pirate hijack[7]

The 2009 hijacking by Somali pirates of the US-flagged *Maersk Alabama*, en route from Djibouti to Mombasa, was one of the most dramatic acts in the many chapters of the piracy story that has played out in recent years. And over the weekend it took a new twist.

More than half of the ship's crew is now suing Maersk's US subsidiary and the crew management company, Waterman Steamship Corporation, for a combined total of $50m in damages, claiming corporate negligence.

The incident turned the vessel's captain, Richard Phillips, into a national hero. Somali pirates attacked the vessel some 250 miles off the coast of Somalia on 8th April, but were unable to assume command because the crew fought back.

Then Capt. Phillips offered himself in exchange for the safety of the vessel and crew. After three days in one of the vessel's lifeboats with four hijackers, US Navy Seals attacked the pirates and freed Capt. Phillips, killing three of his captors in an action that clearly lends itself to Hollywood. [8]

However, the papers filed in Norfolk, Virginia and Mobile, Alabama, allege that Maersk and Waterman, through the actions of Phillips, are guilty of deliberately putting them in grave danger, because two days before the attack the ship had received a warning from the US Maritime Administration that all vessels should sail at least 600 miles off the Somali coast because of pirate activity. This would have added 36 hours to its sailing time and consumed considerably more fuel.

"Defendants knowingly, intentionally and wilfully sent their employees, including plaintiff, into an area where pirates were attacking merchant vessels. Despite knowingly exposing their employees and the plaintiff to such grave danger, defendants failed to take adequate steps to provide appropriate levels of security and safety for their employees.

"Defendants showed a wilful, wanton and conscious disregard for the safety of plaintiff and other officers and crew of the *Maersk Alabama* and did so primarily for financial gain," claimed a paper filed on behalf of crewmember John Cronan, who is claiming $20 million in compensatory and punitive damages as a result of receiving physical injuries and suffering severe post-traumatic stress disorder which has left him with large medical bills and reducing earning potential.

In a filed response, Maersk called the suit "meritless" and claimed that it could not be held responsible for the actions of the pirates, and added that the crew understood the inherent risks of working in shipping and that since the US Coast Guard had approved the *Maersk Alabama's* vessel security plan it has immunity from liability.

There has also been a precedent, of sorts. In December 2009, the Maersk Alabama steward Richard Hicks filed a case against the same two defendants in a similar motion (and interestingly John Cronan later joined him) in Harris County Court in Houston, but the case remains mired in a debate over whether a Texas court has jurisdiction over Virginia-based Maersk and Alabama-based Waterman.

---

[7] Gavin van Marle 28th May 2012

[8] The film *Captain Phillips* is currently shooting; the fact that it's directed by Jason Bourne director Paul Greengrass and starring Tom Hanks gives a pretty clear indication of what cinema-goers can expect when it goes on release March 2013.

The Norfolk case is not expected to go to trial for at least a year, so there is all manner of further twists and turns that could be taken, although one implication is more or less certain: if ultimately the court finds in favour of the 11 crew, it is likely to pave the way for a whole slew of compensation claims from crew that have suffered the nightmare of being a hostage.

During these times of global economic crisis, shipping companies do what they can to cut overheads and taking the most direct route is sometimes a risk that is taken. Some ships are so fast and have very high freeboards that it is not possible to board them by Somali pirates using skiffs and ladders, but as the British flagged MV Asian Glory found out, it only takes a lapse in concentration and the ship has been hijacked. In their case the pilot's door was left open. The high, slab-sided car carrier was deemed untouchable, but the open door was the Achilles heel and the ship was easily and quickly hijacked.

What Capt. Philips did, offering his life in exchange for the rest of the crew was extremely brave and unselfish; the crew should remember this when standing before him in court. It is hoped he is not the scapegoat in this trial and pardoned for his decisions and actions.

Good luck Captain Philips (right)

3. Types of Attack and Methods of Boarding

Pirates and thieves use various methods of climbing on board vessels. All the methods they are currently using are very basic, but are often effective. Attackers are often successful due to the fact that they are unopposed. It is not recommended that the ship's crew go and fight off the pirates in order to save the vessel, but many attacks have been thwarted when the crew have used simple means to stop the attackers getting on board, like setting off fire hoses, throwing items at the pirates or their skiffs, unhooking their ladders and cutting the ropes and grappling hooks. It is a fine balance between being brave and defending initially to stop the boarding and putting the crew in harm's way. This is something that has to be decided by the CSO, Captain, and crew prior to entering hostile waters.

Vessels at anchor.

For smaller, private vessels, attackers will approach by whatever means they have to hand. In Colombia, large pieces of polystyrene are used as boats or rafts for fishing and transport, and these have been used in the past, as have dug-out canoes, old windsurfing boards, and even tenders. If a vessel is at anchor, the lowest points will be the most sought after; the anchor cable will be another. A thief or pirate will usually use a grappling hook or rigid ladder with a hook welded on the end to get on board. The best defence for this is avoidance, with the crew detailed to perform sentry duty for a period each, throughout the night. The use of lights above and below the water line is also good deterrent. There are electronic measures too, such as 'Night Owl', a system that homes in on the target, illuminates them and triggers an acoustic device to repel attackers. On larger vessels, it is recommended to keep the anchor wash turned on, use sentries and avoid leaving Pilot's steps or Jacob's ladders on the ship's sides; all should be fully retracted to the highest position. The vessel and its surroundings should be fully illuminated with deck lighting; if necessary, cover low freeboard areas with high-pressure fire hoses (Nemesis 5000), to make it as difficult as possible for the attackers to climb on board. Other measures to be considered include greasing the railings, erecting electric fences (Secure Marine), installing razor-wire, nets and using PIR guard systems.

When deploying crew to guard the vessel, ensure that they are fully briefed; don't expect them to know exactly what they should be doing or looking out for. Ensure they are well rested, nor have a period of vigilance that is not too long, and have suitable communications with those inside the vessel. All blind spots of the vessel must be patrolled. Should an incident occur, the crew should understand that they are there to detect and deter, but not to put themselves in harm's way.

From an outsider looking inwards towards the vessel, a patrolman at night, wandering around looking professional and assertive, using his torch to shine into key areas and across nearby water will be enough to deter most opportunist thieves; relying solely on cameras is not an option. Well-used anchorages are preferable to quiet ones, with other boats for mutual support; this is especially important with smaller vessels. However, as seen in the Lagos anchorage, Nigeria, mutual support doesn't really work there at night; every vessel is a potential target.

Super yachts have been known to deploy their tender or RIB to patrol around the area of the vessel to ensure the security of the owner or clients on board.
One well-known businessman has an armed team of more than 12 ex-Ghurkha Soldiers that deploy with him when he travels by sea.

On commercial ships ensure that anchor plates are used.

Superyachts with hydraulic sterns that can be opened and lowered into the water should be retracted during the night; an open-ended luxury yacht is a golden opportunity for the poor and desperate thief. Without teaching the mariner how to suck eggs, protection of a vessel at anchor is quite straightforward and common sense prevails, but if night vision cameras are used, or thermal imagers or any other manned technical surveillance equipment then it is only as good as the person who is on watch and reacting to it. The best method is a decent sentry patrolling the boat with a torch and radio depending upon the vessel's location.

For ships with high free boards, the stern is usually the targeted area of entry, so ensure your sentries cover this area, or all doors are securely locked down and access grills are padlocked shut. Once done ensure that the OOW is informed. Often shipping companies and owners are put off by inflated pricing and fancy technical wizardry that may fail as soon as it becomes damp. In that case, the ratings are usually placed on watch, or no guarding is done at all. A simple solution is to cover vulnerable areas with simple PIR activated security lights. At less than £10 each, these lights can be put out when the ship is at anchor, any movement will activate them, so ensure that an item cannot blow around in a draught, thus setting them off. The triggering of a PIR light can be enough to make the intruder go away and alert the ship's sentry. The electrical officer onboard can add a bell or siren to the light so both go off when the circuit is made.

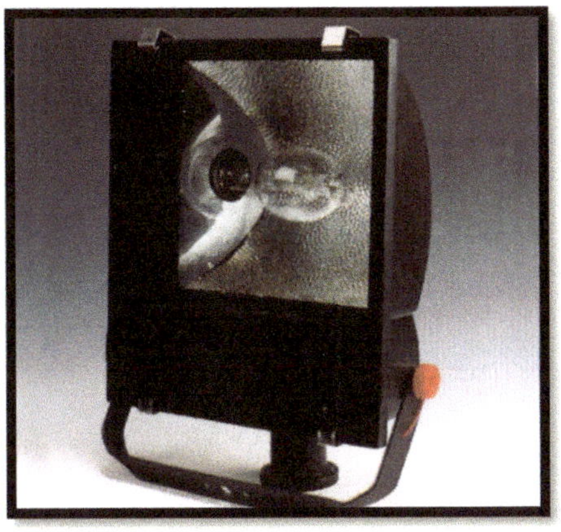

Various PIR lights that can be used to cover 'blind spots' such as the poop deck, thus helping security situations.

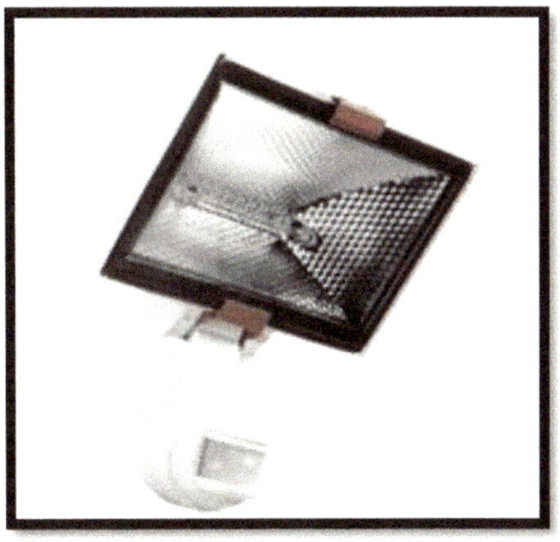

Vessels underway

For vessels underway the determined attackers will have no problem gaining access, as seen constantly in the GoA HRA. The key factors that will make your vessel safer are; freeboard height, speed (very few vessels have been taken over 16kts), sea state (pirates can board up to sea state 5) time of year (monsoon season is much safer to transit in rough waters) day/night (pirates attack visually, so night is safer depending upon lunar illumination), ship is hardened and has all that is mentioned in BMP4 and onboard security either private or military.

Attacks on moving targets used to be within a shortish distance of a shore; now, with the tactic of hijacking vessels to be used as motherships, that has changed. Recently Somali pirates have taken vessels from the Indian coast right down to Mozambique. Motherships have the ability to put their skiffs in the water very quickly; some vessels tow their skiffs, and others have them on board. Only some four years ago, mother ships were not a common tool, now the Somali pirates realise that they can take a ship, use it immediately to attack more using the captured crew to their advantage, as they know their ship inside out.

Some hostages used to be taken ashore, now they are held on the ship, as it has all the provisions required, and so the ships are forced to help capture more ships that are unaware that that particular vessel is now a pirate mother ship. The disguised motherships offers many advantages: it will probably have a decent electronics suite such as radar, AIS, VHF and hi-powered communications – many items the pirates didn't have the luxury of a few years ago – as well as provisions that will last long periods of time and vast amounts of fuel and water.

Small yachts and vessels often think that because of their small size and low cost that they will be left alone, and that the pirates are only interested in the ships containing high value products such as crude oil or containers/bulk. This is far from the truth. The pirates can demand the same ransom for a 36' sailing yacht as they can for a 340m container ship. In 2011 the pirates started to use more powerful skiffs too, previously the small wooden or fibreglass skiff had one or two out board engines that range between 30hp-60hp (Yamaha being the favorite). Now larger, faster lightweight boats are being used with larger twin OBMs that can achieve 30+kts on flat water, and a lot of the time the waters in the GoA and surrounding areas can be dead flat! Even now after so many BMPs being produced and available online or as a hardcopy, sailing yachts still sail through the HRA with full sails up. This is a very dangerous practice and should never happen. The high sails can be seen like a marker beacon from miles away, often over the horizon attracting everyone's attention. Pirates know sailing boats are far less likely to carry armed guards due to space and expense, and are easy to board with low speeds and low freeboards.

Whether 350m or 35m, pirates don't care – it's about the ransom

The below diagram shows the high-risk sectors that should be observed by lookouts on vessels underway at 20kts and over, or when the sea state is 4 or above. For vessels travelling less than 20kts in calm waters, the threat is 360°.

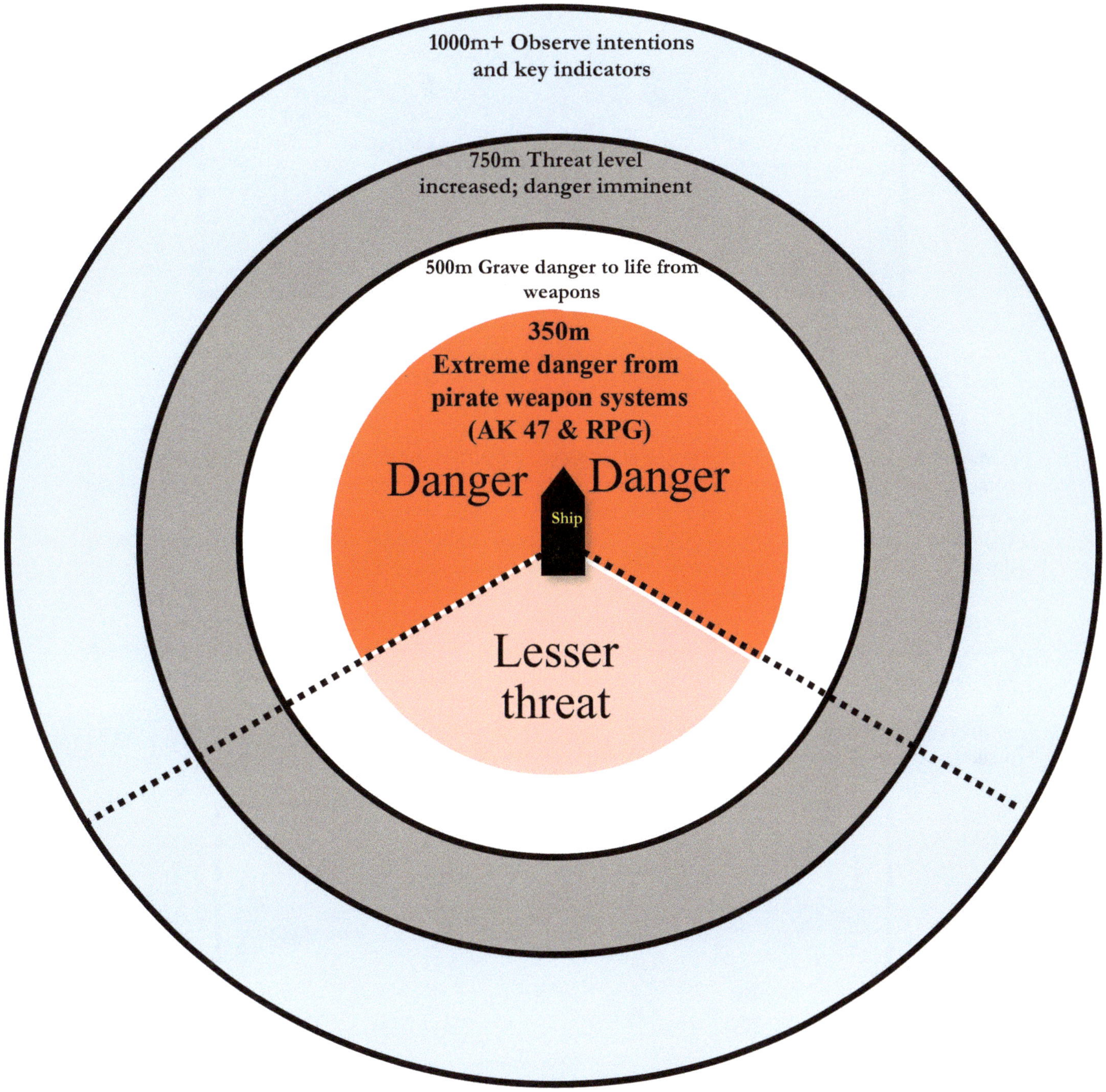

With the current equipment used by Somali pirates, in order to close in on targets, the pirates must start their attack from either forward or flanking positions. On calm seas, skiff speed is around 20kts. Skiffs deploying from abaft 135° or 235° would take too long to catch up with the target vessel and board, especially if the target is 'zigzagging', in rougher seas or turning into sea. Captains should ensure the sentries are aware of their arcs, unless the vessel is slower than 20kts or pirates are using the new high-speed skiffs that have been sighted off East Africa in 2011.

The pirate group MEND from the Niger Delta region is much more brutal and has greater firepower than those found in other areas.

A small boat bouncing around on the sea is an unstable platform from which to fire from. Anyone trying to fire a weapon accurately from a skiff in anything apart from a mirror-flat sea is going to have a very difficult time engaging the target accurately from distances over 100m. There is much more chance of hitting the target purely by luck. The same applies to hand-held rocket launchers such as the RPG. An RPG 7 is a Russian-made, robust, battle proven, shoulder-launched, multiple-use anti-tank weapon. RPG means rocket-propelled grenade and it is a very effective. The grenade itself is not like a hand grenade that explodes in all directions; instead, the warhead has a shaped charge inside. When the warhead strikes its surface, the explosion accelerates forwards and can penetrate up to several inches of solid metal. RPGs are very cheap and extremely common in war-torn countries such as Iraq, Afghanistan and Somalia; they are also very easy to use. The good news for vessels sailing close to countries where these weapons are in abundance, is that to fire one accurately from a distance of over 75m in a choppy sea and hit the target is very difficult.

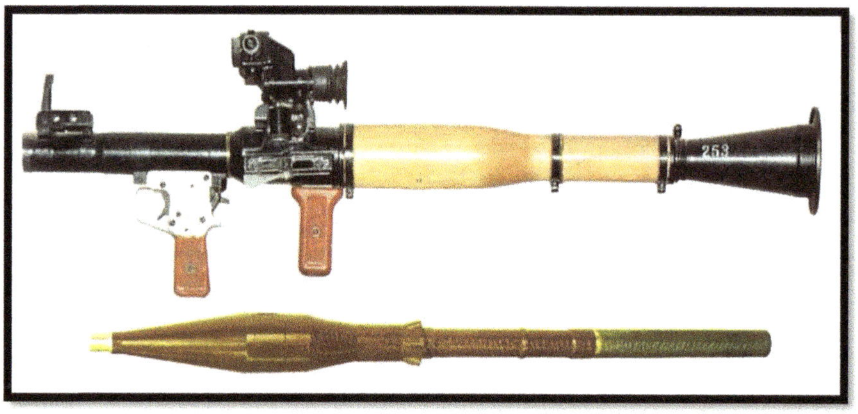

RPG 7 with an optic sight
(sight is not used by Somali pirates)

Pirates in the GoA will fire weapons close to or over the vessel to persuade it to stop. Unless it is unavoidable, the vessel should not stop but keep going at full speed, ideally into a sea that will slow down or stop the pursuers. The RPG has a safe-arming distance, usually around 10+m, so if an RPG is fired and hits an object less than 10m away, the warhead will not detonate.

There is also a safety pin in the nose cone that is often not removed in the height of excitement, so again the head will not explode. These considerations mean that the firer has to get close enough to a vessel to be accurate enough to hit it, and the RPG only has a maximum range of 350m on land. Normally, RPGs will be fired at distances of no more than 200m; a realistic range would be 50-150m. If a skiff is within 150m, well-trained security guards, aboard a much more stable platform definitely have the upper hand and a huge advantage over the small, bouncy skiff and at this range they could target and kill each individual pirate or destroy the engine with a single shot. Pirates are usually warned with flares and warning shots well before 350m, the accurate fire from 7.62 or 5.56mm will engage to 400m and beyond, depending upon the rifle type, the barrel length, and firer's ability.

It could be that the attacker is a battle-hardened warrior, but just as easily they could be young teenagers sent out to sea to go and capture what they can find and bring it back to Somalia. Nevertheless, the potential danger of any pirates should never be underestimated.

The high bow and white wash of a wooden skiff is usually the first things seen in the water. The next thing you should be looking for is the ladder protruding over the end of the bow, a clear target indicator that these men are pirates, not armed fishermen.

On the more tranquil waters of the world, a small tender approaching your yacht off St Tropez, Margarita or the sleepy cays around Indigo Island, can quietly approach in flat calm seas and pull out a weapon such as a handgun, which at close range (20m and less) would be lethal. It is very difficult to say exactly what to do in this situation, but alarms should be pressed to inform the crew and guests; the authorities will be monitoring for such emergency calls and distress signals, such as SSAS or EPIRB. Cooperation without agitation is the best advice.

Years ago, when pirates boarded vessels it was often a matter of giving them what they wanted, usually high-value goods, and they would leave. These days, piracy is a much more organised and serious game.

A sailor in South America was approached on his catamaran by a small tender; the men came aboard armed with knives and a machete and wanted his newer outboard motor for themselves. He fought back using his own machete and lost an arm during the fight. The sailor was lucky not to bleed to death and, in hindsight, was foolish to defend a small-value item at the cost of an arm.

Once thieves and pirates are aboard a vessel, everyone should adopt a passive role and aid the robbers so they can get off the vessel as soon as possible. It should be remembered that all material items are replaceable and most are insured.

Various internal/external pictures of what pirates have done to vessels

Cabins have been ransacked and looted. Rubbish and old khat lies discarded

SY Quest in Djibouti Harbour, full of bullet holes

Bullet holes

Somali Pirates and their underway tactics

Times are desperate for the people of Somali, as one of the poorest countries in the world and cursed with drought that leads to famine; it's hardly a wonder that desperate men turn to piracy. Somali has a colourful and harsh past, there are so many stories and reports from the country it is difficult to decipher what is true and what is not. What is known is that Somali piracy first began in earnest in January 1991 with the hijacking of MV Naviluck. The crew were killed and the ship burnt. Twenty years later it has morphed into an international business from which many are making huge profits, not only the seasoned pirates.
Pirates can range in age from early teens to weathered 40+ year olds. Some will have spent their entire lives upon the seas; others will be ex-combatants or members of the former Puntland Coastguard, the Somali Marines or SomCan. Never presume they are young, desperate men seeking fortune; some will be very well trained with experience.

Somali men working for the Puntland Coastguard. This was relatively effective until the men weren't paid.

All are desperate men wanting a quick fix for easy cash, most chewing khat* and wanting to take that one vessel in order to get a one-off payment that will set them up in business as something legitimate. However, one easy payment can lead to the lure of another, and then a third. Pirates are squanderers and spend their money quickly on luxury items such as new vehicle, on women and Khat and share some with family and friends. Soon the money has gone and another easy fix is simple to obtain despite the risk of death or imprisonment. Don't be sympathetic towards Somali pirates thinking that they have had their fish poached and shores poisoned; these are contributing factors but it doesn't give them the right to take up arms and turn into the cold blooded, torturing murderers that we have seen recently. Look at the recent attacks upon the SY Quest and MV Beluga. * see page 252

The men themselves wear very basic clothing: no Henri Lloyd jackets or Musto shoes here, just simple day-to-day clothing including old military uniforms, leather sandals or flip-flops are common. Onboard they eat a little simple food, have a large drum of water, and use general boat running equipment and climbing equipment. Their technology is about as advanced as handheld VHF, satellite phone, compass and GPS; they're quite brave doing what they do with so little, especially if operating without a mother craft. It is said that some pirates leave the shore on a one way mission; capture a ship or perish. This is due to them only having enough fuel, food and water to last for a few days. This sort of do or die pressure is probably why attacks still take place in the GoA and IRTC where ships are travel in numbers and are escorted by naval patrols.

Who the Somali pirates are.

According to a BBC report, most pirates come from the region of Puntland, in northeastern Somalia. The pirates can be divided into four main groups operating off the Somali coast.

1. The National Volunteer Coast Guard (NVCG), commanded by Garaad Mohamed, is said to specialise in intercepting small boats and fishing vessels around Kismayo on the southern coast.

2. The Marka group, under the command of Yusuf Mohammed SiadInda'ade, is made up of several scattered and less organised groups operating around the town of Marka.

3. The third significant pirate group is composed of traditional Somali fishermen operating around Puntland and referred to as the Puntland Group. *(See page 56 khat)

4. The last set are the Somali Marines, reputed to be the most powerful and sophisticated of the pirate groups, with a military structure, a fleet admiral, admiral, vice-admiral and a head of financial operations.

Reports suggest that Somalia had a thriving fishing industry and foreign poachers would take their fish stocks using huge purse seine nets and modern systems that destroyed the reefs to catch lobster and crab. Other reports say that to make money, licences were sold by the authorities for large sums on a regular basis, this spread and the fishing boats defended themselves using anti-aircraft guns against the Somalis.

Other reports suggest that the Somali shores were a dumping ground for toxic waste; the UN officials say otherwise. Whatever the truth is, what is known is that Somali has had an awful lot of bad luck over the years. It would be nice to see an end to civil unrest and a stable, uncorrupted government be in charge again and stop piracy once and for all.

Stability within Somali: Piracy is temporarily halted.

Somali piracy was halted in early 2006 when the **Islamic Courts Union** (ICU) took control over various states. This is the way to stop the piracy: on land, not on the sea. Unfortunately, the ICU lost control by the end of that same year and piracy continued to flourish in 2007, accelerating out of control.

Background information:

The **Islamic Courts Union** (**ICU**) was a group of Sharia Courts who united themselves to form a rival administration to the Transitional Federal Government (TFG) of Somalia, with Sharif Sheikh Ahmed as head of the ICU. They are also known as the **Joint Islamic Courts**, **Union of Islamic Courts** (**UIC**), **Supreme Islamic Courts Council** (**SICC**) or the **Supreme Council of Islamic Courts** (**SCIC**). Western media often refer to the group as **Somali Islamists**.

Until the end of 2006, they controlled most of southern Somalia and the vast majority of its population, including most major cities such as Jowhar, Kismayo, Beledweyne, and the capital Mogadishu.

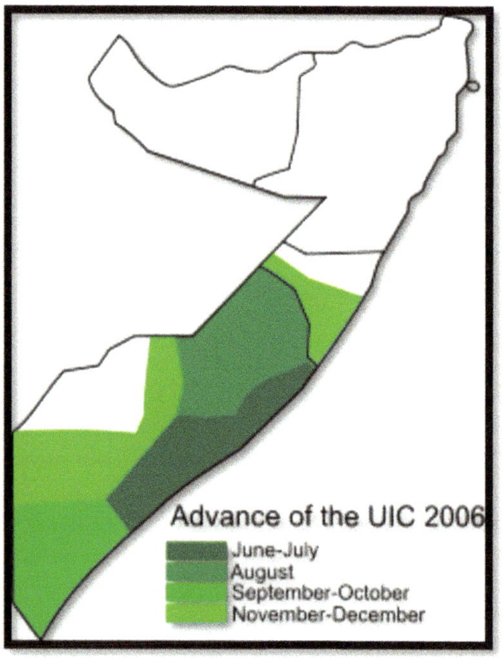

The ICU was supported by warlord Yusuf "Indho Ade" Mohamed Siad who ruled Lower Shabelle but later became defense chief of the ICU, who aided in the defeat of the Mogadishu warlords. Only the Northern regions (Puntland, Somaliland), and the furthest interior regions of the south were outside their control.

In December 2006, the ICU lost much territory after defeats at the battles of Baidoa, Bandiradley, and Beledweyne, retreating to the capital, Mogadishu. On December 28th, they abandoned Mogadishu, leaving the city in chaos while they moved south towards Kismayo, which allowed the TFG and Ethiopian troops to take over the city. After a stand at the Battle of Jilib, the ICU abandoned the city of Kismayo on January 1, 2007. Stripped of almost all their territory, it was speculated the ICU would pursue guerrilla-style warfare against the government.

Instead, hardline Islamists broke ranks from the ICU and formed other militant groups, such as Al-Shabaab and Hizbul Islam, to continue the war against the government. The less-militant members of the ICU went into exile in Eritrea and Djibouti, where they formed the Alliance for the Re-Liberation of Somalia in September 2007. In the two years following the ICU's ouster from Mogadishu, the hardline Islamist groups concentrated their power in the south and west of Somalia, taking ground from both the TFG and ICU.

By January 2009, a reconciliation and powersharing deal was brokered between the Transitional Federal Government (TFG) and the Djibouti contingent from the former Islamic Courts Union which resulted in the expansion of the Parliament and the election of Sheik Sharif Ahmed, former leader of the ICU, as President of the Transitional Federal Government.

Social policies

The Islamic Courts' claimed mission was to bring social justice and combat iniquity thus after capturing Mogadishu it brought Sharia law back to Somalia and re instituted the constitution.

In the year 2000, the courts formed a union of Islamic courts, partly to consolidate resources and power and partly to aid in handing down decisions across, rather than within, clan lines.

In an interview featured in the BBC Online Somali section in June 2006, Sheik Sharif Shaykh Ahmed said "the union of Islamic courts was established to ensure that Somali people suffering for 15 years would gain peace and full justice and freedom from the anarchic rule of warlords who refuted their people to no direction."

- On October 5, 2006 the Islamic Courts had declared the formation of the supreme Islamic Sharia court of Banadir province. The announcement ceremony was attended by all Islamic officials; both consultative and executive councils, intellectuals and civil society members and took place in the former Somalian presidential palace in central Mogadishu. That announcement from the central Islamic Court was destined to end all tribal Islamic Courts in the capital.

- On November 17, 2006, the ICU had banned the use, sale and transportation of *khat* altogether and the Islamic Court of Kismayo banned the sale of cigarettes. This was a controversial move as it was the main source of income for many war widows and orphans and a huge import-export business.

- The ICU fought pirate activity at the Somali coast, which subsequently declined during its rule.

Harakat al-Shabaab Mujahedeen

The Hizbul Shabaab, also known as Al-Shabaab, or simply as "Shabaab", is the Youth Wing of the ICU. It is a radical and somewhat independent organization under the ICU umbrella that is integrated quite tightly with the ICU armed forces, acting as a sort of "special forces" for the ICU.

The Shabab caused difficulties for the ICU in maintaining a good international image on a number of occasions due to their hot-headedness and zealousness, such as abducting critical journalists, harassing overly-hip youngsters, and murdering wounded JVA soldiers in a Bu'aale hospital.

The ICU formally apologized for each of the incidents, and attempted to make it clear that these actions did not reflect ICU policy. Nevertheless, these incidents gave their opponents excellent propaganda ammunition, and aided the global perception of the ICU being like the Taliban.

A few years ago poor Somali fishermen would see a slow-moving superyacht sailing past their location; it soon became known that these vessels were easy to board and that their occupants would hand over high-value assets as soon as knives, machetes and guns were seen. The pirates learned quickly that to pretend to be in distress was a sure way of getting friendly sailors to slow down or stop; begging for water, food or cigarettes was one method, a burning barrel of oily rags was another. Frantic arm waving, the outboard's cowling removed and black smoke was enough to make all but the hardiest stop to help out, not turn away at full speed. These decoys were used for a while, but when the perpetrators turned from opportunist fishermen to full-on professional pirates, such tactics were not needed.

Now pirates in the Indian Ocean and GoA HRAs will use AIS, radar and modern communications (and luck) to choose their targets. Once chosen, they will hunt them down until they have control of the vessel, pirates operating in your local area will often block VHF Ch16 by playing music or similar. Usually more than one skiff will attack; the modus operandi is for a minimum of two skiffs or more. It is common for a skiff to come in close and fire an AK47 at or over the vessel – or worse, they may fire RPG 7 projectiles. This does not mean the vessel has to stop, damage will be sustained by the receiving end, but never stop, continue full speed ahead, and in rougher seas, into the sea. A tanker once had multiple RPG 7 hits on her stern (approximately 18), yet she continued on course at full speed and escaped. It all depends upon the vessel and the damage sustained plus the decision of the master.

Pictorial diagrams of the current modus operandi used by Somali pirates

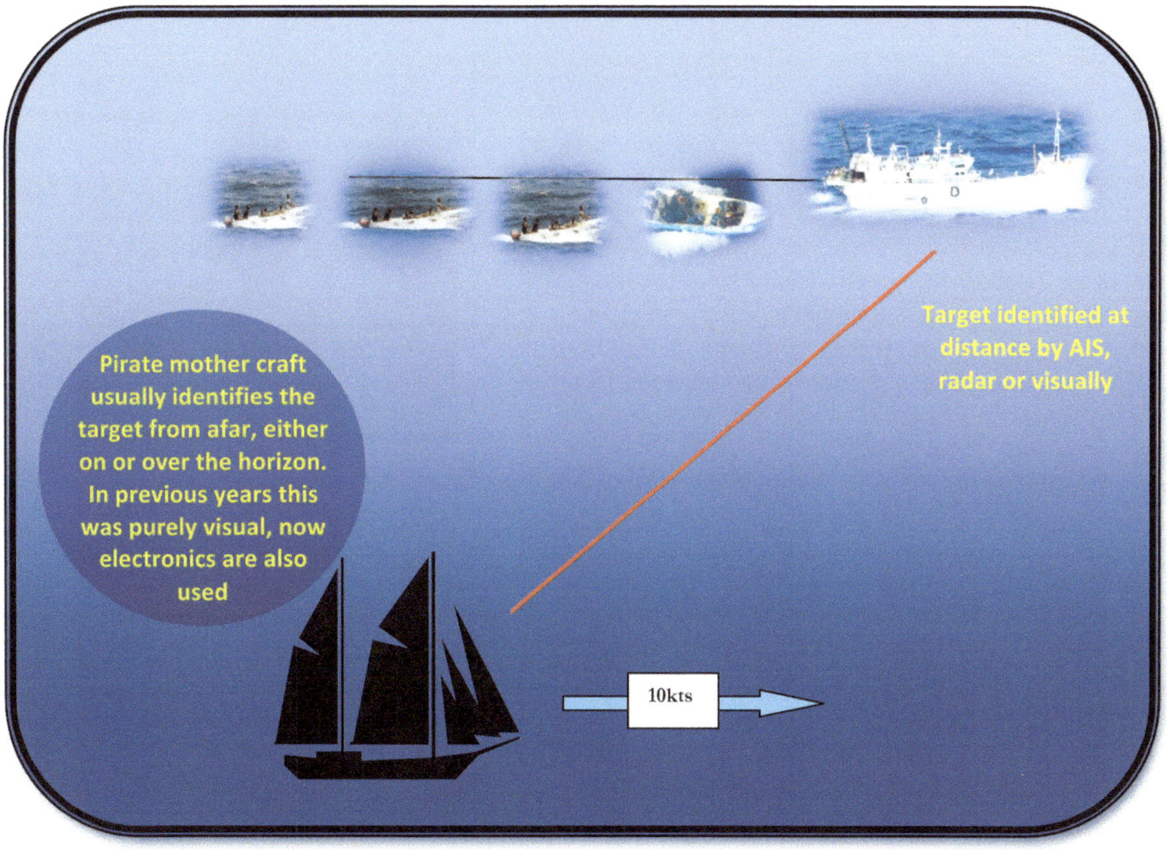

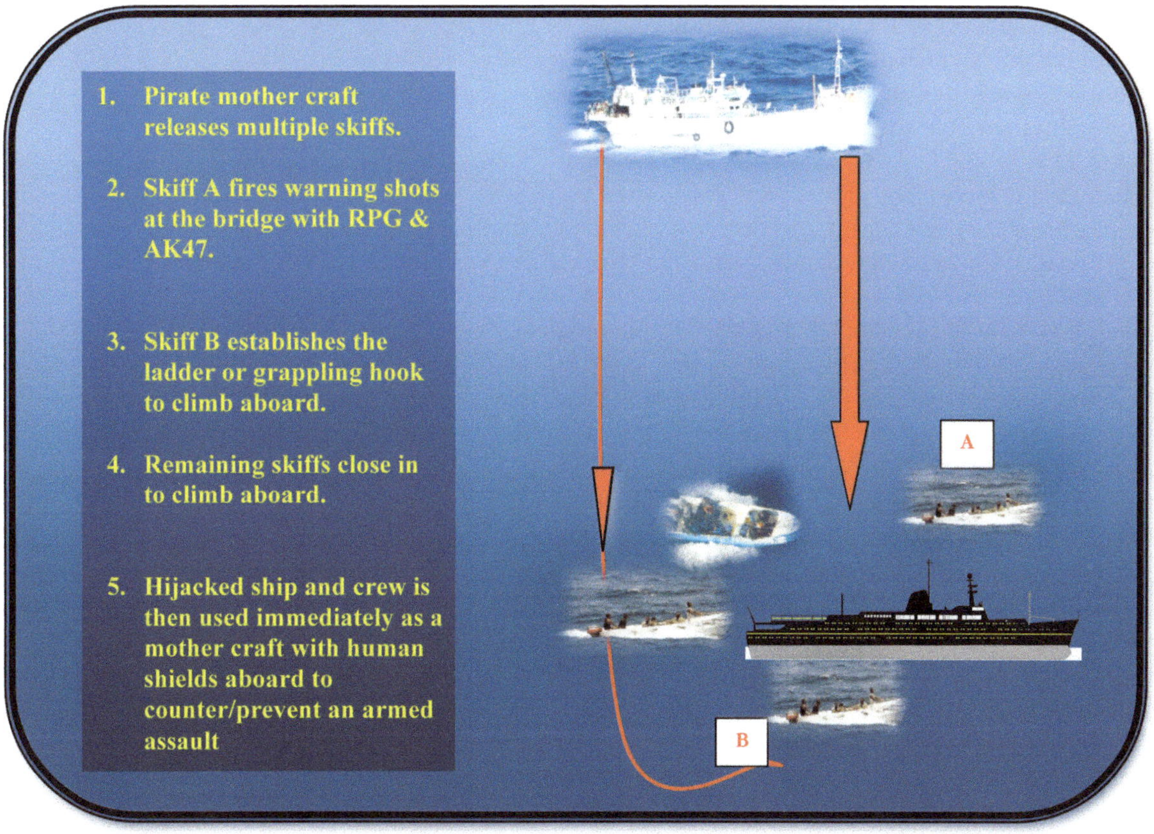

The birth of modern day piracy in Somali waters

Early 2005 the militia of a Suleiman sub-clan, based in Harardheere in central Somali started a new business: maritime piracy, with 'technical assistance' from a number of seasoned pirates from Puntland, a region in the Northeast Somalia. These technical assistants taught the Harardheere militia the tricks of the trade and they became almost immediately successful and received large sums of ransom. Around the 27th June 2005 they hijacked off the coast of central Somalia the WFP chartered MV Semlow on its way to Bossaso, carrying some 750mt of WFP relief rice for the tsunami victims in Puntland. The vessel was held off Harardheere and only released after 100 days in captivity on the 4th October 2005. Note that in the meantime, the Harardheere pirates had split in two groups: the Suleiman militia and the Puntland TAs mainly from around Eyl.

The recent piracy in Puntland waters started in early days, as a by-product of the enforcement of the selling of fishing rights to international fishing boats by the Puntland authorities, which could then fish in Puntland waters. In order to reinforce that foreign fishing boats would indeed buy those licenses, the Puntland 'navy' was born. Once they saw how easy it was to extract money from other vessels passing by, the present day Somali pirate from Eyl were born.

In 2006 the spate of hijackings went on until the take-over of the ICU, which gave a warning that hijacking would not be allowed anymore. In the second week of August 2006 the ICU took control of Harardheere district after lengthy negotiations with the elders and militia of that place. The pirates were disbanded, as per results of the negotiations; their acts were seen as something of the past of which they would not be prosecuted. When some pirates' remnants hijacked the Veesham-1 in early November 2006, the ICU sent boats immediately with their forces to the vessel and when negotiations with the pirates failed, took over the vessel and arrested all eight pirates.

After the fall of the ICU in the end of December 2006, piracy started again. This time even in Puntland waters, where the Eyl group together with some pirates from central Somalia. They hijacked the MV Rozen on Sunday 25th February 2007 off Bargal on the Indian Ocean coast of Puntland. The MV Rozen had just discharged first 900mt of food aid and 100mt+ of FAO fishery equipment in Bossaso and thereafter a further consignment of 900mt WFP food-aid in Berbera. After lengthy negotiations a ransom was agreed and the vessel was freed Thursday 5th April 2007 late at night.

With the downfall of the ICU and the fighting raging in Mogadishu, the old pirate groups apparently thought that the time was ripe to start again their old practice, and until now have been proven right. The Suleiman clan has been assisting the TFG.

It also received support in the form of weapons and ammunition from the Puntland authorities in their clan-fight with the Sa'ad clan, which was based at the border with Puntland, along with others in South- Galkayo. The former TFG state Minister of Marine Transport and Ports was "Honourable" Mohammed Jama M. Furuh, an elder of the Suleiman clan and reportedly the brother-in-law of 'Afweyne' (a nickname for bigmouth), the leader of the Harardheere militia and pirates.

One of the last Ministers of Interior of the TFG was also a Suleiman, and was involved in the piracy of the MV Semlow in 2005. For this reason, the TFG will not act against the Suleiman clan unless under considerable pressure.[9]

(Mr Van de Velden was the WFP coordinator in Somalia for 10 years and on behalf of the United Nations also conducted the operation to find out what toxic waste had been allegedly dumped on the Somali coastline. After an extensive and thorough period of investigation and analysis, the information given to the world's media by Somalia, was mainly untrue. Most of the stories were made up, it was a way to try to trick the world into giving them aid and support. A classic example of this were the two, large, toxic chemical containers that were dumped on the shoreline, supposedly contaminating the local area leading to high mortality with marine life, domestic livestock and the people themselves, were in fact two black rubber fenders that had been ripped off a transported oil rig being towed during a storm and filled with nothing more than stale air.)

There are conflicting reports about toxic waste dumping on Somalia's shores, at some point it did happen and the tsunami certainly did stir up previously buried containers of harmful waste.

Various images of the toxic dumping and its consequences.

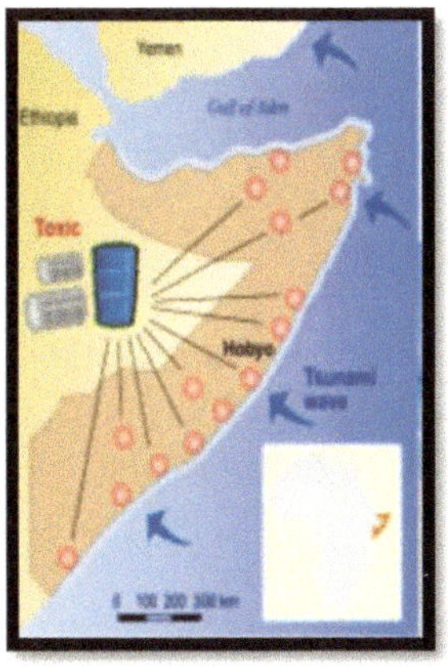

[9] With thanks to Mr L Van der Velden. World Food Programme

Detailed information on Somalia

Somali Flag.

Somalia, officially the Federal Republic of Somalia and formerly known as the Somali Democratic Republic, is a country located in the Horn of Africa. It is bordered by Djibouti to the northwest, Kenya to the southwest, the Gulf of Aden with Yemen to the north, the Indian Ocean to the east, and Ethiopia to the west.

In antiquity, Somalia was an important centre for commerce with the rest of the ancient world. Its sailors and merchants were the main suppliers of frankincense, myrrh and spices, items which were considered valuable luxuries by the Ancient Egyptians, Phoenicians, Mycenaeans and Babylonians with whom the Somali people traded. According to most scholars, Somalia is also where the ancient kingdom of Punt was situated. The ancient Puntites were a nation of people that had close relations with Pharaonic Egypt during the times of Pharaoh Sahure and Queen Hatshepsut. The pyramidal structures, temples and ancient houses of dressed stone littered around Somalia are said to date from this period. In the classical era, several ancient city-states such as Opone, Mosyllon and Malao, which competed with the Sabaeans, Parthians and Axumites for the wealthy Indo-Greco-Roman trade, also flourished in Somalia.

The birth of Islam on the opposite side of Somalia's Red Sea coast meant that Somali merchants, sailors and expatriates living in the Arabian Peninsula gradually came under the influence of the new religion through their converted Arab-Muslim trading partners. With the migration of fleeing Muslim families from the Islamic world to Somalia in the early centuries of Islam and the peaceful conversion of the Somali population by Somali Muslim scholars in the following centuries, the ancient city-states eventually transformed into Islamic Mogadishu, Berbera, Zeila, Barawa and Merka, which were part of the Berberi civilization. The city of Mogadishu came to be known as the City of Islam, and controlled the East African gold trade for several centuries. In the Middle Ages, several powerful Somali empires dominated the regional trade including the Ajuuraan State, which excelled in hydraulic engineering and fortress building, the Sultanate of Adal, whose general Ahmed Gurey was the first African commander in history to use cannon warfare on the continent during Adal's conquest of the Ethiopian Empire, and the Gobroon Dynasty, whose military dominance forced governors of the Omani empire north of the
city of Lamu to pay tribute to the Somali Sultan Ahmed Yusuf.

In the late 19th century, after the Berlin conference had ended,
European empires sailed with their armies to the Horn of Africa.

The imperial clouds looming over Somalia alarmed the Dervish leader Muhammad Abdullah Hassan, who gathered Somali soldiers from across the Horn of Africa and began one of the longest colonial resistance wars ever.

Somalia dominates the Hon of Africa.

Somalia was never formally colonised. The Dervish State successfully repulsed the British Empire four times and forced it to retreat to the coastal region. As a result of its fame in the Middle East and Europe, the Dervish state was recognised as an ally by the Ottoman Empire and the German Empire, and remained throughout World War I the only independent Muslim power on the continent.

After a quarter of a century holding the British at bay, the Dervishes were finally defeated in 1920 when Britain for the first time in Africa used aeroplanes when it bombed the Dervish capital of Taleex.
As a result of this bombardment, former Dervish territories were turned into a protectorate of Britain. Italy similarly faced the same opposition from Somali Sultans and armies and did not acquire full control of parts of modern Somalia until the Fascist era in late 1927.
This occupation lasted till 1941 and was replaced by a British military administration. Northern Somalia would remain a protectorate while southern Somalia became a trusteeship. The union of the two regions in 1960 formed the Somali Democratic Republic.

Due to its longstanding ties with the Arab world, Somalia was accepted in 1974 as a member of the Arab League. To strengthen its relationship with the rest of the African continent, Somalia joined other African nations when it founded the African Union, and began to support the ANC in South Africa against the apartheid regime and the Eritrean secessionists in Ethiopia during the Eritrean War of Independence. A Muslim country, Somalia is one of the founding members of the Organisation of the Islamic Conference and is also a member of the UN and NAM. Despite suffering from civil strife and instability, Somalia has also managed to sustain a free market economy, which, according to the UN, outperforms those of many other countries in Africa.

Somalia is poorly endowed with natural resources. Livestock and livestock products have always been the major exports, followed by crops, such as bananas, which are grown in the riverine region. While chaos and clan fighting continue in most of Somalia, some orderly government has been established in the northern part. In May 1991, the elders of clans in former British Somaliland established the independent Republic of Somaliland, which, although not recognised by any government, maintains a stable existence, aided by the overwhelming dominance of the ruling clan and the economic infrastructure left behind by British, Russian and American military assistance programmes.

Northern Somalia is the world's largest source of incense and myrrh that are forestry products.
There is no national telecommunications operator in Somalia. The telephone network was completely destroyed during the war.

Al-Shabaab

Harakat al-ShabaabMujahideen ('Movement of Warrior Youth'), more commonly known as al-Shabaab is an Islamistinsurgency group in Somalia in the ongoing war there. As of summer 2009 the group was said to control most of the southern part of the Somalia, including a large swathe of the capital, Mogadishu, where it is said to have imposed its own harsh form of Sharia law. Estimates of al-Shabaab's strength, as of December 2006, vary between 3,000 to 7,000.

The group is an offshoot of the Islamic Courts Union, which splintered into several smaller groups after its removal from power by Ethiopian forces in 2006. The group describes itself as waging jihad against enemies of Islam and is engaged in combat against the Somali Transitional Federal Government and African Union Mission to Somalia. It has reportedly declared war on the UN and on Western non-governmental organisations that distributes food aid in Somalia, killing 42 relief workers in 2008 and 2009. It has been designated a terrorist organisation by several western governments and security services, and is known to have ties to al-Qaeda.

Somali Islamists al-Shabaab 'join al-Qaeda fight'

Somali Islamist rebel group al-Shabaab has confirmed for the first time that its fighters are aligned with al-Qaeda's global militant campaign. The group said in a statement that the 'jihad of Horn of Africa must be combined with the international jihad led by the al-Qaeda network'. Meanwhile, several people have died in fighting in Mogadishu after government troops shelled militant positions. Islamist insurgents control much of southern and central Somalia. The government, which is backed by the UN and African Union, holds sway only in a small part of Mogadishu.

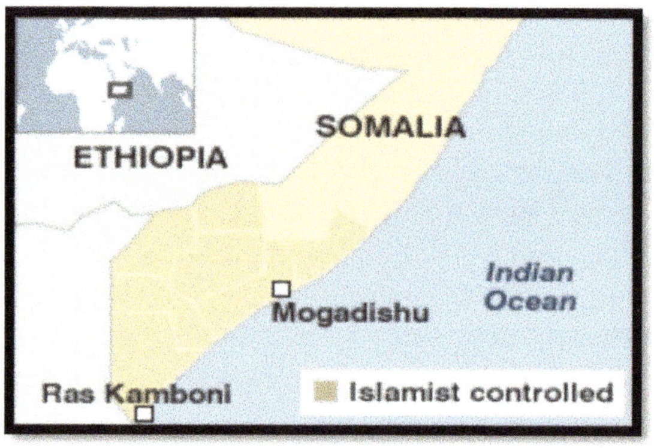

Despite repeated accusations by the US that al-Shabaab is linked to al-Qaeda, the group denied the connection in a recent interview with the BBC.

'Financer of terrorism'

The group's statement also announced that its militants had joined forces with a smaller insurgent group called Kamboni. The group, based in the southern town of Ras Kamboni, was previously allied to Hizbul-Islam - another militant group fighting the government.. Kamboni is led by Hassan Turki, a militant the US accuses of being a 'financer of terrorism'. Al-Shabaab said it was trying to unite all Islamist forces to create a Muslim state under its hard-line interpretation of Sharia law. The group, which controls swathes of Somalia, has carried out public beheadings and stonings.
Don't ever think that because the Somali pirates currently use a code of conduct that they are nice people and may treat you well. In recent times those codes of conduct have been ignored and hostages have been mal-treated, with examples of torture, beatings and mock executions.

Information about Somali pirates and piracy

History

During the Siad Barre regime, Somalia received aid from Denmark, Great Britain, Iraq, Japan, Sweden, USSR and West Germany to develop its fishing industry. Co-operatives had fixed prices for their catch, which was often exported due to the low demand for seafood in Somalia. Aid money improved the ships and supported the construction of maintenance facilities. After the fall of the Barre regime, the income from fishing decreased due to the Somali Civil War.

There was no coastguard to protect against fishing trawlers from other countries illegally fishing and big companies dumping waste which killed fish in Somali waters. This led to the erosion of the fish stock. Local fishermen started to band together to protect their resources. Due to the clan-based organisation of Somali society, the lack of a central government, and the country's strategic location at the Horn of Africa, conditions were ripe for the growth of piracy in the early 1990s.

Precise data on the current economic situation in Somalia is scarce but with an estimated per capita GDP of $600 per year, it remains one of the world's poorest countries. Millions of Somalis depend on food aid and in 2008, according to the World Bank, as much as 73% of the population lived on a daily income below $2.
These factors and the lucrative success of many hijacking operations have drawn a number of young men toward gangs of pirates, whose wealth and power often make them part of the local social and economic elite. Abdi Farah Juha who lives in Garoowe (100 miles from the sea) told the BBC, 'They have money; they have power and they are getting stronger by the day. They wed the most beautiful girls; they are building big houses; they have new cars; new guns.'

Some pirates are former fishermen, whose livelihoods were hurt by foreign ships illegally fishing in Somali waters. Seeing the profitability of piracy - ransoms are usually paid - warlords began to facilitate pirate activities, splitting the profits with the pirates. In most of the hijackings, the bandits have not harmed their prisoners. The attackers generally treat their hostages well in anticipation of a big payday to the point of hiring caterers on the shores of Somalia to cook spaghetti, grilled fish and roasted meat that will appeal to a Western palate. They also keep a steady supply of cigarettes and drinks from the shops on shore.

The Transitional Federal Government has made some efforts to combat piracy, occasionally allowing foreign naval vessels into Somali territorial waters. However, more often than not, foreign naval vessels chasing pirates were forced to break off when the pirates entered Somali territorial waters. The government of Puntland has made more progress in combatting piracy, evident in recent interventions.

Summary of events that took place between 2008 -2010

On 21 November 2008 the Indian Navy received United Nations approval to enter Somali waters to combat piracy.
On 20 April 2009, United States Secretary of State Hillary Clinton commented on the capture and release of seven Somali pirates by Dutch naval forces that were on a NATO mission. After an attack on the Handytankers Magic, a petroleum tanker, the Dutch frigate De Zeven Provincien tracked the pirates back to a pirate mothership and captured them.
They confiscated the pirates' weapons and freed 20 Yemeni fishermen who the pirates had kidnapped and who had been forced to sail the pirate mothership.
Since the Dutch naval forces were part of a NATO exercise but were not on an EU mission they lacked legal jurisdiction to keep the pirates so they released them. Clinton stated that this action 'sends the wrong signal' and that additional co-ordination was needed among nations.

On 23 April 2009 international donors pledged over $250 million for Somalia, which included $134 million to increase the African Union peacekeeping mission from 4,350 troops to 8,000 troops and $34 million for Somali security forces.
Secretary-General of the United Nations Ban Ki-moon told delegates, at a donors' conference sponsored by the UN, 'Piracy is a symptom of anarchy and insecurity on the ground,' and that 'more security on the ground will make less piracy on the seas.'
Somali President Sharif Ahmed pledged at the conference that he would fight piracy and to loud applause said, 'It is our duty to pursue these criminals not only on the high seas, but also on terra firma.' The Somali government has not gone after pirates because pirate leaders currently have more power than the government. It has been estimated by piracy experts that in 2008 pirates gained about $80 million through ransom payments.

On 8 November 2009, Somali pirates threatened that a kidnapped British couple would be 'punished' if a German warship did not release seven pirates. Omer, one of the pirates holding the British couple, claimed that the seven men were fishermen but a European Union naval force spokesman said that they were captured as they fired AK-47 assault rifles at a French fishing vessel. On 30 January 2010, a British couple kidnapped by Somali pirates had been held for 100 days. In a video the kidnapped woman Rachel Chandler was shown to be 'almost skeletally thin'. A Somali pirate by the name of Noor has said that the British couple will be shot if the pirates do not receive a ransom of $3 million.

Effects and perceptions

There have been both positive and negative effects of the pirates' economic success. Local residents have complained that the presence of so many armed men makes them feel insecure, and that their free spending ways cause wild fluctuations in the local exchange rate. Others fault them for excessive consumption of alcoholic beverages and khat.

Khat* (Catha edulis, Somali: qaad), is a flowering plant native to tropical East Africa and the Arabian Peninsula. Khat contains the alkaloid called cathinone, an amphetamine-like stimulant which is said to cause excitement, loss of appetite and euphoria. In 1980 the World Health Organisation classified khat as a drug of abuse that can produce mild to moderate psychological dependence. The plant has been targeted by anti-drug organisations like the DEA. It is a controlled/illegal substance in many countries, but is legal for sale and production in many others.

Examples of Khat, fresh Khat wrapped in Banana leaves and dried Khat.
Other names include:African Salad/Abyssinian Tea/Tea of the Arabs/Bushman's Tea/Flower of Paradise/Qat/Qaat/Mirra/Herari

On the other hand, many other residents appreciate the rejuvenating effect that the pirates' on-shore spending and re-stocking has had on their impoverished towns, a presence which has often provided jobs and opportunity when previously there had been none.
Entire hamlets have in the process been transformed into veritable boomtowns, with local shop owners and other residents using their gains to purchase items such as generators - 'allowing full days of electricity, once an unimaginable luxury'.

Local fishermen in the Malinde area of neighbouring Kenya have reported their largest catches in forty years, catching hundreds of kilos of fish and earning fifty times the average daily wage as a result.
They attribute the recent abundance of marine stock to the pirates scaring away the large factory trawlers of foreign fishing fleets, which they claim have for decades deprived local dhows of a livelihood. Marine biologists agree, saying that the indicators are that the local fishery is recovering because of the lack of commercial scale fishing.

Weaponry and funding
Pirates get most of their weapons from Yemen, but a significant amount comes from Mogadishu, Somalia's capital. Weapon dealers in the capital receive a deposit from a hawala dealer on behalf of the pirates and the weapons are then driven to Puntland where the pirates pay the balance.
Various photographs of pirates in situ indicate that their weapons are predominantly AKM, RPG-7 and semi-automatic pistols such as the TT-30. Additionally, given the particular origin of their weaponry, they are likely to have hand grenades such as the RGD-5 or F1.
The funding of piracy operations is now structured in a stock exchange, with investors buying and selling shares in upcoming attacks in a bourse in Harardhere.

Ransom Payment: Pirates say ransom money is paid in large denomination US dollar bills. It is delivered to them in burlap sacks, which are either dropped from helicopters or cased in waterproof suitcases loaded onto tiny skiffs.
Ransom money has also been delivered to pirates via parachute (Controlled Air Delivery System CADS, a remote controlled steerable ram-air parachute), as happened in January 2009 when an orange container with $3 million cash inside it was dropped onto the deck of the super tanker MV Sirius Star to secure the release of ship and crew. To authenticate the banknotes, pirates use currency-counting machines, the same technology used at foreign exchange bureaus worldwide.
According to one pirate, these machines are, in turn, purchased from business connections in Dubai, Djibouti, and other areas. Hostages seized by the pirates usually have to wait 45 days or more for the ships' owners to pay the ransom and secure their release. However it is not always like that as of October 2012, Somali pirates have released the merchant ship "MV Orna" nearly two years after hijacking the Panama-flagged vessel in the Indian Ocean in 2010.
Somali pirates allegedly get help from the Somali diaspora. Somali expatriates, including reputedly some among the 200,000 Somalis living in Canada, offer funds, equipment and information.

Sovereignty and environmental protection
The UN envoy for Somalia, Ahmedou Ould-Abdallah, has stated, 'Because there is no (effective) government, there is ... much irregular fishing from European and Asian countries,' and that the UN has 'reliable information' that European and Asian companies are dumping toxic and nuclear waste off the Somali coastline. However, he stresses, 'No government has endorsed this act, and private companies and individuals acting alone are responsible.' In addition, Ould-Abdallah told the press that he believes the toxic waste dumping is 'a disaster off the Somali coast, a disaster (for) the Somali environment, the Somali population,' and that what he terms 'this illegal fishing, illegal dumping of waste' helps fuel the civil war in Somalia since the illegal foreign fishermen pay off corrupt local officials or warlords for protection or to secure counterfeit licenses.
However, Ould-Abdallah noted that piracy will not prevent waste dumping: 'The intentions of these pirates are not concerned with protecting their environment,' and 'What is ultimately needed is a functioning, effective government that will get its act together and take control of its affairs.' These issues have generally not been reported in international media when reporting on piracy. Pirate leader Sugule Ali said their motive was 'to stop illegal fishing and dumping in our waters... We don't consider ourselves sea bandits. We consider sea bandits [to be] those who illegally fish and dump in our seas and dump waste in our seas and carry weapons in our seas.' Also, the independent Somalian news-site Wardher News found that 70 percent 'strongly supported the piracy as a form of national defence of the country's territorial waters'.

Waste dumping

Following the massive tsunami of December 2004, there have emerged allegations that after the outbreak of the Somali Civil War in the late 1980s, Somalia's long, remote shoreline was used as a dump site for the disposal of toxic waste.

The huge waves which battered northern Somalia after the tsunami are believed to have stirred up tonnes of nuclear and toxic waste that was illegally dumped in Somali waters by several European firms.

The European Green Party followed up these revelations by presenting before the press and the European Parliament in Strasbourg copies of contracts signed by two European companies—the Italian Swiss firm, Achair Partners, and an Italian waste broker, Progresso—and representatives of the warlords then in power, to accept 10 million tonnes of toxic waste in exchange for $80 million (then about £60 million). According to a report by the United Nations Environment Programme (UNEP) assessment mission, there are far higher than normal cases of respiratory infections, mouth ulcers and bleeding, abdominal haemorrhages and unusual skin infections among many inhabitants of the areas around the north-eastern towns of Hobbio and Benadir on the Indian Ocean coast—diseases consistent with radiation sickness. UNEP continues that the current situation along the Somali coastline poses a very serious environmental hazard not only in Somalia but also in the eastern Africa sub-region.

Under Article 9(1)(d) of the Basel Convention on the Control of Transboundary Movements of Hazardous Wastes and Their Disposal, it is illegal for 'any transboundary movement of hazardous wastes or other wastes: that results in deliberate disposal (e.g. dumping) of hazardous wastes or other wastes in contravention of this Convention and of general principles of international law'.

According to Nick Nuttall of the United Nations Environmental Programme, 'Somalia has been used as a dumping ground for hazardous waste starting in the early 1990s, and continuing through the civil war there,' and 'European companies found it to be very cheap to get rid of the waste, costing as little as $2.50 a tonne, where waste disposal costs in Europe are something like $1000 a tonne.'

Illegal fishing

At the same time, illegal trawlers began fishing Somalia's seas with an estimated $300 million of tuna, shrimp, and lobster being taken each year depleting stocks previously available to local fishermen. Through interception with speedboats, Somali fishermen tried to either dissuade the dumpers and trawlers or levy a 'tax' on them as compensation. In an interview, Sugule Ali, one of the pirate leaders explained 'We don't consider ourselves sea bandits.

We consider sea bandits (to be) those who illegally fish and dump in our seas.' Peter Lehr, a Somalia piracy expert at the University of St. Andrews says 'It's almost like a resource swap, Somalis collect up to $100 million a year from pirate ransoms off their coasts and the Europeans and Asians poach around $300 million a year in fish from Somali waters.'

According to Roger Middleton of Chatham House, 'The problem of overfishing and illegal fishing in Somali waters, is a very serious one, and does affect the livelihoods of people inside Somalia; the dumping of toxic waste on Somalia's shores is a very serious issue, which will continue to affect people in Somalia long after the war has ended, and piracy is resolved.' To lure fish to their traps, foreign trawlers reportedly also use fishing equipment under prohibition such as nets with very small mesh sizes and sophisticated underwater lighting systems.

Under Article 56(1) (b) (iii) of the Law of the Sea Convention:

'In the exclusive economic zone, the coastal state has jurisdiction as provided for in the relevant provisions of this Convention with regard to the protection and preservation of the marine environment'. Article 57 of the Convention in turn outlines the limit of that jurisdiction: 'The exclusive economic zone shall not extend beyond 200 nautical miles from the baselines from which the breadth of the territorial sea is measured'.

Military presence

The military response to pirate attacks has brought about a rare show of unity by countries that are either openly hostile to each other, or at least wary of co-operation, military or otherwise.

Military counter-piracy operations are conducted by naval ships from the Combined Task Force 150 (CTF-150), Russia, China and India.

Countries of the CTF-150 share information during the monthly Shared Awareness and Deconfliction (SHADE) meetings, a mechanism established in December 2008.

In response to the increased activity of the INS Tabar, India sought to augment its naval force in the Gulf of Aden by deploying the larger INS Mysore to patrol the area. Somalia also added India to its list of states, including the US and France, who are permitted to enter its territorial waters, extending up to 12 nautical miles (22 km; 14 mi) from the coastline, in an effort to check piracy. An Indian naval official confirmed receipt of a letter acceding to India's prerogative to check such piracy. 'We had put up a request before the Somali government to play a greater role in suppressing piracy in the Gulf of Aden in view of the United Nations resolution. The TFG government gave its nod recently.' India also expressed consideration to deploy up to four more warships in the region. Similarly, Russia also chose to send more warships to combat piracy near Somalia. This announcement followed the International Maritime Bureau terming the menace as having gone 'out of control'. Germany said it was willing to add 1,400 troops to join an EU mission in the area that would begin in December.

Africom commander, General William Ward, added that the United States was concerned about the rise in piracy, and was involved in multilateral efforts to provide security, 'The United States is participating in those activities currently, but again, and that is not specifically being controlled by the United States Africa Command.' European naval vessels have operated against piracy either independently, or as part of Combined Task Force 150. As a result of increased piracy, the European Union has established Operation Atalanta, to co-ordinate the European naval response to piracy and maintains international law in international waters in the region.
A maritime conference was also held in Mombasa to discuss the rising concern of regional piracy with a view to give regional and world governments' recommendations to deal with the menace. The International Transport Workers Federation (ITWF) organised the regional African maritime unions' conference, the first of its kind in Africa. Godfrey Matata Onyango, executive secretary of the Northern Corridor Transit Coordination Authority said, 'We cannot ignore to discuss the piracy menace because it poses a huge challenge to the maritime industry and if not controlled, it threats to chop off the regional internal trade.
The cost of shipping will definitely rise as a result of the increased war insurance premium due to the high risk off the Gulf of Aden.' Pakistan offered the services of Pakistan's navy to the United Nations in order to help combat the piracy in Somalia 'provided a clear mandate was given'.

VULNERABLE VESSELS
Asia, led by India and China, could take 75 percent of South Africa's 65 million tonnes of thermal coal exports in 2010 as demand shifts from glutted Europe, putting many more ships in the gun sights of Somali pirates, analysts said.Companies involved in this seaborne coal trade said they have already had to swallow higher costs due to taking longer routes to avoid pirate hotspots and insurance premiums. A senior shipper said piracy risk cover on a voyage from South Africa to India added $30,000 on top of the basic insurance cost. A further $40,000 to $50,000 had to be added for longer diversions aimed at avoiding pirates.

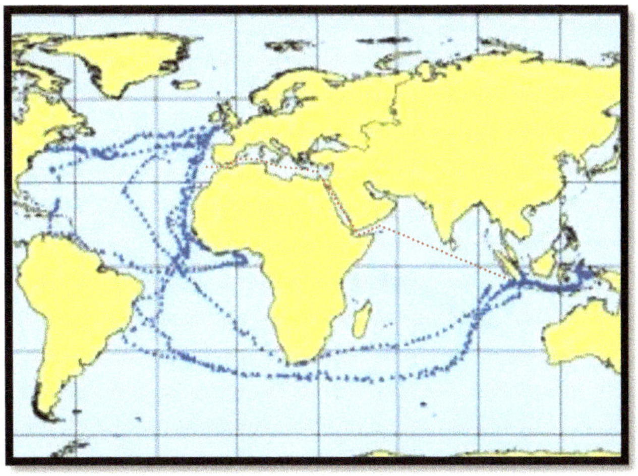

A picture paints a thousand words when it comes to comparing the distances around the Cape or via the Suez Canal, especially for the hydro-carbons coming out of the Middle East heading West.

Below is a first-hand account of how an armed pirate attack took place and how the on board security team reacted, saving the ship from being hijacked. Mr. Nigel Watson Clark is one of Britain's leading anti-piracy consultants and has experienced a great deal in his profession, including being kidnapped by MEND in the Niger Delta in 2006. Details of which are on page 261.

Nigel Watson Clark
Consultant Anti-piracy operations.

I come from Carlisle. Brought up here to enjoy the stunning scenery and countryside of Cumbria. Now living in Bristol, I return north as often as I can to see my family, friends and head for the hills. Early in February 2011 I stumbled across Lank's Tarn above Patterdale having taken a 'wrong' turn on an early morning walk up Hellvellen, its a very long way from the harsh and uncompromising environment of Anti-Piracy Operations in the Gulf of Aden and Eastern Sea Board of Somalia. However, these are the kind of moments that we savour, an unexpected glimpse into the beauty of Cumbria that many of us from the county treasure whilst conducting long bridge watches transiting through the High Risk Areas of this region.

Piracy is a huge modern problem and threatens world trade, the goods we export, oil and gas supplies to Europe with the annual cost estimated at £7 billion. The 'Hollywood' image of swashbuckling and glamorous adventures could not be further from reality. At one point, Six Hundred seamen from 30 hi-jacked vessels were being held hostage against their will in squalid, dangerous conditions by drug fuelled Somalis 'negotiating' a ransom from shipping companies which they have no control over. There's a whole economy, structure developed on the Horn of Africa that is thriving and Piracy Cartels demand vast sums of dollars for the release of valued human and cargo assets, the latest rumoured to be £5,000,000 for one tanker. The cost to the international community for Military Warships to patrol and escort vessels through these shipping lanes is staggering, the human cost incalculable, yet the attacks, hi-jackings and hostage taking continues.

The pirates now operate up to 1000 nautical miles off the Somalian coast from Mother-ships and fast boats called 'skiffs' and the Navies can't secure such a vast sea; The Indian Ocean. I work in the Maritime Security Sector like many, perhaps a disproportionate amount of Cumbrians', mostly ex-Royal Marines, for Private Maritime Security Companies working closely with the International Military effort and the International Maritime Organization to combat the attacks by Piracy Groups. However, the solution to Piracy does not lie at our hands, but we are deployed on vessels by shipping companies as protection for that individual vessel to transit through safely.

When we first embark and introduce ourselves to the Captains, Senior Officers and crews, they are looking only to passage and arrive safely at their next destination, not looking to take on the Pirates, not looking for a fight, but just looking to us to secure their safe passage. There are many levels we use to mitigate the risks of an attack. Visual and physical defensive measures that delay any attempted boarding and good vigilant watchkeeping. There are Security Procedures that we brief, train and drill with the ship's crew so that everyone has a role and everyone does their own job. We have open and closed source intelligence that helps identify the areas of current high risk and recent attacks and we have weapon systems to defend ourselves. I used to get angry at some suggestions we were some kind of Maritime Mercenaries that was occasionally aimed (cheaply) at us, but I've learnt that those with that view are unlikely to be convinced by 'on the ground' reasoning. There's is barely anything more violent then when a pirate commander's first tactic is to intimidate the Captain of the vessel to stop than firing an RPG (Rocket Propelled Grenade) at the bridge. It is simply our role to prevent them from doing so and our strict Rules for the Use of Force (RUF) are robustly enforced.

I have worked in many regions that security is an essential part of any operation. Sadly, Africa and the Middle Eastern counties have the bulk of the world's maritime security related problems.

Iraq, Nigeria, Angola, Sri Lanka, Kenya, Madagascar and Oman are regular stamps in my passport. These are wonderful countries and when time allows in the gap between transits, it's a thrill to visit them and enjoy the palm lined white sandy beaches and relax. I draw the line on Somalia. A dysfunctional state in turmoil since 1991 and recently the emergence of Islamic Insurgency and Pirate Cartels. There is a unique geo-political influence on the Horn of Africa that allows these groups to operate in one of the world's busiest shipping lane and target vessels transiting through for hijacking without government interference and taking them to anchor offshore Somalia, then demanding a ransom for its release. It was on one such transit in April 2011 that we encountered a determined Pirate Action Group, this is my personal account:

As Carlisle United supporters headed North from Wembley having won back the Johnston's Paint Trophy I was heading South through the Gulf of Aden on board a tanker wandering through stories told many times on bridge watches, of Nigeria or hedonistic skydiving days in Florida or Australia. Perhaps I was banging on about previous glamour tasks, 'the mighty blues' or maybe even pure nonsense.... doesn't really matter. What does matter was the instant recognition of sheer fear in the eyes of the Filipino Bridge Wing Watch Keeper as he uttered the words "Two small boats Sir!" At the very same time, over his shoulder I recognised the wakes of the approaching Skiffs, it's normally the first indicator, they were about 3 nm away.

Piracy Attack..... No doubt, absolutely no doubt and I know we were about to be tested again. "Think procedures Nige', think procedures ! Do things in order , we have drilled and practised for this many times and there a lot of things to do, so we set too it". " 30 degrees to Port Sir" is my first command to the Officer of the Watch. That allows us to immediately distance ourselves from the approach and determine if they alter their own.....they did! Mark grabbed his body armour and without instruction drew his weapon. The right people appeared to be arriving on the bridge as the General Alarm sounded. "I believe we have a Pirate attack Captain", monitor the approach, continue to analyse the threat, update the Captain, secure the crew in the Muster Area and then our two other security team members arrived together and my turn to don body armour and take charge.

A piracy attack, a firefight of any kind, even for seasoned ex-military personnel who has been here before, is pure intense; there is a lot at stake. All other distractions are lost and if we get this right, if everyone does their job we will win this fight.... we cannot afford to lose it. As the skiffs continue their rapid approach, I ask... "Fire off a flare, Lee" The rocket flare propels itself skyward and I remember it was a too high trajectory. " and another mate" Jack is on aim but does not fire his opening shot. Of course the flares, designed as a warning for pirates to stay clear, have no effect, but its part of our escalation for Rules for the Use of Force.

*The aggressors continue to close astern of us. The 2 white hulled skiffs have speed on us and close at 30kts while we are still recovering from a sharp turn which has positioned the skiffs behind us but we slow to 7 knots. " "They're getting closer mate" Lee said calmly and I ask the Captain for permission to fire warning shots. " "They're getting closer Nige'" Lee reiterates" "Okay, Fire your shots". **Crack**, the familiar sound of a 7.62mm leaving the barrel, and less then as second later I see the splash barely 10 meters ahead of the aggressors. I ask for another round and it goes down, the same splash and this time had an immediate and dramatic effect. The 'skiff' coxswain has had enough and sharply pulls to port abandoning the fight. One skiff remains, still chuffed that we're only now dealing with one, I ask Mark on the radio... " put two down rounds on that one on the Port side .....and again" as we all observe the remaining more determined incoming pirate 'skiff'. Again I see the sea erupt in front of their boat and still they keep coming. "We're taking incoming Nige!!" and although I never heard the rounds missing somewhere around us I asked for more shots from Mark and Jack. This time, they too had had enough and slowed, disengaged, before regrouping with the other pirate boat, I radioed the guys " Good drills fella's..... I like your work !".*

No real sense of any triumphalism as we unloaded and cleared our weapons, just a calm satisfaction. The two pirate group skiffs heading 180 degrees away from us towards a Mother-ship on the horizon and only then did we allowed ourselves some high fives and big smiles.

The Captain and Senior officers were chattering away excitedly in their native Indian language forgetting momentarily to send word down to the Citadel that the remainder of the mustered crew were now safe to emerge. An alarm still sounding added to the lessening air of excitement but we had overcome our aggressors. Now the reports, now the internal team inquest, Jack had the presence of mind to start his video and we reviewed the action. It showed a team calm under extraordinary pressure.... I was relieved that what was recorded highlighted our professionalism and after a coffee I allowed myself the forbidden weed... a Marlboro Light.

Later that evening, almost a cliché, I 'took the breeze' alone on the bridge wing. The sun golden as it set low over Socotra Island. A Filipino crewman gingerly interrupted my tranquility and head slightly bowed, captured the reason why we are here. " Thank you for saving us Mr Nigel .... from my family, Thank you. These are dangerous waters."

There's more to all this and the Commander from military intelligence (EUNAVFOR) arrived in Mombasa to take my statement a few days later. Our attackers were caught by a Finnish Naval Vessel, two of the pirates are aged 9 and 12, small enough to crawl through Razor wire and window grills. But don't let that distract you from the facts, that they would then make way for ruthless killers and give them access to the superstructure, take the vessel and to cause the same misery as hundreds of seamen banged up right now offshore Somalia. EUNAVFOR want to prosecute and I maybe the main witness. The Finnish warship were denied permission to hand over the pirates to a Flag State with the death penalty and thereby lies a problem. It is a messy and dirty business this Piracy.

A year earlier I was involved in a task to escort back to safety a vessel taken by pirates after they had been released. I will never forget the harrowed look on 25 hardened seafarers as I walked onto the bridge. They were shattered, broken and fragile men who were subjected to nearly 5 months of appalling conditions, mock executions and captivity at the hands of drugged up volatile Somalia's. That image stays with me. Yet, the group that attacked us had the same fate for us in mind and they were released from the Finnish Warship to re-group and have another go.

So what has this got to do with Cumbria? Well,...... please refer to my opening couple of sentences and really enjoy springtime on the fells. ... meanwhile there are ordinary innocent seamen out there just wanting to be their jobs, to passage safely but wake again this morning to an AK-47 to his head.

***Press release 27 April 2011** ..... A group of 18 suspected pirates, who were detained a fortnight ago by Finnish Warship Phojanmaa, have been released, as no country was willing to accept or prosecute them. The group of Somali men, who were arrested as part of the EU Atlanta anti-piracy operation, were set loose on the shores of their own country on Thursday. Spokesman for EU Atlanta, Paddy O'Kennedy, said the 18 were released in an undisclosed location on humanitarian grounds, as no nation was willing take responsibility for investigating or prosecuting the alleged crimes. "Personal items were returned to the Somali men before their release. Confiscated weapons and other items related to piracy were not returned to them," said the skipper of the Pohjanmaa, Commander Mika Raunu, in a YLE report. Pohjanmaa took custody of the suspects after an attack on a Singaporean vessel, but Finland refused to take the cases to trial as no attempt had been made on any Finnish nationals or ships. The EU also decided not to release the men to Singapore as they could have faced the death penalty if found guilty there.*

4. EQUIPMENT USED BY THIEVES AND PIRATES

Various fast boats and skiffs

M.E.N.D in Nigeria

Pirates at Bab el Mandeb, southern Red Sea.

There are many different types of fast boats or skiffs that are being used by thieves and pirates all over the world. Above are just two examples. Basically they fall into two general categories: GRP-fibreglass and wooden. The GRP boats are generally smaller, have a flatter profile and a low bow. They are extremely difficult to spot on a bright sea, especially if there are any white horses around. These boats come with either one or two outboard engines and can reach speeds of 20–30 knots, depending on the sea state and age of the hull.

Gulf of Aden skiffs Wooden with high, pointed bow (used by fishermen and pirates)

These GRP boats are cheap, light in weight and easy to coxswain, the downside is they are not good in rougher seas, so if a vessel is being pursued by a GRP type and has a following sea; it should turn into sea and hope to lose its pursuer. Both types of skiffs can be seen in large numbers in and around the Hannish Islands and Bab el Mandeb and south of the fishing port of Aden. On calm days, these small boats will venture huge distances and cross the IRTC in search of fish. All skiffs should be closely watched in high risk areas and this is where decent, image stabilised binoculars come into their own.

GRP with blunt bow, very common and favoured by Somali pirates

Various photos of Somali pirates and their equipment:

A GRP Skiff and single OBM, piracy equipment includes a ladder, RPG 7, AK47, fuel and water.

A mothership used by Somali pirates, being boarded by Naval Forces.

Pirates with twin OBMs, plenty of fuel drums and their rigid ladder with a large hook.

Pirates seen loading an RPG7 and the top end of their 'hooked' boarding ladder.

Typical, lightweight GoA skiffs and pirates armed with PKM automatic weapons

Weapons are cheap and plentiful in Somalia

Various aids used by Somali pirates

Above, various common weapons including: RPG warhead with charge fitted and without. AK47 variant, Chinese Type 56 with bayonet and broken stock and AK47 with folding stock (all rusty and dirty).

Above, various anchors, not grappling hooks. These cannot be thrown over a ship's railings, they weigh over 10kgs each.

Left: Mobile phone and 2x GPS systems

On the right a Thuraya satellite phone

Below, a captured handmade ladder. In the top, right box are 2 hooks to be fitted to the straight ladder shaft. Point to note; if the railings are too wide, the pirates cannot establish their ladders. Empty 45 gallon drums fixed to the top rails will prevent this and can be done if the rail length is relatively short or you have lots of empty drums. Also consider the benefits of an electric fence.

A Somali 6-man attack team

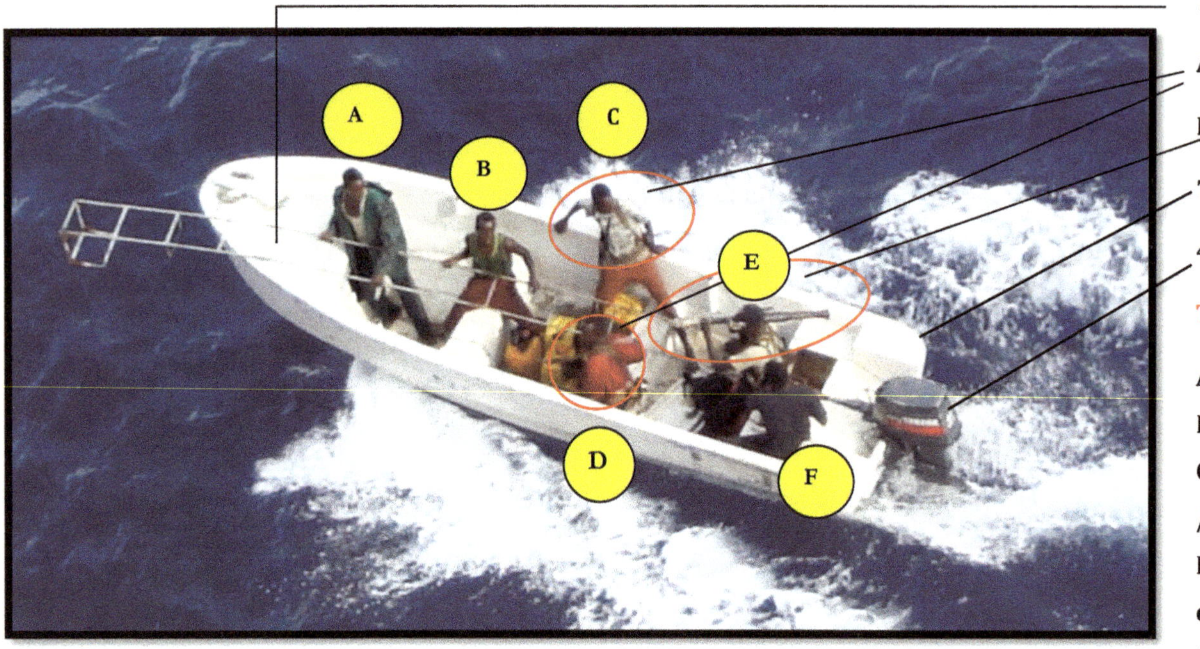

Eventually, all men will board, the skiff will be tied alongside, craned on board or discarded.

How the pirate assault is executed

Once the mothercraft or Pirate Attack Group (PAG) has identified their target, a typical assault by Somali pirates will consist of one or more skiffs approaching the vessel. This will be done normally with the sea, across it, not against it. If the target is moving less than 20kts and has a lowish freeboard, the pirates will come alongside at what they deem to be the easiest place to board. Usually the stern's poop deck is lower than the rest of the ship so that would be a natural 'hook on' point (and should be the most defended by the ship's crew).

The PAG Team Leader (TL) will give the orders to come alongside; the covermen will cover the ship with their weapons; AK47s and RPG. The laddermen will hook the ladder or pole onto a fixed rail or throw a grappling hook with a knotted rope. The coverman and TL will usually climb first, with their weapons slung across their backs. Once onboard the remaining team will board and tie the skiff alongside or if not possible, let it drift.

If the ship is too fast or is difficult to board, the skiff will stay parallel to the bridge at 100-200m to intimidate it and will usually fire shots and an RPG into the side of the bridge (hence why the sides of the bridge need to be hardened). This is to scare the Master into slowing down or stopping, but should never be done.

The assault group will normally use the external stairwells to get to the bridge, then force their way inside using any means available. If the pirates have boarded the vessel, then the entire crew should be locked in their secure, unobvious citadel, having raised the alarms on all available means and close down the ship's propulsion and power. In the vast Indian Ocean, it may take days for a coalition warship to reach you, hence the need for a professionally prepared citadel that can sustain the entire crew for up to 5 days.

If the ship is correctly 'locked down' then access to the internal should be extremely difficult, with each and every door locked and reinforced along the way.

The pirates only have a certain amount of time to gain entry, after a few hours of trying their patience will wear thin and fear of coalition forces arriving will make them give up and search for an easier target.

There is another method that some pirates have adopted which is much more successful, but this will not be published as it will inform all global pirates of the most effective method to use. This and other restricted information can be obtained during a pre-deployment brief from IMAAG.

An example of a small mothercraft that gives the PAG longer distances to search for shipping away from the heavily patrolled areas of the GoA.
Photo courtesy of E. Carter

It is incredible to think that these men go way offshore in these open top boats in order to capture huge ocean-going vessels. One large wave could easily overturn or swamp the boat.

Skiffs will usually travel at least as a pair (but usually more) boarding on the Port and Starboard quarter or lowest area; they will use one or two outboard engines and can have speeds of up to 25+ knots, depending upon the sea state. Inside they will have climbing aids such as a bamboo pole, aluminium or metal ladder, knotted rope and grappling hook, or a combination of these. Narrow ships' rails and lips will allow easy access for the pirates' hooking system; the wider the lip or rails, the more difficult it will be to climb aboard.
On the metal fixed ladders the hooks are usually quite wide, up to 30cm (1ft); that will hook on most rails.

A brave crew can easily unhook the ladder manually or blast off a climber with a high-pressure fire hose, and once the ladder is without the weight of the person it can be dropped into the depths. Spares are not usually carried. With smaller vessels, it's a case of cross decking from the skiff to the low freeboard found on motor and sailing vessels.

The Captain knows his vessel intimately and should think what he can do to avoid illegal boarders. Pirates will take the easy option; they will soon give up and pursue another target if a vessel is proving too difficult or hazardous to board. Men in body armour will sometimes be enough to deter an attack once they are identified by the attackers. Attacks underway usually happen during daylight hours, with slow speeds, low freeboards or easy access points.

Only a small percentage of vessels are attacked, and only a small percentage of those will be hijacked successfully. The Maersk Alabama was not taken the second time she was attacked, because on the second occasion she had an armed security team on board.

Motherships such as these are stolen and used by the pirates, and carry their fast skiffs on board or are towed; see left.

Commercial vessels, fishing boats and Dhows are hijacked and used as mother ships; wooden dhows are the pirates' favourite.

As Somali pirates become more advanced, as their tactics change. They realise that using mother ships is the way ahead, now they are using larger ships to reach further distances and leaving the crew onboard to help them in running the vessel and help them in their activities, thus using the hostages as human shields as and when coalition forces arrive. Some people choose to run the gauntlet and try to pass through the GOA or other high-risk areas without the necessary precautions, usually to cut costs. The most famous example is the case of the Chandlers. As this book goes to press, hundreds of hostages are still being held in Somalia waiting for ransoms to be paid, and each month more are captured. A two-man, armed security team could have deployed with the Chandlers for the passage through the GoA and Indian Ocean; this would almost certainly have guaranteed the safe passage to friendly waters; unfortunately good guards are expensive, costing £500- £1500 a day per person. This cost should be weighed up against the stress of being held captive in a hostile environment and having to pay a large ransom, or even worse being killed. The option of having a yacht transported to a destination should also be considered. The British government will never back down to terrorism; past evidence of this can be seen with kidnap cases in Iraq such as the horrific Ken Bigley incident. Other governments will negotiate, but Britain won't, and that should also be considered before making any hazardous trip.

Below, a typical vessel that pirates would use as a mothership.

Somali pirates seen using their typical GRP skiff with a single 40HP OBM. These are capable of 20kts on a calm sea. Often tarpaulins are covering their obvious pirate equipment, but the long ladders are difficult to conceal. Note as of 2011, larger faster skiffs are in use with twin OBMs and higher speeds (30kts).

An average skiff carries between 4-6 pirates. Weapons are usually kept out of sight until the last moments and are slung whilst climbing

Below are various photographs of some of the skiffs/mothercraft that have been used by Somali pirates up until 2011.

Be aware though that pirates now use larger, recently-kidnapped commercial vessels. When in the HRA, it is essential that the OOW knows which vessels these are as you identify them by electronic means (AIS/Radar/VHF) or visually.

Fishermen in their skiffs in and around the GoA are known to carry weapons; this does not make them pirates. Fishermen do not carry ladders though. When pirates attack your vessel, if possible try to film it for evidence.

The Is'Hak (above) was boarded and released as no evidence was found. As a result, she was later used as a mothership for attacks on merchant vessels

Many of these mother craft will be out of service by the time you read this, but this shows you the variation of craft they use and prefer.

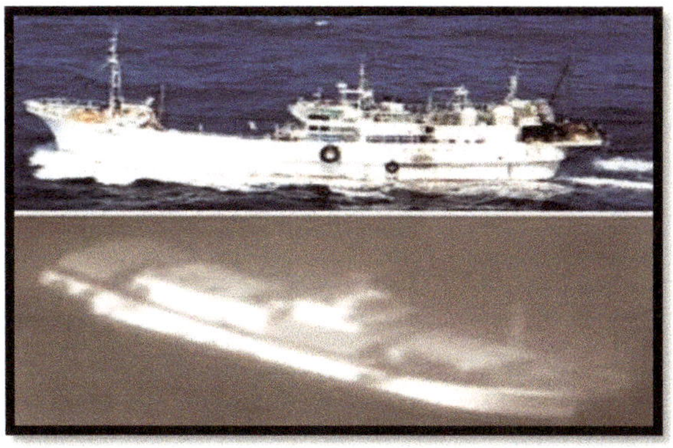

A dhow towing a fishing boat, or a pirate mothercraft and skiff? It could be either

Pirates with their captured vessel

A pirate poses with Russian PKM 7.62mm belt-fed machine gun
One of the most commonly used photos.

An 10kg anchor, often confused with a grappling hook; too heavy to be thrown!

A simple, lightweight, grappling hook 1kg

Pirates seen with a GRP skiff, single OBM and AK47

Pirates around the captured MV Faina carrying dubious Russian T72 battle tanks amongst other war stocks in 2008.

5. Friendly forces, group transits and convoys

Safety in Numbers

Details of Gulf of Aden convoy timings can be obtained from the Maritime Safety Corridor Horn of Africa www.mschoa.eu . Convoys usually run at pre-set speeds of varying knots (see below). A convoy does not guarantee 100% safety; thinking this will only lead to a false sense of security; counter measures must still be taken as pirates do attack during convoys.

The French forces operating in the GoA have had a lot of success there.

Fishing dhows being checked by Royal Marines Fast RIBs deployed from the nearby RN warships.

Safety in numbers has always been good advice in general and for transitting through high-risk areas in particular. The problem is trying to co-ordinate it. Vessels moving through the Gulf of Aden now have the possibility to travel in large convoys, often with a coalition warship. There are factors to consider though: the vessel needs to be able to maintain a minimum required speed for the duration of the transit, and it has to be at the start line at the correct time and date; the convoy will not slow down or wait for stragglers. **Most vessels that have been taken have been solo, with a low freeboard, and have been transitting under 15 knots.**

NATO Submarines:

The Dutch submarine monitored communications between pirate vessels and their warlords on shore.

This was the first submarine to contribute to NATO's anti-piracy mission "Operation Ocean Shield" off the horn of Africa. As one of four Walrus-class submarines belonging to the Royal Netherlands Navy, it is one of the most modern non-nuclear submarines. Built with stealth technologies, it is very difficult to detect – even by other submarines – and can remain submerged for long periods.

US coastguard and DEA have reduced piracy around parts of the Caribbean to minimalistic levels

Naval convoy heading South in the Suez Canal.

Various International Friendly Forces

Yemeni patrol boats at Aden Harbour

Omani Patrol Boat at Salalah Harbour.

This tanker not only has a Naval presence, but still deploys its fire hoses, which is good to see. Just because the ship is unladen and has a high freeboard, probably 10m+, doesn't make it safe.

A Warship shadows a commercial vessel in the G.O.A.

French Dauphin Helicopter patrolling the IRTC.

Nigeria Naval, fast boat patrol; Niger Delta

American RIBS capture Somali Pirates, overseen from the Blackhawk Heli-sniper; 'The Eye in the sky'.

A Greek Navy Commando is seen detaining a skiff with suspected Somali pirates tied up alongside a Greek frigate in the GoA after a failed attack on a Norwegian cargo ship. April 1, 2009.

French security forces test their Famas assault rifles in the late afternoon

Various friendly 'small arms' include the belt fed 'Vulcan' Mini Gun and GPMG, as well as the HK A2 rifle (SA80).
The 'Vulcan' GAUSE-17/A has 6 counter-rotating barrels that fire 2000-4000 7.62mm rounds per minute.

Warship deploys a RHIB to check a suspicious dhow

Soldiers of Chinese Navy Special Forces rehearse an anti-piracy drill

Armed RIBs are the perfect boat for interdiction operations, preferred by the world's Special Forces groups, light, fast and extremely seaworthy. The best are made by Halmatic and Fabio Buzzi Design.

Below is description of just one of the types of aircraft that are operating 24-7 in the GoA HRA to help detect, deter and stop piracy.

On 8 March 2010, the Swedish coastguard Maritime Patrol Aircraft (MPA) conducted its first formal mission for EU NAVFOR's anti-piracy operation – Op Atalanta. The Swedish coastguard aircraft, a DASH 8, monitors the waters off the coast of Somalia, providing the force commander with essential information on the movements of ships in the area. The authorities report directly to the force commander and document any incidents.

The MPA's DASH-8 Q-300 is equipped with several advanced surveillance systems that makes it one of the world's most advanced sea surveillance aircraft. The MPA is manned by a civilian crew.

What follows are details of the sophisticated equipment it carries – exactly what is needed to help the vulnerable mariners.

The EL/M-2022(V)3 search radar incorporates a number of electronic features that will assist the operator in detection, classification and tracking of all targets of potential interest. These include ISAR (Inverse Synthetic Aperture Radar) and size measurements which aid in target identification, SAR (Synthetic Aperture Radar) which greatly enhances the surface mapping capability, and MTI (Moving Target Indication).

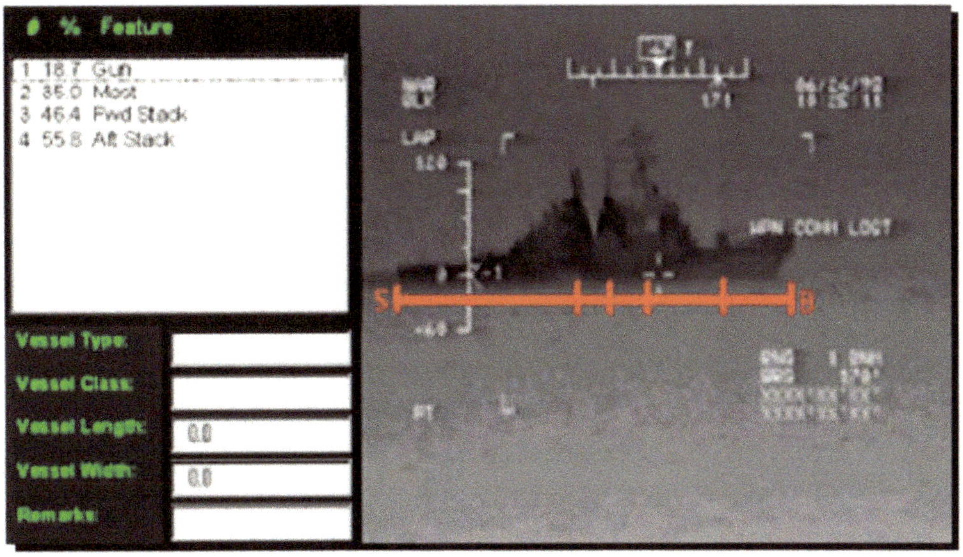

To facilitate closer inspection of targets where such action is warranted, the MSA is equipped with a Wescam MX-15 Electro-Optic/Infrared Sensor (EO/IR) which provides stabilized day and night imagery. The EO/IR pod includes multiple cameras and sensors that will allow the SCG to positively identify ships and read ships names at long ranges under very low light conditions.

The EO/IR sensor is installed under the aircraft's nose section and has, similarly to the radar, a full and un-obstructed 360º field of view. The EO/IR sensor can be pointed to a target by the search radar, be manually controlled or be kept on a designated target via its own auto-tracking system. Images from the EO/IR sensor are annotated with position, time and other data that are relevant to further analysis and legal proceedings.

THE GULF OF ADEN'S FRIENDLY FORCES

The Combined Task Force 151 (CTF 151) was formed on 8 January 2009 with the specific mission of conducting counter-piracy operations in the Horn of Africa maritime region. CTF 151 will assume the lead role in fighting piracy and will be augmented by Combined Task Force 150 (CTF 150). CTF 150 was formed just after the launch of Operation Enduring Freedom to conduct Maritime Security Operations (MSO) in the Gulf of Aden, Gulf of Oman, the Arabian Sea, Red Sea and the Indian Ocean. CTF 150 was not a dedicated counter-piracy force; its primary mission was the deterrence of destabilising activities, such as drug smuggling and weapons trafficking.

French Naval helicopter checks for pirate equipment.

INS Tabar F-44 patrols in the IRTC, Gulf of Aden

A point to note, when the sea state is as calm as this, skiffs can be deployed from over the horizon, out of sight, and be upon a vessel very quickly. It is paramount that vigilance (both visual and radar) is 100% thorough for a full 360° when in high-risk areas

In 2009 heavy naval presence in the GoA forced pirates out into the deeper oceans. There have been attacks from India right down to Tanzania and Mozambique. Ships heading to, or coming from, East Africa should not follow the coastline. It is recommended to sail east of Madagascar and come in that way. It is not a guaranteed safety route, but will be much safer than hand-railing the coast.

An empty skiff on the receiving end of a coalition warship's weapon system

HMS Cumberland F85 takes a brief resupply in the Omani port of Salalah

**A military sentry covers an approaching skiff with his GPMG.
With the current maritime law, and ROE the soldier cannot engage unless
he is fired upon initially. Somali pirates know this.**

A RHIB deploys from the nearby warship to interdict suspect pirates

The patrolling naval ships and aircraft in the GoA and Indian Ocean give great moral support to those passing through those waters.

The Arleigh Burke class guided missile destroyer USS Farragut foils pirate attack, and sinks mother ship

The flagship of the international Combined Task Force (CTF) 151, USS Farragut, operating off Somalia and in the Indian Ocean, has rescued an oil tanker from suspected pirates in the Somali Basin area of the western Indian Ocean. The US Navy News reports that the tanker MV Evita was attacked some 500 kilometres northwest of Seychelles, which is on an approximate line between Mogadishu, the Somali capital, and the Seychelles. The Evita was fired on from three alleged pirate skiffs, which also shot rocket-propelled grenades at the tanker in an attempt to make it stop. However, the tanker was able to evade the alleged pirates by using "best management practices" recommended to merchant vessels, which included increasing its speed and firing flares at the skiffs. The vessel's Master radioed the International Maritime Bureau (IMB) based in Kuala Lumpur, Malaysia, and the UK Maritime Trade Operations Offices (UKMTO) in Dubai. UKMTO then sent an urgent message to international forces operating in the area.

A Swedish Maritime Patrol Aircraft from the international force's EU component, EUNAVFOR, got it touch with the MV Evita and was able to find the suspected pirate skiffs. The force flagship, USS Farragut, was dispatched to monitor and board the skiffs.
The boarding party found 11 suspected pirates aboard the skiffs, as well as fuel drums and grappling hooks.
The suspected pirates were not held, but were disarmed and released on two small skiffs, while the mother ship was destroyed and sunk.

Military robocopters gain pirate ship recognition technology [11]

11 April 2012

The US Navy has announced plans to test a new 3D sensor system that can be attached to an unmanned helicopter to help swiftly and accurately identify pirate vessels lurking among legitimate shipping. The sensor package, called the Multi-Mode Sensor Seeker (MMSS) comprises of high definition cameras, mid-wave infrared sensors and laser radar (Ladar) technology. This will be placed into a robotic helicopter called Fire Scout, which will then be able to autonomously identify small boats on the water and reduce the workload of sailors operating it from control stations on Navy ships. Ken Heeke, programme officer at the Office of Naval Research's Naval Air Warfare and Weapons Department, explains: "Sailors who control robotic systems can become overloaded with data, often sifting through hours of streaming video searching for a single ship."

The MMSS system features automatic target recognitions software that allows the robocopter to distinguish target boats in congested coastal waters with Ladar, cross-referencing the precise dimensions of the boats with a database of known pirate ships. That information can then be sent to human operators who can analyse the 3D images of the vessels.

The software has been integrated into the robocopter by an international team including BAE Systems, the Naval Air Warfare Center Aircraft Division NAWCD, UK defence technology company Raytheon and Utah State University.

The system will be thoroughly tested off the coast of California in the summer of 2012.

[11] Thanks to Olivia Solon

NATO Shipping Centre

NATO's point of contact with the Maritime Community

Telephone: +44(0)1923 956574 info@shipping.nato.int Fax: +44(0)1923 956575

Operation Ocean Shield The aim of the NATO Shipping Centre (NSC) Counter Piracy webpage is to inform all interested parties and stakeholders – shipping companies, shipping organisations and international organisations, national shipping authorities and indeed ships' masters, about the steps the NSC has taken to broadcast information about the piracy situation in the Horn of Africa. Also, the webpage will keep you informed of the NATO Counter Piracy Operation Ocean Shield, which commenced on 17 August 2009, as the follow on operation from Operation Allied Protector, which ended the day before. This operation, which spells an extension by NATO of counter piracy operations, will entail the following military tasks:

(1) Deter, disrupt and protect against pirate attacks, rendering assistance to ships in extremis as required.
(2) Actively seek suspected pirates and prevent their continued activity through detention, seizure of vessels and property, and the delivery of suspects and evidence to designated law enforcement authorities, in accordance with NATO agreements.
(3) Facilitate and support the development of regional states' capacity to conduct effective counter-piracy operations, in coordination with other related international efforts.
(4) Coordinate NATO operations and initiatives with coalition maritime forces, EU naval forces, and other non-NATO forces conducting counter piracy operations off the Horn of Africa.

Of course, all counter piracy efforts are closely coordinated with the EU Maritime Security Centre Horn of Africa (MSC HOA). MSC HOA also has the lead role in the coordination of the group transits through the Gulf of Aden.

- Essential Contact Information
  - UKMTO: ukmto@eim.ae, +971 50 552 3215
  - MARLO: marlo.bahrain@me.navy.mil, +973 3940 1395
  - NATO Shipping Center: info@shipping.nato.int; +44 1923 9566574
  - MSCHOA: postmaster@mschoa.org, +44(0)1923 958545
  - IMB PRC piracy@icc-ccs.org, +60 3 2078 5763

NATO-OTAN OPERATION OCEAN SHIELD

MARITIME LIAISON OFFICE MARLO

MARLO MISSION

The Maritime Liaison Office (MARLO) facilitates the exchange of information between the United States Navy, Combined Maritime Forces, and the commercial maritime community in the Middle East. Our liaison officers travel regularly throughout the Gulf and East Africa to foster communication, stay apprised of changes in local port infrastructure and management, and proactively address your concerns and questions.

USS Momsen assisting M/V Lehmann Timber

Operation ACTIVE ENDEAVOUR

As a result of the 11 September 2001 terrorist attacks in the U.S., NATO launched Operation Active Endeavour as part of the Global War on Terrorism. The operation commenced in October 2001 and is still ongoing. NATO Maritime Component Commander Naples commands the operation to deter terrorism in the Mediterranean and contribute to the peace, stability, and security of all nations in the area. Operation Active Endeavour is based on international law and directly supports United Nations resolutions against threats to international peace and security caused by terrorist acts. Any suspicious behaviour at sea might be considered as a potential indication of illegal or terrorist activity.

More than 1200 well-trained military personnel onboard warships, submarines, and aircraft are fully dedicated to ensure the success of Operation Active Endeavour. Non-NATO nations such as Russia and Ukraine are trained to participate in Operation Active Endeavour. Other nations such as Morocco, Algeria, Croatia, Israel and Albania see the benefits of cooperation or participating in Operation Active Endeavour, and are willing to do so. Cooperation with Operation Active Endeavour forces provides for the safe and secure movement of vessels at sea and reduces the time spent on inspections at sea and ashore. This is an important contribution to the peace, stability and security of all nations and peoples in the area

Operation Endeavour is a NATO maritime operation in the Eastern Mediterranean as part of the international campaign against terrorism. This operation started 26 Oct 2001. The operations area was extended in March 2004. Its area now covers the whole of the Mediterranean Sea including the Straits of Gibraltar. This was confirmed in the North Atlantic Council on 16 March 04. The operation's mission is to conduct naval operations, initially in the Eastern Mediterranean, to actively demonstrate NATO's resolve and solidarity. Operation AE is one of the measures resulting from NATO's decision to implement Article 5 of the Washington Treaty, expanding the options available in the campaign against terrorism. Merchant ships transiting the area can expect to be called on VHF by patrolling naval units. They will ask questions on the ships identity and activity. The fact that NATO is operating in these areas is not only a political gesture but also an indication of the importance of these sea areas. Boarding by naval forces has been authorised. At the same time the anti terrorism operations in the W-Indian Ocean, Persian Gulf and Red Sea continue. These developments are followed in the NATO Shipping Centre (NSC).

The 14 December 2001 NATO's civil and military authorities were requested to support the NATO Shipping Centre in providing shipping information to warships. The Shipping Centre is also acting as a point of contact for the merchant marine. The national authorities were asked to forward this request to their shipping authorities. Reporting is on a voluntary basis. Operation Active Endeavour has been extended several times, the end date of the Operation has not yet been decided.

Counter Piracy news

The NSC web site offers several useful tools/sources of information when it comes to enhance a safe voyage through the area where pirates are active.

Alert map:

The alert map displays position, time and nature of the reported incidents. The map is updated immediately after the appearance of an official alert. Information put on the alert map can be downloaded as an XML-file by clicking the RSS symbol, in the .

PAG (Piracy Attack Groups) map:

The PAG map is manually created, and shows areas with recent and confirmed piracy activity. The PAG map is a jpg picture, and can be copied and used by CSOs etc.

Piracy updates:
The NSC publishes daily and weekly Piracy updates describing the latest assessments regarding piracy activity within the area.

Newsletter: Every month the NSC publishes a newsletter.

A summary of what the EU counter-piracy group does; from the MSCHOA.

Pirates armed with 7.62mm short ammunition fired from AK47 Kalashnikovs and short-range RPG 7 fired from the shoulder on unstable skiffs are no match against a pintle-mounted, fully automatic .50calibre machine gun (12.5mm), fired by a weapon specialist (VPD) standing on a very stable platform. He should consider wearing a cap though, Keeping the sun's glare from his eyes.

Over the weekend of 5-7 March 2010, EU NAVFOR units were involved in concerted operations to interdict and disrupt pirate action groups before they had the opportunity to pirate vessels in the Indian Ocean.
Six pirate action groups have been intercepted, motherships and skiffs have been destroyed and over 40 pirates have been taken into custody.

As reported by EU NAVFOR on 5 March 2010, the force commander of Operation ATALANTA, tasked a French EU NAVFOR warship to intercept and disrupt a pirate attack group, which had previously been repelled by the Vessel Protection Detachment embarked on board a French vessel. The warship intercepted the group of one mothership and two skiffs and found pirate paraphernalia in the skiffs including an RPG rocket launcher, grappling hooks and several fuel barrels. The pirates were arrested and the mothership destroyed.

GROUP ANCHORAGES

Safety in numbers: **you never know who's watching!**

As well as travelling in numbers, consider anchoring in small groups too. Always check previous reports when planning journeys into remote locations. In other areas such as South America, East/West Africa or the Malacca Straits, try to travel in groups rather than solo; safety in numbers may be enough to put off a chance attack. Many owners enjoy and want the solitude and tranquil anchorages such as in a Venezuelan backwater or creek. However, the captain or travel planner should carefully consider the situation and best option. Supposedly safe anchorages may well be prize locations for the local armed thieves.

The below anchorage off the Venezuelan coast has been viciously attacked twice in 2008. An American citizen was shot and killed, and his friend wounded when pirates boarded their sailboat SY Chill in an apparent robbery attempt. The yacht was reported to be anchored off a small island in Mochima, a national park along Venezuela's northeastern coast. The author has worked in this region providing superyacht security; it is recommended to have night watches during the sleeping hours.

One of the many beautiful bays in the Mochima National Park, Venezuela

7. The Internationally Recommended Transit Corridor Gulf of Aden (IRTC - GoA),

The Amended Maritime Security Patrol Area (MSPA) in the Gulf of Aden was established in support of the International Maritime Organisation's (IMO) on-going efforts. The corridor was implemented from 31 August 2008. As of 1 February 2009, the existing Maritime Security Patrol Area introduced by Coalition Navies in 2008, was replaced by two separate, five-mile-wide eastbound and westbound routes, separated by a two-mile buffer. The organisation ISAF recommends that sailing yachts sail in the 2-mile buffer zone or on the flanks of the east and westbound lanes. Westbound vessels should stay in the north lane and vice versa.

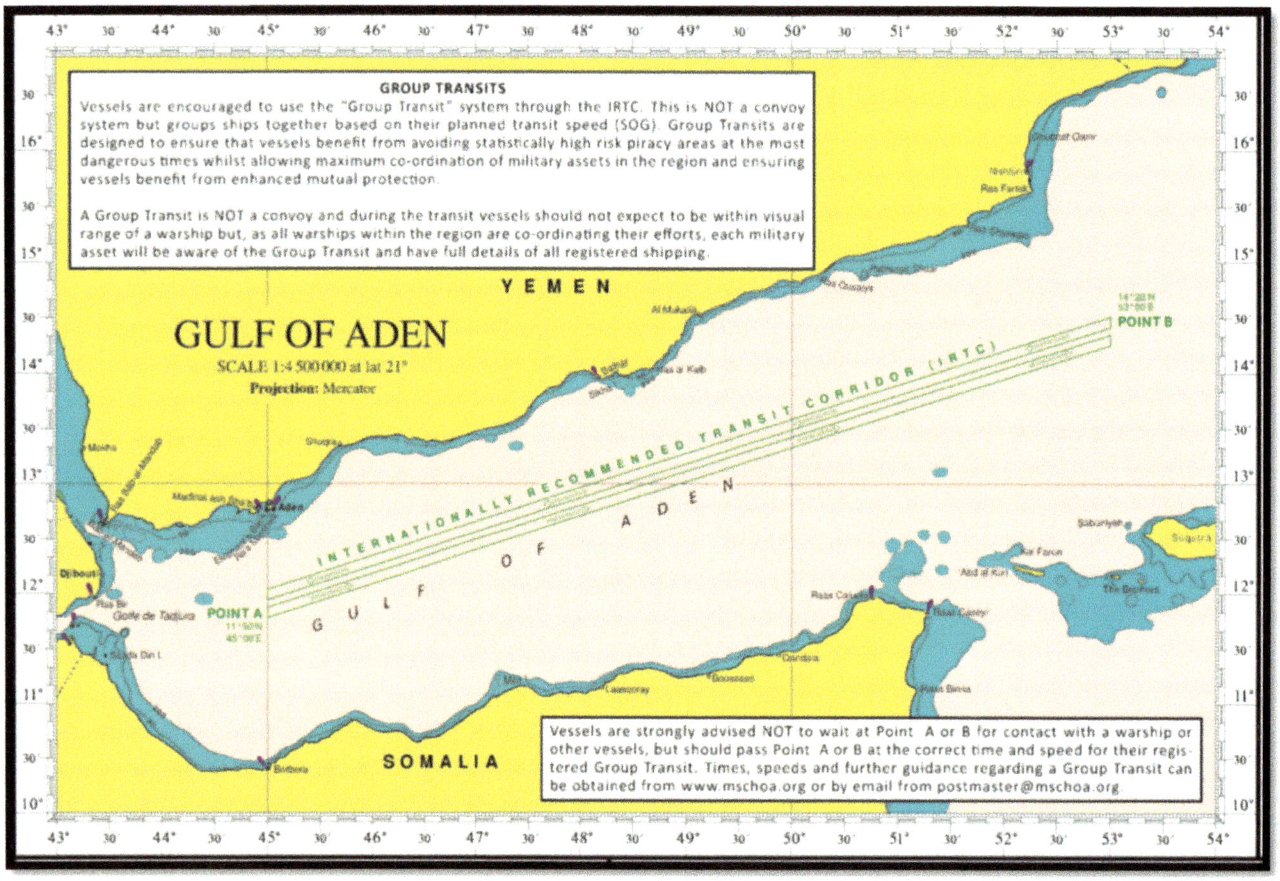

Above: the current IRTC in the GoA

Convoys will also use this area too; there are plenty of vessels going in both directions that can offer mutual support, but be aware of vessels both large and small running 'darkened ship' at night. For smaller vessels, it is advisable to sail parallel either north or south of the busy lanes or in the 2-mile wide buffer zone in the centre. Large ships should stay clear of the smaller vessels such as yachts; the chances of collision are much higher than that of being boarded by pirates.

Note: do not transit in the YTT Yemeni Territorial waters, as EU NAVFOR (coalition warships) cannot engage pirates or help there.

The change came on account of the increase in number and repositioning of warships in the region, and is also designed to reduce risks of collisions. The exact and up to date details of the MSPA can be obtained from the MSCHOA website: www.mschoa.org. Originally there was no point in broadcasting such details so freely, as it can only be surmised that the criminals will read this guidebook too, in the original draft copy a large percentage of sensitive information was removed, however almost all antipiracy information is readily available on the Internet, of which criminals and pirates do read.

Masters using the IRTC are not relieved of their obligation and should continue to maintain a strict 24-hour lookout using all available means to get an early warning of an approaching threat. Some vessels have been attacked and/or hijacked in the corridor. Ships and owners are advised to register their details on the MSCHOA website and obtain further information regarding the close support protection details for ships transitting the GoA. Ships are encouraged to conduct their passage through the IRTC in groups based on their transit speed.

This yacht decided to take an extra fuel bladder with it for a southeast bound trip through the GoA.
Ensure that the fuel is transferred to its internal tanks prior to sailing in high-risk areas.
Even though it is diesel, it's a Health and Safety nightmare as it is, sat above the aft cabins.
The author was is rough seas off Tanzania on a 20m boat; the two 1200l fuel bladders were torn away from their fixings and were lost overboard, thankfully without ripping and were later recovered.
Ensure they are lashed sufficiently when being used.

6. Transits, Escorts and Convoys

Group transits, as previously mentioned are whereupon a group of ships passes through the IRTC from point A at the west end and point B at the east end. Ships may join the transit depending upon its speed. The idea being that it will pass through longitudes 45-47°W during the hours of darkness. Sailing yachts and slow moving vessels should plan their passage during the time of the month when there is no moon. Transits may not have a coalition warship with them, but usually there is one not far away.

For ships in the GoA IRTC, UKMTO recommends that a master should delay the pirates from boarding or gaining internal entry by at least 30 minutes; this has proved enough time to send military assistance to the ship.

Convoys are where a group of ships travel together at the same speed, normally with an escorting warship. For this service, you have to pay the sponsoring country. Convoys (or escorts) are normally done by national warships from China, Malaysia, India, Russia, Korea, and Japan. These countries' ships can escort either single of multiple ships through the high-risk area as often seen.

Below is the IRTC explanation, with courtesy of the MSCHOA:

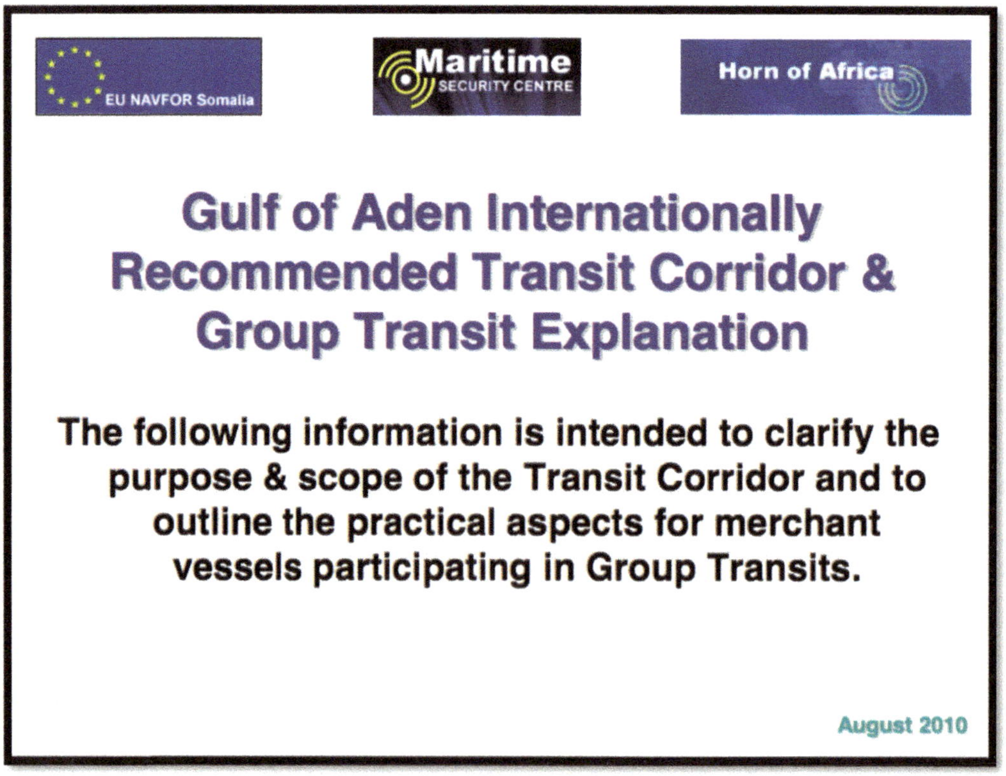

IR Transit Corridor

EU NAVFOR Somalia

The IRTC was amended in 2009 to reflect revised analysis of GOA pirate activity and shipping industry feedback. The new corridor has been positioned further from established fishing areas resulting in a decrease in false piracy alerts.

The corridor is 492 miles long and has an East bound and a West bound lane. Each lane is 5 miles wide with a 2 mile separation between the lanes.

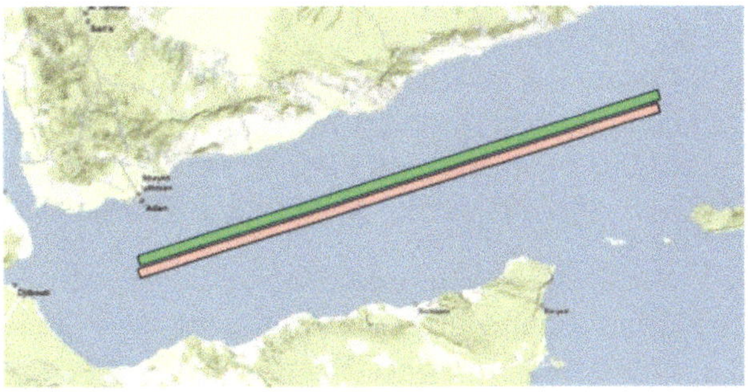

The corridor is not marked or defined by navigational aids, and is not intended to be a TSS. However to make warship patrols more effective, vessels transiting the GOA are strongly recommended to adhere to the Transit Corridor and Group Transit guidelines.

IR Transit Corridor

EU NAVFOR Somalia

The East bound corridor starts at 45°E between 11°53'N & 11°48'N and ends at 53°E between 14°23'N & 14°18'N.

The West bound corridor starts at 53°E between 14°30'N & 14°25'N and ends at 45°E between 12°00'N & 11°55'N.

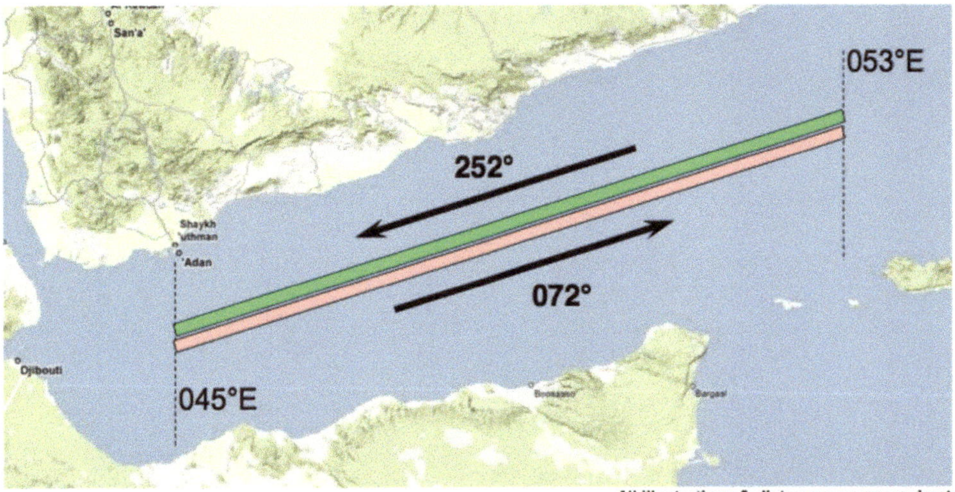

All illustrations & distances are approximate

Group Transits

EU NAVFOR Somalia

"GROUP TRANSITS" ARE NOT "CONVOYS"!

"Group Transits" are designed to put ships into different speed groups in order to exploit the additional protection and assurance of being in a group. The times for different groups to enter the IRTC are calculated so that they pass through the area of statistically greatest danger, between 47E & 49E, at night and ensures that all ships, regardless of speed, are together at first light. This allows the military forces in the area to best position their assets in the area so as to protect ships against piracy and to give assistance in case of attack.

Analysis of successful and attempted pirate attacks in the region clearly indicate that attacks during darkness are rare and, to date, have a zero success rate. Many of the successful attacks have occurred around first or last light in the area between 47E & 49E.

In 2010 statistics show that there have been no successful attacks on ships keeping to "Group Transit" times & speeds.

Group Transits

EU NAVFOR Somalia

Area of greatest threat – statistically – **between 47E & 49E**
(This is area is constantly reviewed and may be changed.)

Night time / darkness transit section (approximate)

Most vulnerable time / area of GT

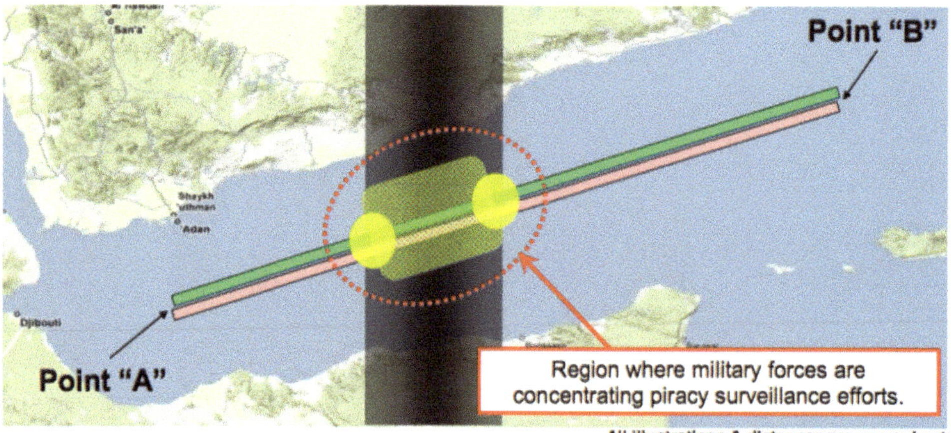

All illustrations & distances are approximate

Group Transit Groupings

EU NAVFOR Somalia

Speed (SOG)	Eastbound Point "A"		Westbound Point "B"	
10 kts	01:00 Z	04:00 LT	15:00 Z	18:00 LT
12 kts	05:30 Z	08:30 LT	21:00 Z	00:01 LT
14 kts	08:30 Z	11:30 LT	01:00 Z	04:00 LT
16 kts	11:00 Z	14:00 LT	05:30 Z	08:30 LT
18 kts	13:00 Z	16:00 LT	07:00 Z	10:00 LT

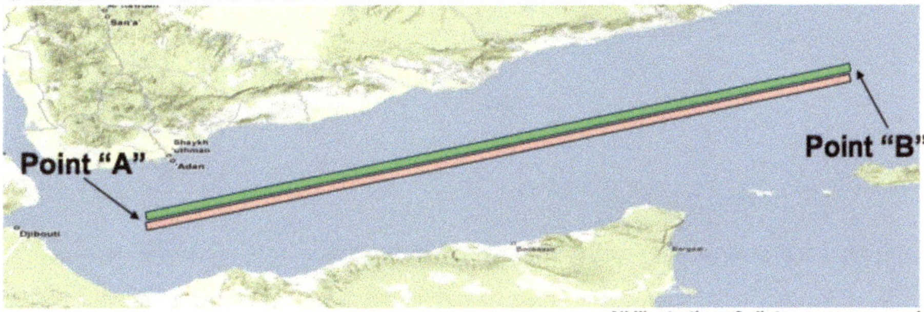

All illustrations & distances are approximate

Westbound GT Case Study

EU NAVFOR Somalia

Vessel ID	Vessel Type	Transit Speed	Vessel ID	Vessel Type	Transit Speed
Ship A	VLCC	12 kts	Ship D	Offshore Supply	10 kts
Ship B	Bulk Carrier	14 kts	Ship E	Car Carrier	14 kts
Ship C	LNG Carrier	18 kts	Ship F	General Cargo	12 kts

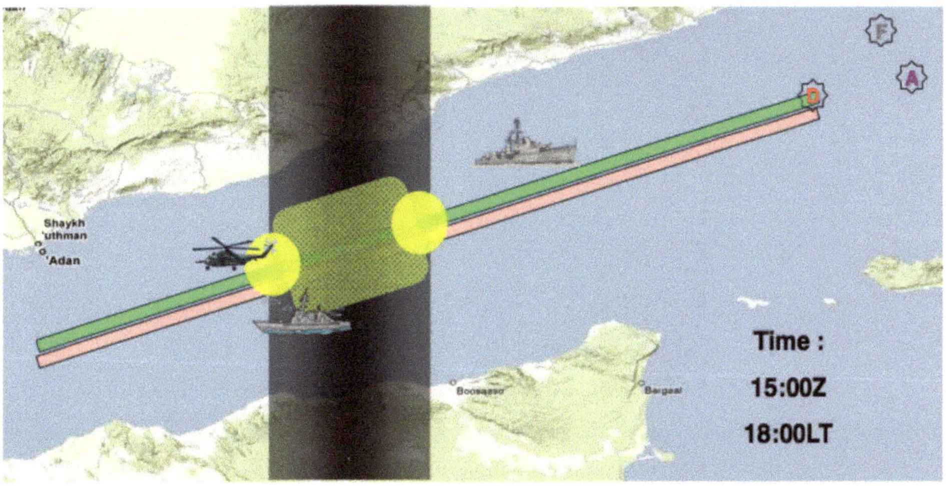

All illustrations & distances are approximate

Westbound GT Case Study

EU NAVFOR Somalia

Vessel ID	Vessel Type	Transit Speed	Vessel ID	Vessel Type	Transit Speed
Ship A	VLCC	12 kts	Ship D	Offshore Supply	10 kts
Ship B	Bulk Carrier	14 kts	Ship E	Car Carrier	14 kts
Ship C	LNG Carrier	18 kts	Ship F	General Cargo	12 kts

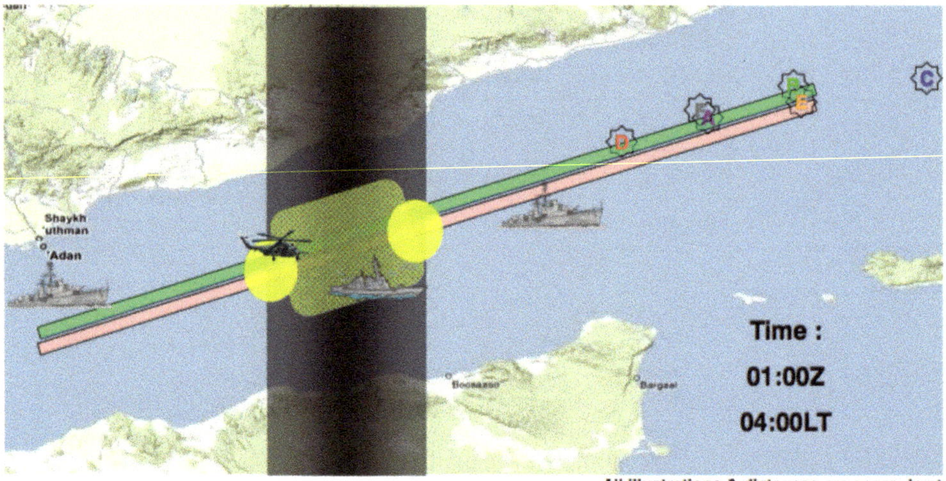

All illustrations & distances are approximate

Westbound GT Case Study

EU NAVFOR Somalia

Vessel ID	Vessel Type	Transit Speed	Vessel ID	Vessel Type	Transit Speed
Ship A	VLCC	12 kts	Ship D	Offshore Supply	10 kts
Ship B	Bulk Carrier	14 kts	Ship E	Car Carrier	14 kts
Ship C	LNG Carrier	18 kts	Ship F	General Cargo	12 kts

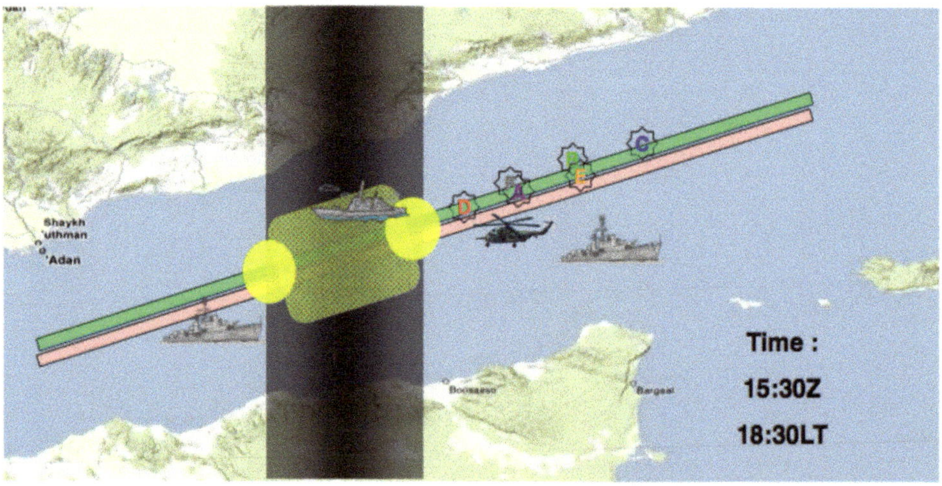

All illustrations & distances are approximate

Westbound GT Case Study

EU NAVFOR Somalia

Vessel ID	Vessel Type	Transit Speed	Vessel ID	Vessel Type	Transit Speed
Ship A	VLCC	12 kts	Ship D	Offshore Supply	10 kts
Ship B	Bulk Carrier	14 kts	Ship E	Car Carrier	14 kts
Ship C	LNG Carrier	18 kts	Ship F	General Cargo	12 kts

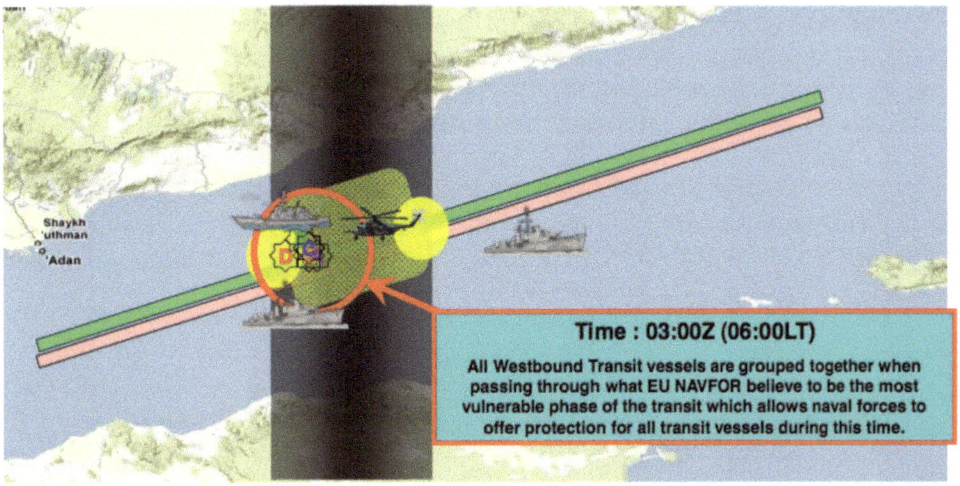

All illustrations & distances are approximate

Westbound GT Case Study

EU NAVFOR Somalia

Vessel ID	Vessel Type	Transit Speed	Vessel ID	Vessel Type	Transit Speed
Ship A	VLCC	12 kts	Ship D	Offshore Supply	10 kts
Ship B	Bulk Carrier	14 kts	Ship E	Car Carrier	14 kts
Ship C	LNG Carrier	18 kts	Ship F	General Cargo	12 kts

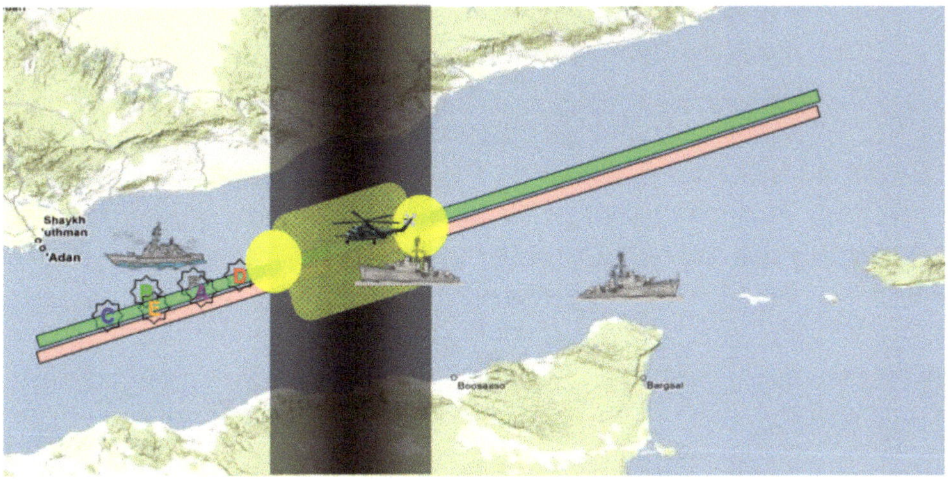

All illustrations & distances are approximate

Important Considerations

EU NAVFOR Somalia

"GROUP TRANSITS" ARE NOT "CONVOYS"

Group Transits may not be closely accompanied by a warship.

As shown in the Case Study, although a vessel may see no other vessels at the start of her transit, other vessels participating in the same transit will converge during the critical stage of the transit. For this reason it is most important that a vessel enters the IRTC at the correct time and does NOT stop and wait for other vessels. Also they should, as far as possible, maintain the group speed over the ground.

Even if in a Group Transit each vessel must still employ all possible anti-piracy security measures in compliance with "BMP3" and keep a VHF watch on Ch. 16 & 8 throughout the transit.

Without registering a vessel movement with MSCHOA and transmitting regular position, course, speed & ETA at IRTC entrance updates to MSCHOA, EU NAVFOR will be unable to provide warships with information regarding which vessels are in each transit and when/where they should expect to see them.

Further Information

EU NAVFOR Somalia

WWW.MSCHOA.ORG

A website created by EU NAVFOR Somalia in order to inform the Merchant Shipping community with regard to the continued threat of Piracy off the Horn of Africa.

(User registration is required to access all areas of the website)

POSTMASTER@MSCHOA.ORG

Email address monitored by EU Maritime Security Centre military and merchant navy personnel where questions regarding the Transit Corridor and Group Transits may be directed.

Maritime SECURITY CENTRE

Horn of Africa

Below is the UKMTO Standard Message Format to be used when sailing through the GoA IRTC.

A message should be sent every 6 hours between points A & B

UKMTO STANDARD MESSAGE FORMAT

1	Ship Name	
2	Flag	
3	IMO Number	
4	INMARSAT Telephone Number	
5	Time & Position	
6	Course	
7	Passage Speed	
8	Freeboard	
9	Cargo	
10	Destination and Estimated Time of Arrival	
11	Name and contact details of Company Security Officer	
12	Nationality of Master and Crew	

NOTES:

EMERGENCY CONTACT

- **UKMTO Dubai**

United Kingdom Maritime Trade Operations
Email: ukmto@eim.ae
Tel: +971 50 552 3215

SECONDARY CONTACTS

- MSC-HOA

Maritime Security Centre – Horn of Africa
Email: postmaster@mschoa.org
Tel: +44 1923 958 545
Fax: +44 1923 958 520
Website: www.mschoa.org

- NATO Shipping Centre

Email: info@shipping.nato.int
Tel: +44 1923 956 574
Fax: +44 1923 956 575
Website: www.shipping.nato.int

- MARLO Maritime Liaison Office – Bahrain

Email: marlo.bahrain@me.navy.mil
Tel: +973 1785 3925
Cell: +973 3940 1395
Website: www.cusnc.navy.mil/marlo/

- IMB Piracy Reporting Centre

Email: piracy@icc-ccs.org
imbkl@icc-ccs.org
Tel: +603 2031 0014 (24 hr Helpline)
Fax: +603 2078 5769
Telex: +84 34199 (IMBPC1 MA34199)
Website: www.icc-ccs.org

FURTHER INFORMATION

Further information and guidance can be obtained from the following organisations, websites or publications:

- UKMTO Dubai, MSC-HOA, MARLO and the IMB-PRC.
- Best Management Practice Guidelines – "BMP3" (available from Admiralty Distributors, OCIMF and INTERTANKO).
- Oil Companies International Marine Forum (OCIMF) Publication "Piracy – The East Africa / Somalia Situation".
- IMO Marine Safety Committee (MSC) Circular(s).
- Admiralty Annual Summary of Notices to Mariners.
- Admiralty List of Radio Signals (ALRS) Volumes 1 and 6.
- Relevant Navigation Warnings and EGC SafetyNet broadcasts on Inmarsat C.

7. OPEN-ENDED SUPERYACHTS AND VESSELS

As can be seen at most prestigious marinas, some superyachts have sweeping teak steps cascading down from the upper decks all the way to the water line, allowing guests to come down from the sundeck and mount jet skis easily and elegantly with the minimum of fuss. These designs are truly beautiful and work very well; unfortunately, they present a very easy method of boarding for pirates. Such vessels present such a tempting invitation to board, unfortunately for the Captain the BMP 4 ship's hardening cannot be applied.

Most motor superyachts are open ended;
the above type of stern is much more secure than below.

French Commando Zodiac boats arrive at French cruise ship Le Ponant, whose crew was taken hostage by pirates, off Somalia's coast April 12, 2008. The open end offers easy boarding for all.

The same applies to open-ended vessels such as work- or tugboats. For the vessel's security men, these workboats create a lot of extra effort; however, with some good common sense-type thinking most open-ended vessels can be secured using basic materials to hand.

It's not only working boats and superyachts that frequent the beautiful islands of the Seychelles, but as of 2009 pirates are attacking all vessels in and around these waters including the Spanish Tuna Fleet.

Use anything to hand to protect your vulnerable areas. Situations like the above are at extreme risk and a good tug will provide the perfect mother craft for long-range pirate operations

For superyacht Captains it is very difficult to harden the most luxurious of private vessels, some times it just isn't feasible, in these cases that is where a PCASP team from a reputable company would be needed. Companies such as Veritas and Ironside Associates specialise in such services and use men that know how to conduct themselves on such prestigious vessels. Some PCASP men have only worked upon commercial ships and would not ne suitable for the superyacht industry unless they have prior training before embarkation.

On one occasion, a deckhand secured his vessel by placing large two-metre fenders in the stairwells and inflating them, thus wedging them in and preventing access. All of the open areas between decks were covered with fishing nets, and lastly with cod-lines that had triple hooks attached every 30cm.

This combination certainly makes boarding more difficult, especially if the vessel moves away at full speed with aggressive turns thrown in. Open sterns will certainly draw in the pirates/thieves, in this case, trailing lines will be very effective, see page 103, 140 & 147 for details.

A Captain knows what materials he has to hand on his vessel and with some pre-transit planning and additional input from the engineer and crewmembers it is easy to orchestrate some methods to prevent or slow or stop illegal boarding. The use of bio-grease can be used too on open-ended boats and their railings; it may take the deckhands a day or two to completely remove it, but that's better than months in Somalia waiting until a ransom is paid. If hardening the vessel is not an option then the crew must take shifts as sentries.

Nets will certainly slow down anyone trying to board illegally, but won't guarantee safety.

On expensive yachts such as 'A' below, the use of Razor wire is not an option

Quite often such workboats are moved across the HRA at slow speed, these types of boats need to ensure that they have every type of ship's hardening available and if possible pay for a convoy in the IRTC. PCASP should be considered, as pirates will do their best to obtain your vessel. With it they can deploy further afield and hijack, other vessels before taking you to Somali for a long boring wait for the ransom to be paid.

Razor wire, electric fencing, water cannons, sandbag walls, trailing lines, swinging oil drums should all be installed prior to the journey. Read BMP4 and consider PCASP to ensure maximum safety.

Captains and Chief Officers should employ the ratings to protect the ship as much as possible using all materials to hand

8. Preventative measures and Ship's Hardening

Two things are widely known amongst pirates and thieves: Firstly commercial ships are relatively easy to board/capture and owners/insurers pay huge ransoms in order to release them and secondly that to own a private boat you must have surplus money and therefore fall into the 'wealthy' category. Boats are expensive to buy, run and maintain. Their contents are usually equally expensive, especially on the bigger, private vessels or super-yachts and offer rich pickings for the poor.
Piracy is as old as sailing itself. Anti-boarding techniques and preventative measures go back centuries and have changed with technology, unfortunately there is not a decent, up-to-date guidebook that a Captain can quickly refer to that mentions all of the necessary subjects they need to know; hence this book was produced.
Let us take a classic example of a medium sized sailing vessel that is being pursued by a pirate skiff. The Captain should immediately call for assistance, increase his speed away from the threat, and inform the crew to move to a safe area. It may be that there is a heavy sea, by turning into it will prevent the small skiff from keeping up with their target and will certainly make boarding very difficult. If the seas are calmer and the Captain continues on his course and zig-zags, he should have old ropes, trailing lines, nets or rope launchers to deploy into the water by a crew member. These will hopefully foul the prop' of the skiffs, thus stopping the attack. Should they avoid these and the chase continues, deploy smoke and airborne rocket flares to attract the attention of any nearby coalition warships, helicopters etc, and then consider firing flares close to the skiffs.
The next stage would be to try to prevent the men from climbing on board. High pressure, pre-placed fire hoses can be turned on, the yacht's rails should be pre-greased, and electric fences can be turned on. If ladders or grappling hooks are established on the boats gunwales or rails, then you've done all that you can and you should adopt a passive role as soon as they board. Don't be putting yourself at risk by trying to beat them off or fire rope launchers at them, they will most probably shoot you, especially if you are on a small sailing yacht.

Most ships have 45-gallon drums. These filled with water or sand will make simple defences that will stop most bullets and RPGs, even when hit with multiple strikes they will slow down the incoming rounds sufficiently to make the inner bridge much safer. Anti-blast film on the windows, such as that made by 3M should also be used.

For sailing yachts, simple items on sailing yachts, such as water-filled fenders, Dynema and Kevlar ropes, tightly coiled, can all provide protection from incoming bullets; they are not guaranteed to stop them, but they will certainly slow down bullets considerably and are better than nothing at all. A low velocity bullet wound is very different to a high velocity one, the latter being extremely traumatic to the body.

Large fenders filled with water worked well on this sailing yacht, note fishing nets taped on the aft rails

On commercial vessels, empty 45-gallon drums filled with sand or water make good barriers too.*

Captains and crew who follow all of the above measures may prevent the pirates from boarding; they are desperate measures, some of which have worked in the past, but small boats offer very little protection or defence. Should the attackers gain access to the vessel, and then once they are onboard, a completely passive role should be adopted. The taking of vessels by Somali Pirates is a game of cat and mouse, albeit a deadly game. When being chased or attacked the Captain should use all legal methods possible to avoid capture whilst keeping his crew in a safe location. Attacks have been thwarted by the ship's crew throwing items such as crockery or Molotov Cocktails at the pursuing skiffs. The author is definitely not recommending that petrol bombs are even considered, but these past, failed attacks show us that with a bit of guts and some quick, clever thinking your vessel can be saved. The Somali Pirates do, or did abide by a code of conduct, of which hostages are looked after during their period of capture. There is a fine line between antagonising the pirates too much and doing too little to protect the vessel.
For a breakdown of the above methods, details will be enhanced in the following chapters.

More examples of containers filled with water. Skeptics would say that once shot or penetrated they will be useless. The chances of being attacked twice on one transit are slim, but yes, it may happen, so have spare drums to replace the damaged ones in a time of emergency. Should anyone require to see a bullet penetration demonstration using various calibers including the AK47 7.62x 39mm bullets, IMAAG can provide this.

Above, this Rickmers ship used chainmail fencing to protect the multi-level superstructure, containers filled with water and sand, steel plates were welded shut over the low level windows. Below were double coils of Razor wire, topped with an electric fence, high pressure water cannons, trailing lines and a 4-man VPT on the bridge. Nothing more could have been done to protect this vessel; the company obviously has a very professional CSO.

Coils of heavy-duty rope are put to good use to help protect the vulnerable cockpit of this sailing yacht. It is very difficult to protect yourself on sailing yachts, use what you can if you must sail in high-risk areas. Like the UKMTO say, best avoid such places, but that is difficult when we have areas of natural beauty such as the Seychelles and other Indian Ocean islands.

Keeping low to avoid being shot, a Chinese sailor lights a Molotov cocktail before throwing it at Somali pirates trying to board his ship. He and his crewmates were expecting trouble and had prepared dozens of the makeshift grenades to repel an invasion. Their cargo vessel was attacked in the Gulf of Aden by pirates using speedboats and armed with heavy machine guns and rocket launchers in December 2008, the standoff lasted 5 hours, the ship was boarded, but the crew locked themselves away until coalition warship and helicopter saved them.

Concertina wire, Barbed wire and Razor wire

This information has been included as the knowledge and erection of Razor wire is often sub-standard.

Concertina wire (or Dannert Wire) is a type of barbed wire or razor wire that is formed in large coils which can be expanded like a concertina. In conjunction with plain barbed wire and steel pickets, it can be used to form wire obstacles as well as a multitude of other security barriers. It comes in various types of diameter (see below) with differing types of barbs. During World War I soldiers manufactured concertina wire themselves, using ordinary barbed wire. Today, it is factory made.

Origins

In the First World War, barbed wire obstacles were made by stretching lengths of barbed wire between stakes of wood or iron. At its simplest, such a barrier would resemble a fence as might be used for agricultural purposes. The double apron fence comprised a line of pickets with wires running diagonally down to points on the ground either side of the fence. Horizontal wires were attached to these diagonals. More elaborate and formidable obstructions could be formed with multiple lines of stakes connected with wire running from side-to-side, back-to-front, and diagonally in every possible direction. Effective as these obstacles were their construction took considerable time. Barbed wire obstacles were vulnerable to being pushed about by artillery shells and in the First World War this frequently resulted in a mass of randomly entangled wires that could be even more daunting than a carefully constructed obstacle. Learning this lesson, First World War soldiers would deploy barbed wire in so-called concertinas that were relatively loose. Barbed wire concertinas could be pre-prepared in the trenches and then deployed in no-man's-land relatively quickly under cover of darkness.

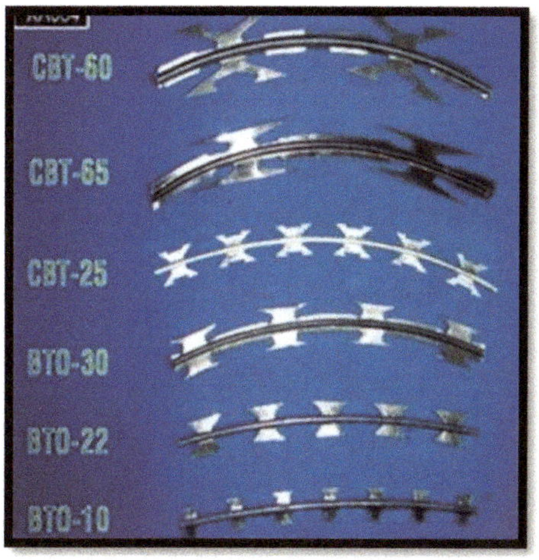

There was what might be called a concertina craze on: innumerable coils of barbed wire were converted into concertinas by the simple process of winding them round and round seven upright stakes in the ground; every new lap of wire was fastened to the one below it at every other stake by a twist of plain wire; the result, when you came to the end of a coil and lifted the whole up off the stakes was heavy ring of barbed wire that concertinaed out into ten meter lengths. Concertina wire packs flat for ease of transport and can then be deployed as an obstacle much more quickly than ordinary barbed wire. A platoon of soldiers can deploy a single concertina fence at a rate of about a kilometer per hour. Such an obstacle is not very effective by itself, and concertinas are normally built up into more elaborate patterns as time permits. Today, concertina wire is factory made and is available in forms that can be deployed very rapidly from the back of a vehicle or trailer.

Razor wire is a mesh of metal strips with sharp edges whose purpose is to prevent passage by humans. The term "razor wire", through long usage, has generally been used to describe barbed tape products. While razor wire is much sharper than the standard barbed wire, it is not actually razor sharp.

Types of concertina Razor wire

Blade Size	Style	Thickness	Diameter of center line	Length	Width	Distance
BTO-10		0.5±0.05	2.5±0.1	10±1	13±1	26±1
BTO-12		0.5±0.05	2.5±0.1	12±1	15±1	26±1
BTO-18		0.5±0.05	2.5±0.1	18±1	15±1	33±1
BTO-22	Blade Length / Core Wire Dia / Blade Space / Blade Width	0.5±0.05	2.5±0.1	22±1	15±1	34±1
BTO-28		0.5±0.05	2.5	28	15	45±1
BTO-30		0.5±0.05	2.5	30	18	45±1
CBT-60		0.6±0.05	2.5±0.1	60±2	32±1	100±2
CBT-65		0.6±0.05	2.5±0.1	65±2	21±1	100±2

Outside Diameter	No. of Loops	Standard Length per Coil	Type	Notes
450mm	33	8M	CBT-65	Single coil
500mm	41	10M	CBT-65	Single coil
700mm	41	10M	CBT-65	Single coil
960mm	53	13M	CBT-65	Single coil
500mm	102	16M	BTO-10.15.22	Cross type
600mm	86	14M	BTO-10.15.22	Cross type
700mm	72	12M	BTO-10.15.22	Cross type
800mm	64	10M	BTO-10.15.22	Cross type
960mm	52	9M	BTO-10.15.22	Cross type

Razor-wire has a central strand of high tensile strength wire, and a steel tape punched into a shape with barbs. The steel tape is then cold-crimped tightly to the wire everywhere except for the barbs. Barbed tape is very similar, but has no central reinforcement wire. The process of combining the core wire with the steel tape was invented by the current owner of Razor Wire International, Renne Cano.

Concertina wire Technical List

A. Materials:

1. The concertina wire made of high tensile wire. The core wire shall be high tensile wire ranging between 1400 to 1500Mpa in 2.5mm diameter, and be of galvanized steel wire, zinc coating: 245g/m2.

2. The blades shall be of 0.5mm thickness stainless steel 304 grade sheet.

B. Design as follow

Razor Wire Specification List

Reference Number	Blade Style	Thickness	Wire Dia	Barb Length	Barb Width	Barb Spacing
BTO-10		0.5±0.5	2.5±0.1	10±1	13±1	26±1

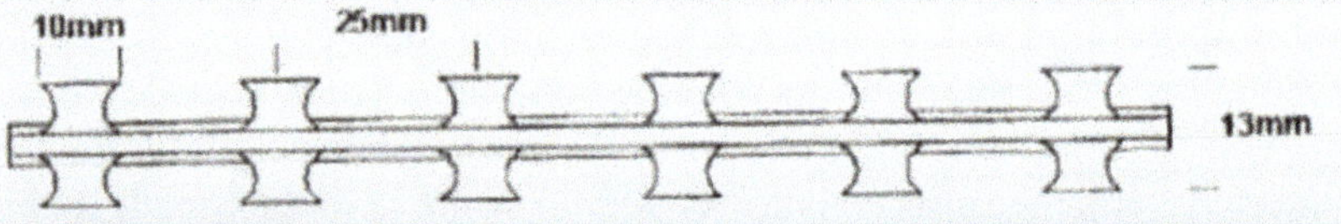

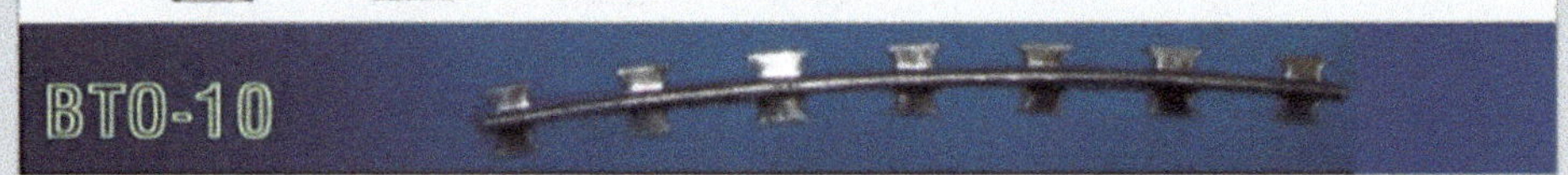

The multiple blades of a razor wire fence are designed to inflict serious cuts on anyone attempting to climb through and therefore have a strong psychological deterrent effect. In many high-security applications, barbed tape supplanted barbed wire, which could be circumvented relatively quickly by humans with tools, while penetrating razor wire barriers without tools is very slow and difficult, giving security forces more time to respond. Starting in the late 1960s, barbed tape was typically found in prisons and long-term mental hospitals, where the increased breaching time for a poorly equipped potential escapee was a definite advantage. Until the development of reinforced barbed tape in the early 1980s, it was rarely used for military purposes or genuine high security facilities because, with the correct tools, it was easier to breach than barbed wire. Since then some military forces have replaced barbed wire with barbed tape for many applications, mainly because it is slightly lighter for the same effective coverage and it takes up very little space compared to barbed wire or reinforced barbed tape when stored on drums. More recently barbed tape has been used in more commercial and residential security applications. This is often primarily a visual deterrent since a well prepared burglar can breach barbed wire and barbed tape barriers in similar amounts of time, using simple techniques such as cutting the wire or throwing a piece of old carpet over its strands. Residential usage of barbed tape has been criticized by some as the aggressive appearance of the barbs is thought to detract from the appearance of a neighborhood. Due to its dangerous nature, razor wire/barbed tape and similar fencing/barrier materials is prohibited in some locales. Norway prohibits any barbed wire except in combination with other fencing, in order to protect domesticated animals from exposure. Some local jurisdictions further regulate or prohibit barbed wire altogether.

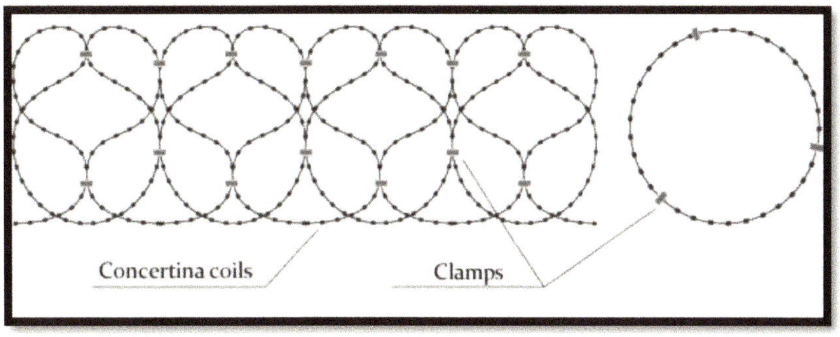

Types

Like barbed wire, barbed tape is available as either straight wire or spiral concertina wire. Unlike barbed wire, which usually is available only as plain steel or galvanized, barbed tape is also manufactured in stainless steel, to prevent the points from rusting to bluntness. Typically the core wire is galvanized and the tape is stainless, although fully stainless barbed tape is used for expensive permanent installations or under water. Barbed tape is also characterized by the shape of the barbs. Although there are no formal definitions, typically short barb barbed tape has barbs from 10 mm to 15 mm long, medium barb tape has barbs 20 mm to 25 mm long, and long barb tape has barbs from 60 to 66 mm long. There does not seem to be much available research to indicate whether longer barbs are actually more effective in resisting penetration, but they provide a stronger psychological deterrent.

Barbed tape was first manufactured by Germany during World War I, as an expedient measure during a shortage of wire. Since it was simply punched out of a rolled ribbon of steel tape, it could be manufactured much more quickly. This early barbed tape had triangular barbs and no reinforcing wire; consequently, it was more difficult to cut with ordinary wire cutters, easier to cut with shears, and was generally of lower tensile strength.

Barbed tape on a fence. Note the absence of a reinforcement wire running down the middle

From the early 1970s, unreinforced barbed tape was commonly used in perimeter barriers of US prisons. In the early 1980s, several manufacturers began offering barbed tape with an embedded reinforcing wire and the product has been the subject to a patent dispute. Early brand names of reinforced barbed tape included "Man Barrier" and "Razor Ribbon". The latter probably lent its name to the modern slang term.

Razor wire on ships

The use of Razor wire on ships works very well. Like all systems it has to be the right material and erected corectly. The Captain or Chief in charge of erecting ship's defences should ensure that the wire is placed as effectively as possible. If the wire is likely to be reused many times, then the higher grade stainless razor wire coils should be bought, using cheap ferrous wire will rust and weaken very quickly due to its location next to sea spray. Ideally the larger diamaters are better such as 75 or 90cms. However if multiple rolls are to erected then 50cms can be used too. Ensure that the wire is connected to each roll and to the ship's railings or stancions every 1-2 meters. This is crucially important. Heavy seas will destroy a badly erected fence if these connections are not close enough together. Again, pirates will throw a grappling hook tied to a bucket, the hook snags on the wire, the bucket is dropped into the sea and the drag factor will rip down the wire.

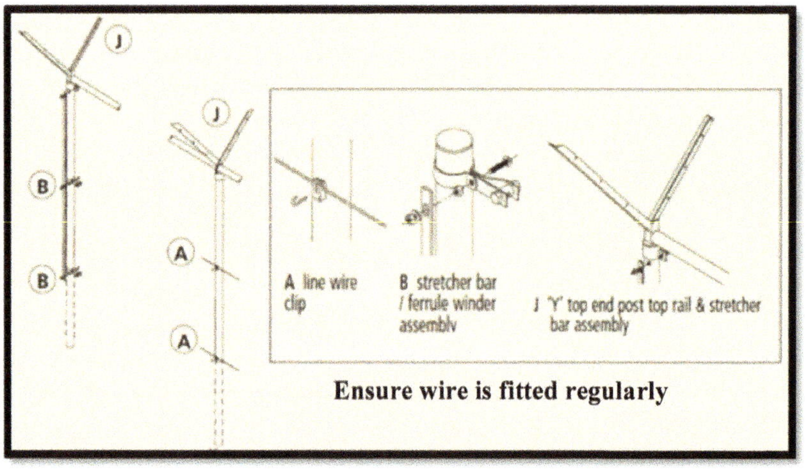

Ensure wire is fitted regularly

There have been instance whereupon the ratings have erected the wire so badly that the pirates' ladder has dragged down the wire enough for the ladder to hold onto the railings. The best examples of concertina razor wire can be seen where 4 rolls have been erected on all vulnerable sides. The lowest areas should be defended the most, followed by the aft areas, only the bow area is normally not attacked, but to be 100% reassured, put it everywhere you deem a threat when you conduct your ship's security assessment prior to the voyage. Ratings must be well supervised when erecting the wire, normally in the equatorial regions it is very warm or too hot, workers begin to take short cuts, erecting the defences as fast as possible. Plastic connectors should never be used as permanent fixings, cable ties can be used to hold the wire in place until the wire/metal fixers are connected.

Badly erected Razorwire will soon be dislodged

Below is a picture of a stainless steel connector, which is perfect. Twisted wire can be used, ensure it's strong enough, or double it over to make double-strand twists.

Even if you use the most expensive stainless steel 100mm diameter coils, and have four high, 360 degrees around your vessel, with fixers every 1m, don't think that this alone will stop determined pirates from climbing aboard, it may stop them, it will slow them, but it doesn't guarantee.

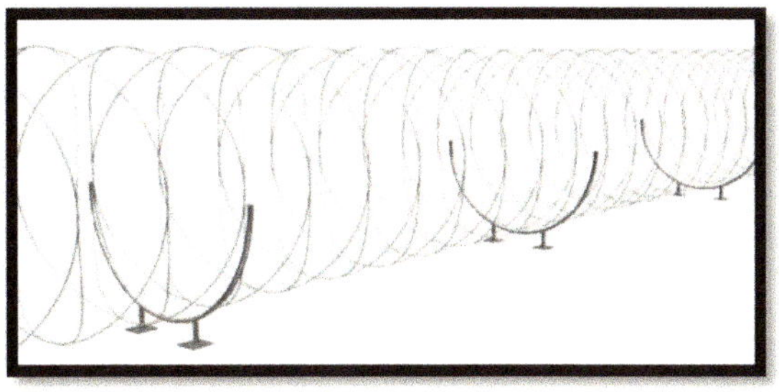

Some ships have rigged coils of wire to be thrown overboard when skiffs approach, they are dragged through the water to foul the propellors and make coming alongside very difficult. This may work, but there downsides too, it takes time to deploy the wire into the water, which will expose the workers to a possible lethal threat, the coils snag on each other so don't trail the 100m or so that you intended, thy may snag your ship's propellor, and they cannot be left in situ in the water as they will snag every piece of debris on the passage.

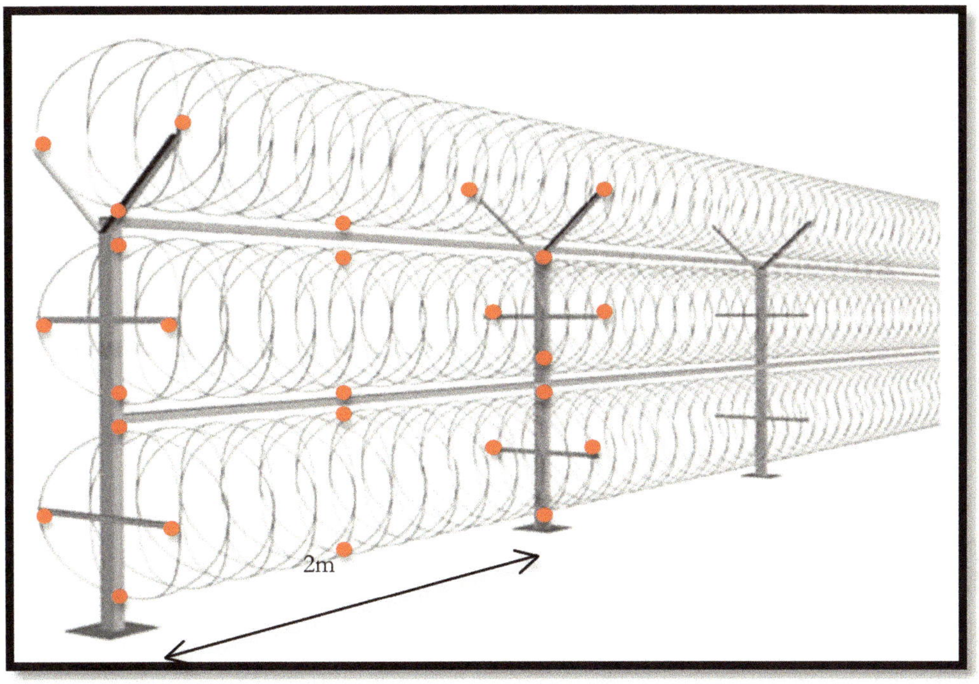

Where ever you decide to fix your Razorwire to, ensure that the connectors are made from metal, not plastic and those connectors are fitted every 1-2 meters to withstand various pulling forces (Sea swell, gales, pirates etc)

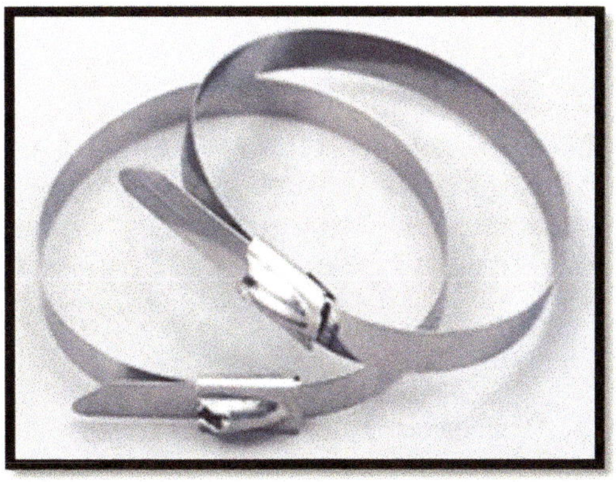

Stainless steel connectors = ●

Various hardening examples on commercial ships:
Photos courtesy of Steve Jackson & IMAAG

Regardless of armed security and other protective methods, always use plenty of razor wire, the more the better. Three rolls of concertina wire is perfect

Stanchions should be robustly fixed in place as pirates will try to rip off or pull down the wire

Ensure full PPE safety equipment is worn when erecting Razor wire

Open access areas should be thoroughly blocked, even at anchor

Weld shut vulnerable openings, even if they are to be removed later. Right: block all stairwells.

Left are lower windows with welded covers preventing entry.

Right, the watertight door handle (dog) can be secured simply by welding a heavy-duty nut in place. One per dog is recommended

All access points should be blocked internal and externally with items to hand such as barrels and razor wire

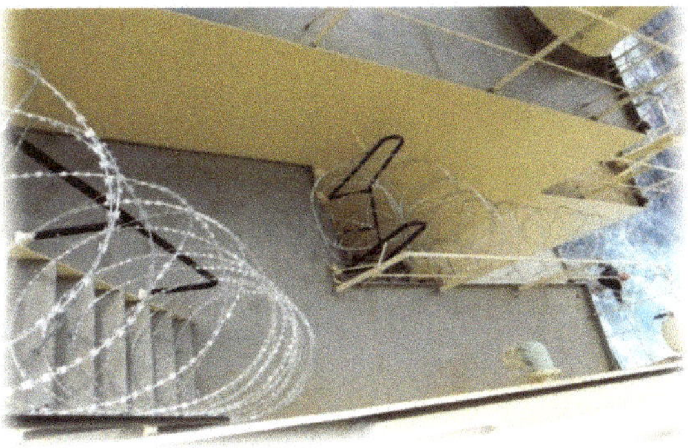

Steel grating is ideal; it can be bolted, welded or hinged into position.

Razorwire used correctly is very effective

Sand Bags.

In the past ships have used sandbags either suspended or built into a wall. This should be done as a latter option. The relentless sun found in and around the equatorial HRA will destroy the fabric of the sand bags and will cause the bag to disintegrate, leaving sand everywhere. Sand weighs a lot, is difficult to manoeuvre and has to be brought onboard at a cost. Much better is to use empty 45 gallon drums, placed on matting and lashed to the rails. Once in place they are filled with water, these will stop bullets and RPGs. If punctured, replace them. They are cheap (€5 each for brand new ones at Algeciras Port, Spain), easy to move and simple to store.

A newly made sandbag wall is a good defence; this is one way of using them, but is full of gaps, so not ideal. A solid wall is much better, as used for flood defences or by the military.

After a few months in the fierce equatorial sun, the UV rays will quickly damage the synthetic fibres, they will become brittle and break open. The sand will eventually spill out causing further problems, such as blocking drainage and being blown into well-greased machinery, davits etc. Cover your sandbags with canvas sheeting or similar. If you are going to use sand bags, order enough; 400 is suitable for most commercial ships and have them craned directly on to the bridge wing areas.

Next is a better method of securing the bridge's flanks and vulnerable areas.

Bridge hardening possibilities. The best defence to stop bullets and RPGs is to continue the sheet plate around the bridge flanks; this will not interfere with vision from the OOW.

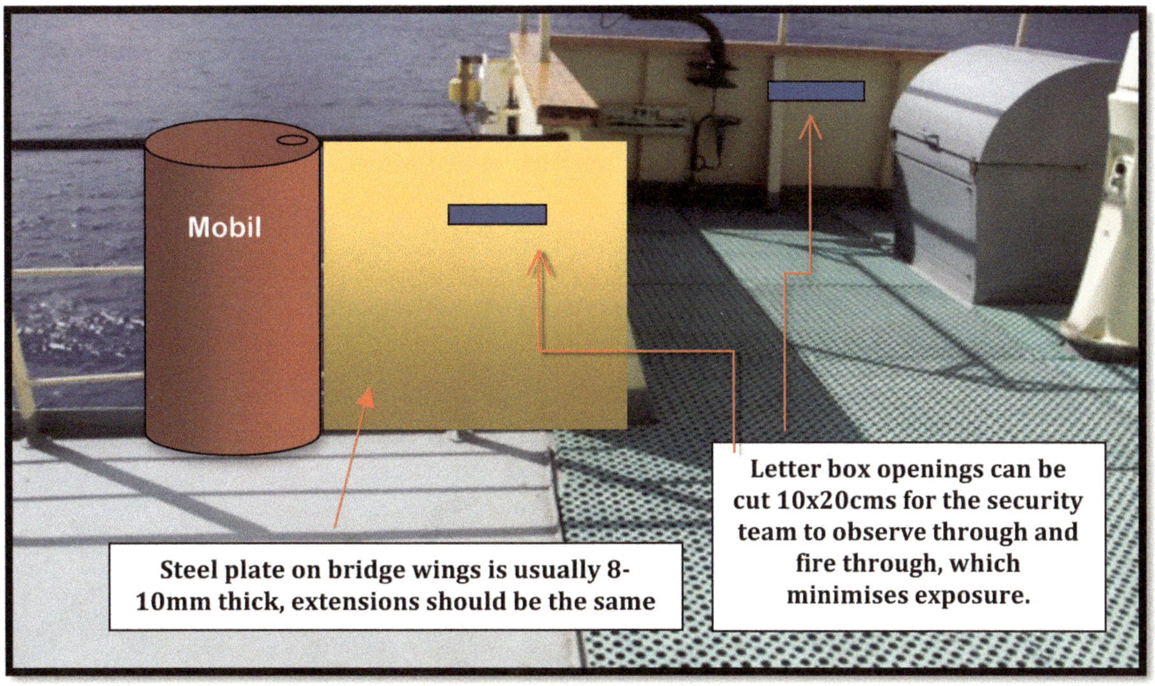

***If that cannot be done then place a line of 45-gallon drums along the bridge's port and starboard sides to prevent incoming projectiles such as RPG rockets and bullets from striking the bridge (as Somali pirates often do this when attacking).**

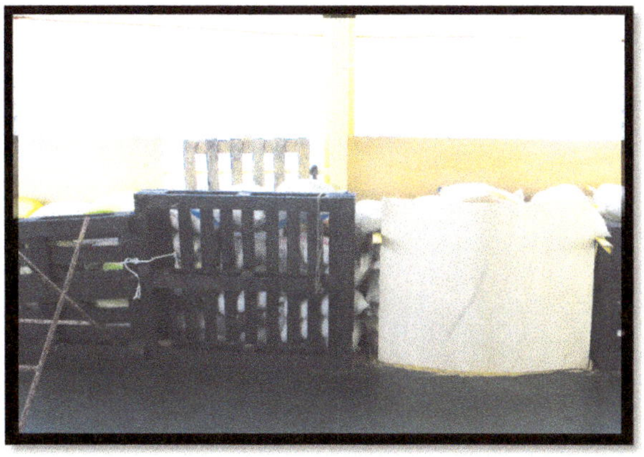

Above left: The empty drums are cheap, common and can be moved very easily by security and O.Ss /A.Bs. Once in place, they should be securely lashed to the rails, and then filled with water. They can be stood on anti-slip matting, as used on the bridge wings. Once the vessel has moved out of the high-risk area, they can be emptied and stored until the next high-risk passage. Wooden pallets can also be used but are not bulletproof; they will cause RPGs to explode before hitting the bulkheads (which is what is needed).

Above right: there weren't enough oil drums so sand bag walls were made, sandwiched between plywood and pallets to maintain rigidity

A wall of 45-gallon drums is not high enough so as to ensure maximum protection. Single or double chain mail fencing or weldmesh should be used. Any RPGs that impact it will detonate with less effect, as opposed to an RPG striking the bridge itself, which will be devastating and could be lethal.

Chainmail as seen above; this does not interfere with ship's husbandry and maintenance, it is better and more effective to have it mounted to the ship's rails creating a standoff from the bridge. Internally anti-blast film should be permanently fixed to the windows; neither will impair the vision of the OOW.

These empty rice sacks filled with sand and re-stitched closed made a very impressive sandbag wall, the crew changed the shape from curved to parallel as to offer as much protection as possible to the bridge's vulnerable flanks.

Removable anti-RPG screens required for front and flanks of standard bridges

Weldmesh welded to upright poles that can be removed easily when out of the high risk area, it must be light enough to man-handle and strong enough to withstand heavy weather and heavy seas and stop an RPG strike.

An unprotected vessel was hit by a Somali Pirate's RPG that caused this damage.

External damage **Internal damage.**

Below diagram of an anti-RPG screen that can be fitted and removed easily by 2 men

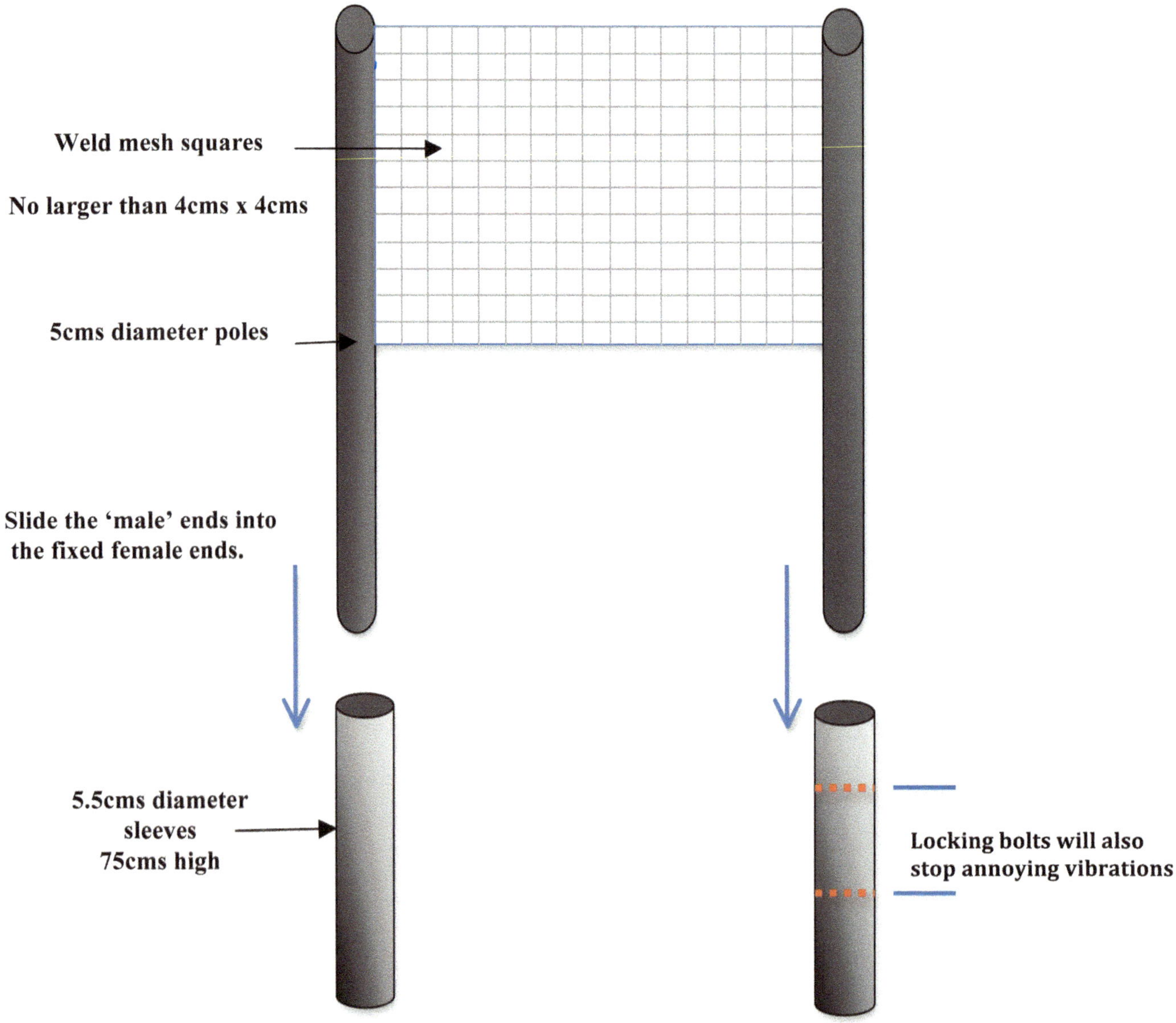

An RPG is much more effective when it has a direct strike, but if it hits the mesh that is .5m+ in front of the target, the mass of the lethal force is dispersed enough that only debris and a lesser pressure wave will impact. In war zones you will see anti-RPG mesh at least .5m in front of vehicles and checkpoints.

9. Sentries

Picture courtesy of Ironside Associates

In the Gulf of Aden, the author watches a skiff's course at sun set

When transiting through, or operating in, areas of high risk, it is imperative to use sentries. The more the better, when in hostile waters; any spare crew should be posted on the upper decks or bridge to assist with the spotting of small, low-lying boats or suspicious activities. If possible, there should be a sentry on watch at any given time in conjunction with the Officer of the Watch (OoW), on larger vessels ensure that 2 outer sentries are posted. To make life easier, the sentry should be equipped with his own equipment such as good quality binoculars, polarised sunglasses, a two-way radio and a night-vision device, rather than sharing the ones from the bridge. Sentry handover times should stagger with those of the OoW. Ideally, the sentry should not be on watch for a period of more than four hours. It takes a great deal of concentration to do the job correctly and professionally. Searching the horizons and studying radar screens in the heat of the day is extremely tiring; a lapse in concentration could lead to dire circumstances.

When choosing binoculars, without doubt one of the best pairs of image-stabilising, waterproof binoculars is the Canon 10 x 42 L IS WP – expensive (approx. £750), but worth every penny for identifying craft in rougher seas or vibrating ships. There is also an 18x magnification version, but field of view is minimised, there is the excellent 10x30 (£200-400), but the 10x 42 are the best. The sentry should be briefed upon what he is looking for and should bear in mind that an incoming skiff may be a poor local fisherman trying to sell some fresh fish. In the area of the Lagos Fairway Buoy, Nigeria, there are dozens of small friendly boats nipping around trying to make a living by selling cigarettes and fruit. It must be remembered that not all approaching skiffs are ransom-seeking, armed pirates. When the sentry sees a suspicious incident he should inform the OoW or Captain; if security guards are on board they too should be notified as soon as possible. The easiest way to point things out in the open ocean is to use the clock-ray method as used by NATO Forces. Use the bow as the 12 o'clock position, so if the suspicious boat is 90° off the starboard side at four nautical miles, then the correct target indication should be: 'Suspicious vessel, 3 o'clock at four nautical miles.' That will ensure everyone is looking in the correct area.

Correct target indication orders;

the 'Clock-Ray' method.

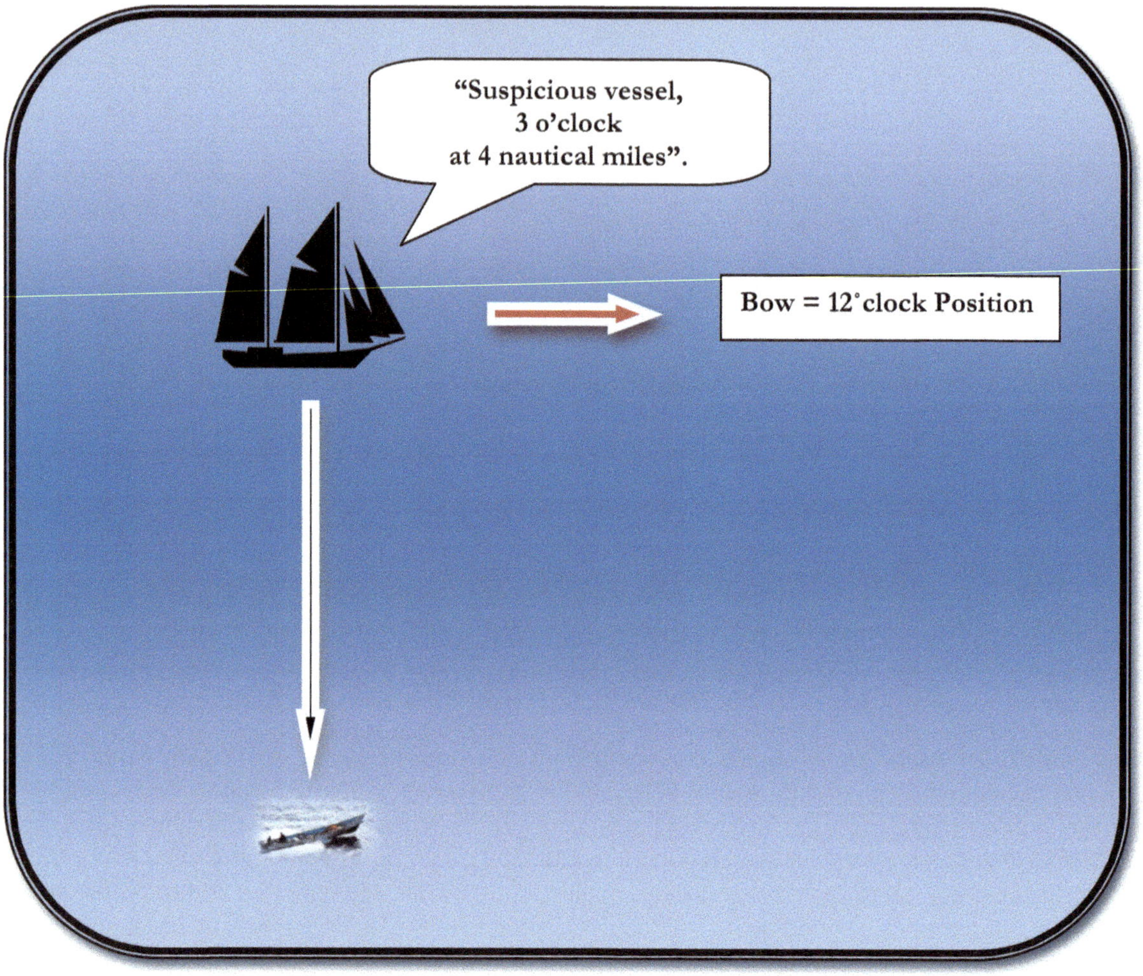

At night the sentry should avoid using white light, as this will affect night vision for up to 35 minutes; he should use red light instead. The bridge should also be using red lights, as warships do. Walking out to a bridge wing from a white-lighted bridge will leave that person ineffective until their night vision is fully restored. White lights can be reddened using red cellophane if red bulbs are not available. The red cellophane wrappers from Babybel cheeses will work as a last-ditch effort on fixed and torch lights. A decent head torch, such as those made by Petzel, can come with both white and red LED functions, red being perfect for night duties.

If the vessel's watches are worked in pairs, then if possible, the timings should be staggered; the same applies to sentries. That way, rather than having two persons changing at the same time, one changes, allowing the remaining sentry to brief the oncoming person. The person already in place knows what has happened since starting his watch, knows from the radar and visually where other vessels lie, and his eyes will be fully adjusted to the dark. It is essential to use good-quality sentries who have short shifts and plenty of rest periods. Two-three hours per shift is ideal, four hours is the maximum.

Good vigilance is a must!

In the mid-afternoon light there are two skiffs less than 1.5nautical miles away (Niger Delta)

Below: Same photo with increased magnification

Same photo with x20 magnification. Ensure you use good quality sentries who have short shifts and plenty of rest periods. 2-3 hrs per shift is ideal, 4 hrs is the maximum.

A skiff on a flat sea can be on a vessel's stern within three minutes of initially being spotted; prior training and slick drills will come into their own if this occurs. International Maritime Antipiracy Advisory Group (IMAAG) can provide this.

The below vessel was selling cigarettes, fruit and beer in the area of the Lagos anchorage, Nigeria. What a perfect way to conduct an innocent reconnaissance of possible targets to steal from at night.

A sentry from Neptune Maritime Security monitors a pair of suspicious fishing vessels in an area where a PAG has been reported. Due to their course and CPA, the security team don full equipment and watch until the threat has passed.

The security team monitors the threat and remains 'stood to' until it the ship is well away from possible danger.

The following photos show exactly why the need for alert sentries and armed guards are required:

Photos courtesy of maritime security expert: Steve Jackson

10. Radar and AIS

It is imperative that on-duty personnel constantly man and observe the radar and track targets when in dangerous waters. Often small vessels cannot be identified by average radar systems. Worse news still is that small vessels that are attacking or approaching are easily hidden by a slight swell, even from the best of radar units.

In May 2007, the wary Captain of a prestigious sailing superyacht saw a contact on his radar lying 10 nautical miles to his port side. The fishing vessel, of a similar size to a large dhow, was on a parallel course but making way a few knots slower than his speed. The vessel stopped dead in the water, not usual when in the centre of the Gulf of Aden. Small skiffs were seen in and around the vessel. The Captain turned away from the potential threat and increased speed. Within minutes, the superyacht was being approached by six fast skiffs, presumably pirates intent on boarding. They then withdrew when they saw multiple armed security men, overtly standing on the upper decks, and the attack was thwarted. In another instance, a commercial vessel transiting past Somalia at night, was supposed to have a crew member constantly observing the radar. One of the security men radioed to the team leader that a boat was alongside, underway. It turned out that the ship had almost run over a fishing boat, and that no one had been manning the radar.

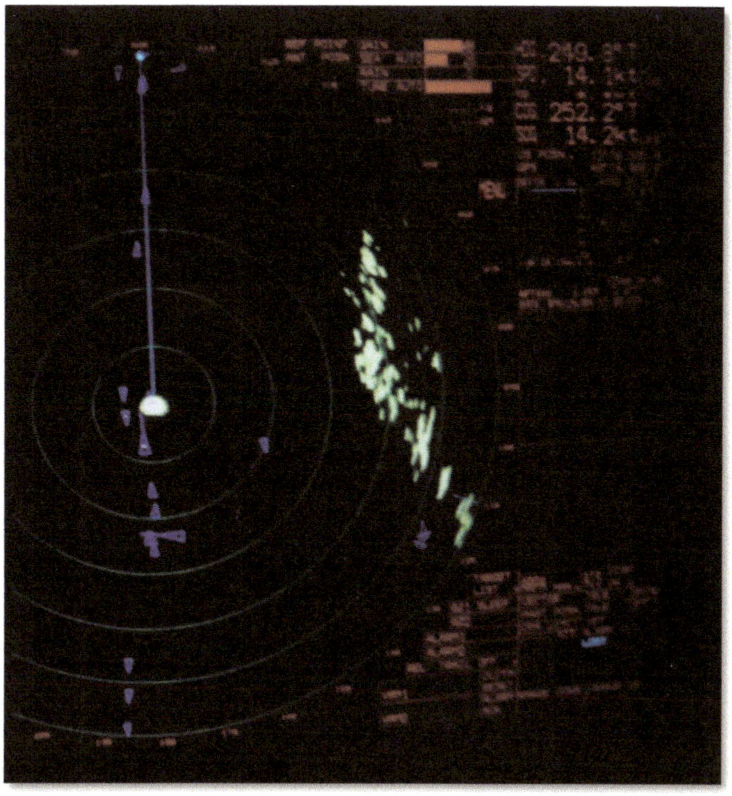

Above and below: GoA commercial convoys.

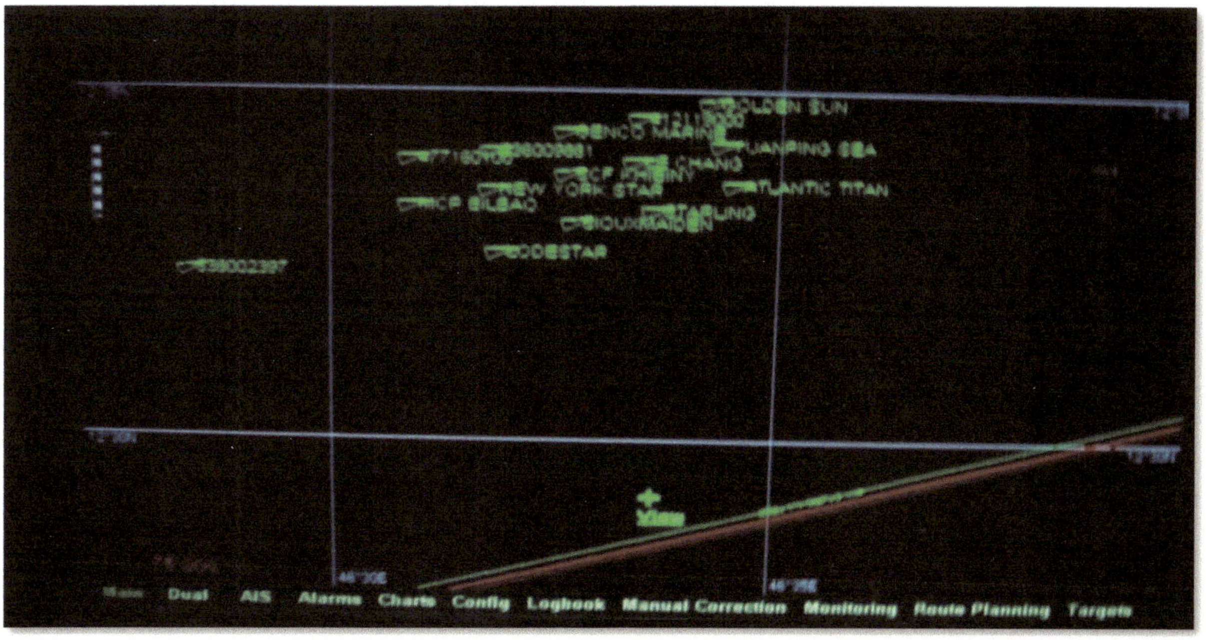

If possible consider using X and S band radars at distances such as 6 and 12 miles. Set alarms also to warn of approaching craft at a suitable and realistic distance depending upon your location.

Below an X band radar set to 6nm, try to have this as dark as tactically possible at night.

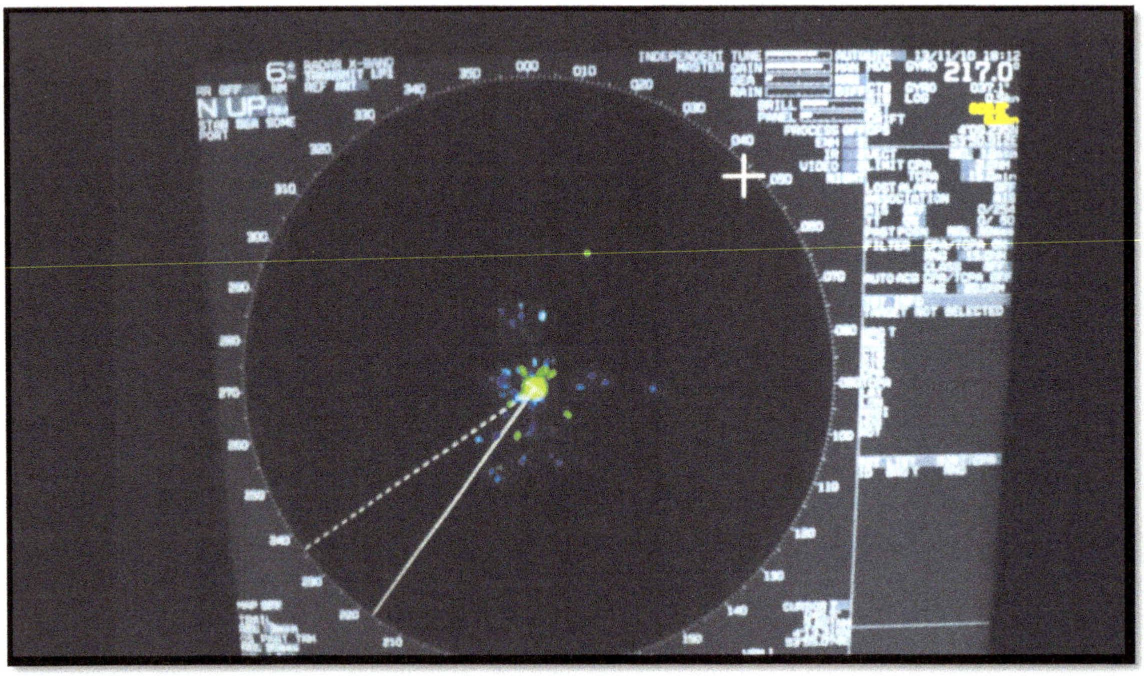

Most vessels have the S band set to 12nm and X band on 6nm when in the GoA HRA.

Below, whilst in the GoA HRA, the upper target* began to act suspiciously during the night, the client ship* altered course many times to avoid close contact, the vessel eventually gave up and sailed away.

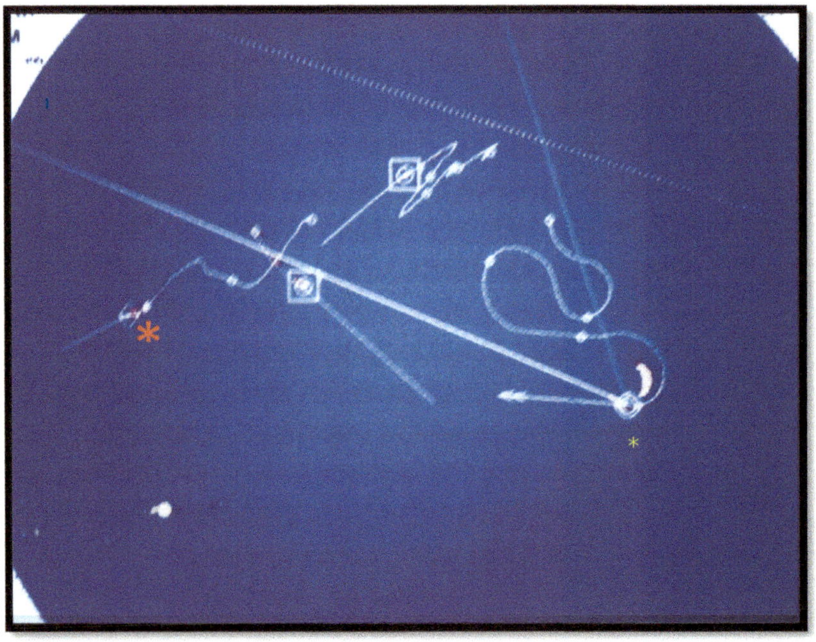

Probability of attacks; Natural factors

Sea state related boarding probability

Sea state	0	1	2	3	4	5	6	7	8	9	10
Chance of boarding from a skiff	100%	100%	100%	90%	70%	40%	10%	5%	0%	0%	0%

= Easy to board

= Difficult, but possible

= Not possible

©

Moon phase related attack probability (for 100% darkened vessels)

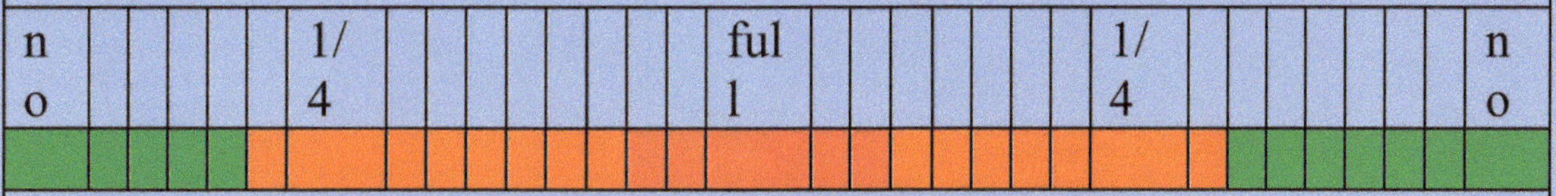

= Very slim, unless pirates encounter a target by chance

= Possible due to the ambient light from a partial moon

= Very possible due to high lunar illumination

©

When pirates start using night vision devices and radar as standard, the above table will become obsolete.

THE ATTACK UPON USS COLE

The following case study shows that you never be too careful. A USS warship was attacked successfully by terrorists right on the doorstep of Aden Harbour.

On 12 October 2000, USS Cole set in to Aden harbour (GoA) for a routine fuel stop. A small craft approached the port side of the destroyer and an explosion occurred, putting a 40 x 60-foot gash in the ship's port side: 17 crew died and 39 were injured - the ship was saved. Following that terrorist attack, any US warship that needed an enhancement to its existing radar has chosen to fit the Sigma S6 Radar Processor at a cost of approximately $50,000 each. These units are publicly available for private and commercial shipping; their enhancement is so good that they will detect the smallest of objects in rougher seas (including icebergs, oil slicks and combat swimmers), targets that standard, modern radar systems would normally miss.

Below, the image shows where and how the attack took place:
SS Cole after the devastating attack 12 October 2000 while refueling at Aden Harbour, Yemen

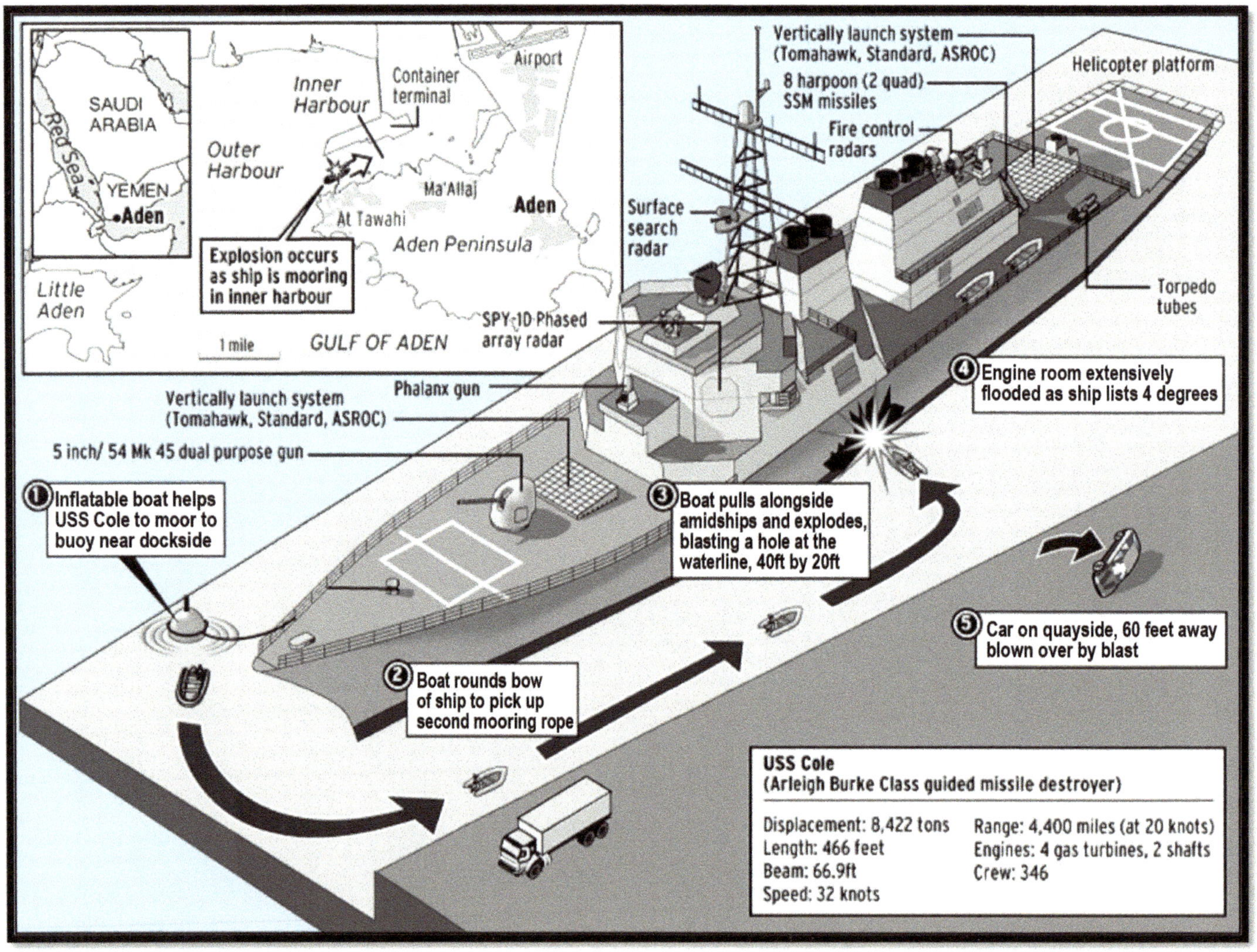

USS Cole after the devastating attack 12 October 2000 while refueling at Aden Harbour, Yemen

The problem of corruption from officials and even worse from crewmembers is something worth bearing in mind. Upon exiting Port Suez it is not uncommon to be asked many times for the vessel's details, over and over again. It is never clear who is on the receiving end or where that information is being sent. It is important not to freely let people know if the vessel is or isn't armed, information should be released only sparingly. In the South China Sea, Malacca Strait, and areas around Malaysia, it is common for crewmembers to release information to thieves and pirates, often for financial gain. Confiscation of personal mobile phones could be one way to help the situation, but would certainly lower morale and may breach human rights.

MV Limburg also attacked in Yemen 2004 by Al Qaeda

Automatic Identification System: AIS

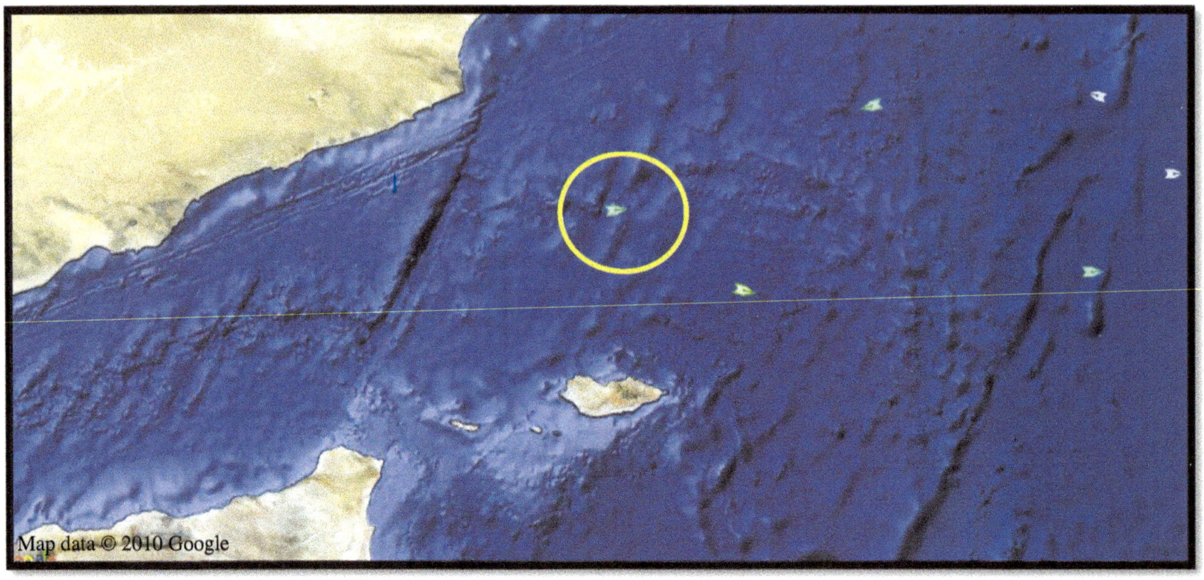

Pirates and thieves must absolutely love AIS. They can choose their target and vector their vessels onto it, knowing the speed, course, cargo etc.

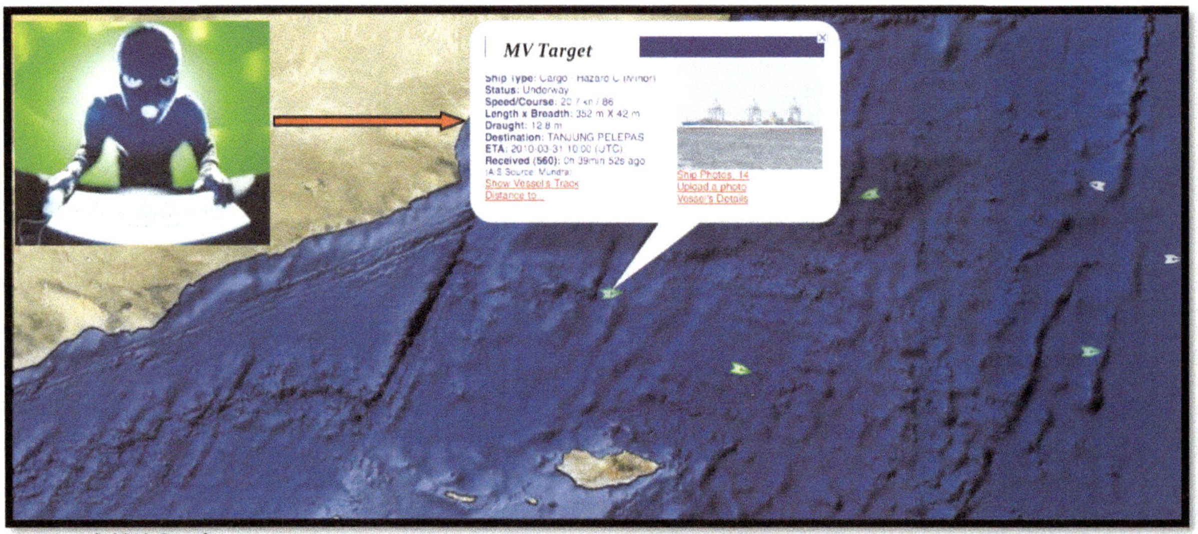

Map data © 2010 Google

Automatic Identification System (AIS): telling the whole world too much information. Pirates don't even need an AIS unit to see the vessel's details thanks to certain websites! Don't make life easy for them

The Automatic Identification System (AIS) was brought into the maritime world in the early 2000s, to aid mariners with navigation and identification of vessels at sea. Unfortunately, when used by professional pirates it gives them all the information they need to sit back in a coastal office and choose which vessel to take. The AIS gives information about the vessel's cargo, where it's coming from, its destination, speed, and dimensions. Similar information may also be leaked from corrupt official sources that are financially rewarded for such material. It is therefore recommended to switch the AIS unit to 'receive only' when transiting through high-risk waters. MSCHOA, UKMTO, various organisations and naval forces recommend different options; some advise leaving it on, others prefer to turn it off. If a vessel is attacked, then it must be turned ON!

Some vessels can be seen in the HRA with "Armed Team onboard" on their AIS information.

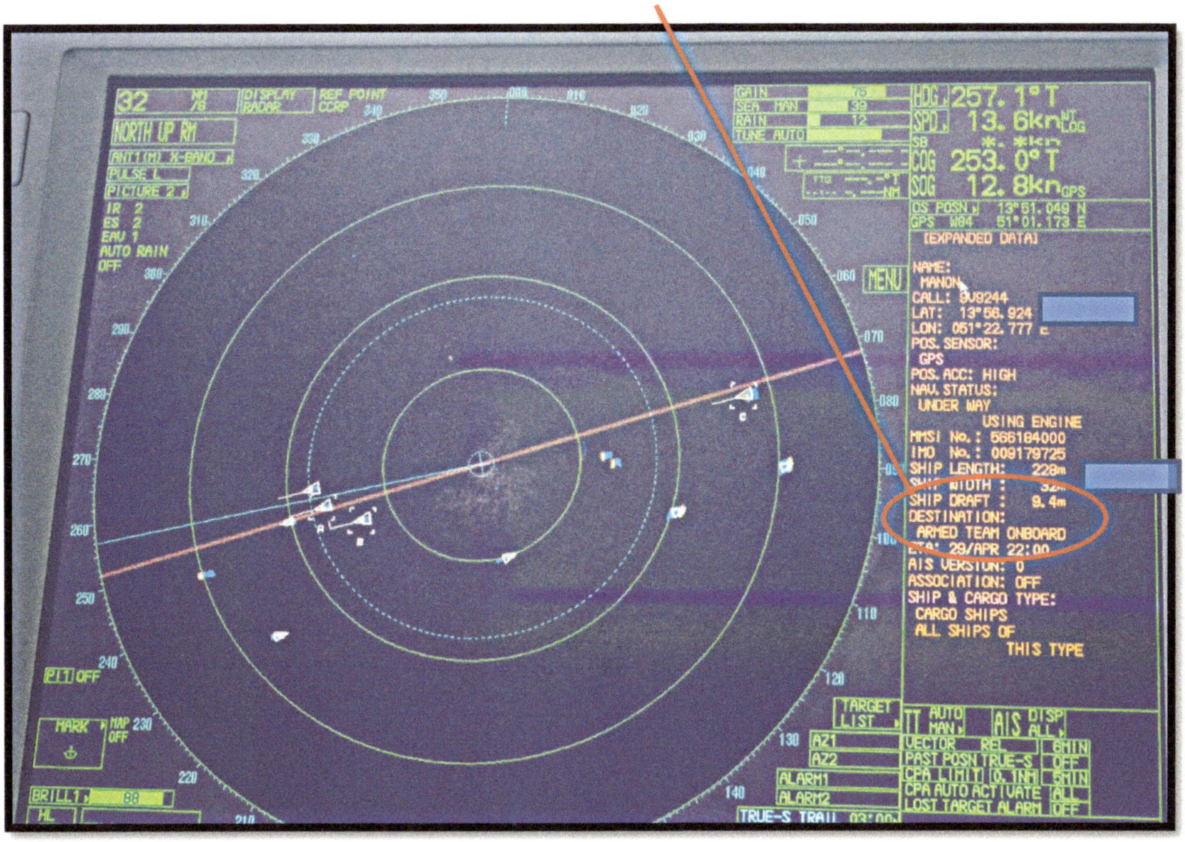

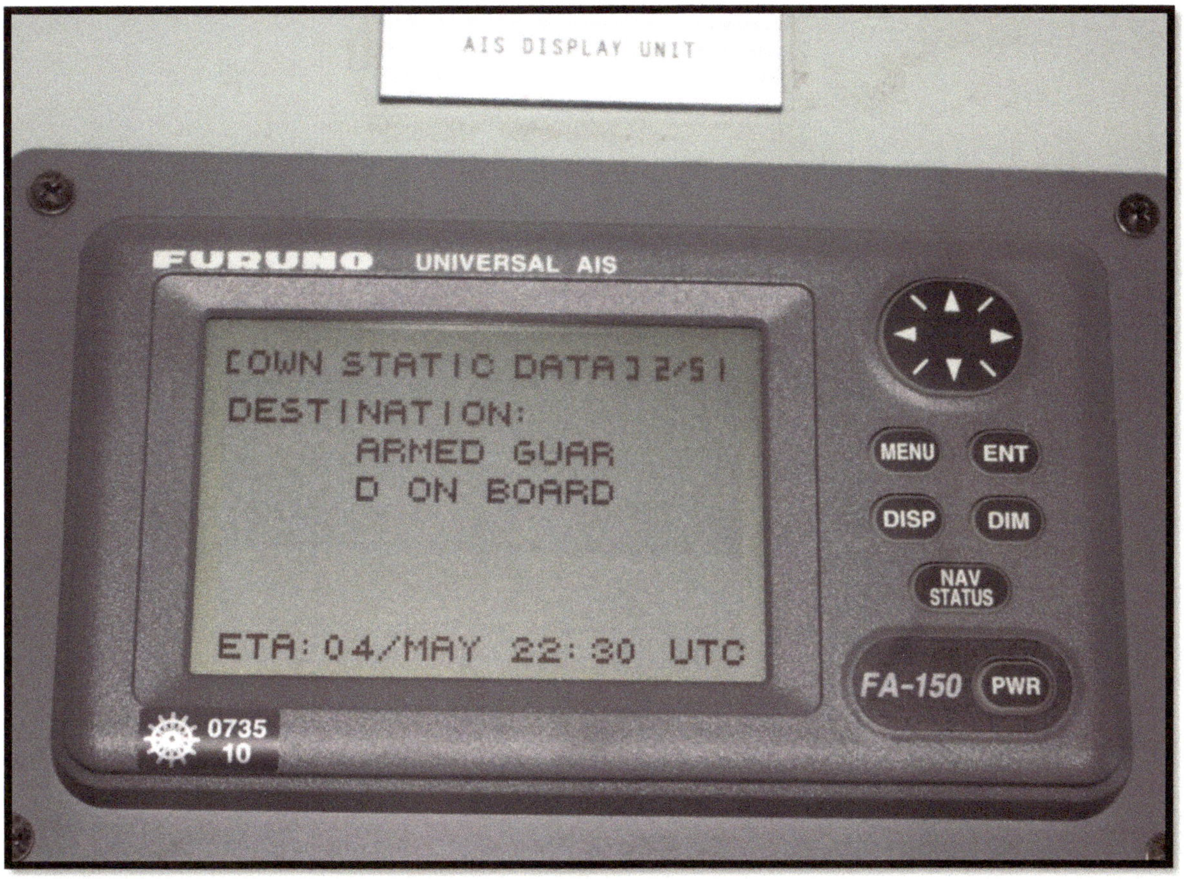

If you can change your AIS settings in the HRA, you should; motherships with AIS will see this.

11. PASSIVE MEASURES

There are many non-lethal ways of protecting a vessel, whether it is with high-pressure hoses, electric fences or technical devices such as LRAD (long-range acoustic device). The following pages cover the various ways, from simple to complex, in which to defend a vessel.

A. THE LONG RANGE ACOUSTIC DEVICE (LRAD)

The Long Range Acoustic Device (LRAD) is a crowd-control and hailing device developed by American Technology Corporation. It is a speaker/amplifier that is capable of projecting very high volume sound signals, up to 151Db, that can be intolerable to humans. It has been developed for crowd or riot control by the USA and is now used also in maritime roles for passive defence. It has successfully thwarted attacks in the Gulf of Aden, preventing Somali pirates from illegally boarding vessels underway. Advantages of this system are that it is passive, not lethal; it is very simple to use and install. However, it is expensive and one unit is not enough against multiple attacks; also, it can cause permanent hearing damage, and it is often difficult to mount without the user experiencing reflection from rigging and ships' structures and is not guaranteed to stop boarding. The LRAD 500X can be heard at distances of around 1500 metres, but it is much more effective at closer ranges. See the LRAD information pages in the back of this book.

On 7 November 2005, LRAD was first used to foil a pirate attack on a luxury cruise liner. The system was installed as a part of the ship's defence systems, and was activated when pirates attacked the ship with RPGs, 60 kilometres off the Somali coast. In recent times the LRAD's popularity has fallen dramatically since the MV Biscaglia was hijacked. The ship had three unarmed security men and an LRAD, see pages 190-192.

The LRAD 500X and Maxa Beam torch in operation off the Nigerian coastmanned by the author.

B. Fire Hoses

Some larger vessels carry high-pressure and ballast pumps. Many attacks have been thwarted when the ship's personnel have used hoses against pirates trying to board the vessel. It is a good idea for larger ships to position fire hoses so that their angles cover the areas most likely to be climbed, such as lower freeboards or from amidships to the stern. If the hoses are on constantly, potential pirates can see this from afar and will hopefully be discouraged from approaching. The ideal angles of the hose nozzles should be so that they cover the ship's sides 0-20 degrees, rather than pointing out to sea.

The left-hand vessel **A** has its hoses firing 90° away from the ship, which is virtually a waste of time and effort. Ships **B and C** clearly show the ballast pumps pouring water down the ship's sides, but this unfortunately does not protect the ship's rear. Fire hoses need to be placed in order to cover this arc as in ship **D**.

A

B

C

D

This photograph shows the varying high-pressure water systems, Razor wire and dummy sentries, all recommended in the BMP4 and enhanced by the security team.

The same tanker used its fire fighting water cannons to great effect; be aware that this does expose the operator to the high risk threat

ANCHOR WASH.

Another consideration is to leave the anchor wash on. Anchor cables are extremely easy to climb; a cable with a high-powered anchor wash is blasting down is almost impossible to climb. If there are anchor plates on bigger vessels then they should be used securely. For smaller vessels, the chains could be greased, or large, anti-rat type plates could be used to prevent climbers; a powerful light should be focused on this vulnerable access point. There are now tailor-made, high-pressure water systems available for ships; an example of one is the Nemesis 5000.

You don't have to be in the SBS to be able to climb an anchor cable; it's extremely easy, as shown here by Greenpeace.

Nemesis 5000 - Marine Anti-Piracy System:

Non-lethal visual and physical deterrent

Developed with leading marine security experts, Nemesis 5000 is simply the most effective water canon system on the market. Designed to be easy to install and operate the Nemesis units are light weight (only 15kg) and durable. The units are flexible and can be mounted on brackets manufactured to suit any handrail, gunwale or fish plate.

Nemesis 5000 takes seawater from the vessel's fire water system and creates a moving curtain of water jets, each with an impact equivalent to a ten pin bowling ball travelling at over 60 mph.

Key Benefits

1. Increases crew safety
2. Effective, unmanned response to a hostile boarding attack
3. Continuous 360 degree vessel coverage or focused protection of vulnerable areas
4. Uses existing vessel utilities to best advantage
5. Intrinsically safe for all vessels
6. Does not require Class Approval for installation

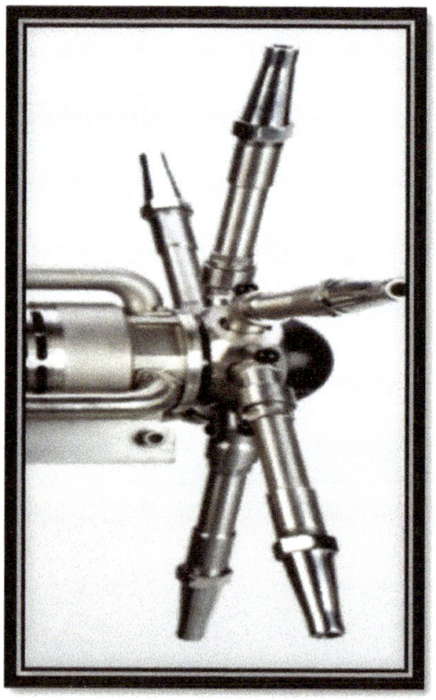

Above: The effectiveness of Nemesis 5000 as a deterrent has been proven during trials on an anchored vessel. Former SBS personnel simulating an attack from a small craft failed to board the protected ship. For further information contact Maritime Protective Services, Inc. www.mpsint.com

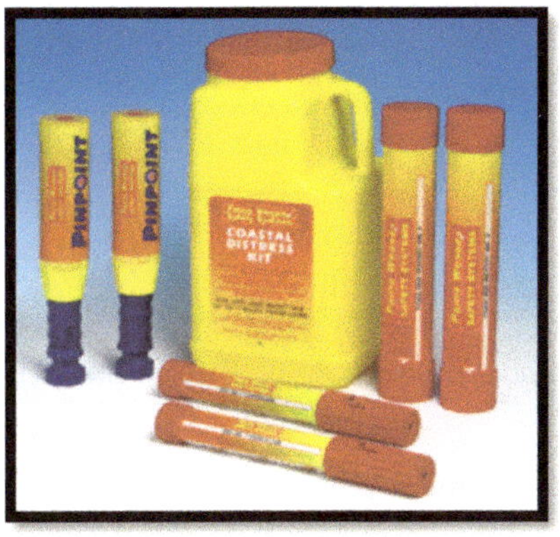

Photo courtesy of Pains-Wessex

C. Flares

All vessels have to carry an assortment of flares, hand-held, once-only types or Very pistols. These can be fired over or in the area of a boat that has been positively identified as a hostile threat. There was a case where a pirate boat was close enough for a smoke grenade to be tossed into the pursuing vessel, and this action alone prevented the vessel from being boarded. A simple action such as this may be enough to delay or deter pirates or thieves from attacking a vessel. However, it may also antagonise the attackers and make them much more violent. Flares can be used to try to deter an attack by armed security, before using firearms. Firearms should only be used in self-defence if every other method has not worked and human lives are being threatened. Lastly, flares fired into the air will attract the attention of nearby vessels and possibly low-flying aircraft, as will smoke grenades - the more attention that can be attracted, the better. For more information on the legality of firing flares directly at pirates and robbers in self-defence, a maritime lawyer would have to be consulted. Pains Wessex is a very good company from which to buy both flares and smoke grenades.

D. Evasive Steering

If it looks inevitable that a vessel is about to be illegally boarded whilst underway, then during the last few moments before the attackers come alongside, the vessel should start radical, evasive steering: throwing the vessel hard over from one side to the other makes it very difficult to board from a small skiff or speedboat. The bow wave and rough waters produced by such actions make boarding very difficult, and if trailing lines are out in position it is likely that the attacking boat will become entangled and stalls. If the sea state is producing a swell and waves, then if possible the vessel should turn into it; such measures have saved smaller vessels in the past. A small attack boat can catch up with a vessel that is running with the sea, but if that vessel turns into sea and continues at approximately 10+ knots, it becomes very difficult for the smaller boat to catch up and attempt to board; it is better to do this and go in the wrong direction for an hour or two, than to continue running and become a victim.

Aggressive steering from port to starboard, with smaller vessels will make boarding more difficult and it increases the likelihood of the pursuer becoming entangled with a trailing line.

Even small sailing boats can make themselves difficult to board just by throwing the boat hard over to port and starboard. It may be hard to believe that this will have any effect on hardened pirates, but in fact in 2008 pirates tried to gain access onto the same vessel three times in succession. The first time the OBM broke down; the attackers fixed it and caught up. Then the pirate leader fell overboard; his colleagues collected him and tried again, only to be swamped by the zigzagging ship. It pays never to give up and to keep fighting to the bitter end. Evasive steering works well with smaller vessels, but for the larger commercial ships, radical steering is slow and difficult and usually less than 15 degrees, thus not effective at all.

E. Steam and Irritant Curtains

Secure-Marine

Secure-Waters

This is a system invented by a Dutch security company Secure-Marine. It works simply by surrounding the ship with a 360° hot-water curtain at 80° Celsius. An irritating agent mixed in with the scalding water is a further deterrent.

Custodia Security Consultants

Maritime Operations Anti-Piracy Solution

Custodia Security Consultants are in a unique position being the only security company in the world offering the MOAPS systems for maritime protection, in conjunction with our maritime security teams.

- Unlike many other anti-piracy solutions available, MOAPS can be effectively deployed while vessels are transiting, at anchor or in port.
- MOAPS....Maritime Operations Anti-Piracy Solution is an irritant.
- It is a liquid that has been synthetically engineered from a food ingredient.
- It is designed to cause a sensory overload of the nervous system by inducing ocular pain.
- The discomfort is transitory, the sensory overload recovers after 20 minutes and there are no adverse effects.
- MOAPS has been extensively evaluated and unlike other irritant incapacitants it is non-carcinogenic.
- It can be delivered as a liquid, vapour aerosol or powder.
- The specific gravity is only slightly higher than water with a variable surface tension dependant on the application.
- To date 2 delivery systems have been trialled and evaluated and found to be cost effective.

Vapour and Fog.
The vapour system is a man portable SOLAS compliant 13 litre backpack discharging 130 litres of (vapour) irritant per shot from the discharge unit. The vapour discharges at a rate of 140 meters per second to a distance of about 30 meters, the vapour cloud is then carried by the prevailing wind, neutralising all persons in its path.

It is intended as an indirect fire system, the operator discharging the device upwind of the threat. If deployed at close range of 8 meters or less the pressure of discharge will knock a man off his feet. This unit is SOLAS approved based on a proven fire fighting/riot control system.

The fog delivery system delivers a dense cloud of irritant 500 cubic meters per minute with a run time of 20 continuous minutes. MOAPS when atomised creates a film carried within the fog/smoke. The irritant remains well above the minimum particle size recommended by the Home Office and is therefore deemed safe. Operators are trained to observe prevailing wind conditions to minimise the risk of contamination.

For all enquiries about MOAPS, please visit their website: www.custodiasecurityconsultants.com

F. Electric Fences

Secure-Ship

Another great product from Secure-Marine is a 9000-volt electrifying fence that surrounds the ship. It is non-lethal, so no one will die from it. It is similar to systems used to protect military installations and is another way to protect the crew and ship if a crew does not wish to use firearms.

For further information see: www.secure-marine.com

Secure-Marine Electric fence

A double strand electric fence circumnavigates this ship, it was turned on permanently during the hours of darkness.

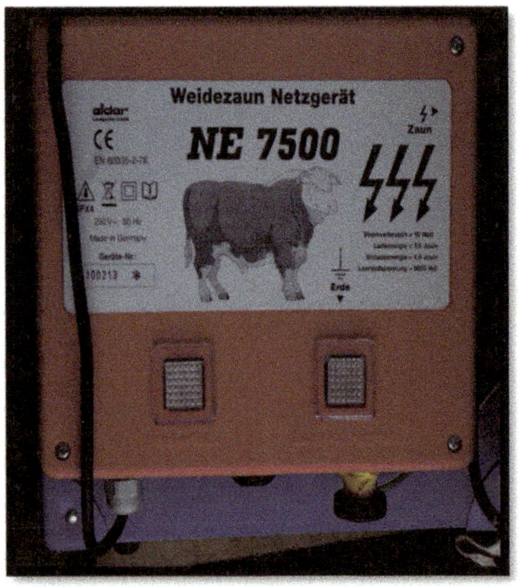

12. LIGHTS AND LIGHTING EQUIPMENT

Almost all pirate attacks in GoA take place during daylight hours; pirates there operate without lights or night-vision systems. Pirates and thieves operating from the Niger Delta, South America and other areas across the world operate both day and night. They all use simple tactics and work visually as opposed to using vision enhancing equipment. However, as always, it is better to be prepared for the worst eventuality. If a vessel is boarded during the hours of darkness, the pirates or thieves will be using some sort of ambient light: in the open ocean this will be the light of the moon or an artificial white light. Somali pirates have only attacked a few times at night and in each instance, the attack took place under a near-full moon. Since 2009, however, attacks became far more common in twilight conditions, the cloak of half-darkness making it difficult to spot speeding skiffs.

Navigation lights. Maritime law (International Rules for the Prevention of Collisions At Sea) states that to avoid collisions at sea, vessels must display navigation lights whilst underway at night. This is normal practice. However, it is commonplace for vessels moving through dangerous waters to have their navigation lights turned off. This should only be carried out by competent personnel who are not close to other vessels. The radar must be of a high quality and checked frequently. The IRTC in the Gulf of Aden can be extremely busy, so rather than sailing through it at night, a vessel should parallel it some miles on either side, to reduce the danger of collision. The ratio of vessels being attacked in the GoA in 2008 was approximately 1:100. The chances of a collision at sea are far greater than being attacked by pirates, so should the OoW have any doubt whilst underway, he should turn on his navigation lights until the situation has improved. Many ships will call on the VHF or flash a white light or, more alarmingly at night, will approach, illuminate the vessel with all its searchlights and start to interrogate the OoW over the VHF. If a vessel is underway without lights, it is imperative to have a nominated, reliable person to check at dusk, from the outside, that the vessel is blacked out; it is all too easy to open a blind during the day and forget about it when darkness falls. If in doubt, the lights should be left on, or a lower-watt bulb used. Commercial vessels should not have their deck lights on, just their navigation lights.

On all vessels, powerful hand-held torches should be to hand; the best is probably the Maxa Beam (www.peakbeam.com). A very rugged, military-grade unit, it has 6-million candle power and throws a beam 1.5 miles. The Maxa Beam CSWL offers several unique capabilities, including a remote-controlled beam width feature in which the operator can alter the beam width between a 1-degree spot and a 40-degree flood. It also has a non-lethal strobe function that effectively disables and disorients a target in situations where lethal force is not warranted. This unit can also be mounted on top of the LRAD.

The Maxa Beam hand held torch

With smaller vessels: it is recommended that halogen 'work lights' or similar wide-angle, high-intensity lighting be fixed to the stern and boat's sides in the areas where boarding is easiest. These lights should be wired into the mains and have an on/off switch that can be easily operated by the vessel's crew.

If these lights are shone into the eyes of pirates just as they are coming alongside, the attackers' night vision will be rendered useless for the next few minutes, and they will be unable to judge distances, use ladders and operate weapons. This gives the defenders the upper hand, enabling them to defend themselves with whatever means they have to hand. However, crewmembers should not stand behind the lights when robbers approach, as lights usually draw fire if shooting takes place.

For larger commercial vessels, if they come under attack then all deck lighting can be turned on as well as AIS if both were off.

Some larger vessels have high-power spotlights with pan and tilt capabilities that can be used too, but experience shows that these are slow moving and difficult to use; the last thing a crew wants is to illuminate the vessel, thereby giving attackers the upper hand. Fixed lights are the way ahead. This picture shows the areas most likely to be climbed, covered by 500-watt units.

Stern halogen security lights, entanglement nets and 150m trailing lines

When at anchor

At anchor it is recommended to fully illuminate the vessel to cover the sides and the surrounding waters. All thieves prefer to work in the shadows, away from prying eyes and possible onlookers. Underwater lighting systems are available on some vessels including the larger superyachts. It is unlikely that divers or swimmers will attack a vessel, but it should not be ruled out as a possible option. Commercial vessels are generally very well illuminated at night; however, lights alone should not be relied on as a deterrent to prevent thieves from boarding. It is necessary to have at least one sentry, equipped with a fully charged torch and radio, to patrol the vessel constantly. The vessel should be locked down, with the exception of an access door for the sentry; that door should also be locked, with the key held by the sentry. Smaller vessels that want to anchor in what looks to be a safe and sheltered bay, inlet or creek, should be able to if someone sleeps in the wheelhouse. Often, with the smaller yachts, there is not enough crew to use sentries, but as in the military, it is better to have someone on watch for an hour at a time and be a little tired the next day than risk being taken by surprise. Most small sailing yachts are often ignored when it comes to anti-piracy and boat security.

These high power halogen lights were perfect when this supply boat was at anchored off Dar es Salam.

It is many a couple or family's dream to sail for a period of time on their beloved yacht and all too often are put off some of the nicer parts of the world due to the heightened threat of kidnap, theft or violence. Razorwire and steam curtains do not work for smaller craft; many companies specialise only in the commercial market.

However the skippers of the minority market should do their best to defend their crew and vessels. Electric fences for example should be considered. Almost every decent house in South Africa is surrounded by these small, neat electric fences, they on a boat, only need to be switched on at the last moment thus reducing the danger of harming the passengers. When at anchor or ashore, a simple device that makes an empty yacht appear occupied is the use of electrical timers. Just plug these into lamps, electric blinds and music systems, as you would do at home. It will give the casual thief the impression that the boat is occupied when you have that onshore sun-downer or fishing trip. Many casual thieves will want to take the tender, its out board motor, hand held VHF and anything that can quickly be lifted and moved.

If you feel vulnerable and must leave the boat unattended then it's worth considering leaving low value items such as second wallets, an old handbag, a faulty camera, laptop or VHF handset. Don't leave them on display; you'll only be asking for trouble, put them in drawers and places that would be searched in time of break in. Very loud burglar alarms are very off-putting as are mobile PIR halogen lights, most chandlers or marina based electrical companies can give in depth advice on what works and what doesn't. The best method is to employ armed security if possible.

For larger vessels, Razorwire, electric fences, steam curtains, anchor washes, and electronic systems such as 'Sea Owl' can all be enabled to help protect the vessel. It is imperative to notify everyone on board that the vessel has counter measures enabled in order to avoid harming the crew. Razorwire can be used to block all areas, such as external stairwells, ladders and climbable frames.

External doors should have obvious signage altered in the HRA. Pirates may want to gain access to the engine room, but not have much time. If signage is swapped for the garbage locker, including all the H&S signs, then the intruders may spend an hour or more trying to open the false door, buying you much needed time. Lights with PIR facility are very good for covering blind spots and areas where boarding might be expected. Ensure that the surface of the water does not cause the light to turn on and off, otherwise people will not take notice of such a useful asset.

On larger vessels, ensure grills are locked shut

Dogs.

Some vessels do have dogs on board; their bark is very useful for warning people that intruders are approaching and the possibility of an attack by dogs may deter the criminal from boarding. However, for armed or determined thieves a dog can soon be dispatched with poisoned food or a couple of bullets.

Dogs have been used by the military for centuries, especially so during the Second World War, both by the US Navy and Coastguard. Families often take their pets with them on longer sailing trips and a dog sleeping on deck will act as a great lookout during the hours of darkness.

Night Vision.

Night vision equipment has been available for some years now. In the military, it has been used extensively since the Vietnam War in the 1970s. Night vision comes in various shapes, generations (grades) and sizes; there are monocular and binocular systems, rifle scopes and camera lens. Shape and size is not what matters, the quality of the unit is measured by 'generation'. Generation 1 (Gen 1) is the lowest quality and cheapest. Units start at around £350. The best commercially available are Gen. 4. These are much more expensive, but much, much better. Helicopter pilots can use Gen. 3 quite easily for flying at night, as can military drivers. Apart from high costs, there are laws concerning night-vision systems (NVS). In the UK, only lower-generation units are allowed, such as Gen. 1 NVS. In the USA you can buy and own higher generations, such as Gen. 4, but they cannot be exported. So it is not legal to buy Gen. 4 from the Internet and ship it overseas, nor can you own it in the UK. Most units use standard batteries, such as AA. A Gen. 1 NVS unit will work if there is ambient light such as the moon. It is very good for finding ships' lights at night when humans or binoculars cannot see what the radar is identifying. Without moonlight, Gen. 1 NVS in the open sea is not good at all. Gen. 3 or 4, however, are very good even without ambient light. Thermal images are available; they too are very good, but extremely expensive. Units cost £10-20,000. A good NVS is a better buy.

Night vision equipment

UK legal Yukon Gen' 1

Night Vision System by ITT Gen' 2a

The night will look like day under a full moon, albeit, green.

The ATN Night Spirit monocular

PVI escort boat DM1 seen under a full moon

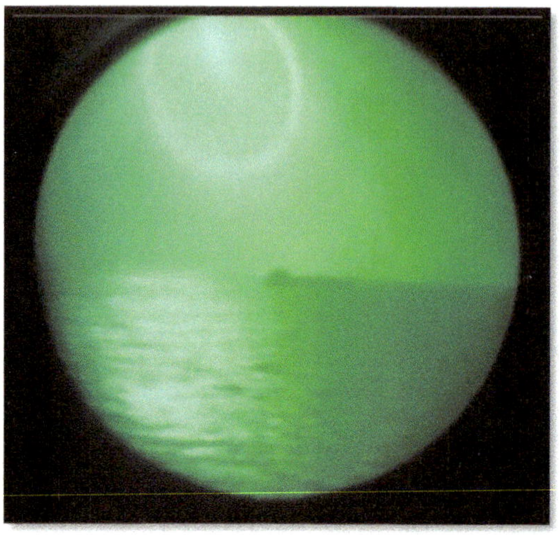

This photo' was taken at Bab el Mandeb, ¾ waxing moon

On another transit, these photos are at Bab al Mandeb under a quarter moon using the above ATN 'Night Spirit'.

On the east side of the shipping lanes are the hundreds of small squid boats with their bright fluorescent lights.

Although expensive, night vision sights are a necessary piece of equipment. Even out of the high-risk areas of the world, they are suitable for identifying small targets such as fishing boats or navigational buoys. Ship's lights can be seen at great distances even without ambient light, up to 18nm.

From a safety point of view they are perfect for nighttime man overboard scenarios. A small salt water activated light may look bright when testing them on the STCW 95 course, but out in the open ocean with a sea state they are very difficult to see at distances over 300m, a night vision will easily spot the victim. Some ships have night vision systems on the bridge, but are better suited as paperweights. Often its difficult to know which piece of equipment is better, especially with something so specialist as a ship's night sight. IMAAG is an advisory company and will help mariners with such decisions and where to purchase them.

13. ENTANGLEMENT: ROPES AND NETS

In past cases, vessels have been closely followed by their pursuer, being assessed and waiting for the right location and time of day to strike. If this occurs, a very simple way to slow down or stop the pursuers is by throwing a line, rope or netting in front of their vessel's course. Try to establish radio link firstly, warn them to stay away or counter measures will be used, tell them you are armed, a plywood black silhouette held high may be enough to deter them, this has worked in the past. Such measures should be taken after all other methods and evasive manoeuvres, have been used.

Test firing the Pains Wessex rope launcher, this model throws to 250m. Photo: Ironside Associates

Alternatively, vessels can tow long lengths of line or rope behind them, for example four lines of 8mm polypropylene of 200m lengths. With smaller yachts, there needs to be a weak point that will snap when entangled, to avoid the risk of towing a skiff or ripping out the boat's fittings. This weak point should be close to the point of attachment, such as the cleat. Rocket-propelled line throwers are very good; they throw lines up to and over 250 metres. A 5mm polypropylene line is perfect to entangle small propellers used with outboards. A very good example can be bought from Pains Wessex.

It works very well if two rope launchers are connected together and then fired simultaneously, port and starboard. The launcher can be reused, so the bitter ends of each line should be connected to each other; this will give 500m of potential buoyant entanglement - very difficult for pursuers to avoid.

Another rope launcher from Hansson Pyrotech

Rope launchers here are connected to each other & pre-fitted to the Port & Stbd rails. This method will give 500m of lateral coverage.

A box of old pre-cut ropes can be stored at the aft end; these can be thrown one at a time into the water by either one person, or ideally two. The line then floats lengthways across the path of the pursuit boat and is much harder to avoid - not very eco-friendly, but this measure can save lives.

Again, old fishing nets are perfect for uses such as this. In the picture below the sailing yacht pre-positioned six lengths of net (each 12m x 12m), rolled and attached to the stern guardrail. If required, two people can quickly rip off the retaining masking tape and drop the nets slowly into the water. The transparent monofilament net is very difficult for the pursuit boat to see and will snag the pursuers' propeller very easily.

Transparent fishing net to foul the attackers' propeller.

Taped to the aft rail for quick deployment

Trailing lines

Handmade trailing lines work very well, with small vessels such as sailing yachts, ensure there is a weak spot close to the point of attachment. Ideally there should be 4 trailing lines at the stern, care must be taken if parallel trailing lines are used as to not foul your own propellers. The below example is from a tanker in the HRA, ensure that a weight is used to keep the lines at water level, otherwise the first 30m of line/rope will be suspended above the water. The weight does need to be substantial, such as a 40kgs; the thicker the rope, the more weight required. Do not attach anything on to the end, not even a knot, this will cause spray and will make the location of the lines obvious.

Below is a commercial example of an enhanced system using multiple trailing lines.

P-Trap

On February 17th, a cold but sunny winter's day, the Coast Guard's Esvagt Connector sailed out of the port of Den Helder carrying the prototype of the —P-Trap, as Westerbeek has called his invention. The weather couldn't have been better for the trial. A rendezvous had been arranged with the Joke Dijkstra of the KNRM and the Gouwe of the Royal Dutch Navy on the open seas.

Two RIB's (rigid inflatable boats) were mobilised specially for this purpose. Lieutenant Frank de Ridder was in charge of the trial. The crew of the RIB's wanted to experience what it was like to be a pirate and threw themselves into their role. One member had even hoisted a pirate flag.

They would show the Esvagt Connector just how easy it was to board it. The test was first carried out cautiously, but gradually with more speed. The test was carried out four times with overwhelming results. The pirates were unable to get any closer than 5 metres from the ship. Their propeller jammed completely and their boat stalled. This happened so abruptly during the last test at high speed that the crewmembers were flung forward, with one member incurring minor injuries. Afterwards they said that the outcome had given them quite a fright.

P-Trap

The construction of the P-Trap

The principle of the P-Trap rests on a bundle of thin lines that are towed through the water, forming an impenetrable zone alongside and behind the ship. An extension bracket keeps the lines at the right distance from the ship. The extension bracket can be folded up and the lines can be rolled up. The lines are long enough so as not to get caught up in the propeller of their own ship.

As soon as the ship approaches a piracy hazard area the extension brackets are unfolded and the lines are rolled out, creating a safety zone around the ship through which pirate boats cannot approach.

It is impossible to see the thin lines under water from a small boat on the surface. Pirates who approach the ship in their high-speed boats run into the lines, immediately jamming their propeller. The lines break as a safety measure for their own ship. The pirate boat cannot navigate because the propeller cannot function. Because the ship has let out a large number of lines the system continues to work when attacked by several pirate boats. The lines can be rolled out so that broken off pieces can quickly be replaced and there are always lines in the water.

Simple and inexpensive

The effectiveness of the system was proven during the trials. A fast RIB ran at full speed into the protective zone and immediately came to a standstill. The exceptional thing about the invention is that it is extremely simple and affordable. —That's what I was always striving for, says Westerbeek.

Simplicity. He applied for a patent on his P-Trap in the early stages of his invention. Ships that use the P-Trap are protected day and night. Pirates don't even need to be spotted in advance.

The device always works and the crew never comes in contact with the pirates. They are kept off the ship. Another advantage is that no special training is required to operate the device and no additional crew is needed to install it. It takes only one person half a day to get it up and running. The device is made to measure and weighs no more than approximately 1500 kg. Due to its simplicity it can be made quickly so ships can have it at their disposal in no time. Ship owner Dockwise is the first to purchase the system. Preventing piracy has always been one of the ship owner's top priorities.

Conclusion of the P-Trap

Despite the invention's success it should be put into perspective and not be considered the one and only means to combat piracy. Present day piracy with armed pirates is too complex for that. The P-Trap is, however, a worthy contribution to measures for protecting ships against piracy. It is an impenetrable corridor that prevents pirates from boarding and even coming close to ships. A P-Trap website is currently in the making. Henri L'Honoré Naber is the former Chief Minister of the Netherlands Merchant Navy Staff and now runs his own consultancy, Safer Seas Consultancy (saferseas@gmail.com).

14. Decoys and props

If a vessel doesn't have the benefit of security guards on board, a proven method that on previous occasions has prevented armed pirates from continuing with their attack is to construct decoys. These 'props' are limited by the imagination of the makers. There are ships that have cut out silhouettes of Browning .50cal machine guns and mounted them on the bridge wings or in areas where incoming boats can clearly see the weapons. In one incident, two ex-Marines picked up the plywood machine gun, ensuring the silhouette was facing the correct direction (90° from the target), gently lowered the gun onto the false pintle mount, where a third man attached the fake mounting pins (in fact three bent nails). A false belt was loaded into the gun; the gunner cocked the gun in a realistic fashion and pointed it out to sea. The inbound skiffs turned around and were never seen again on that transit. False body armour can be made from bin bags, cardboard or canvas. Weapons can be made from simple plywood, using a jigsaw, and painted matt black. False ammo magazines can be loaded into weapons in full view of inbound boats by using Velcro on the 'magazine' and on the side of the false weapon, making the whole drill look convincing.

Decoys can be made in the silhouette of a sentry wearing body armour, standing holding his weapon in a vigilant manner, or even in a firing position. These dummies can be lowered and raised whenever required. A decoy should not be left in the same place for days on end; it needs to be moved around and slight changes made, such as adding a cap or a woolly hat. Simple measures like these may well prevent the attackers from continuing their attempt. In BMP4 it is recommended to use dummy sentries. However with a weapon slung across its chest or back, will make it much more intimidating. Pirates don't want or need a hard time - they will pursue easier targets. It is imperative that a vessel does not tell other boats that they have decoys; if word gets out that decoys are on board, there is a very good chance potential pirates will find this out too and pursue the vessel in the knowledge it has little else in the way of security. Seagoers should not think they can save money by replacing security with plywood cut-outs - these are just another measure that could be considered.

If you must use dummies, ensure they are realistic, this one looks like a drunk who has been run over!

If this silhouette was viewed from more than 200m with the naked eye, it would be hard to say whether it was real or not? If your crew had realistic weapon silhouettes and were seen on the bridge wings, bow and stern, it could prevent the pirates from attacking your vessel. Do not rely on this alone: it should be a last option!

Make your own dummy weapons.

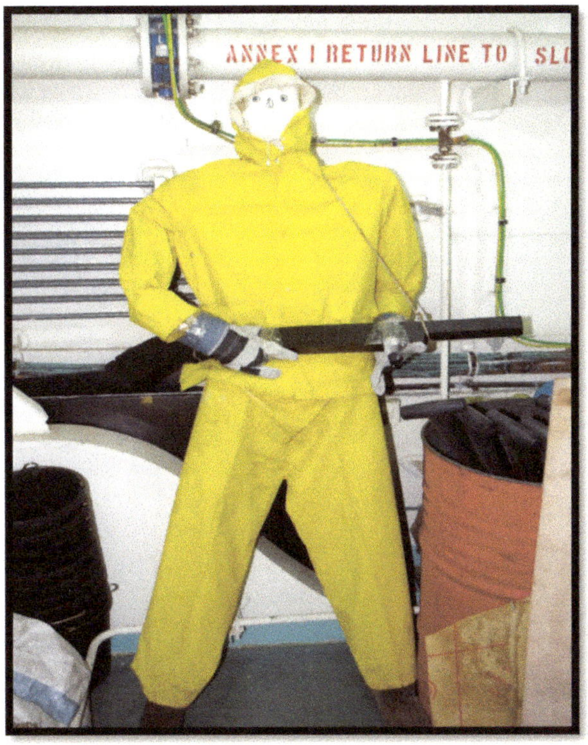

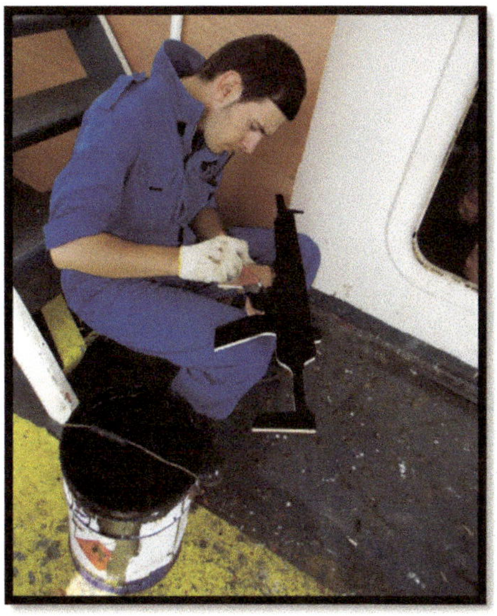

The above dummy was originally unarmed, the bosun made this weapon, which isn't bad for a seaman, but during the safe days in the northern Red Sea the author used a jigsaw on a spare piece of 10mm plywood and within 20 minutes had a painted weapon silhouette, much more realistic than the latter. A dummy guard with a weapon slung across his chest is 10x more effective.

SILHOUETTE TEMPLATES

Here are a few templates and silhouettes that could be cut from basic materials such as 10mm plywood and painted matt black to be placed across the chest of your dummy sentry. If you have an armed team on board, ask the TL to draw around his weapon onto plywood and cut on the inside of the line for a realistic copy.

AKM

M16

Browning M2 .50cal MG

GPMG M60

RGP 7
(Rocket propelled grenade launcher)

12 gauge/bore
Pump-action shotgun

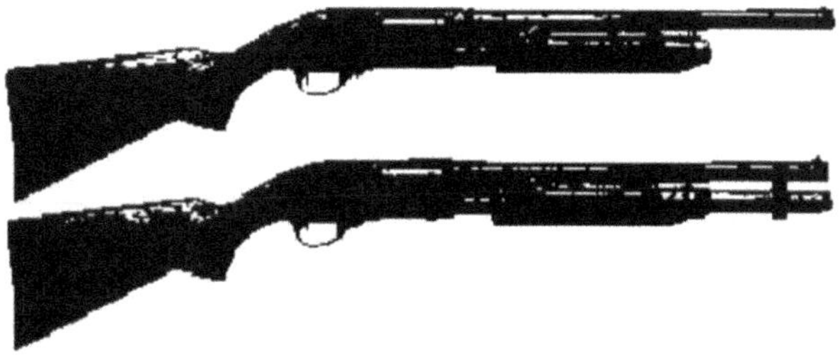

VARIOUS SILHOUETTES OF ARMED SECURITY GUARDS.

GUARD & GPMG GUARD & .50CAL MG

GUARDS AIMING WITH A COLT AR15 ARMALITE

15. Non-passive measures (Armed Security)

Weapons

Introduction: The following chapter is very in depth. The author is a weapons expert and was asked by Captains and consultants to include more information on this chapter, hence the present detail. He fully endorses facilities such as Shooting Solutions, Euro-tactical, Miris, BoB Dunkley, etc, as a firearm must only be handled by a competent and safe user. There is information that now states that security companies provide 1 or 2 security personnel to a ship, and that a total of 4 weapons are taken on board so that crew members can be taught how to use the weapon in times of need. Even the best firearms instructor cannot expect to turn an Able Seaman -AB into a safe and accurate shot, with discipline and an understanding of perfect English. **This is something that should definitely not happen, ever.** The AB is now putting himself in harms way by exposing himself to hostile incoming fire from armed pirates, there are legal issues with this and the AB's insurance would not cover him for such duties. The sooner that private armed security guards are internationally regulated, the better.

Shipping is realising that as of early 2011 that the arming of ships is a realistic need to stop, not prevent illegal boarding. Over the next two years the laws will probably change to allow the carriage and use of firearms much easier for vessels. At the end of this chapter are some examples of meetings that have taken place to support this, as only the previous year this was a taboo subject and most authorities did not recommend this practice.

Guns for Hire: Just because an armed security team are deployed on board, it does not mean that firearms will be used or pirates will be shot. This is not the purpose of the security men; their role is to give the vessel Best Management Practices and recommendations to make the passage as safe as possible, whilst tying in with the ship's own security plan (SSP) and procedures as laid down by the shipping company's CSO and flag state.

When pirates are spotted and close upon their target, the armed security team abide by the strictest of Rules of Engagement (ROE) as used by UK based armed forces and Police. There is a scale of escalation with all approaching vessels; warnings take place and the security team will only use weapons as a last option in self-defence. The media's well used phrase "Guns for Hire" is completely wrong and paints a bad image within the industry.

No ship has ever been taken that has had an armed team onboard. The distance that pirates become a lethal threat is around 350m. Their AK47 rifles and RPGs have a maximum effective range of 350m, but are dangerous up to 900-1000m. The security team need to react and to deter the pirates by using all other means available to hand. At distances over 350m, a verbal warning by mouth or LRAD/PA system will not be heard, so the security men make it obvious to the pirates that they are onboard, seeing 4 men dressed in body armour, helmets and holding rifles above their heads is enough to make the pirate abort; this visual warning deters most approaching skiffs intent on boarding. The use of flares fired in the direction of the skiffs is the next deterrent, often this is enough to ensure the pirates turn around, if the flares haven't worked then a couple of well-aimed shots in and around the pirate skiff (but never at them) is the next step, this is done by the team marksman/ex-military sniper using a sniper rifle or accurate rifle with a telescopic sight. This has been done numerous times by security guards in the last two years (2009-11) and has worked almost 100% of the time in deterring/stopping the attack.

The use of shotguns at these distances is not ideal, 350m is too great a distance for shotguns, even with solid slugs or SG/LG rounds, plus the firer cannot guarantee accuracy at that range. In compliance with maritime law, many of the best armed security companies are not buying the cheaper firearms available, instead are using modern sniper rifles with bipods and telescopic sights (sometimes silenced) and used by marksmen/snipers. With these firearms, the men can guarantee that warning shots will land away from the skiff and not accidentally hit someone as could happen with a cheap rifle. A determined pirate who continues his pursuit of the target can have his out board motor (OMBs) disabled with accurate fire from these men with these weapons, the skiff now disabled can be apprehended by a coalition warship later on, and even better cannot be used to attack an undefended vessel that happens to pass by.

This subject has many pros and cons; some prefer this method, but most do not. If crewmembers are going to carry firearms for use in self-defence then they must comply with maritime law, however the author does not recommend this practice; a former soldier having had years of combat experience in areas such as Afghanistan and used to handling lethal firearms in close proximity to danger is completely different to a crew person branding a shotgun. This generally doesn't happen on commercial vessels, but does occur on superyachts and sailing yachts. For further advice, a good maritime lawyer should be consulted.

A very rough guideline is that, whatever the situation, only the minimum amount of force can be used to protect human life. All other methods of preventing thieves and pirates from boarding the vessel must be tried prior to the use of firearms.

A verbal warning must be issued prior to shots being fired, unless that warning will further endanger lives or the attacker is well out of earshot but firing upon your vessel.

The use of cameras with fish-eye lens to film and record the event are tools that should be used in the event that an armed response is necessary (Oregon and GoPro make such cameras that can be mounted on weapons and helmets).

A great advantage of having weapons on board lies in the fact that many thieves and pirates will not attack when they see that the vessel is armed - they prefer an easier target. As of early 2012, less than 35% of shipping has armed security.

Shotguns. Weapons such as pump-action or semi-automatic shotguns are cheap and cheerful. There are stories of ships and yachts that have bought shotguns just for their transit through a high-risk area. Once clear of the dangers and back in safe waters, the guns' ammunition has been used and the weapons dismantled and sunk in deep waters.

In 2012, the price of a cheap shotgun started at around £350. High-quality names such as Browning and Beretta make very good firearms, but do cost more. When choosing shotguns, models with a longer magazine capacity, such as eight or 10 rounds of ammunition, are the ones to go for, (ideally with a 3 inch magnum chamber).

In the UK, gun laws enforced over the last 20 years state that a magazine can only hold up to two rounds. Guns intended for use on the foreshore for wildfowling (shooting ducks and geese) are ideal.

They will be much hardier, have a higher 'proof' rating and be more resistant to rust than 'blued' metalwork that can rust from a mere sweaty thumbprint, or the humidities of the HR areas. Shotgun laws are more lenient than rifle laws when dealing with shipping, especially when dealing with military style assault rifles.

Flare pistols and 12-bore pump-action shotguns

With the correct ammunition, such as solid slugs (Brenneke) or SG (Buckshot), shotguns are the perfect firearms for close-range work (up to 150m). However, with conventional shot, such as No. 7, distances are greatly reduced, down to 30m, and shotguns are then not recommended.

A variety of firearms should always be test-fired before a choice is made, wearing the correct protective equipment. In a situation where a vessel is being fired upon at close range from a boat full of pirates, just one shot from a shotgun loaded with Buckshot SG ammunition will be enough to kill and incapacitate multiple persons. At a range of up to 75m these cartridges can be lethal. Buckshot SG has the same ballistic co-efficiency as firing nine .38 special handguns all at once at the same target. So if a person is hit at close range by SG Buckshot, it will be a lethal strike.

The best <u>12 bore</u> ammunitions for maritime security:
solid Buffalo slugs and 00 Buckshot

The nine lead balls in a SG Buckshot cartridge have a tendency to drop quickly with range. This trajectory should be assessed prior to entering the high-risk area. Like all multiple-shot cartridges, lead shot is designed to spread out with distance. If a shotgun has a multi-choke fitting in the end of the barrel, the full-choke option should be inserted for SG Buckshot; that way, the shot pattern will remain tighter at longer distances, giving a longer range of tighter spread and greater accuracy. Above 150m, shotguns are not effective.

Brenneke slugs, Buffalo or solid shot are an extremely powerful round. Police forces around the world use them for stopping moving cars, as one shot to the engine block will punch a hole in it and stop it almost immediately; the same applies to an outboard motor that is made from light, cast alloy. Solid slugs will travel for long distances with huge amounts of kinetic energy.

Again, shotguns should be test-fired so the user knows how much to aim above at certain distances. The cartridge instructions should be referred to when fitting choke tubes and using solid slugs, as different manufacturers recommend different settings. Some makes of solid slug will be more accurate with a tight choke; others could cause a bursting barrel. If in doubt, an 'open choke' setting should be used, or the choke tube not fitted.

Approximate costs for 2012:

12-BORE Semi-Autos:

WINCHESTER SUPER X3 - Mossy Oak or composite stock, 28 or 30in barrel. From £900.
BROWNING MAXUS - Mossy Oak, composite or standard stock, 26, 28 or 30in barrel, about £1,200; Phoenix Special Canard, 28 or 30in barrel, £760.
HATSAN ESCORT - 3.1/2 in Magazine, 24, 26, 28 and 30in barrels. Approx. £450.
BENELLI SUPER BLACK EAGLE - 26 or 28in barrel, £1,700 importer's recommended price. (These guns are inertia-fed; others listed are gas-fed).
BERETTA A400 XPLOR - 26, 28 and 30in barrels, available with or without Kick-Off anti-recoil system. Prices from £1,615 (importer's recommended price).

Pump Action Shotguns

MOSSBERG 535 WATERFOWL - £429 or Winchester Super X3 Pump, 26, 28 and 30in barrels, from £870.
REMINGTON 870 - Hard to find, but there might be a few around with 3.1/2in. New price around the £500+ mark.

Definition of a gun's 'Proof':

A gun's proof marks are a permanent safety aide memoire to give you the correct information for choosing a cartridge that can be used safely in your particular gun. When you buy a box of cartridges, always read the manufacturer's data printed on it and use that information to satisfy yourself that its contents are safe to use in your gun.

Before the technical details, we need to understand the history of the way in which shotguns have been proofed in modern times. From 1896 onwards, British guns were always marked with the maximum service load – in ounces – of shot for which the gun was proved.

Additionally, the type of powder – black or smokeless – was specified. This was normally just in the simple terms of 'nitro proof', though specific nominated powders, such as Schultze, sometimes appeared instead.
After 1925 and until 1989, this information was supplemented by the inclusion of the chamber length in inches. Thus, armed with these three pieces of information, the shooter could choose a cartridge that fell within their limits, knowing this was safe to use in his gun.

In 1955, the first metric markings appeared, with the option to have the chamber length marked in millimetres. Table one gives the metric equivalent for the imperial chamber length.

From 1984 to 1989, where metric proof was used, it was marked in kilograms per square centimetre, for example 900 or 1,200kg. These were the standard and magnum proof pressure values respectively. Alternative imperial proof marks introduced in 1954 gave service pressures in tons per square inch, marked as '3 tons'. In the case of the Birmingham Proof House, this was marked as '3 tons per square inch' until 1954.
In 1989, all proof data was marked in metric using the bar as the unit of measurement. The use of kilograms per square centimetre was dropped. Under this system, 850 bar represented standard proof, with 1200 bar being special or magnum. While it is possible to use a mathematical factor to convert one pressure unit to another, this conversion is only valid if the two sets of values have been arrived at using the same pressure measuring system. For example, the 1954 Rules of Proof used the Lead Crusher Radial system. This measured pressure in units of tons per square inch.

Today, all International Proof Commission (CIP) Proof House use the Radial Transducer system to measure pressure, with bar as the unit of measurement. The two systems are not simply convertible by mathematical means. However, there is sufficient data to give approximate conversions.

1954 Rules of Proof converted to CIP values (courtesy of Bill Harriman BASC)

BASC
The British Association for Shooting & Conservation

Chamber length	Highest mean service pres. Tons per square inch (1954 Rules) lead crusher system	Converted to CIP Copper Crusher (bar)	1954 Proof Pressure converted to CIP Copper Crusher (bar)
12-2 ½	3	542	867
12-2 ¾	3 ¼	587	939
12-3	3 ½	632	1011
12-3 MAG	4	722	1155

Pattern and choke

Shot, small and round and delivered without spin, is ballistically inefficient. As the shot leaves the barrel it begins to disperse in the air. The resulting cloud of pellets is known as the shot pattern, or shotgun shot spread. The ideal pattern would be a circle with an even distribution of shot throughout, with a density sufficient to ensure enough pellets will intersect the target to achieve the desired result, such as a kill when hunting or a break when shooting clay targets.

In reality the pattern is closer to a Gaussian*, (*In probability theory, the normal (or Gaussian) distribution is a continuous probability distribution that has a bell-shaped probability density function, known as the Gaussian function or informally the bell curve) or normal distribution, with a higher density in the centre that tapers off at the edges.

Patterns are usually measured by firing at a 30 inch (76 cm) diameter circle on a large sheet of paper placed at varying distances. The hits inside the circle are counted, and compared to the total number of pellets, and the density of the pattern inside the circle is examined. An "ideal" pattern would put nearly 100% of the pellets in the circle and would have no voids—any region where a target silhouette will fit and not cover 3 or more holes is considered a potential problem.

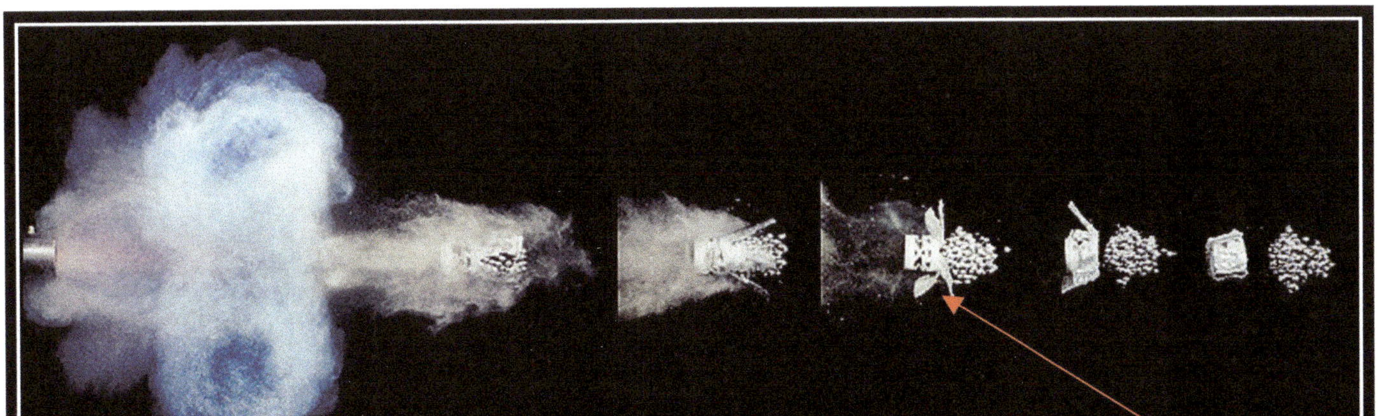

Separating powder from shot, known as wadding, in this case the 'plaswad'.

A shotgun cartridge has 'wadding' to separate the powder from the shot/slug, this can be biodegradable card/felt of more commonly used plastic, known as the plaswad. The above diagram shows how the mass of pellets is contained within the plaswad until it departs the barrel. Air friction will cause the plaswad to quickly slow down as the expanding pattern of the shot heads towards the target, the same as a 'sabot' round. Velocity, barrel length and shot size will all affect the pattern and range.

A constriction in the end of the barrel known as the choke is used to tailor the pattern for different purposes. Chokes may either be formed as part of the barrel at the time of manufacture, by squeezing the end of the bore down over a mandrel, or by threading the barrel and screwing in an interchangeable choke tube, as seen here.

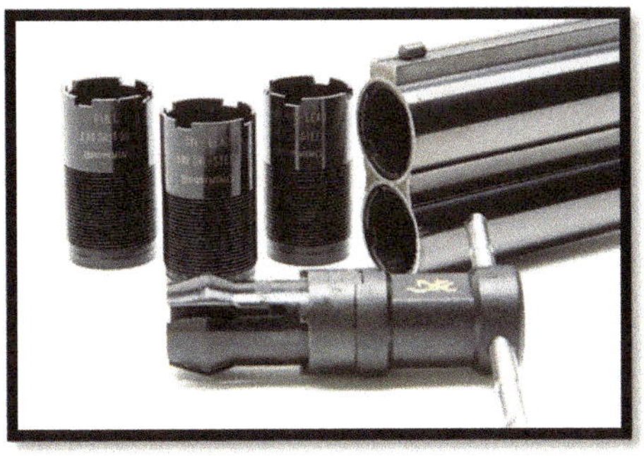

The choke typically consists of a conical section that smoothly tapers from the bore diameter down to the choke diameter, followed by a cylindrical section of the choke diameter. Briley Manufacturing, a maker of interchangeable shotgun chokes, uses a conical portion about 3 times the bore diameter in length, so the shot is gradually squeezed down with minimal deformation. The cylindrical section is shorter, usually 0.6 to 0.75 inches (15 to 19 mm). The use of interchangeable chokes has made it easy to tune the performance of a given combination of shotgun and cartridge to achieve the desired performance.

The choke should be tailored to the range and size of the targets. The use of too much choke and a small pattern increases the difficulty of hitting the target, the use of too little choke produces large patterns with insufficient pellet density to reliably break targets or kill game. "Cylinder barrels" have no constriction.

Other specialized choke tubes exist as well. Some tubes have constrictions greater than "Super Full", or additional features like porting to reduce recoil, or "straight rifling" that is designed to stop any spin that the shot column might acquire when travelling down the barrel. These tubes are often extended tubes, meaning they project beyond the end of the bore, giving more room for things like a longer conical section. Shot spreaders or diffusion chokes work opposite of normal chokes—they are designed to spread the shot more than a cylinder bore, generating wider patterns for very short range use. A number of recent spreader chokes, such as the Briley "Diffusion" line, actually use rifling in the choke to spin the shot slightly, creating a wider spread. The Briley Diffusion uses a 1 in 36 cm twist, as does the FABARM Lion Paradox shotgun.

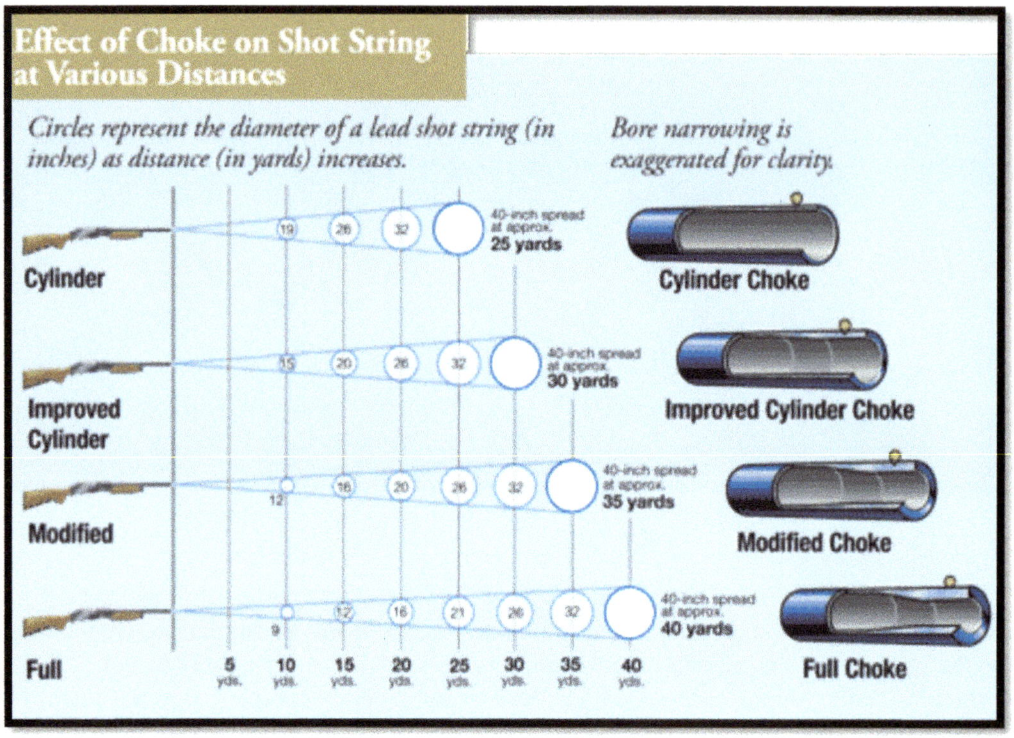

Oval chokes, which are designed to provide a shot pattern wider than it is tall, are sometimes found on combat shotguns, primarily those of the Vietnam War era. They were available for aftermarket addition in the 1970's from companies like A & W Engineering. Military versions of the Ithaca 37 with duckbill choke were used in limited numbers during the Vietnam War by US Navy Seals. It arguably increased effectiveness in close range engagements against multiple targets. Two major disadvantages plagued the system. One was erratic patterning. The second was that the shot would spread too quickly providing a very limited effective zone.

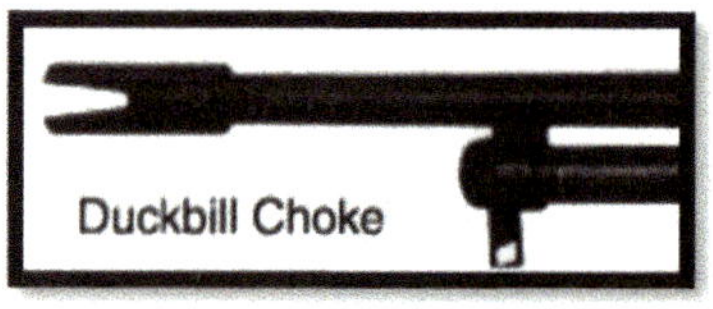

Barrel length

Shotguns generally have longer barrels than modern rifles. Unlike rifles, however, the long shotgun barrel is not for ballistic purposes; shotgun shells use small powder charges in large diameter bores, and this leads to very low muzzle pressures and very little velocity change with increasing barrel length. According to Remington, modern powder in a shotgun burns completely in 25 to 36 cm barrels.

Since shotguns are generally used for shooting at small, fast moving targets, it is important to lead the target by firing slightly ahead of the target, so that when the shot reaches the range of the target, the target will have moved into the pattern.
On uphill shooting, this means to shoot above the target. Conversely, on downhill shooting, such as from a ship's bridge wing, this means to shoot below the target, which is somewhat counterintuitive for many beginning hunters. Of course, depending on the barrel length, the amount of lead employed will vary for different barrel lengths, and must be learned by experience.

Shotguns made for close ranges, where the angular speed of the targets is tend to have shorter barrels, around 24 to 28 inches (610 to 710 mm). Shotguns for longer range shooting, where angular speeds are less tend to have longer barrels, 28 to 34 inches (860 mm). Barrels for shotguns have been getting longer as modern steels and production methods make the barrels stronger and lighter; a longer, lighter barrel gives the same inertia for less overall weight.

Shotguns with shorter barrels are not ideal for maritime security guards and shotguns with barrels of less than 24" (inches) must be held on a Firearms Certificate in the UK as the same for solid slugs such as Brenneke.

Ammunition

12 bore Cartridges are the most commonly used round, filled with lead or lead substitute* pellets (*the use of lead is banned in the UK for shooting wildfowl, such as geese and ducks, due to the fact that these birds swallow the poisonous lead pellets which are stored and used in the gizzard to grind up the grain types that they feed upon. Types of alternate shot metals include: Bismuth, Steel, Tin, and Tungsten). Of this general class, the most common subset is birdshot, which uses a large number (from dozens to hundreds) of small pellets, meant to create a wide "kill spread" to hunt birds in flight. Shot shells are described by the size and number of the pellets within, and numbered in reverse order (the smaller the number, the bigger the pellet size, similar to bore gauge). Size nine (#9) shot is the smallest size normally used for hunting and is used on small upland game birds such as snipe, dove and clay pigeons (Skeet). Larger sizes are used for hunting larger upland game birds and waterfowl. In Europe and in other countries that use the metric system of measurement, except Canada, the shot size is simply the diameter of the pellet given in millimetres.

Buckshot is similar to but larger than birdshot, and was originally designed for hunting larger game, such as deer (Totally illegal in the UK!). While the advent of new, more accurate slug technologies is making buckshot less attractive for hunting, it is still the most common choice for police, military, and home defence uses. Like birdshot, buckshot is described by pellet size, with larger numbers indicating smaller shot. From the smallest to the largest, buckshot sizes are: #4, (called "number four"), #1, 0 ("one-aught"), 00 ("double-aught"), 000 ("triple-aught") and 0000 ("four-aught"). A typical round for defensive use would be a 12 gauge 2¾" (7 cm) length 00 buck shell, which contains 9 pellets roughly 8.4 mm (.33 inch) in diameter, each comparable to a .38 Special bullet in damage potential. New "tactical" buckshot rounds, designed specifically for defensive use, use slightly fewer shot at lower velocity to reduce recoil and increase controllability of the shotgun. There are some shotgun rounds designed specifically for police use that shoot effectively from 50 yards (46 m) with a 20" diameter grouping of the balls.

Slug rounds are rounds that fire a single solid slug. They are used for hunting large game, and in certain military and law enforcement applications. Modern slugs are moderately accurate, especially when fired from special rifled slug barrels. They are often used in "shotgun-only" hunting zones near inhabited areas, where rifles are prohibited due to their greater range.

Shotgun Rifled Slugs

Many shotgun slugs are designed to be stable when fired from a smoothbore barrel, which lacks the rifling normally used to stabilize the projectile. Rifled slugs have what looks like rifling cast into the surface. This acts like fins to impart a spin on the slug as it exits the smooth barrel, and thus stabilizes the slug. Foster slugs are designed with a deep cup in the back, so that the centre of mass is far forward and drag will tend to keep the slug moving point first. Many Foster slugs are also rifled; the forward mass of the slug helping keep it stable until the rifling begins to provide spin. A variation on the Foster design is the Brenneke slug. Brenneke and Foster type slugs have the same basic configuration as normal slugs, but have increased accuracy. The hollowed rear of the Foster slug improves accuracy by placing more mass in the front of the projectile, therefore inhibiting the "tumble" that normal slugs may generate.
The Brenneke slug takes this concept a bit further, with the addition of a wad that stays connected to the projectile after discharge, increasing accuracy.

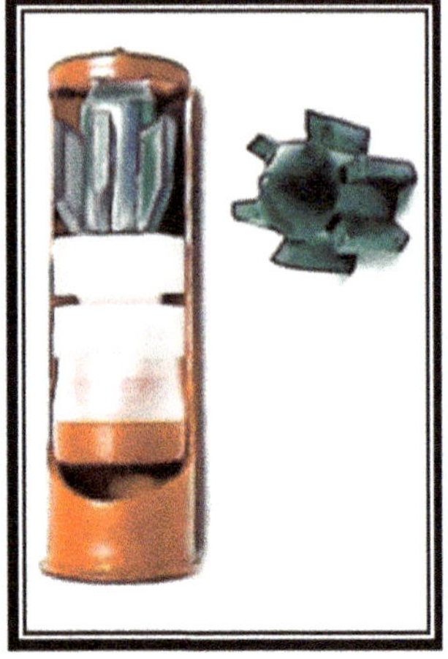

Both slugs are commonly found with fins or rib, which are meant to allow the projectile to safely squeeze down during passage through chokes, but they do not increase stability in flight.

Shotgun slugs intended for use in smoothbore barrels need to be made out of very soft lead alloys as they must be able to fit through the restrictive choke present in most shotgun barrels. Even so, it is not recommended to fire slugs through very constrictive chokes, as the effort of compressing the slug will eventually flare the end of the barrel, effectively reducing the degree of choke. Rifled barrels for shotguns are an unusual legal issue in the United States of America. Firearms with rifled barrels are designed to fire single projectiles, and a firearm that is designed to fire a single projectile with a diameter greater than .50 calibre (0.5 inch, or 12.7 mm) is considered a "destructive device" and as such is severely restricted. The ATF has ruled that as long as the gun was designed to fire shot, and modified (by the user or the manufacturer) to fire single projectiles with the addition of a rifled barrel, then the firearm is still considered a shotgun and not a destructive device. Rifled barrels in the UK are very rare and would have to be held on a firearms certificate, not a shotgun certificate.

Many U.S law enforcement agencies now are training their deputies in the use of shotguns with the rifled slug. At short to medium range shooting, the slug has awesome stopping power. The decision to use these rounds probably came about as a result of the Los Angeles shootout where the bank robbers were fully protected by body armour. The police at that time had no weapons available to stop them. Now they do...after the incident was over.
Using a rifled shotgun barrel is great for use with the rifled slug only. If you purchase one of these, then the other optional shells (following) will be of no use since the rifling makes the balls fly out into an oval pattern that is not predictable. For general use, the smooth bore shotgun is best.

Sabots are a common type of slug round. While some slugs are exactly that—a 12-gauge metal projectile in a cartridge—a sabot is a smaller but more aerodynamic projectile surrounded by a "shoe" of some other material. This "sabot" jacket seals the barrel, increasing pressure and acceleration, while also inducing spin on the projectile in a rifled barrel. Once the projectile clears the barrel, the sabot material falls away, leaving an unmarked, aerodynamic bullet to continue toward the target.

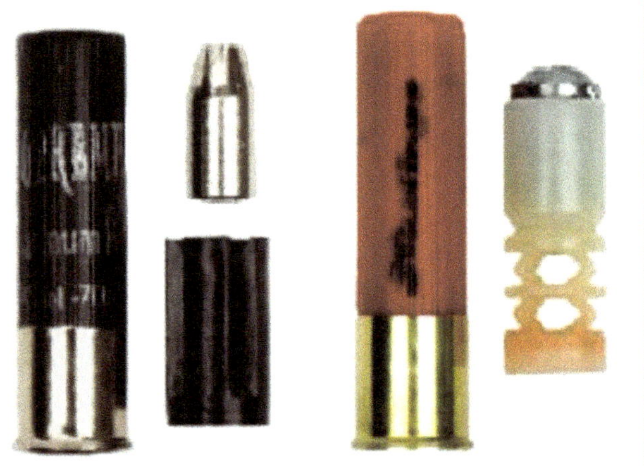

	Range	50m	100m	125m
Left: **Winchester platinum Tip**	Drop	0"	2.7"	5.7"
Right: **Hastings Magnum**	Above	1.9"	Drop 0'	3.6"

The advantages over a traditional slug are increased shot power, increased bullet velocity due to the lighter-mass bullet, and increased accuracy due to the velocity and the reduction in deformation of the slug itself. Disadvantages versus a traditional slug include lower muzzle momentum due to reduced mass, reduced damage due to smaller bullet diameter, and significantly higher per-unit cost.

NB: UK Police do not like private users having access to these sabot rounds available in rifle calibres too, such as the .308 accelerator. This is because in a crime scene it is extremely difficult to identify the weapon that has fired the round due to lack of forensics such as rifle twist marks on the projectile and other tell-tale signs.

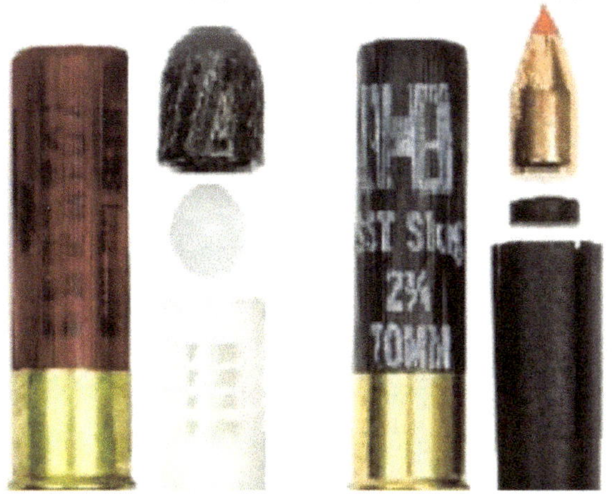

	Range	50m	100m	125m
Left: **Federal Tru Ball**	Drop	0"	7.3"	15"
Right: **Horrady SST**	Drop	0"	5'	6.6"

	Range	50m	100m	125m
Left: **Rottweil Blitz**	Drop	N/A	N/A	N/A
Right: **Winchester PowerPoint**	Drop 0"	4.7"	9.9"	6.6"

Non-Lethal Shotgun Ammunition.

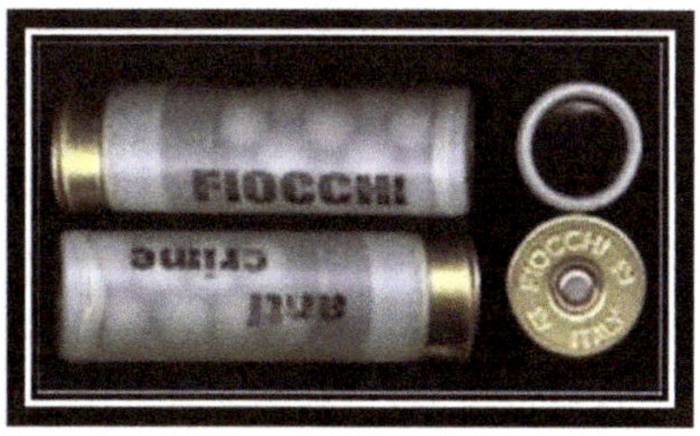

Two rounds of Fiocchi
12 gauge rubber buckshot

Less Lethal rounds, designed for riot control, but could be used for fending off pirates, rather than 'lethal' ammunition as currently used.

Flexible baton rounds, commonly called bean bags, fire a fabric bag filled with birdshot or a similar loose, dense substance. The 'punch' effect of the bag is useful for knocking down targets; the rounds are used by U.S police to subdue violent suspects. The bean bag round is by far the most common Less Lethal round used.

Due to the large surface area of these rounds, they lose velocity rapidly, and must be used at fairly short ranges to be effective, though use at extremely short ranges, under 3 m (10 ft.), can result in broken bones or other serious or lethal injuries. The rounds can also fly in a frisbee-like fashion and cut the person or animal being fired at. For this reason, these types of rounds are referred to as Less Lethal, as opposed to less-than-lethal.

Gas cartridges spray a cone of gas for several meters. These are primarily used by riot police. They normally contain pepper gas or tear gas. Other variations launch a gas-grenade-like projectile.

Rock salt cartridges are hand loaded with rock salt, replacing the standard lead or steel shot. Rock salt shells could be seen as the forerunners of modern less-lethal rounds. In the United States, rock salt shells were and are sometimes used by rural civilians to defend their property. The brittle salt was unlikely to cause serious injury at long ranges, but would cause painful stinging injuries and served as a warning. Some Spanish police forces, like the Guardia Civil and Cuerpo Nacional de Policía, use special rock salt shells called SAL-90 in their riot control units.

Rubber slugs or rubber buckshot are similar in principle to the bean bag rounds. Composed of flexible rubber or plastic and fired at low velocities, these rounds are probably the most common choice for riot control. Shapes range from full bore diameter cylinders to round balls of varying sizes, to a patent pending design "star round".

TASER International announced in 2007 a new 12 gauge eXtended Range Electronic Projectile or XREP, which contains a small electroshock weapon unit in a carrier that can be fired from a standard 12-gauge shotgun. The XREP projectile is fin stabilized, and travels at an initial velocity of 100 m/s (300 ft./s).

Barbs on the front attach the electroshock unit to the target, with a tassel deploying from the rear to widen the circuit. A twenty-second burst of electrical energy is delivered to the target. Breaching rounds, often called Disintegrator or Hatton rounds, are designed to destroy door-locking mechanisms without risking lives. These should not be fired at people under any circumstances.

Bird bombs are low-powered rounds that fire a pyrotechnic that is fused to explode a short time after firing. They are designed to scare animals, such as birds that congregate on airport runways.

Screechers fire a pyrotechnic whistle that emits a loud whistling sound for the duration of its flight. These are also used to scare animals.

Blank cartridges contain only a small amount of powder and no actual load. When fired, the blanks provide the sound and flash of a real load, but with no projectile. These may be used for simulation of gunfire, scaring wildlife, or as power for a launching device.

Stinger is a type of shotgun cartridge which contains 16-00 buck balls made of zytel, and is designed as a non-lethal ammunition ideally used in small spaces.

Home made; it is not unusual for qualified sportsmen/women to 'homeload' their own ammunition. The author does this with his deer stalking ammunition, it is much more accurate than standard grade hunting ammunition for various reasons. Gamekeepers and landowners would often change the contents of a shotgun cartridge for shooting at poachers and trespassers alike. Often rock salt or rice would be used. In 1980 when the author was ferreting on the nearby estate, he opened the gamekeeper's hut door, centrally located within the wood. There was an alarm gun inside (that is designed to fire a blank 12 bore cartridge to alert the 'keeper) pointing at the door on a tripwire, the cartridge was loaded with carpet tacks of which were blasted into the hut door, his Barbour jacket and his forehead. He and 'Jock' Law were lucky not to be blinded or seriously injured, not good at the tender age of 12. After that they avoided that private estate.

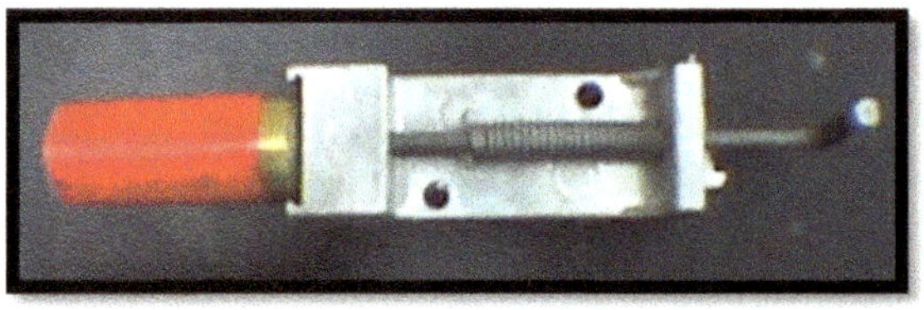

Typical 12bore alarm gun, only to be used with blank ammunition

Rifles.

Originally, shotguns were commonly used for maritime security, but in the last five years (2007-12) more companies are using the preferred rifles with longer ranges and greater accuracy. Generally, rifles require more complex paperwork and have complicated legal issues, such as bullets ricocheting and hitting other targets or people. A rifle will cost around £750-£1500, AK47 types will be less, however military or assault rifles with an automatic capability are not allowed and have to be converted to single shot. In the UK there are various categories as deemed by the Home Office regarding to types of weapons. For example a shotgun must have a smooth bore, have barrels of more than 24 inches and not magazine fed, if the weapon is semi-auto or pump action then the tubular magazine must not hold more than 2 cartridges. Weapons that do not conform to that must be held on a firearms certificate. For sporting rifles, such as target weapons or hunting weapons, these normally will be held on a 'Section 1' firearms licence, but for a weapon such as an M16 or AK47, these are held on a 'Section 5' firearms licence. Shipping and security companies need to be fully aware of the licensing implications when considering weapons and ammunition (as types of ammunition do need careful consideration, such as the Brenneke slug) and should seek legal advice.

Some authorities and people believe that weapons will only lead to further bloodshed and an increase in fatalities. There are two sides to that story. A professional security team will ensure that pirates do not get close to the vessel and do not gain access by climbing aboard; a professional team can fend off even the largest of pirate attack groups with two marksmen on each bridge wing or other protected fire position. On the other hand, an unprofessional team using the wrong tactics and weapons, ammunition and equipment could be out-gunned, over run and end up with the pirates boarding the ship which then would lead to a fire fight onboard, in this scenario, yes persons on both sides could be injured and killed and the shooting could also lead to an incident such as a major fire if the ship is carrying volatile fuels such as LPG, Hydrocarbons etc. On self-protected vessels, such as private yachts, if a pirate or thief gets hold of a crew member's weapon, it often makes a situation much, much worse and can end in fatalities. If the vessel wants an armed option, it is recommended to use only professional private security companies such as those mentioned in chapter 17. Note: It is not recommended for a vessel to arm itself: robberies where the crew remain passive usually end peacefully; in instances where crew have used weapons, there have often been casualties or deaths. Weapons and ammunition must be declared to every port the vessel visits, and are often taken away by customs and returned prior to departure or sealed in the ship's bonded store and only opened when exiting. Sometimes this can be complex and time consuming; often a departing vessel restrained by its draft can be delayed until the next high tide or next day due to the time it takes to receive the weapons from customs (such as Port Victoria Harbour in Mahe, Seychelles). Some countries will not allow this, hence the use of armed security onboard not being a viable option on some HRA transits. Weapons come in all sorts of shapes and sizes, fully automatic are not allowed, so weapons with that capability, such as an AK47 or M16 must have the trigger sears altered so that the weapon is semi-automatic and fires a single shot only each time the trigger is squeezed. A good firer never pulls a trigger! In most action movies, people fire weapons at each other on fully automatic, with endless bullets striking accurately on their targets. Nothing could be further from the truth, but incredibly, untrained firers adopt this unprofessional manner, with the butt under the arm, as seen in many pictures taken the Liberian civil war.
The two key features of a weapon to be used for maritime security are that it must be safe and it must be accurate. Bolt-action weapons work very well, but usually have smaller magazines holding only 5-10 rounds. Semi-automatic weapons work by varying ways, this could be blowback (where the backward pressure of the detonating projectile pushes the working parts to the rear), or delayed blowback as found with the awesome H&K G3, or gas operated as found with AK47, M16 or Browning Longtrac.

The benefit of these types of weapons is that they do come with high capacity magazines, so should a security guard need to use his weapon his needs not to change a magazine, or disturb his firing position or point of aim.

An important consideration is the barrel length as shorter barrels will cause a loss in barrel pressure that leads to an increased drop in the bullet's trajectory (dropping curve), whereas a longer barrel will increase the rifle's accurate range, that is why sniper rifles have such long barrel length, cut at a specific length due to resonance and harmonics.

The Browning BAR Match 7.62x51 with magazines of 20 and 10 rounds. Semi-automatic, highly accurate and hard hitting; a perfect choice.

A perfect, battle proven weapon calibre for defence would be a 7.62mm x 51mm (standard NATO) cartridge, these have a much harder hitting power than the NATO standard 5.56 x 45mm SS109. The 5.56mm round was brought into service for two reasons. Firstly the soldier can carry more ammunition because each round is smaller and lighter. And secondly the rounds are designed to injure the enemy soldier -so his men have to assist him off the battlefield - rather than to kill him. An accurate 7.62mm round is usually fatal as soldiers who fought in the Falklands War of 1982 and deer stalkers will testify.

The Geneva Convention prohibits the use of soft-nosed or expanding ammunition in armed conflict, and rightly so. So never buy hunting ammunition to protect your vessel with; the cartridges should be what NATO call ball, which is full metal jacket (FMJ), where upon the lead bullet head is totally enclosed in a copper case.

An ideal weapon type would be the 7.62mm Self Loading Rifle (SLR), this was the in-service weapon between 1958 and 1987, when eventually the 5.56mm SA80 replaced it. The SLR is a battle proven weapon; strong, accurate, heavy hitting up to ranges of 600m.

The sights however are not luminous, so they either have to be altered, changed or an optical sight with illuminated sight picture be used (such as an Eotech or Aimpoint). These weapons are so reliable, they have magazines that hold 20 cartridges and are well priced.

The very good EoTech 510 weapon sight

The original weapon that the SLR was copied from was the FN 7.62mm, as used by the Argentinians back in the 1980s. Similar to the SLR, but made to a higher quality by Fabrique Nationale, the same company involved with Browning, who make some of the best hunting weapons available. Above the Browning BAR Match or Long Trac are also very good. Some companies use bolt action hunting rifles, such as the Steyr Scout, a very accurate and reliable weapon, whereas other companies have used second-hand, short barrelled and far from ideal weapon types. There are online blogs where the security guards are not happy with the security company providing them with shotguns and no6 shot that has a lethality of no more than 40m!

Converting conventional 'iron sights' for night time use.

History

The author wrote this article whilst on an armed transit for a well known maritime company whose rifle's iron sights did not have illumination. The conversion is tried and test and works very well.

Since 2007 Somali piracy has exploded, however 98% of attacks have taken place during daylight hours, the other 2% were either under moonlight or by luck. Not all of the weapons used by maritime security companies come equipped with telescopic or red dot type sights. There is nothing wrong with iron sights and a competent shooter will shoot as accurately with iron sights as he will with optical means up to 400m (especially from a moving ship).

For the weapon systems with non-illuminated iron sights, here is a simple guide to show you how to convert you rifle (or shotgun). The pictures here are of the H&K G3s.

Equipment required:

1. Self-illuminating safety sign.
2. Scissors.
3. Superglue
4. Lighter
5. Clean cloth

Method:

1. The ship's no 3 officer is usually the safety officer, ask him for a spare luminous sticker, he should have some in his possession.

2. Cut a 1mm sliver off the edge.

3. Remove any oil from the front/rear sights, then using a cigarette lighter heat the area for about 10 seconds. Once it's cooled, remove soot with cloth.

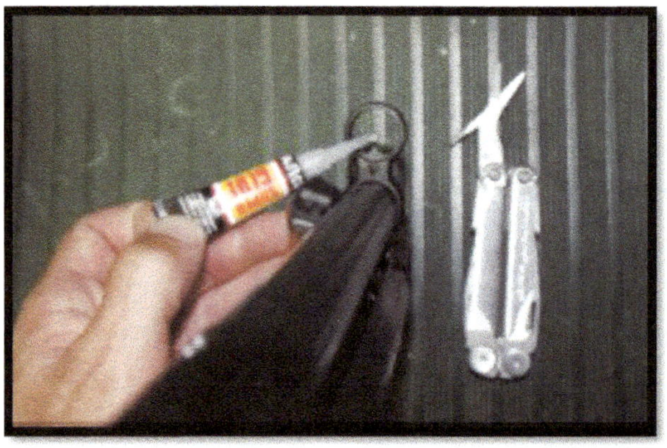

4. Ensure you remove the wax paper off the back of the 1x1mm square of luminous sticker. When you place the 'dot' onto the sight use the tip of a needle or similar, not your finger. Adjust the position until it's at the top of the blade. Once happy put a drop of glue on and around the 'dot'.

5. Do the same sequence for the rear sight. You should apply 2 'dots' though, one either side of the Vee or circular hole (diopta). This will appear the same as the sight picture found on Sig or Glock pistols during daytime use. The smaller the dots on the rear sight, the better, but it is difficult to work with dots smaller than 1x1mm.

6. Let the sights dry, then try them at night; the rear sights will appear slightly blurred, that's normal, but now you can aim the rifle accurately should you have that rare nocturnal encounter.

7. Check the accuracy

The below table shows the differences in velocity and energy between 3 common calibres as used by Private Maritime Security Companies

Velocity in feet-per-second (Muzzle, 100, 200, 300, 400, 500 yards)						
Distance in Yards	**Muzzle**	**100**	**200**	**300**	**400**	**500**
5.56 NATO (63 grain):	**3200**	**2862**	**2521**	**2198**	**1900**	**1612**
7.62 NATO (168 grain):	**2700**	**2513**	**2333**	**2161**	**1996**	**1839**
.30-06 (150 grains)	**2700**	**2473**	**2257**	**2052**	**1859**	**1664**

Kinetic Energy in Ft-Pounds (Muzzle, 100, 200, 300, 400, 500 yards)						
Distance in Yards	**Muzzle**	**100**	**200**	**300**	**400**	**500**
5.56mm NATO (63 grains @ 3200 FPS):	**1432**	**1146**	**889**	**676**	**505**	**364**
7.62 NATO (168 grains @ 2700 FPS):	**2719**	**2355**	**2030**	**1742**	**1486**	**1261**
.30-06 (150 grains @ 2700 FPS):	**2428**	**2037**	**1697**	**1403**	**1150**	**922**

A Layman's explanation:

The easiest way to describe the above table is to compare the 5.56mm bullet to a golf ball and the 7.62mm to a cricket ball. The **velocity** is the speed that the bullet or ball travels at, the **Foot/ pounds** (Ft/Lbs) is the energy that is within the projectile.

Foot/pounds: If a golf ball were thrown at you, full speed, it would travel quickly on a relatively flat trajectory and would hurt when it struck you.

If the cricket ball was thrown at you full speed, the speed would be less, the trajectory would be more curved, but when it strikes you, you'd be in a great deal of pain because of the inertia /energy within. This energy within a moving bullet is known as Ft/Lbs.

The larger and heavier the bullet, the more Ft/Lbs it has, an example of this is the Barrett .50 calibre sniper rifle. The staggering ballistic performance is as follows:

Bullet type = Speer, Velocity 3,044 ft/s (928 m/s), weight/ 647 grain (41.9 g), Energy 13,144 ft-lb's (17,821 J).

With self-protection, laws state "Using the minimum force possible' so shooting at pirates with a .50cal rifle is not recommended at this point of time. Maybe in years to come, it could be the recommended weapon in BMP10?? Let's hope piracy has ceased by then and they (the pirates) resort to fishing and farming again in their peaceful, prosperous, and governed country.
When the author was a gamekeeper, he heard reports of poachers cutting the top off a 12 bore cartridge and pouring liquid candle wax into the lead shot. This simple method turns a common shotgun cartridge into a long distance, hard hitting solid projectile that was used primarily for close range deer shot at night (lamped). The homemade 'frangible' round would break up and all the energy would be expended within the deer, albeit, not ideal for eating with over 300 leads pellets within. The same could be done for shooting at skiffs at longer ranges than a 12 bore using multi-pellet cartridges would allow, however, this practice is illegal and very unsafe for the firer (due to over-pressure within the thin barrel, which could cause an explosion).
When at sea, guns, like all metallic objects, will rust much more quickly than if stored on land. The guns must be fully serviced, oiled and cleaned. Thicker oils should be used, rather than thinner penetrating oils such as WD40, as the thicker oil will reside much longer.
Guns should always be stripped and assembled inside, not on the open decks. It is all too easy to lose a return spring over the side or a firing pin down a drain. Consider using trigger locks for additional security.

Gun safety rules must be understood and applied in all situations involving firearms. The IMO recommends that private security guards have a certificate to state that they are confident, safe and competent to use firearms (the guard must also have a criminal background check and a Doctor's letter stating that he is sane and healthy to use such weapons). Shooting ranges providing this facility can be found around the UK, the leading facility is Shooting Solutions based in Dorset.

The fundamental rules of gun safety must always be applied simultaneously when handling or using a gun:

General Safety Rules:

Always keep the gun in a secured, locked gun safe, out of sight

Always treat the gun as if it were loaded

Never touch a gun unless you are permitted to do so

Always be aware of the direction in which the muzzle of your weapon is pointing and NEVER point it in an unsafe direction.
Always keep your finger off the trigger until ready to shoot

When in use:

Always keep the gun unloaded until ready to use

Always keep the gun pointed in a safe direction

Know your target and what is beyond

Be sure the gun is safe to operate

Know how to use the gun safely

Use only the correct ammunition for your gun

Wear hearing and eye protection as appropriate

Never use alcohol or medicines before or while shooting

All weapons, such as the above M4, should be kept locked away and unloaded until the threat increases to a level that the team leader deems it necessary to use them. However, "Neither the Master nor the security team leader can command a member of the security team against that person's own judgment to use lethal force or to not use lethal force" Some companies require that the weapon be with the security guard throughout his period of duty, in this case, the weapon should be unloaded and well-oiled against the corrosive conditions found at sea.

A very good paper written by INCE & CO can be downloaded from their website.
http://incelaw.com/news-and-events/News/ince-welcomes-fac-report-into-piracy/
www.incelaw.com

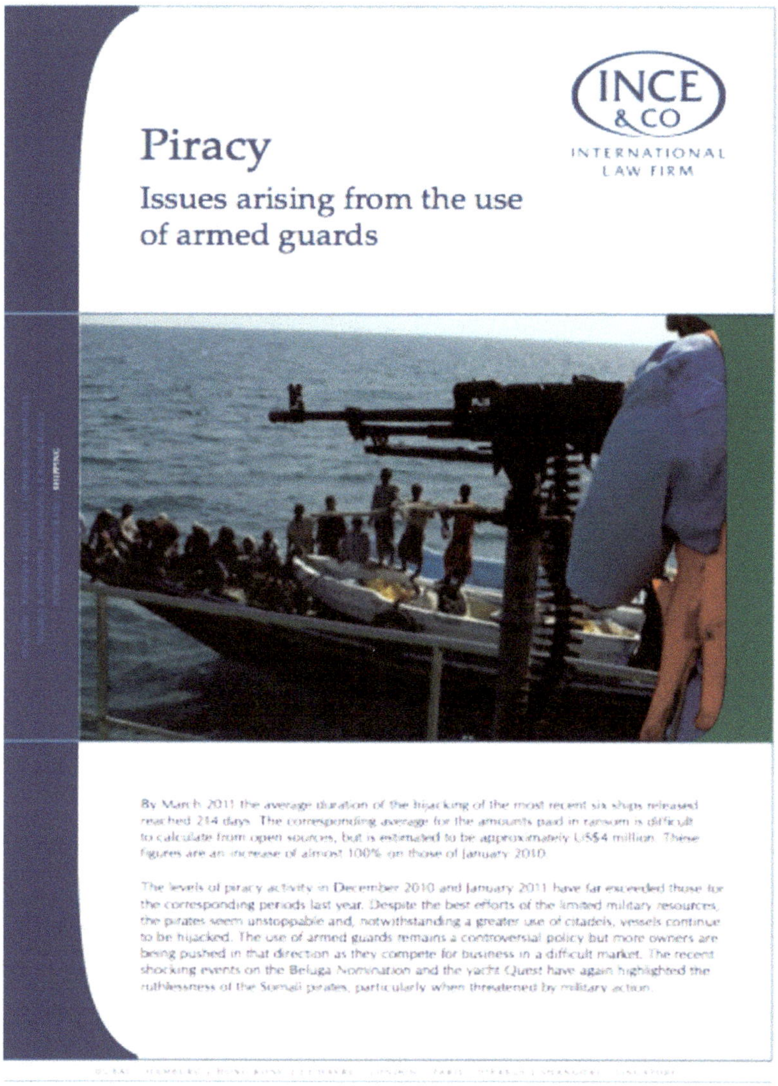

INCE & CO
INTERNATIONAL LAW FIRM

Piracy

Issues arising from the use of armed guards

By March 2011 the average duration of the hijacking of the most recent six ships released reached 214 days. The corresponding average for the amounts paid in ransom is difficult to calculate from open sources, but is estimated to be approximately US$4 million. These figures are an increase of almost 100% on those of January 2010.

The levels of piracy activity in December 2010 and January 2011 have far exceeded those for the corresponding periods last year. Despite the best efforts of the limited military resources, the pirates seem unstoppable and, notwithstanding a greater use of citadels, vessels continue to be hijacked. The use of armed guards remains a controversial policy but more owners are being pushed in that direction as they compete for business in a difficult market. The recent shocking events on the Beluga Nomination and the yacht Quest have again highlighted the ruthlessness of the Somali pirates, particularly when threatened by military action.

16. Privately Contracted Armed Security Personnel And Private Maritime Security Companies

Armed guards to protect British ships from pirates

British ships are to be allowed to carry armed guards to protect them from pirates, David Cameron has announced. 30th Oct 2011

British merchant ships sailing off the coast of Somalia will soon be able to carry armed guards to ward off pirate attacks, Prime Minister David Cameron said on Sunday. Britain is one of only a few countries with major shipping fleets to currently ban armed guards on its vessels, alongside the likes of Japan, Greece and the Netherlands. However, owners of ships from other countries are increasingly putting guards onboard as national navies struggle to combat Somali piracy in the vast Indian Ocean, a problem which is costing the world economy billions of dollars a year.

David Cameron is to allow the use of armed guards on ships as of October 2011

In an interview with the BBC, Cameron said that Britain now planned to license guards to carry firearms on ships. "The evidence is that ships with armed guards don't get attacked, don't get taken for hostage or for ransom and so we think this is a very important step forward," Cameron said.
"The fact that a bunch of pirates in Somalia are managing to hold to ransom the rest of the world and our trading system I think is a complete insult..." he added.

The planned exemptions to Britain's strict firearms laws could allow guards to carry revolvers, automatic weapons or even rocket launchers on board.
A spokeswoman for Britain's Home Office (interior ministry) said that a licensing scheme would start within a month, and that the weaponry allowed would be "appropriate and proportionate".
Licences would restrict use of the weapons to off the Somali coast, the Gulf of Aden, the Arabian Sea and parts of the Indian Ocean. Britain's Transport Ministry said it expected around half the 200 British ships which sail through those waters to want to use armed guards.
Somali pirates, operating from the shores of the lawless state in the Horn of Africa, have raked in millions of dollars a year in ransoms from scores of hijacked ships from around the world, including oil super tankers.

Last month the shipping industry called on the United Nations to create an armed military force to be deployed on vessels to counter the escalating menace from the armed seaborne gangs.
Better armed and increasingly violent pirate gangs are set to ramp up attacks in the coming weeks in the Indian Ocean as the monsoon ends.
The Prime Minister said radical action was required because the increasing ability of sea-borne Somali criminals to hijack and ransom ships had become "a complete stain on our world".
He unveiled the measure after talks at a Commonwealth summit in Australia with leaders of countries in the Horn of Africa over the escalating problem faced in waters off their shores.
Under the plans, the Home Secretary will be given the power to license vessels to carry armed security, including automatic weapons, currently prohibited under firearms laws.
Officials said around 200 were expected to be in line to take up the offer, which would only apply for voyages through particular waters in the affected region. It is expected to be used by commercial firms rather than private sailors - such as hostage victims Paul and Rachel Chandler.

Asked if he was comfortable with giving private security operatives the right to "shoot to kill" if necessary, Mr Cameron told BBC1's Andrew Marr Show: "We have to make choices.
"Frankly the extent of the hijack and ransom of ships round the Horn of Africa is a complete stain on our world. " The fact that a bunch of pirates in Somalia are managing to hold to ransom the rest of the world and our trading system is a complete insult and the rest of the world needs to come together with much more vigour.
"I want to help lead this process and as part of that we are going to be taking the step of putting armed guards on our ships." Evidence from other countries with more relaxed regulations over armed guards was that their ships did not get targeted, he said.
"We are going to have to license that in a proper way, the Home Office has agreed to do that. But I think this is a big step up for our campaign against this piracy."
Other counter-piracy measures being taken include offering support from Treasury officials to Kenya to help them track down pirates' assets.

Mr Cameron also said help could be given to countries such as The Seychelles and Mauritius, both represented at the Commonwealth Heads of Government Meeting in Perth, who were acting to bring pirates to court and imprison them. Around 17 ships are currently being held by the pirates who can operate hundreds of miles from the Somali coast.

Negotiations often take many months before the ships and crews are released for ransom. The Socotra 1, a Yemeni-owned ship, was seized on Christmas Day 2009 and is still being held.

USA-Change in best practices regarding self-protection

While the non-wartime, 20th-century tradition has been for merchant vessels not to be armed, the US government has recently changed the rules so that it is now best practice for vessels to embark with a team of private security guards. The USCG leaves it to the shippers' discretion to determine if those guards will be armed. After some mixed messages from the IMO and the Chamber of Shipping it is good to hear the British government take a clear line. The IMO has said that it does not support the use of armed guards but will advise ship owners and managers on how to use security services if they need to use them. Similarly the Chamber of Shipping has voiced valid concerns about encouraging the use of weapons on merchant ships. David Cameron's statement, 30th Oct 2011, has brought clarity to the British maritime industry by closing the gap between what is needed and what the IMO will advise.For the past two years at least we have seen private security firms and London insurance companies fill a vacuum and offer much needed services to the international maritime industry from the UK.

Our maritime security industry is already well placed in setting a global standard in maritime security, based on a long history of military, merchant shipping and oil and gas expertise. Security providers like Britannia Maritime Security have shared a solution focused approach with the UK insurance industry and UK shipping management companies for some time now. Britain has played an integral part in developing what is very soon to be a kite mark for the international maritime security industry; and some individual providers are now at the forefront of developing anti-piracy solutions in the Gulf of Aden.

However, ironically, British ships, up to now, have not been able to take advantage of British maritime security expertise in the same way as other state flags have. This is likely to change overnight and it will be interesting to see if cooperation between British ship owners and UK based private security companies raises the bar further in the regulation and improvement of security services to the maritime industry.
Demand for best practice and well managed maritime security services is likely to go up in 2011. We will almost certainly see more demand from other countries, for example India; the Indian government is slightly ahead of the UK government, in allowing the use of privately contracted armed guards on their ships. David Cameron's statement is most welcome in that it sets the scene for further cooperation between the UK and other countries to develop improved anti-piracy solutions.

The use of professional private security guards is recommended as the gold standard, but not all agree. They are expensive and create problems regarding to weapons and national laws, but compared with what may lie ahead; it should be considered money well spent. Also, many insurance companies now insist on security guards when a vessel is transitting through the GoA HRA.
Guards should be chosen well; many have excellent pedigrees, having had careers in amphibious military units such as the Royal Marine Commandos, Special Air Service (SAS) or Special Boat Service (SBS) they are now working for or own specialist, maritime security companies. However, there are also opportunist businessmen who have set up low-budget companies, employ cheap labour and provide vessels with 'hired muscle' for lower, more attractive prices. There is a famous saying within the private security industry (aka 'the circuit'): 'Pay peanuts, get monkeys!'
Ex-bouncers, Walter-Mittys, testosterone-pumped gym queens and 'Rambo' types are quickly drawn to highly-paid, hostile environments where they can participate in bodybuilding, take steroids and patrol the streets looking like something from a Schwarzenegger movie. With mirrored glasses and assault vests, these cowboys have no prior training or real experience; some of the stories they tell back in the pubs and clubs are quite unbelievable and mostly false!

Ironside Associates use only former Special Forces men for their maritime security

Unfortunately, as work in countries such as Iraq becomes less, some of these men are now focusing on anti-piracy and giving the security sector a bad name in certain circles. In the UK, the Security Industry Authority (SIA) is licensing trades such as doormen, security guards and bodyguards, but the maritime industry remains at present unregulated, so guards should be chosen carefully. The UK's leading company that trains private security guards solely for the maritime industry is Trident Operations. Run by former UKSF officers, Trident, like the SIA, ensures that its employees have a thorough grounding and high proficiency in maritime security consultation. Other leading companies are 3RG, Blue Mountain Group, Mandusc and Transafe Maritime.
There are other companies too who employ security men from all types of backgrounds, and a few from the SAS such as; Blue Mountain Group, MAST, Minimal Risks and SPS. There are ex Special Boat Service men who have proven companies dealing with maritime security, as this is the SBS's field of expertise, these include: Ironsides Associates Ltd, Neptune Maritime Security, Veritas International, Solace Global Maritime, MPS, HadCon, PGS Group, PVI, Salama Fakira and Cerberus-International, all of which employ former maritime special forces men to man the client's vessels and can provide many more security-related services.

Veritas International is one of the world's leading maritime security companies that specialise in chaperoning and close protection to its clients within the superyacht industry.

Case study: *Somali pirates firing automatic weapons attacked the Maersk Alabama on Wednesday 18 November 2009, the second attack on the ship. Private guards on board the US-flagged ship repelled the attack with gunfire and a high-decibel noise device, proof – if any is needed – that private security is a sound investment. It is far better to pay for this service and have a secure vessel and reassured crew, than to run the risk of capture, possible death, loss of income and ultimately a multi-million dollar ransom.*

As previously mentioned: Maersk Alabama was attacked twice, in 2008 and 2009. An armed security team thwarted the second attack

In November 2009 the Captain of the hijacked chemical tanker MV Theresa VIII paid the ultimate price when he died as a result of gunshot wounds inflicted by pirates.

The only guaranteed way to prevent this is by employing professional armed security or have armed military guards on board.

Ex-military security guards

Most UK based security companies employ men who are former UK military, or Police. Very few are from other backgrounds. The industry needs a man who smart, inteligent, experienced, who understands law, has self discipline and remains calm in times of stress. These are just a few of the qualities required for maritime security work. They are not just hired muscle, or employed to shoot pirates, that is completely incorrect; they ensure that the Captain and his crew and ship have the best possible protection during the transit, that BMP4 is completely adhered to, that the ships passage plan is correct and the ship's hardening is as robust as possible.

Whilst underway the team will reassure the crew that they have the best possible protection when away from the patrolling warships, that the citadel is fortified, and has sufficient water, rations, medical equipment and communications to last up to five days in the Indian Ocean. They will do everything possible to deter pirates from coming close to the vessel, abiding by rigid rules of engagement, their weapons are there as a last resort and only used in self defence when every other means has failed and bullets and RPG warheads are being fired at the ship. It is too easy for those who are not informed, to sumise that 'gun totting Rambo types' are there to shoot at any nearby boat, regardless of it's occupants.

This image is what all security companies try their hardest to stay away from, hence the need for formal training and regualation to ensure that the guards are of the best pedigree and had correct training, such as that supplied by Trident Operations , Blue Mountain Group and 3RG. The now famous case of two Italian soldiers who killed two Indian fishermen whilst deployed on a ship is a clear example of what can happen if the on board guards are not trained to a high enough standard.

One of the three leading companies in Britain is **Neptune Maritime Security**, based in Dorest, England, again compromising of former military personnel who are all fully vetted and trained to the highest of standards. They were recently seen on the BBC when a report was aired on Somali piracy.

NEPTUNE
MARITIME SECURITY

Another leading company is Solace Global Maritime Security, comprising of former Special Boat Service and Royal Marine manpower.

Below, the late Orlando Rogers (co- founder Solace) erecting ships defences in the GoA

Privately contracted security guards come from various backgrounds; there are many good men out there, but to employ the very best it is recommended that former maritime Special Forces are used. These men are the cream of the UK's military and have had years of maritime experience in hostile environments and deliver very high standards.

Below is an advert from PVI, a company that provides armed escort vessels and vessel protection teams in high risk areas such as the GoA/Indian Ocean, they are one of the world's largest, armed, maritime security companies.

The death of a suspected pirate off the coast of Somalia has drawn attention to the use of armed private security contractors on board merchant vessels.

The incident, which involved guards aboard the Panamanian-flagged MV Almezaan, is believed to be the first of its kind. But several organisations, including the IMB, have previously expressed concerns over the use of armed security contractors.

'While we understand that owners want to protect their ships, we don't agree in principle with putting armed security on ships,' IMB director Captain Pottengal Mukundan told the BBC News website. 'Ships are not an ideal place for a gun battle.'

One argument is that the use of armed operatives could encourage pirates to use more violence when taking a ship. Mr Mukundan said he had seen no evidence that there had been much of an increase in the use of armed guards by merchant ship owners. Dozens of warships patrol the waters off the Somali coast, but this has not deterred pirates. The amount of ocean to patrol is vast, and pirates have responded to the increased naval presence by moving attacks farther out to sea. 'The naval forces are displacing the threat - they can't be everywhere at once. Almost the whole of the Indian Ocean region - some five million square nautical miles - is a security risk.'

Many vessels prefer to use non-lethal counter measures.

Seen here is an armed US Navy sailor manning the LRAD (this combination is sometimes used as non-lethal preventative measures should always be used primarily when a threat approaches).

Prevention

The shipping industry has, so far, largely resisted arming their boats – not least because this would deny them port in some nations. Furthermore, arming the ships can raise liability issues and increase insurance costs. A director of a maritime security firm says the use of private operatives is not necessary and that ship owners can find other ways to protect themselves, such as boosting training, carrying out more drills and purchasing equipment that could prevent pirates boarding a vessel. 'Private security guards are not necessary, they simply muddy the water,' he said. 'They are often foreign to the crew themselves and they don't know the ship well.

Many are former soldiers that have been in Iraq or Afghanistan and they think they can shake the dust off their shoes and make it as a private security guard. Their day rate is pretty high and the crew have to find ways to get them on and off the vessels.' Their presence, he said, would only lead to 'more spilt blood'. This international shipping law firm Ince and Co released a report highlighting the issues arising from the use of armed guards.

It pointed out that a fundamental question arose as to who would authorise the use of force. Stephen Askins, a lawyer with Ince, told the BBC News website that the debate on the use of armed guards was one that polarised the industry. 'Most industry bodies and ship owners are against them,' he said. 'But no ship with an armed guard has been hijacked, so there are those – particularly those who have had hijacked ships – who think they are necessary.' He said private security companies had come into their own in places like Iraq and had seen the maritime sector as potentially lucrative. 'Many have moved across but there is no system of accreditation, so there is no way of knowing the good from the bad,' he said. Mr Askins said some firms provided armed escort vessels, but that these did not have any status in international law. 'The various conventions dealing with piracy relate to states and their navies,' he said. 'The rights that they are given, like the right of innocent passage relate to military ships. There are also issues over the use of armed force. The relevant law is the law of the flag state, but a merchant ship could, for example, be Panamanian and the escort ship could be, say, UK flagged.'

'Lethal force for them would come after a series of steps including warning shots. The good companies would follow that procedure. Normally that would be enough to deter an attack.' In May 2009, the US coastguard drafted a maritime security directive that would require US-flagged ships sailing around the Horn of Africa to post guards, and ship owners to submit anti-piracy security plans for approval. At the time, the coastguard's director of prevention policy, Rear Admiral James Watson, said that they expected to see 'additional security' that could 'involve the use of firearms'. He added that they were 'looking for things that work but that don't make the situation worse'. The directive has not yet passed into law. For now, the handling of the shooting by a private security operative will be watched closely by legal experts. An independent inquiry is planned, but first investigators will need to establish who had jurisdiction – the flag the vessel was flying, its owners or the nationality of the contractors – and who was responsible for the security contractors.

A lot has changed since Somali piracy began making headlines in the summer of 2008. The US and European Union have deployed warships off the Somali coast, the US is putting Marines aboard some commercial vessels, and shipping companies are hiring armed guards for others. But after American and Dutch forces captured and then released pirates after two separate incidents, it's no secret that the international community still hasn't figured out what to do with captured brigands. Most navies patrolling the coast of Somalia are content to confiscate pirates' weapons, destroy their faster boats and put them back in the water. U.S and other naval forces released roughly 60 percent of the 706 pirates they captured between August 2008 and December 2009. Of the 269 that they turned over for prosecution, 46 have been convicted and 23 acquitted so far

Maritime Security Standards

UK STANDARDS FOR MARITIME PRIVATE SECURITY COMPANIES BY END 2012[13]

Draft Standards to ensure service quality and reduce risk in hostile maritime environments

At the Inaugural Conference of the Security in Complex Environments Group (SCEG) today (Monday), the Chair of SCEG, Chris Sanderson, announced that standards designed to ensure high levels of quality and professionalism of all Private Security Companies operating in a maritime environment would be in place before the end of 2012. The Security in Complex Environments Group (SCEG) is a Special Interest Group within ADS. It brings together private security companies operating on land and sea around a common agenda of raising standards and introducing robust and independent accreditation for companies operating in complex and high-risk environments. ADS was appointed by UK Ministers as the government's industry partner for the regulation and accreditation of private security companies in June 2011, and an announcement was made in Parliament.

ADS believes that the high levels of risk of piracy in the seas off Somalia makes the development of maritime standards and independent accreditation a high priority, to reduce risks to private security companies and their employees, to ship owners and seamen, and to ship and cargo insurers and brokers. The SCEG has been working on standards, and will shortly be consulting with government officials, client groups and others such as intergovernmental bodies and certification bodies. The draft standards will be then submitted to government Ministers. It is intended that the government will play an important role in the selection of independent certification bodies that will audit individual private security companies against the standards, when they are finalised. Our intention is to have an independent accreditation process in place by the end of 2012. This will also address accreditation for private security companies operating in complex or high-risk land environments such as Iraq and Afghanistan.

Rees Ward, CEO at ADS, said:

"Piracy on the high seas is increasingly a problem, both for the areas and communities it affects as well as the commercial shipping which suffers from its attentions. The human and financial costs to ship owners and companies are potentially very high. Having a set of standards endorsed by the UK government and implemented by independent accrediting bodies will reduce levels of uncertainty and risk. ADS' Security in Complex Environments Group has this as its top priority, working with the UK government."

FCO Minister for Counter-Piracy and Conflict issues, Henry Bellingham, said:

"Given the importance of the private security sector to the UK economy, I am delighted that our partner association, ADS, is leading the way globally in the drafting of maritime standards for British companies. It is vitally important for British security companies, working both at sea and on land, to operate with the highest professional standards that are consistent with the principles of the International Code of Conduct for Private Security Service Providers."

---

[13] Mark Lowe (Marsec Review)

SAMI | Security Association for the Maritime Industry

www.seasecurity.org

SAMI: Britain's SAMI is doing a very professional job of ensuring that the private maritime security companies are recognised, verified and represented by and to the international shipping industry.

What is the overall aim of SAMI?
The guiding philosophy and vision is to create an organisation which is positive for both sides of the shipping equation – it allows the best security operators to proudly show their standards, it will allow companies to apply continuing, benchmarked improvement, while providing the rest of the shipping industry with the reassurance it wants and needs.

As well as SAMI there is also IAMSP, details follow:

Welcome to the International Association of Maritime Security Professional's website (IAMSP). As an independent body, we provide the Maritime Security Industry with a credible home and voice for those individuals and companies that adhere to, or that are seeking to adhere to, the highest standards of professionalism today.

We are an enabling organization. We understand that maintaining professional status is something that requires ongoing effort. For that reason, our community provides its members with guidance, tools, training and developmental forums that assist them in attaining, maintaining and demonstrating that professional status.

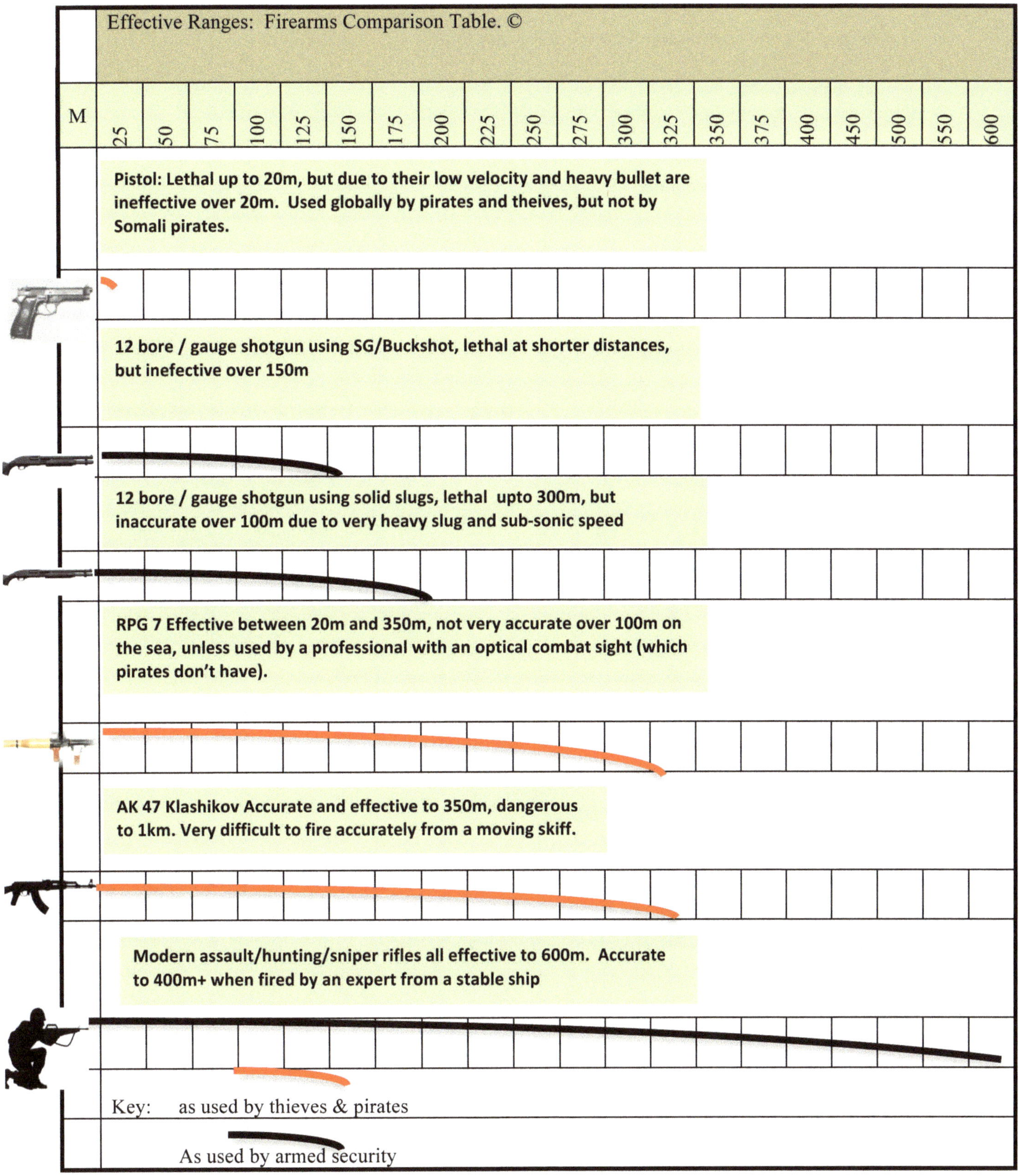

***The red lines represent the ranges of weapons currently used by Somali pirates; MEND and Indonesian pirates will use any weapons including weapons that can match and outreach the above examples, such as the 7.62x51mm GPMG (General Purpose Machine Gun)**

15 February 2011; **Shipping Industry Changes Stance on Armed Guards**

The International Chamber of Shipping (ICS) is the principal international trade association for shipowners, representing all sectors and trades and about 80% of the world merchant fleet.

ICS - whose Executive Committee comprising representatives of national shipowners' associations from over 30 countries met in London last week - has decided to clarify its stance on the use of private armed security guards to defend merchant ships against attacks by Somali pirates. ICS members have also identified a vital need for the military to disable the hijacked 'motherships', which the pirates are now using to launch attacks throughout much of the Indian Ocean.

ICS Chairman, Spyros M Polemis, explained:

"ICS has had to acknowledge that the decision to engage armed guards, whether military or private, is a decision to be made by the ship operator after due consideration of all of the risks, and subject to the approval of the vessel's flag state and insurers. The consensus view amongst shipping industry associations remains that, in normal circumstances, private armed guards are not recommended, and are a clear second best to military personnel. However, in view of the current crisis in the Indian Ocean - with over 700 seafarers held hostage and, most recently, a seafarer being executed - ship operators must be able to retain all possible options available to deter attacks and defend their crews against piracy. Many shipping companies have concluded that arming ships is a necessary alternative to avoiding the Indian Ocean completely, which would have a hugely damaging impact on the movement of world trade.

Mr Polemis added:
"The eradication of piracy is the responsibility of governments. Frustratingly, politicians in those nations with the largest military navies in the region show little willingness to increase resources to the extent that would be necessary to have a decisive impact on the problem of piracy. Western governments, at least, appear to give the impression that this otherwise unacceptable situation can somehow be tolerated. Sadly, until we can persuade governments otherwise, the use of armed guards by ships is very likely to continue increasing."

ICS advises that the shipping industry will meanwhile be looking at all possible options, including alternative routes, which could have a very dramatic effect on transport costs and delivery times. Piracy is already estimated to cost the global economy between US $7-12 billion per year. If increasing numbers of ships decide to divert around the Cape of Good Hope, this will almost certainly have a major impact on inventories and costs throughout the whole supply chain and, most particularly, on the cost of oil. It could also greatly damage the economies of Africa and the Middle East at this very politically delicate time.

Growing calls for armed guards to defend ships against piracy menace

23 March 2011

Shipping industry experts have raised a clear voice in favour of deploying armed guards on merchant vessels to repel piracy attacks. Many maritime professionals who previously opposed the measure for fear of escalating the violence say they have changed their minds, while retaining various reservations. The switch in mood has been reflected in a decisive vote at the 2011 'hot topic' Debate of WISTA-UK (part of the Women's International Shipping & Trading Association), for the tough approach.

Passionate contributions to the debate came from both sides, and those who declared themselves neutral on the issue.

The industry is agonising over what is the best response to the mounting number of pirate attacks, mainly originating from citizens of Somalia, and the growing ordeal of hostages who are subjected by their captors to cruel treatment. Participants at the WISTA Debate resolved by 42 votes to 16, with 13 declared abstentions, to support the motion: "This House believes that vessels should have armed guards on board."

In total, some 100 men and women from shipping, law, insurance, private security and other services were present at the meeting, in the City of London. The Debate is organised every March, the month in which International Women's Day is celebrated.

The International Maritime Bureau reported that there were a total of 440 attacks on shipping in 2010, of which 218 were attributed to Somali pirates in the Gulf of Aden, off the Coast of Somalia and in the Western Indian Ocean, and there have been further outrages in the first quarter of 2011.
Opening discussion at the WISTA event, Peter Hinchliffe, secretary general of the International Chamber of Shipping, said that proposing the motion was a task he "would not and could not have undertaken a few weeks ago," and it was important to put this into context.

Citing rising brutality in recent cases, Mr Hinchliffe insisted that one needed "to fight the current version of piracy" being perpetrated by Somali youth, who were financed by a murky underworld of organised crime. What was important was that this lucrative business of piracy was removed with speed. The military presence in the Gulf of Aden had caused piracy to shift almost as far as the coast of India. Sea control in the northern Indian Ocean was being ceded to armed gangs.

Some 600 seafarers are at present held for ransom, and the average time in captivity has extended to around eight months. No nation had a strategy to tackle the problem, and seafarers were daily running the gauntlet of armed pirates, with ships' superstructures being penetrated by rocket propelled grenades, said Mr Hinchliffe. Unfortunately most flag states did not have the resources at their finger tips to provide military guards in the theatre of operation. "In these exceptional circumstances, it is our belief that the use of armed guards, private security, be permitted by the flag state when considered appropriate."
He added: "We must not send [ships'] masters into the area with their arms tied behind their backs, but let us not institutionalise a precedent that could encourage the use of armed guards."

Seconding the motion, Maria Dixon of ISM Shipping Solutions, who is president of WISTA-UK, spoke of the experience of her niece when employed as a third officer and her niece's fiancé as IT manager on a passenger ship, the Oceanic, during a Gulf of Aden cruise in 2009. Six pirates, aboard two skiffs, began shooting at the ship and the crew ran inside for cover, although some intrepid Japanese passengers went out to the deck.

When ship was in contact with a Greek NATO warship 20 miles away, the pirates heard the radio message and fled. "I certainly think that there should be armed guards on board," said Ms Dixon. "It is not the same as combating common thieves. The crews may be subject to panic attacks. Firing weapons will keep pirates away. The crew are seafarers meant to sail the ship, not to defend it!"

Opposing the motion, Leslie-Anne Duvic-Paoli of the Royal United Services Institute for Defence and Security, referred to the principle that nation states should have a monopoly of violence. She questioned how trustworthy were some private security companies, in a market which was unregulated and a legal framework that was vague.
Private security businesses were mainly involved in a land-based environment, and the maritime environment was completely different. She warned that having security guards on board would lead to an escalation of violence. One consequence would be that pirates would attack ships without armed guards on board, and "when pirates see that there are armed guards on board they will resort to more violence." She spoke of an incident in February 2011 in which American hostages were killed by pirates who felt threatened by a US Navy ship.

Angus Galbraith, an ex-seafarer on tankers, who is a member of the London committee of the Nautical Institute and a Lloyd's broker with Lloyd's underwriting authority, opposed the motion, warning that the laws of many countries forbade carrying guns on board merchant ships. This meant any armed guards on board had to be kept outside port limits.
Mr Galbraith said that in cases where P&I (protection and indemnity) and hull insurers agreed that armed guards should be on board, he was somewhat relaxed about the situation (as P&I insurers then would be committed to legally defending the master who could be held liable for manslaughter for any deaths that occurred onboard), but said that most of the security people were ex-SAS officers and had no experience of tankers. Firing shots around posed a big problem, an environmental problem: an explosion on a gas carrier or a tanker of 200,000 dwt would create a serious issue.

He said it was critical for shipping companies to be appropriately insured (kidnap and ransom), as the insurance side could usually expedite the release of the crew and ship. He urged rejection of the principle of guards on board, but he was in favour of military convoys and armed guards positioned one or two miles from a ship.

Taking a 'neutral' stance, that ship owners should be left to make their individual decisions, Nick Platt, vice-president of Gard P&I Club (UK), admitted: "Sometimes the P&I clubs are seen as the solvers of all problems, but we are not, when it comes to piracy." What they did do was to vet security company contracts. Until quite recently, Gard was against the idea of armed guards, but "we are now neutral together with the other clubs in the International Group [of P&I Cubs]."
Mr Platt said: "Pirates are very clever people. They are doing very good business." We were one step behind, when we should be one step ahead of them. "What happens if they put 30 to 40 pirates on the ship with heavy weapons. Are your three or four armed guards good enough?"

Also on the 'neutral' side was Peter Cook, a founding member of the Security Association for the Maritime Industry, which positions itself as the maritime security industry's regulatory body.
Mr Cook said: "Piracy is a complex problem. It is not something that will be solved by putting armed guards on board." Whether armed guards should be embarked depended on the risk assessment made of the ship. Of the guidelines in BMP3 (Best Management Practices to Deter Piracy in the Gulf of Aden and off the Coast of Somalia), he said that as a document of consensus, it was not as explicit as it could be. BMP was developed by shipping industry organisations, in cooperation with navies, to offer practical advice to companies and ships. It was the basic minimum to observe, said Mr Cook.

He observed: "There is a marked increase in physical abuse of seafarers. I do not see any reason why that will decrease. I think that we are looking in the near future at a greater number of events where people are injured, tortured or killed." He said that using maritime security companies was a short-term solution, "but we have to have something."

From the audience, Janet Strode, general manager of the International Parcel Tankers Association, said that after a long time being against the deployment of armed guards, the association was now in the middle of a discussion on the issue.
Sue Williams, a London-based hostage negotiator, said she had changed her opinion and was in favour of the armed guards option.

The average incarceration period had risen to 155 days, from 66 days, and the world had to wake up to the degree of such torture, said Ms Williams.
Julie Lithgow, a member of WISTA-UK, cautioned that armed reaction was not the answer. She said: "We talk about finding the solution ashore, about wanting governments to do something. We don't specify what that something is. We already have clear lessons from other developing nations that prove that the best way for a society to develop socially, economically, politically and securely is through universal access to education and equal rights for women.

"But I acknowledge there is a need for short term action to reduce the numbers of seafarers taken, held hostage, beaten, tortured and killed by Somali pirates. After years of legislation to make our ships safer and safer for seafarers, putting guns on ships, however skilled the armed guards may be, makes our ships intrinsically less safe.
"BMP has a number of suggestions that can make our ships safer, and so far, no vessel with BMP correctly and robustly implemented has been taken by pirates. One of the simplest and cheapest recommendations within BMP is to inform UKMTO [UK Maritime Trade Operations office in Dubai] and MSCHOA [Maritime Security Centre - Horn of Africa} when your ship enters the high risk zone. And yet, more than 30% of ships entering the zone fail to take even this first step.

"So my short term solution suggestion is that BMP become mandatory, and vessels can be held by port state control for no- compliance with BMP at ports before entering the zone," said Ms Lithgow.
In further contributions, a former ship's master said that crews had been reduced substantially in recent years, to a level of 15 or 16 people expected to carry out many duties. He said there must be some form of protection for seafarers or shipping would die as potential recruits to the industry were deterred. "I feel the seafarer has been let down." Another ex-master complained of lack of official strategy in dealing with the menace, and suggested that navies might be able to stop pirates leaving the shore, although that would mean taking over the beaches.
John Faraclas, a shipping commentator and consultant, said that the piracy-hit area should be declared a war zone "with whatever this entails." He added: "We should go and smash them there."
Participants had no hesitation in responding to the call by the moderator of the debate, Paul Gunton, executive editor of IHS Fairplay, for a robust discussion and for the meeting to explore alternatives to armed guards.

Ms Duvic-Paoli said: "The alternative is political, everyone knows it. The solution is on land, not at sea." She urged insurers to insist that every ship owner followed the Best Management Practices code if they wanted to secure cover.

Jim Davis, chairman of the International Maritime Industries Forum, and a WISTA-UK Ambassador, presided over the event. He said that the problem of maritime kidnapping called for a short-term approach of carrying armed people on board, as crews of just 15 on very large ships could not be expected to look after themselves without help.
He felt that the problem of rules of engagement had not been raised clearly during the debate: the present rules of engagement were shackling such forces as there were.
In the medium term, said Mr Davis, "we must get the United Nations behind us. In the long term, there is the need to address the question of an anarchic, totally poor country [Somalia]."

Mr Davis summed up: "The freedom of the high seas and trading thereon is one of the oldest legal requirements. That must be reinforced. On land, too, in Somalia we have a big job to do."

ICoC
International Code of Conduct for Private Security Service Providers

International Code of Conduct for private security providers: a multi-stakeholder Initiative of the 21st century?

In Geneva, November 2010, nearly 50 global private security firms came together to sign an International Code of Conduct (ICoC) with the objective of strengthening respect for human rights and humanitarian law within their operations. In addition to those who participated in the Geneva meeting, more companies have endorsed the Code by letter with the number of signatory companies now at 70. These companies are a diverse group – ranging from small and medium sized service providers to the largest in the sector. Some specialise in governmental services as well as protection services for extractive industries.

Representatives of NGOs, media and maritime security took part in the event, as did armed security providers for National Parks and endangered species in Africa. In addition to CEOs and senior management representatives, high-ranking officials from endorsing governments, such as the United Kingdom and the United States of America also participated in the signing of the Code. A number of other interested governments including Afghanistan, Australia, Canada and South Africa together with representatives from civil society, humanitarian organizations and academia also took part.

The signatures commit these companies to a set of principles set out in 70 paragraphs guiding employees and managers in their conduct as well as overall company management in ensuring respect for human rights and international law.

The International Code of Conduct was developed through a multi-stakeholder process (for background documents see: BHRRC facilitated by DCAF). Why is this new Code necessary? Indeed, many label private security industries "guns for hire" or "21st century mercenaries", indicating their unlawfulness.

The fact that these companies often operate in contexts in which governmental authority is absent or the rule of law is compromised does not mean that they operate outside of the law, nor does it mean that the provision of security services aims to replace governmental state sovereignty over the use and legitimate exercise of force.

There is no one solution that fits all and regulatory efforts range from a restatement of international law such as was achieved by the Montreux Document to a new convention, elements of which have been presented by a UN working group.

Different legal regimes have different means and abilities to ensure that private security providers operate in a manner which is consistent with international human rights standards. But in certain circumstances these traditional regimes fail to provide accountability for human rights abuses. Therefore the ICoC is important: "for by bringing together all of the key stakeholders—states, civil society organizations, relevant experts, clients, and the private security companies themselves — this initiative has the potential to address gaps in oversight and accountability left by traditional regimes" in the words of legal advisor HaraldKoh who spoke at the Geneva signing event.

The ICoC is more than just a "gap filler" or a normative reaffirmation by non-state actors. The Code is a practice-oriented tool. Not only is the number of signatory companies impressive (three times more members than currently participate in the Voluntary Principles on Security and Human Rights for example) but so too is the substance of the principles the Code affirms. It refers specifically to the UN "Protect, Respect, Remedy" framework on human rights and business developed by SRSG John Ruggie as well as to the Montreux Document on governmental obligations.

The Montreux Document clearly links with the "Protect Pillar" of the UN framework. Similarly, the ICoC is addressing the "Respect Pillar" while the commitment of the industry to develop measurable standards, external oversight and an accountability mechanism within the next 18 months reinforces the UN framework's "Remedy Pillar".

The commitment goes further. Take for example the Code's provisions concerning use of force and firearms: Under current international humanitarian law, personnel of private security providers would lose their status as civilians if participating in hostilities in armed international conflicts. When properly incorporated into armed forces they might even enjoy privileges as combatants. Under the ICoC these activities are not legitimate. Furthermore, the use of firearms is restricted to the exceptional use for "self-defence or defence of others against the imminent threat of death or serious injury, or to prevent the perpetration of a particularly serious crime involving grave threat to life." Suggesting that these codes of conduct are "soft law" wrongly indicates that they are not binding on those involved and that violations have no consequences.

Those who witnessed the negotiations between governments, clients, NGOs and service providers leading up to the ICoC will attest to the fact that discussions had anything but a soft character. Apart from being the basis for the development of an external oversight and accountability mechanism, the ICoC will be stronger than any other existing multi-stakeholder tool for ensuring corporate responsibilities.

The Code is meant to be included in service contracts and the U.S. and U.K. governments will include its provisions in their own security service procurements. Other governments and clients are encouraged to do the same. Once the ICoC is included into a contract, the violation of human rights becomes a reason for contract litigation. Such litigation and the possibility of exclusion from being signatory to the ICoC could go far beyond any consequences of violations of "hard law".

Unfortunately, the breaching of human rights treaty obligations cause few legal and political consequences, which makes the impact of being signatory to the International Code of Conduct all the more important.

The ICoC concludes: "Those establishing this Code recognize that this Code acts as a founding instrument for a broader initiative to create better governance, compliance and accountability. Recognizing that further effort is necessary to implement effectively the principles of this Code, Signatory Companies accordingly commit to work with states, other Signatory Companies, Clients and other relevant stakeholders after initial ndorsement of this Code to, within 18 months: to establish objective and measurable standards [..] and to establish external independent mechanisms for effective governance and oversight."

This timeline for institution building, including development of external oversight and accountability mechanisms, presents an ambitious agenda for the next 18 months. But it is not an impossible agenda to achieve. Commitment and hard work are always necessary to turn an idea into reality. The ICoC should come into effect in Mar-Apr 2012.

As of Nov 2012, no modern ship has ever been hijacked with an armed security team onboard.

Unfortunately some authorities, P&I clubs and shipping companies have no real understanding of maritime security and make decisions upon inaccurate information or self-assumptions. A pair of covert marksmen can accurately shoot the outboard motor (OBM) of a skiff that is attempting to board, thus disabling it without even having to engage the pirates themselves. If a former Royal Marine sniper can shoot bulls eyes at 900m at Bisley Shooting Ranges, and eliminate terrorists in dusty, high-stress battles, then to calmly place warning shots in non-dangerous areas, or need be destroy the OMB of a skiff at less than 100m, is very easy for him to do even from the rolling and pitching ship. It makes no difference whether it is a single skiff attack or 30 skiffs, they cannot board with these men on the bridge wings. If those men are from an unprofessional background, or inadequately trained, then that is something different again and that guarantee cannot be made.

Actual event 7th Dec 2008 Gulf of Aden[14]

Names have been removed.

The brave trio defied the gun-toting gang by every means possible – including using home-made weapons.
But the odds were just too great… and they were forced to jump 50ft into the shark-infested sea to avoid being killed or held as hostages.

They endured 40 agonising minutes being shot at in the water before a rescue helicopter arrived.

The three, working as security men on the ship, are the first Britons to escape from the pirates holding the world to ransom by ambushing ships off the coast of Somalia, East Africa.

MV Biscaglia

Ex-Para M said: "It was terrifying. The pirates shot at us with AK-47s while we tried to tackle them with anything we had to hand – scaffolding poles and flare guns. We intended to take them out and grab the ship back, but there were too many of them. We knew if they caught us we'd be dead. We had to take our chances with the sharks."

Ten days later, Mike, 36, ex-Royal Marine C, 44, and another ex-military pal who does not want to be named, were paid £10,000 a month to safeguard the MV Biscaglia as it sailed through the same treacherous waters.

Long before the pirates boarded, the crew should all have been in the citadel

Maritime law banned any weapons being taken on board, but their employers,……… Security Services of Poole, Dorset, promised the ship would be equipped with "deterrents". C said: "The ship had water cannon and a sonic device which we were told was so painful any pirates would scarper. We also made a bazooka from a scaffolding pole and flares." The Biscaglia and 18 other cargo vessels at first sailed with a French frigate for protection. But two days out of Oman, 300 miles off the Somali coast, it fell behind. M, from Dublin, said: "We noticed a skiff about three miles off our port side – and knew it was pirates."

---

14 Story courtesy of the Susie Boniface Daily/Sunday Mirror

The Biscaglia sent a distress signal to the frigate as the skiff circled the tanker staying well out of range of water cannons.M said: “We used our makeshift bazooka but it was wildly inaccurate and the pirates started firing rocket-propelled grenades.”

The security men decide to abandon ship

While two pirates stayed in the skiff, six scrambled on board, firing AK-47s at the bridge where the three men were masterminding the defence.
C, from Poole, said: “They started shooting at me and I ran with them coming after me. They were only about 18, skinny and looked high on the local drug, called khat. They were spraying bullets everywhere.”
The men decided to use the sonic weapon, called an L-RAD. M said: “We thought it would make the pirates back off, but they just laughed. It was a total waste of time.”

The trio locked all the hatches and doors and retreated to the roof of the bridge. Half an hour after the attack had begun, a helicopter from the French warship appeared. Although it was armed, it is against maritime laws in the area to board a vessel by force after it has been taken by pirates. So the helicopter crew were forced to hover and photograph events from above.
M said: “We decided the best thing to do was maybe hiding somewhere and then take the pirates out. We heard shooting and glass breaking and realised they’d got onto the bridge. “The pirates made the crew kneel outside the bridge with their hands on their head.
A couple stood over them with guns. In one of the pictures, you can see I’ve crept forward to the edge of the roof. The pirates don’t know where we are. “C is behind me. We found some iron bars and our plan was for C to jump off the roof, bringing a bar down on the head of one pirate. “We thought there were only three of them and after taking out one we’d be able to handle the other two. But then one of the crew gestured at us that there were six pirates – and we knew we had no chance of taking them on.” C added: “We didn’t want to leave the crew. They have families too. But we’d p***** the pirates off and the chances were we’d get a bullet each.

“At best we’d have a beating and, because of our British passports, be high-value hostages. So we decided the only option was to go over the side.” The pirates shot at the men as they made a dash for it.
And they continued trying to kill them as they floated in the water. Eventually, a second helicopter arrived with a winch and hauled them to safety. Now home, they say there needs to be a drastic change in the way the world deals with the bandits – who net millions in ransom from firms in return for crews and cargo.

Luckily the unharmed men were saved by a Lynx Helicopter

C said: "They know we can't really fight back. It's easy money – and something must be done." It is easy to look back in hindsight and make judgement, but on this particular task, errors were made and the plan didn't work. It was a difficult job for the unarmed security men, but the company promising them that no pirate would board the vessel with the equipment provided, was not correct.

The LRAD is a very good piece of equipment when used in the correct environment or in the perfect conditions. It was designed for urban use; for the confined streets of a city where the sound is channelled, not for a skiff full of determined pirates sitting next to one or two high-decibel engines, with the sound of wind rushing past their ears. The surface of the sea will alone dissipate the sound waves. It has been used in the past and has contributed to pirates not boarding a vessel, but don't rely 100% on this piece of equipment alone.

A bad situation, becoming worse.

There are drills and there is a scale of escalated threat where upon the ship's crew should have reacted accordingly. The above scene should never have happened. When the pirates successfully boarded the ship, personnel should have been locked securely away, the ship immobilised and distress calls made.

When in HRAs abide by the information given in BMP4 and in addition use a reputable, professional security company. Use equipment that is proven to work. Ensure that a thorough briefing has been given prior to departure and that drills are frequently rehearsed by ALL onboard.

If the three men were armed then the outcome would have much different. Maritime law should be updated to allow vessels to easily have weapons onboard, perhaps in future the larger shipping companies will have their own weapons in the ship's armoury and place their own company security men onboard for the high risk transits, thus lowering expenditure on insurance and private security.

If your onboard security team look and behave like this, then chose another security company!

As of May 2012, there is footage of an American vessel security team (VPT) engaging pirates with no self discipline or fire control at all. This 'spray and pray' attitude is one that has been seen in conflict zones such as Iraq and Afghanistan. There is no need for this type or irresponsible and unprofessional behavior. It is exactly the type of footage that gives the industry a bad name. Authorities such as the IMO do not recommend armed security, only that it should be considered once every possible other action has been carried out. With cowboy behavior like this, armed security will never be recommended. Those individuals should never be allowed to work with/carry firearms again.

The scale of escalation: This is what should occur when armed pirates approach:

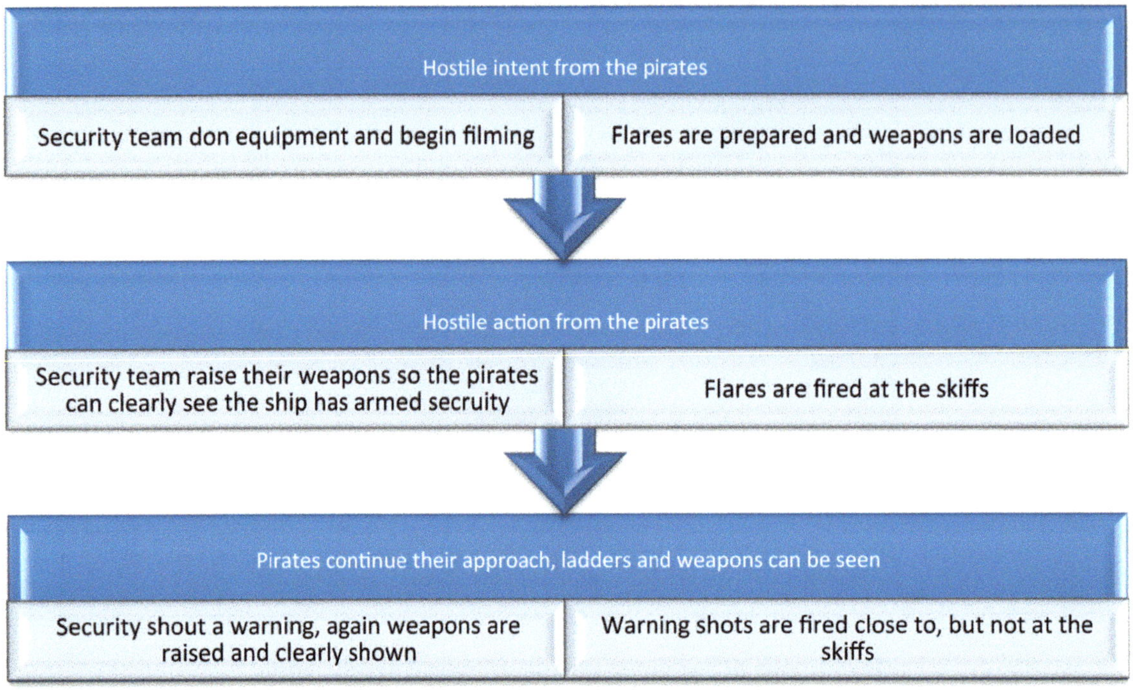

Normally at this point, the pirates will abort their assault and pursue an unarmed vessel.

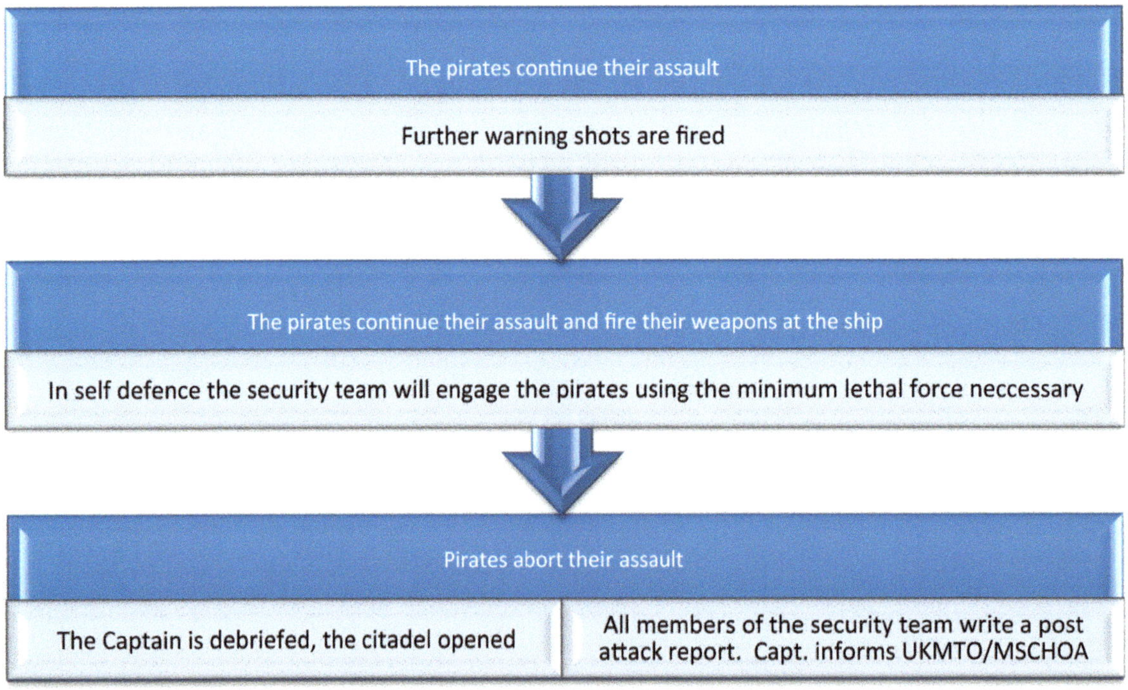

Armed security personnel are not employed to kill people; they are there to protect the crew, the ship, and her cargo from pirates and thieves. If used, they must be professionally trained and certified.

Scale of escalation

(Pictorial) Permission from Neptune Maritime Security

Scenario: The ship is 5 nautical miles SE from Point B of the IRTC, Gulf of Aden.

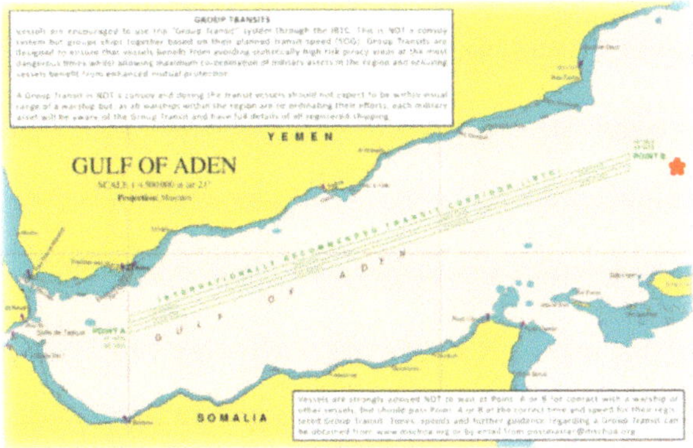

A wooden fishing dhow has been spotted by the MSO, on the horizon, with two whites skiffs close to it The Captain has reported the situation to the local coalition warship on VHF Ch16.

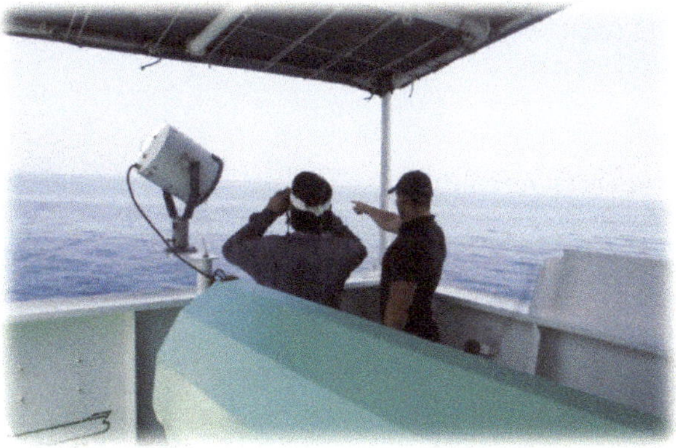

The MSO points out the target to the port sentry and calls the remaining team members.

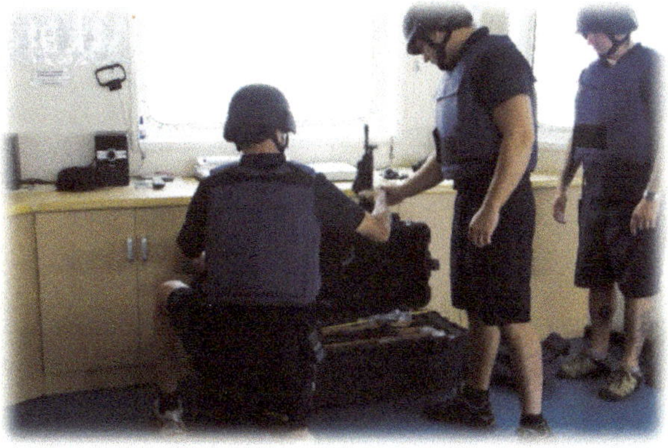

The VPT immediately move to the port bridge wing and the skiffs are shown to the team using the clock-ray method: 2 skiffs, 9 o-clock, 6 miles. They don their equipment ensuring wpns are kept 'muzzles up'.

Safely, quickly and methodically the weapons are moved outside and loaded, facing out to sea.

The team leader issues a verbal warning, most likely not heard, so the team visually shows the skiffs that there is an armed team on board.

The VPT fire two rocket-flares close to the skiffs, the team leader films the action with an image-stabilised camcorder for legal evidence. Again, the VPT show they are armed and look for piracy equipment such as ladders and weapons.

A ladder, RPG and AK47 have been seen; the pirates continue their hostile intent. Whilst filming the team leader tells each member to fire 2 warning shots close to the skiffs.

The Captain is updated via the 4th team radio; the crew moves from the muster point to the citadel.

As soon as the 4 shots were fired, the pirates broke off their attack and returned to their mothership. The weapons are unloaded and checked by the team leader before being cleaned and returned to their box. The Captain informs the citadel and sends the attack report to the UKMTO/MSCHoA. The VPT then inform the security company of the incident and burn the video footage to DVD and write the post incident report.

Piracy Warnings via Inmarsat

Next is a message sent from the IMB to all stations via the Inmarsat C system. Although many people, companies and global authorities don't like, encourage or endorse armed security onboard vessels, the below information gives a very clear picture that all vessels with armed security prevented pirates from boarding, hijacking or the harming of the crew. The firing of flares and warning shots by security personnel was enough to deter all attacks. The vessel that didn't use armed security was successfully boarded, the citadel was breached and that vessel and crew are now in the hands of the Somali pirates.

LES 328 - MSG 4145 - NavWarn Safety Call to Area: 30+60 S 20+120 E - PosOK
FROM 165.21.245.44 13-APR-2011 00:03:51 MSG712913 SENTOSA C LES
130001 UTC APR 2011
ANTI PIRACY SITREP MSG: P086/2011
THIS BROADCAST WARNS SHIPS IN PASSAGE IN EAST AFRICA, THE INDIAN SUB CONTINENT AND SOUTH EAST ASIAN WATERS REGARDING PIRACY AND ARMED ROBBERY.

WARNING WARNING WARNING

East Africa

Gulf of Aden, south Red Sea/Bab el Mandeb, off Yemen, Arabian Sea/off Oman, off eastern, northern and southern Somali coast, off neighbouring Kenya, off Tanzania, off Seychelles, off Madagascar, off Mozambique, Indian Ocean and west and south India and west Maldives. Somali pirates also seen attacking vessel close to coast of Tanzania, Kenya, Yemen and Oman. Vessels hogging these coasts should take additional measures and maintain effective lookout/watch. All ships are advised to monitor IMB PRC warnings that are transmitted when an actual or attempted attack takes place. Warnings will also include the description of the pirate skiffs and/or location of pirate mother vessels and other details if available.

Recently, Somali pirates are using hijacked ocean going fishing vessels and hijacked vessels to conduct piracy operations. Ships are advised to maintain a strict 24 hr visual and radar watch as early detection and assessment will allow masters to take evasive actions and increase speed to escape. At the same time to report to the authorities and request for assistance. Monitor and keep clear of all small boats if possible. Adhere to the latest BMP recommendations. Somali pirates are well armed with automatic weapons and RPG using mother vessels to conduct attacks far from Somali coast. For Gulf of Aden transit, ships are advise to follow recommended schedule and register with EU at www.mschoa.org .

Actual and attempted incidents

12.11.2011: 1218 UTC: Posn: 13:40n - 049:56e, Gulf of Aden.

Six pirates armed with RPG and guns in a skiff chased and fired upon a product tanker underway with intent to hijack. Master raised alarm. Armed security team onboard the vessel exchanged fire with the skiff resulting in the skiff moving away.

11.04.2011: 1005 UTC: Posn: 12:31n - 043:38e, Gulf of Aden.

A passenger ship underway noticed a group of about 20 skiffs near the port bow at a distance of 3nm. Five skiffs were seen to break out from this group and head towards the vessel.
At a distance of around 600-700 meters the armed security team noticed around five to seven pirates armed with RPG and guns were seen in each skiff and instructed all crewmembers to stay inside the ship. As the skiffs approached closer the security team fired warning shots and the skiffs moved away. At the same time three more skiffs approached the vessel from the Stbd side at a distance of 800 meters. The security team noticed arms onboard these skiffs and fired warning shots when the skiffs closed to a distance of 600 - 300 meters. The pirates aborted the attempted attack and moved away. Master informed a warship in the vicinity and all ships in the area via vhf channel 16.

Part (ii) recently reported incidents

Actual and attempted attacks

10.04.2010: 1115 UTC: Posn: 12:02n - 045:08e: Gulf of Aden.

While underway a chemical tanker noticed one white and one blue skiff heading towards the vessel. Four persons were seen in the white skiff and five persons in the blue skiff. Crew alerted and armed security guards made themselves on the bridge wings. The skiffs approached to around 500 meters and the security team fired warning shots resulting in the skiffs moving away. The skiffs continued to follow the vessel for around 15minutes before finally moving away.

08.04.2011: 0234 UTC: Posn: 18:25n - 057:27e: 30nm of Ras al Masirah, Oman.

About ten armed pirates boarded a general cargo ship underway. The ten crewmembers went into the citadel and requested for assistance. Pirates managed to get access into the citadel and took hostage the crewmembers and took command of the vessel.

05.04.2011: 0430 lt: Posn: 01:45.22n - 101:22.17e, Indopalm terminal, Lubuk Gaung, Dumai, Indonesia.

Five robbers in a small boat approached and came alongside a chemical tanker at berth. One of the robbers attempted to climb onboard using the fire wire. Duty crew noticed the robbers and informed other crewmembers. The robbers aborted the attempted boarding upon seeing the crewmembers on deck.

05.04.2011: 0628 UTC: Posn: 16:00.6n - 059:52.1e, around 375nm ne of Socotra island.

Two large white hulled skiffs were noticed approaching a tanker underway at a distance of 2.5 nm. Master raised alarm and all crew except for the duty crew mustered in the safe room.
The security team onboard fired rocket flares as a warning. The skiffs ignored this and continued to approach the tanker at high speed and at a distance of 600meters the security team fired warning shots. One skiff stopped while the other continued its approach. The security team reported that this skiff fired upon the vessel as it approached. The security team returned fire resulting in the skiff aborting the attempted attack.

03.04.2011: 0205 UTC: Posn: 05:35s - 040:20e, around 30nm se of Pemba Island, Tanzania.

Pirates in two skiffs armed with RPG and guns chased and fired upon a bulk carrier underway with intent to hijack. Master raised alarm, increased speed and commenced evasive manoeuvres resulting in the skiffs moving away. After a while the skiffs resumed the chase but aborted after a while.

03.04.2011: 0100 lt: Posn: 01:07s - 117:15e, Samarinda anchorage, Indonesia.
Robbers boarded a general cargo ship at anchor. They broke the padlocks on the bosun store and stole ship's stores and escaped upon seeing the duty crew on patrol. Port authorities informed.

02.04.2011: 0745 UTC: Posn: 15:21.9n - 051:59.3e, around 17nm se of Qishn, Yemen, (Gulf of Aden).

A skiff with three pirates onboard came within 10 meters of a bulk carrier underway. Onboard security team fired warning shots and the skiff moved away. Small arms were sighted in the skiff.

01.04.2011: 1232 UTC: Posn: 14:05n - 051:43e, Gulf of Aden.

A chemical tanker underway noticed a suspicious fishing vessel. After monitoring the vessel for some time it was observed that a skiff as being launched which then headed directly for the tanker. Alarm sounded and navies contacted. Armed security team fired rocket flares in the direction of the approaching skiff. The pirates continued to approach the vessel and fired RPG and guns towards the vessel. The security team onboard returned fire and the pirates aborted the attack and moved towards their mother vessel. No injuries to crew and damages to the tanker.

The picture is very clear that professional armed security teams do work. If you do decide to use them, as the IMO and IMB state, ensure that they are from a reputable company and are verified as being safe and competent.

Training companies Trident Ltd and 3RG both run courses to teach the on board security teams to the highest possible standard. Having attended an ISPS SSO's course and a STCW 95 course will not make a person a professional armed guard, a more thorough training package such as these mentioned is required.
Hopefully the UK government will regulate the industry in the future as the SIA regulated Close Protection Officers and bodyguards. This will standardise the industry and shipping companies will know that their security teams are trained and regulated.

If armed guards are to be used, ensure they are from a reputable and professional company.
Photo: Solace Global Maritime

The Montreux Document in a nutshell

What it is:

The Montreux Document is an intergovernmental document intended to promote respect for international humanitarian law and human rights law whenever PMSCs are present in armed conflicts. It is not legally binding as such; rather, it contains a compilation of relevant international legal obligations and good practices. The Montreux Document is the result of an international process launched by the Government of Switzerland and the ICRC. It was finalized by consensus on 17 September 2008 by 17 States:

Afghanistan, Angola, Australia, Austria, Canada, China, France, Germany, Iraq, Poland, Sierra Leone, South Africa, Sweden, Switzerland, the United Kingdom of Great Britain and Ireland, Ukraine and the United States of America. The number of participating States is growing steadily.

For up-to-date information on participation, see www.eda.admin.ch/psc

What it does: The Montreux Document.

• recalls the pertinent international legal obligations of States, PMSCs and their personnel in situations of armed conflict;
• contains a compilation of good practices designed to help States take national measures to implement their obligations;
• highlights the responsibilities of three types of States: Contracting States (countries that hire PMSCs), Territorial States (countries on whose territory PMSCs operate) and Home States (countries in which PMSCs are based);
• makes it clear that States have an obligation to ensure respect for international humanitarian law and to uphold human rights law; as a result, they have a duty to take measures designed to prevent misconduct by PMSCs and ensure accountability for criminal behaviour;
• recalls that PMSCs and their personnel are bound by international humanitarian law and must respect its provisions at all times during armed conflict, regardless of their status;
• recalls that misconduct on the part of PMSCs and their personnel can trigger responsibility on two levels: first, the criminal responsibility of the perpetrators and their superiors, and second, the responsibility of the State that gave instructions for directed or controlled the misconduct;
• provides a toolkit for governments to establish effective oversight and control over PMSCs, for example through contracts or licensing/authorization systems.

Why it is useful? The Montreux Document is useful because it enhances the protection afforded to people affected by armed conflicts. It does so by clarifying and reaffirming international law, by encouraging the adoption of national regulations on PMSCs designed to strengthen respect for international law, and by offering guidance on how and in what light this should be done, based on lessons learnt.

'Pirate' death puts spotlight on 'guns for hire'[15]

The death of a suspected pirate off the coast of Somalia has drawn attention to the use of armed private security contractors on board merchant vessels.

The incident, which involved guards aboard the Panamanian-flagged MV Almezaan, is believed to be the first of its kind. But several organisations, including the International Maritime Bureau (IMB), have previously expressed concerns over the use of armed security contractors. "While we understand that owners want to protect their ships, we don't agree in principle with putting armed security on ships," IMB director Capt Pottengal Mukundan told the BBC News website. "Ships are not an ideal place for a gun battle." One argument is that the use of armed operatives could encourage pirates to use more violence when taking a ship. But Mr Mukundan said he had seen no evidence that there had been much of an increase in the use of armed guards by merchant ship owners. Dozens of warships patrol the waters off the Somali coast, but this has not deterred the pirates. The amount of ocean to patrol is extremely vast and pirates have responded to the increased naval presence by moving attacks farther out to sea. "The naval forces are displacing the threat - they can't be everywhere at once," says Nick Davis, chief executive of Merchant Maritime Warfare Centre, a not-for-profit organisation. "Almost the whole of the Indian Ocean region - some 5 million square nautical miles - is a security risk."

Prevention

But the shipping industry has, so far, largely resisted arming their boats - not least because this would deny them port in some nations. Furthermore, arming the ships can raise liability issues and increase insurance costs. Christopher Ledger, director of security firm Idarat Maritime, says the use of private operatives is not necessary and that ship owners can find other ways to protect themselves, such as boosting training, carrying out more drills and purchasing equipment that could prevent pirates boarding a vessel. "Private security guards are not necessary, they simply muddy the water," he said. "They are often foreign to the crew themselves and they don't know the ship well. "Many are former soldiers that have been in Iraq or Afghanistan and they think they can shake the dust off their shoes and make it as a private security guard. Their day rate is pretty high and the crew have to find ways to get them on and off the vessels." Their presence, he said, would only lead to "more spilt blood". This month, international shipping law firm Ince and Co released a report highlighting the issues arising from the use of armed guards. It pointed out that a fundamental question arose as to who would authorise the use of force. Stephen Askins, a lawyer with Ince, told the BBC News website that the debate on the use of armed guards was one that polarised the industry. "Most industry bodies and ship-owners are against them," he said. "But no ship with an armed guard has been hijacked, so there are those - particularly those who have had hijacked ships - who think they are necessary." He said private security companies had come into their own in places like Iraq and had seen seen the maritime sector as potentially lucrative. "Many have moved across but there is no system of accreditation, so there is no way of knowing the good from the bad," he said.

Legal status

Most security operatives are former British servicemen, but there are also operatives from the US, Australia, New Zealand and South Africa. Mr Askins said some firms provided armed escort vessels, but that these did not have any status in international law. "The various conventions dealing with piracy relate to states and their navies," he said.

[15] By Kathryn Westcott BBC News

"The rights that they are given, like the right of innocent passage relate to military ships. There are also issues over the use of armed force. The relevant law is the law of the flag state, but a merchant ship could, for example, be Panamanian and the escort ship could be, say, UK flagged." But he also pointed out that there were some very good companies that had "robust rules of engagement". "Lethal force for them would come after a series of steps including warning shots. The good companies would follow that procedure. Normally that would be enough to deter an attack." In May 2009, the US Coast Guard drafted a maritime security directive that would require US-flagged ships sailing around the Horn of Africa to post guards, and ship owners to submit anti-piracy security plans for approval.

At the time, the Coast Guard's director of prevention policy, Rear Admiral James Watson, said that they expected to see "additional security" that could "involve the use of firearms". He added that they were "looking for things that work but that doesn't make the situation worse". The directive has not yet passed into law.

For now, the handling of Tuesday's shooting by a private security operative will be watched closely by legal experts. An independent inquiry is planned, but first investigators will need to establish who had jurisdiction - the flag the vessel was flying, its owners or the nationality of the contractors - and who was responsible for the security contractors.

EU calls for rules on ship guards after Italy-India spat 15th March 2012

The European Union called for international rules on the use of armed guards aboard ships amid a diplomatic spat between Italy and India over two Italian marines jailed in the south Asian country. EU foreign policy chief Catherine Ashton discussed the issue with Italian Prime Minister Mario Monti in Brussels after the two oil tanker guards allegedly killed two Indian fishermen they mistook for pirates last month.

"She underlined the need to put this incident into the broader context of international cooperation on counter-piracy and more specifically on the issue of regulating the protection aboard ships," her office said in a statement.

Several nations have allowed shipping companies to hire armed guards to protect their ships sailing through pirate-infested waters off the Horn of Africa, stirring a debate about their use. The two Italian marines have been imprisoned in India's southern state of Kerala pending a murder investigation despite pressure from Italy for them to be handed over to Rome for prosecution.
Italy argues India does not have jurisdiction in the case as it involved an Italian-flagged vessel and occurred in international waters near India. India disputes this, saying the incident happened in waters under its jurisdiction. Ashton's spokeswoman, Maja Kocijancic, told reporters that the EU was in contact with Italian and Indian authorities in the hope of finding a "satisfactory resolution of this case as soon as possible."

She said the EU, which has deployed navies to police the coast of Somalia since 2008, would like the use of armed guards regulated within the International Maritime Organization, a UN agency."This is a much broader issue that needs to be addressed in order to make sure we do not see incidents and problems that we are faced with in this particular case, and that's why we are keen to take this forward," Kocijancic said.

17. Maritime Law

It is strongly recommended that a reputable maritime lawyer is contacted for expert and detailed information regarding armed security on vessels. However, listed below are some of the many maritime laws that may and most probably will affect a sailor's position with regard to self defence and the systems used.

A BRIEF OVERVIEW

The United Nations Convention on the Law of the Sea (UNCLOS), also called the Law of the Sea Convention or the Law of the Sea Treaty, is the international agreement that resulted from the third United Nations Conference on the Law of the Sea (UNCLOS III), which took place from 1973-1982. The Law of the Sea Convention defines the rights and responsibilities of nations in their use of the world's oceans, establishing guidelines for businesses, the environment and the management of marine natural resources. The convention, concluded in 1982, replaced four 1958 treaties. UNCLOS came into force in 1994, a year after Guyana became the 60th state to sign the treaty. To date, 158 countries and the European Community have joined in the convention. However, it is now regarded as a codification of the customary international law on the issue.

UNCLOS sets the limit of various areas, measured from a carefully defined baseline. (Normally, a sea baseline follows the low-water line, but when the coastline is deeply indented, has fringing islands or is highly unstable, straight baselines may be used.)

The areas are as follows:[16]

- Internal Waters
- Territorial Waters
- Archipelagic Waters
- Contiguous Zone
- Exclusive Economic Zones
- Continental Shelf

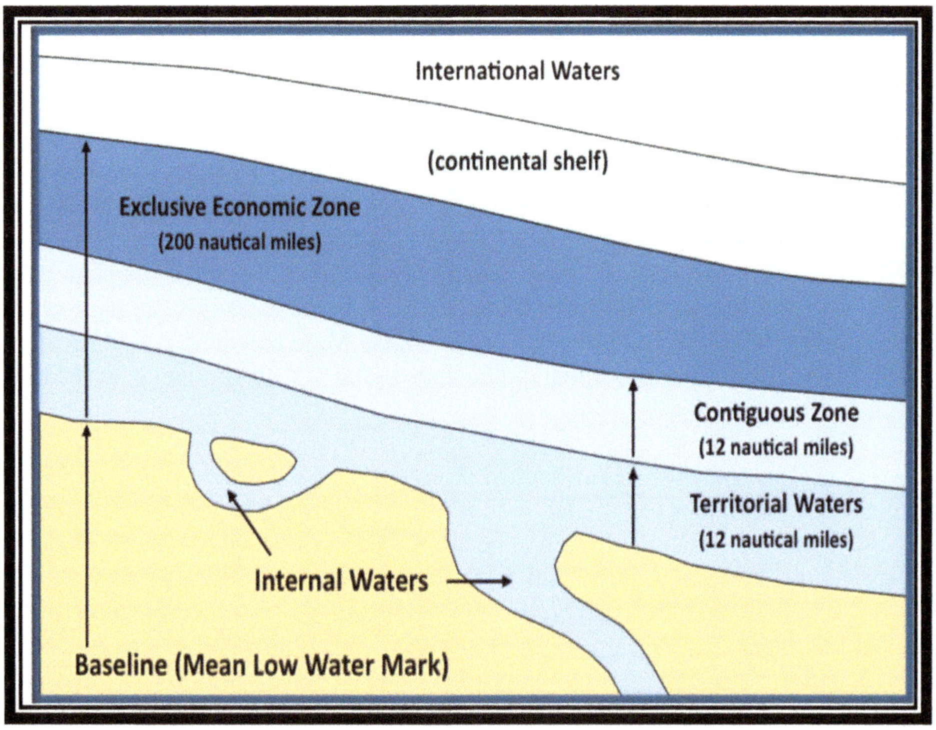

Internal Waters

---

[16] Diagrams courtesy of the IMO

Covers all water and waterways on the landward side of the baseline. The coastal state is free to set laws, regulate use and use any resource. Foreign vessels have no right of passage within Internal Waters.

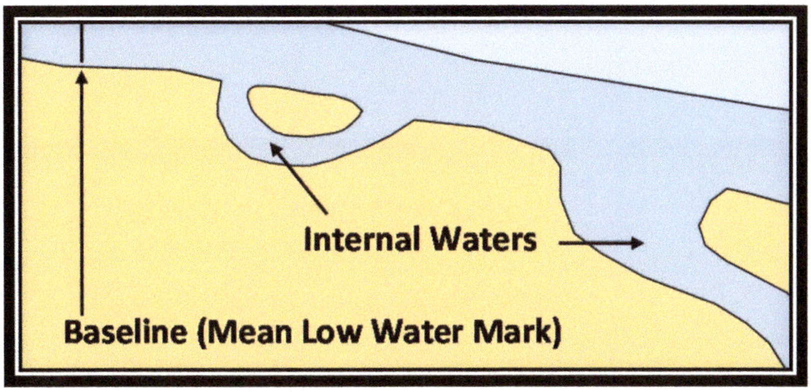

Territorial Waters
Out to 12 nautical miles from the baseline, the coastal state is free to set laws, regulate use and use any resource. Vessels were given the right of 'innocent passage' through any Territorial Waters, with strategic straits allowing the passage of military craft as 'transit passage', in that naval vessels are allowed to maintain postures that would be illegal in Territorial Waters. 'Innocent passage' is defined by the convention as passing through waters in an expeditious and continuous manner, which is not 'prejudicial to the peace, good order or the security' of the coastal state. Fishing, polluting, weapons practice, and spying are not 'innocent'. Nations can also temporarily suspend innocent passage in specific areas of their Territorial Waters, if doing so is essential for the protection of its security.

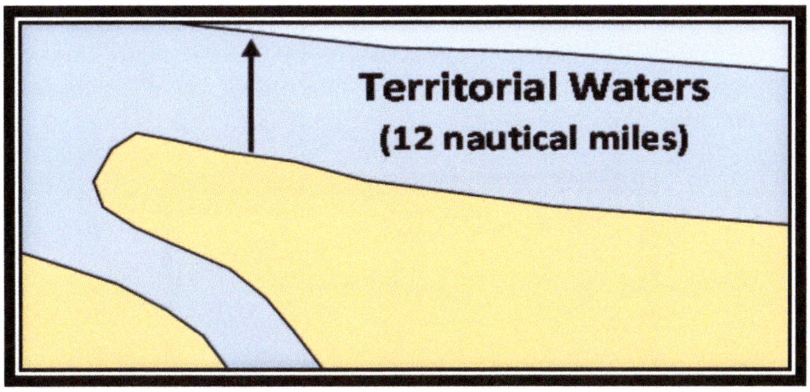

Archipelagic Waters
The convention set the definition of Archipelagic States in Part IV, which also defines how the state can draw its territorial borders. A baseline is drawn between the outermost points of the outermost islands, subject to these points being sufficiently close to one another. All waters inside this baseline are designated Archipelagic Waters. The state has full sovereignty over these waters (like internal waters), but foreign vessels have right of innocent passage through Archipelagic Waters.

Contiguous Zone

Beyond the 12 nautical mile limit there was a further 12 nautical miles or 24 nautical miles from the territorial sea baselines limit, the Contiguous Zone, in which a state could continue to enforce laws in four specific areas: pollution, taxation, customs, and immigration.

Contiguous Zone

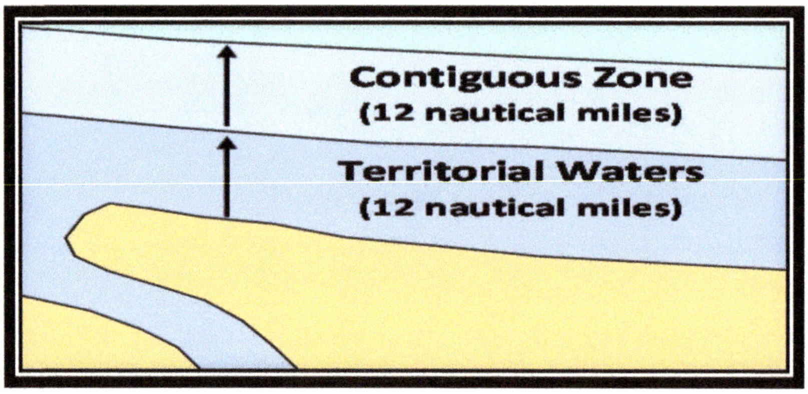

Exclusive Economic Zones (EEZs)

Extend from the edge of the territorial sea out to 200 nautical miles from the baseline. Within this area, the coastal nation has sole exploitation rights over all natural resources. In casual use, the term may include the Territorial Waters and even the Continental Shelf. The EEZs were introduced to halt the increasingly heated clashes over fishing rights, although oil was also becoming important. The success of an offshore oil platform in the Gulf of Mexico in 1947 was soon repeated elsewhere in the world, and by 1970 it was technically feasible to operate in waters 4000 metres deep. Foreign nations have the freedom of navigation and over flight, subject to the regulation of the coastal states. Foreign states may also lay submarine pipes and cables.

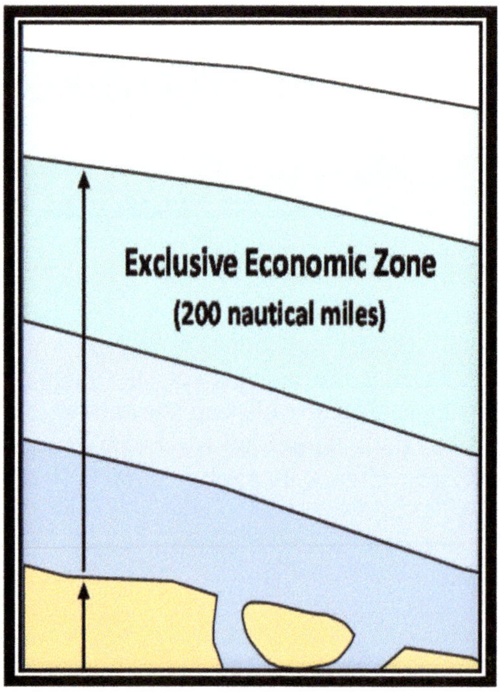

Continental Shelf
The Continental Shelf is defined as the natural prolongation of the land territory to the continental margin's outer edge, or 200 nautical miles from the coastal state's baseline, whichever is greater. A state's Continental Shelf may exceed 200 nautical miles until the natural prolongation ends. However, it may never exceed 350 nautical miles from the baseline; or it may never exceed 100 nautical miles beyond the 2,500-metre isobar (the line connecting the depth of 2,500 metres). Coastal states have the right to harvest mineral and non-living material in the subsoil of their Continental Shelf, to the exclusion of others. Coastal states also have exclusive control over living resources 'attached' to the Continental Shelf, but not to creatures living in the water column beyond the Exclusive Economic Zone.

International Maritime Law – UNCLOS

The following definition of piracy is contained in Article 101 of the 1982 United Nations Convention on the Law of the Sea (UNCLOS):

'Piracy consists of any of the following acts:

(a) Any illegal acts of violence or detention, or any act of depredation, committed for private ends by the crew or the passengers of a private ship or a private aircraft, and directed:

> (i) On the high seas, against another ship or aircraft, or against persons or property on board such ship or aircraft;
> (ii) Against a ship, aircraft, persons or property in a place outside the jurisdiction of any State;

(b) Any act of voluntary participation in the operation of a ship or of an aircraft with knowledge of facts making it a pirate ship or aircraft;

(c)Any act inciting or of intentionally facilitating an act described in sub-paragraph (a) or (b).

Maritime Security Circular MSC.1/Cir 1333 – 26 Jun 09: Recommendations to governments for preventing and suppressing acts of piracy and armed robbery against ships.

Maritime Security Circular MSC.1/Cir 1334 – 23 Jun 09: Guidance to ship owners and ship operators, shipmasters and crew on preventing and suppressing acts of piracy and armed robbery against ships.

Regional Cooperation Agreement on Combating Piracy and Armed Robbery against ships in Asia (ReCAAP)
Regional cooperation among states has an important role to play in solving the problem of piracy and armed robbery against ships, as evidenced by the success of the regional anti-piracy operation in the Strait of Malacca and Singapore. The Regional Cooperation Agreement on Combating Piracy and Armed Robbery against ships in Asia (RECAAP), which was concluded in November 2004 by 16 countries in Asia, and includes the RECAAP Information Sharing Centre (ISC) for facilitating the sharing of piracy-related information, is a good example of successful regional cooperation which IMO seeks to replicate elsewhere.

UNCLOS Flag State of Vessel

UNCLOS specifies the territorial limits of a country and defines whether a vessel is under the laws of its flag state or those of the state whose waters it is lying in.
Vessels are free to navigate the High Seas within the laws of their flag state and only a warship of their own nation has the right to intercept them (other than to confirm the nationality of the vessel) unless they are committing an international crime such as piracy.

Under UNCLOS vessels have a rite of passage through the territorial waters of another country; all vessels exercising this rite of passage must undertake a continuous and expeditious passage though Territorial Waters and may not engage in any activity which does not have direct bearing on the passage.
They must also abide by international conventions – such as Safety of Life at Sea (SOLAS), the International Regulation for Preventing Collisions at Sea (COLREGS) – and the coastal state has the jurisdiction to ensure that they do so.
The coastal state may also have laws and regulations which such vessels must adhere to, to ensure safe navigation, regulation of maritime traffic, protection of navigational aids, facilities, pipelines, and cables, conservation and preservation of the environment and the living resources of the sea (including fisheries laws) and to prevent against infringement of customs, fiscal, immigration or sanitary laws and regulations of the coastal state.
The majority of cruising yachts will not, however, be regarded as being on a continuous and expeditious passage as they may be cruising along the coast, perhaps anchoring for lunch and they may also visit several ports within the coastal state. These activities bring pleasure boaters under the jurisdiction of the coastal state and they could then be required to adhere to all of their regulations.

Flag State of Vessel

UNCLOS also defines a country's Internal Waters (waters which are landward of the baseline) which include many ports, harbours, estuaries and bays and, of course, inland waters such as rivers and canals.
If a vessel makes a continuous and expeditious passage though Territorial Waters to a destination within Internal Waters such as a port, the rite of passage ends on entering Internal Waters. By voluntarily entering a port or the Internal Waters of another country a vessel submits to the jurisdiction of that country, i.e. the coastal or port state, as Internal Waters are considered to be an integral part of a country. The authority of a state over foreign vessels in its Internal Waters is the same as those for a foreigner on its soil, which of course includes boat crews going out for dinner, sightseeing, shopping and generally making use of facilities ashore in their destination port.

The coastal state, however, will generally refrain from interfering with the internal affairs of foreign-flagged vessels as a matter of 'comity' – courteous recognition accorded by one nation to the laws and institutions of another. So unless you attract the attention of the authorities, for example because your boat is deemed not to be seaworthy, you will generally be allowed to go about your business as a visitor without hindrance.

SUA Convention 1988:
Suppression of Unlawful Acts Against the Safety of Maritime Navigation

Adoption:
Entry into force: 1 March 1992

The convention obliges contracting governments either to extradite or prosecute alleged offenders. The main purpose of the convention is to ensure that appropriate action is taken against persons committing unlawful acts against ships. These include:
The seizure of ships by force;
Acts of violence against persons on board ships; and
The placing of devices on board a ship which are likely to destroy or damage it.

International Convention for the Safety of Life at Sea (SOLAS) 1974

IMO's Maritime Safety Committee and Maritime Security Working Group reviewed measures and procedures to prevent acts of terrorism which threaten the security of passengers, crews and the safety of ships.
Amendment to SOLAS Chapter XI-1 (Safety) and new Chapter XI-2 (Security). Used as a vehicle to establish and implement the International Ship and Port Facility Security (ISPS) Code.
International Maritime Law – ISPS (this is covered in Chapter 23)

International Maritime Law – UNSCR

UN Security Council Resolutions:

- In response to growing international concern over the piracy off the coast of Somalia, the UN Security Council adopted Resolution (UNSCR) 1816 in June 2008;
- Encouraged 'states interested in the use of commercial maritime routes off the coast of Somalia, to increase and coordinate their efforts to deter acts of piracy and armed robbery at sea';
- Later that year the Security Council unanimously adopted UNSCR 1838, 1846 and 1851.

Resolution 1846 (2008)

- The Council expressed its concern over the findings of a 20 November report of the Monitoring Group on Somalia that escalating ransom payments were fuelling a growth in piracy off the Somali coast. It called upon states, the IMO and the shipping and insurance industries to appropriately advise and guide ships on how to avoid, evade and defend themselves against attack – Best Management Practices (BMP).
  Adoption of UNSCR 1846 (2008) under Chapter VII:

- UN Council decided that for 12 months states and regional organisations co-operating with the Somali Transitional Federal Government (TFG) may enter Somalia's Territorial Waters and;
- Use 'all necessary means', i.e. deploying naval vessels and military aircraft, as well as seizing and disposing of boats, vessels, arms and related equipment used for piracy;
- To fight piracy and armed robbery at sea off the Somali coast, in accordance with relevant international law.

1851: Adopted 16 December 2008

- Security Council decided that, for 12 months, states and regional organisations co-operating in the fight against piracy and armed robbery at sea off Somalia's coast* could undertake all necessary measures 'appropriate in Somalia', to interdict those using Somali territory to plan, facilitate or undertake such acts.

*For which prior notification had been provided by Somalia's Transitional Federal Government to the Secretary-General.

UN Resolution 733 – Arms Embargo:

- The Security Council first imposed a general and complete arms embargo on Somalia on 23 January 1992 with the adoption of resolution 733.

Armed pirates in the Indian Ocean near Somalia

After the picture was taken, the skiff's crewmembers opened fire on a US navy ship and the US Navy returned fire. One suspected pirate was killed and 12 were taken into custody.

Armed or Unarmed Security Escorts?

International Maritime Law

Who's Law?

- Flag State of Vessel
- US, Russia, Britain and Spain empower private security and ships crews to bear arms

Who is liable?

- Master?
- Individual Security Guard?
- Maritime Security Team Leader?
- Security Company (MST provider)?
- Flag State?
- Owner of the Vessel?

What are the complications?

- Certification of Weapons
- Transport of weapons and documentation
- Recording of weapons – inventory
- Issuing, maintenance and storing of weapons
- Training of armed security guards
- Rules of engagement
- Impact of an armed exchange – leading to lethal force

Use of unarmed security guards

Maritime Security Circular MSC.1/Cir 1333, 1334, 1405 & 1406:

- Use of unarmed security personnel is a matter for ship owners, companies and ship operators to decide
- It should be fully acceptable to provide an enhanced lookout capability this way

Carriage of firearms

Maritime Security Circular MSC.1/Cir 1333, 1334 & FAL 1:

- Flag State should be informed
- Flag State should be informed if entering the Territorial Waters or ports of another state, subject to that state's legislation
- Importation of firearms is subject to the port or coastal state regulations
- Use of firearms may create a greater danger if ship is carrying flammable cargo

Montreux Document:

On 17 September 2008, 17 states including UK finalised the so-called 'Montreux Document on Pertinent International Legal Obligations and Good Practices for States related to Operations of Private Military and Security Companies during Armed Conflict'.
The first international document to describe international law as it applies to the activities of private military and security companies (PMSCs) whenever these are present in the context of an armed conflict. It also contains a compilation of good practices designed to assist states in implementing their obligations under international law through a series of national measures.

Foreign Enlistment (Mercenary) Act 1870

- An offence under the Foreign Enlistment Act 1870 of enlisting oneself or others (except under licence of the Crown) for armed service with a foreign state that is at war with a state with which the UK is at peace
- A foreign state includes part of a province or persons exercising or assuming powers of government
- It is also an offence under the act to build or equip any ship for such service or to fit out any naval or military expedition for use against a state with which the UK is at peace.

Guidelines from the International Maritime Organization

E
MSC.1/Circ.1405/Rev.1
16 September 2011

REVISED INTERIM GUIDANCE TO SHIPOWNERS, SHIP OPERATORS, AND SHIPMASTERS ON THE USE OF PRIVATELY CONTRACTED ARMED SECURITY PERSONNEL ON BOARD SHIPS IN THE HIGH RISK AREA[1]

1 The Maritime Safety Committee, at its eighty-ninth session (11 to 20 May 2011), approved the interim guidance to shipowners, ship operators and shipmasters on the use of privately contracted armed security personnel on board ships in the High Risk Area.

2 Given the importance and urgent nature of the issue, and the need to further develop and promulgate detailed guidance and recommendations as soon as possible, the Committee approved and the Council authorized the convening of an intersessional meeting of the Maritime Security and Piracy Working Group (13 to 15 September 2011) to update the guidance.

3 The Revised interim guidance to shipowners, ship operators and shipmasters on the use of privately contracted armed security personnel on board ships in the High Risk Area is set out in the annex.

4 The attached revised interim guidance should be read in conjunction with the interim recommendations set out in MSC.1/Circ.1406/Rev.1 on Revised interim recommendations for flag States regarding the use of privately contracted armed security personnel on board ships in the High Risk Area, and MSC.1/Circ.1408 on Interim recommendations for port and coastal States regarding the use of privately contracted armed security personnel on board ships in the High Risk Area, and the information provided in MSC-FAL.1/Circ.2 on the Questionnaire on information on port and coastal State requirements related to privately contracted armed security personnel on board ships, as well as the other recommendations and guidance developed by the Organization for preventing and suppressing piracy and armed robbery against ships.

5 Member Governments are urged to bring this circular to the attention of all national agencies concerned with anti-piracy activities, shipowners, ship operators, shipping companies, shipmasters and crews.

6 Member Governments are also urged to take any necessary action to implement, as appropriate, the revised interim guidance given in the annex.

7 Member Governments, international organizations and non-governmental organizations with consultative status are invited to bring to the attention of the Committee, at the earliest opportunity, the results of the experience gained from the use of the revised interim guidance so as to assist the Committee in deciding on any action to be taken.

8 MSC.1/Circ.1405 is hereby revoked.

---

[1] High Risk Area: an area as defined in the Best Management Practices for Protection against Somalia Based Piracy (MSC.1/Circ.1339) unless otherwise defined by the flag State.

ANNEX

REVISED INTERIM GUIDANCE TO SHIPOWNERS, SHIP OPERATORS, AND SHIPMASTERS ON THE USE OF PRIVATELY CONTRACTED ARMED SECURITY PERSONNEL ON BOARD SHIPS IN THE HIGH RISK AREA[1]

1. Introduction

The increased threat to commercial shipping by Somalia-based pirates has led to extended use of armed guards and a marked expansion in the number of firms offering armed maritime security services for vessels transiting the High Risk Area. The Organization, whilst not endorsing the use of privately contracted armed security personnel (PCASP), understands that shipping companies may find it difficult to identify reliable, professional private providers of armed security.

The decision on the employment of PCASP on board ships is a complex one for a ship owner. The absence of applicable regulation and industry self-regulation coupled with complex legal requirements governing the legitimate transport, carriage and use of firearms[2] gives cause for concern. This situation is further complicated by the rapid growth in the number of private maritime security companies (PMSC) and doubts about the capabilities and maturity of some of these companies. Significant competence and quality variations are present across the spectrum of contractors offering services.

The purpose of this guidance is to assist shipowners, ship operators and ship masters considering the use of PCASP on board ships to provide additional protection against piracy.

It is important to note that flag State jurisdiction and thus any laws and regulations imposed by the flag State concerning the use of PMSC and PCASP apply to their vessels. Furthermore it is also important to note that port and coastal States' laws may also apply to such vessels.

The use of PCASP should not be considered as an alternative to Best Management Practices (BMP) and other protective measures. Placing armed guards on board as a means to secure and protect the vessel and its crew should only be considered after a risk assessment has been carried out. It is also important to involve the Master in the decision making process.

1.1
Definitions

High Risk Area: an area as defined in the BMP unless otherwise defined by the flag State.

Private maritime security companies (PMSC): Private contractors employed to provide security personnel, both armed and unarmed, on board for protection against piracy.

Privately contracted armed security personnel (PCASP): armed employees of PMSC.

---

[1] High Risk Area: an area as defined in the Best Management Practices for Protection against Somalia Based Piracy (MSC.1/Circ.1339) unless otherwise defined by the flag State.

2 In the present guidance, all references to firearms include the associated ammunition, consumables, spare parts and maintenance equipment for use by PCASP, and all references to security-related equipment include protective and communication equipment for use by PCASP.

1.2 Risk Assessment

Shipowners should ensure that the flag State is consulted at an early stage in their consideration of the decision to place PCASP on board to ensure that any statutory requirements are met.

Whether to use PCASP within the High Risk Area is a decision for the individual shipowner after a thorough risk assessment and after ensuring all other practical means of self protection have been employed.

The risk assessment should include and document the following factors and considerations, prior to making the determination to take such actions:

.1 vessel and crew security, safety and protection;

.2 whether all practical means of self protection have been effectively implemented in advance;

.3 the potential misuse of firearms resulting in bodily injury or death;

.4 the potential for unforeseen accidents;

.5 liability issues;

.6 the potential for escalation of the situation at hand; and

.7 compliance with international and national law.

2. PMSC Selection Criteria

2.1
General

As with any other type of contractor it is important to undertake the usual due diligence, which normally includes investigation and enquiries in relation to:

.1 Company structure and place of registration;

.2 Company ownership;

.3 financial position (e.g. annual accounts/bank references);

.4 extent of insurance cover (in particular covering third-party risks);

.5 senior management experience; and

.6 quality management indicators – e.g. ISO accreditation.

2.2 PMSC Background Information

To assess the capability of the PMSC to carry out a proposed task, a thorough enquiry regarding the prospective PMSC should be undertaken, particularly in the absence of a robust accreditation scheme for PMSC.

The PMSC should be able to provide documentary evidence which may include:

.1 maritime (as opposed to land-based) experience;

.2 written procedures on management including team-leading skills, chain of authority, change in command, responsibilities in life saving;

.3 understanding of flag State, port State and coastal State requirements with respect to carriage and usage of firearms;

.4 availability of written testimonials/references from previous clients in the maritime industry;

.5 availability of documentary evidence that firearms are procured, transported, embarked and disembarked legally;

.6 understanding of the Somalia-based piracy threat including the military operations in the area, and the means to maintain current knowledge;

.7 understanding of BMP and, in particular, ship protection measures; and

.8 access to legal advice (e.g. in-house counsel / external legal advisers) on a 24/7 basis.

2.3 Selection and Vetting of PMSC

As the quality of the service delivery depends to a very great extent on the quality and experience of the individuals that make up the onboard PCASP team, the quality of the selection and vetting of that team is essential. The PMSC should demonstrate that they have verifiable, written internal policies and procedures for determining suitability of their employees.

The PMSC should be able to provide documentary evidence which may include:

.1 criminal background checks;

.2 history of employment checks;

.3 military and law enforcement background checks, where applicable;

.4 records of medical, physical, and mental fitness of personnel (including drug and alcohol testing);

.5 verifiable system in place to ensure continued suitability for employment of their personnel;

.6 documentary evidence of relevant experience and certification in the use and carriage of firearms to be deployed; and

.7 systems for provision of security identity documentation, travel documents and visas.

2.4 Training of PCASP

As the quality of professional training given to PCASP is of extreme importance, the shipowner should verify that the PMSC have adequate training procedures in place. The records of that training should give confidence that the PCASP have been provided with appropriate knowledge and skills.

The PMSC should be able to provide documentary evidence which may include:

.1 comprehensive and detailed records of training, both initial and refresher training, available for inspection;

.2 subject to any additional requirements of the flag State, PCASP have received, as a minimum, ship-board familiarization training, including communication protocols;

.3 personnel trained and qualified to documented company standards in the appropriate use of force following recognized principles/guidelines recognized by the flag State;

.4 personnel trained to operate the specific firearms and other security equipment that will be used on the vessels on which they will be deployed;

.5 personnel given medical training to a recognized international standard; and

.6 personnel given appropriate training and/or briefing with specific reference to the vessel type, where that vessel will be trading, and the provisions of the International Ship and Port Facility Security (ISPS) Code, International Safety Management (ISM) Code and the BMP.

3. Service Provision Considerations

3.1 Insurance

Owners should verify that PMSC maintain insurance cover for themselves, their personnel and third-party liability cover and that the PMSC terms of engagement do not prejudice or potentially prejudice the shipowners' insurance cover.

Shipowners insurance cover

Liabilities, losses and expenses arising out of the deployment of PCASP may impact on the shipowner's property and liability insurance cover. Shipowners are strongly recommended to consult with their insurers prior to contracting with and embarking PCASP to assess the potential impact on their insurance cover, particularly as it relates to armed engagements and liability insurance held by the PMSC.

PMSC insurance cover

PMSC should provide evidence that they hold and will maintain for the duration of the contract:

.1 public and employers liability insurance cover to an appropriate level and as required by the shipowner; and
.2 personal accident, medical expenses, hospitalization and repatriation insurance.

The PMSC should insure its personnel to carry and use firearms on the high seas and territorial sea(s), for accident, injury and damage arising from the use of firearms and liability for any claim that might arise from the carriage and the use of firearms.

It is vital that shipowners, charterers and underwriters review all provisions in their charters and policies and ensure adequate attention is paid to the questions raised.

3.2 PCASP Team Size, Composition and Equipment

The size, composition and equipment of the proposed PCASP team should be carefully discussed and agreed as necessary by the shipowner contracting with the PMSC. Factors for consideration may include:

.1 **Size of the PCASP Team** – this will be influenced by factors including: length of the estimated time of the vessel transit, latest threat assessment, the agreed duties of the PCASP team (will they act as additional lookouts, assist with rigging self protection measures?) and the size and type of vessel.
The analysis should indicate the minimum number of persons that should form the security team, taking into account the need for continuity of protection in the event of injury or illness.

.2 **Ship safety certificate** – the size of the PCASP team plus the crew should not exceed that specified in the Ship's Safety Certificate. If the ship safety certificate requirements cannot be met due to added security personnel, then the flag Administration should be consulted.

.3 **Composition** – it is important that there is an appropriate hierarchy, experience and skill mix within the onboard PCASP team. The team leader should be competent in vessel vulnerability and risk assessments and be able to advise on ship protection measures. It is recommended that one of the PCASP personnel be qualified as the team medic.

.4 **Equipment requirements** – this will be influenced by factors including: length of the estimated time of the vessel transit, latest threat assessment, the agreed duties of the PCASP team, (will they act as additional lookouts, utilize day and night vision equipment, assist with rigging self protection measures?) and the size and type of vessel. Enhanced medical equipment is recommended.

.5 **Firearms** – the appropriate firearms package to be employed in accordance with the applicable flag State national legislation pertaining to the type, carriage and use of firearms by PCASP, in order to provide an accurate and graduated level of deterrence, at a distance.

3.3 Command and Control of Onboard Security Team – including relationship with the Master

A shipowner / operator when entering into a contract with a PMSC should ensure that the command and control structure linking the ship operator, the Master, the ship's officers and the PCASP team leader has been clearly defined and documented.

Further, prior to boarding the PCASP, the shipowner should ensure that the Master and crew are briefed and exercises are planned and conducted so that all the roles and responsibilities are understood by all personnel on board prior to entering the High Risk Area.

In order to provide the required clarity, the documented command and control structure should provide:

.1 a clear statement that at all times the Master remains in command and retains the overriding authority on board;

.2 a clearly documented set of vessel and voyage-specific governance procedures, *inter alia*, covering procedures in 3.4, 3.5 and 3.6 which include procedures for conducting exercises based on these procedures;

.3 a documented list of duties, expected conduct, behaviour and documentation of PCASP actions on board; and

.4 transparent two-way information flow and recognizable coordination and cooperation between the shipowner, charterer, PCASP, PMSC and the vessel's Master, officers and crew.

Factors to determine such success may include:

.1 providing regular updated intelligence-based threat assessments throughout the contracted period on board, and utilizing this information to offer suggestions as to the vessel's proposed routeing, amending same if required, and under the ship's contractual arrangements;

.2 monitoring the daily activities of the onboard PCASP;

.3 having a 24-hour Emergency Response and a Contingency Plan in place covering all potential actions; and

.4 providing feedback on crew training and ship hardening requirements based upon reports received from the PCASP.

3.4 Management of Firearms and Ammunition from Embarkation to Disembarkation

An essential requirement of the PCASP team will be to demonstrate responsible management and use of weapons and ammunition at all times when on board.

Issues to be considered should include:

.1 documented compliance with the relevant flag, coastal and port State legislation and relationships governing the transport and provision of firearms, ammunition and security equipment to the point of embarkation and disembarkation or ports/places at which the vessel may call as part of its intended voyage whilst the PCASP team is on board. PCASP should be able to prove that actual inventory carried matches all documented declarations;

.2 appropriate containers for firearms, ammunition and security equipment at the point of transfer to the ship;

.3 documented standards and procedures for a complete inventory of all firearms, ammunition and security equipment available upon arrival aboard the vessel (inventory should detail make, model, calibre, serial number and company end user certificate and proof of purchase of all firearms and accessories; and details of ammunition and amount);

.4 control procedures for separate and secure onboard stowage and deployment of firearms, ammunition and security equipment;

.5 areas where firearms may or may not be carried, together with the weapon state (e.g. unloaded & magazine off, magazine on and safety catch on and no round chambered) and what will initiate a change in that state should be confirmed;

.6 detailed and exercised orders for when firearms can be loaded and "made ready" for use should be confirmed, trained and documented during certain periods as listed in the PCASP contract, to ensure the highest of safety and operational capabilities for use of firearms aboard the vessel; and

.7 the inventory should be reconciled on disembarkation of all firearms and ammunition from the vessel.

3.5 Rules for the Use of Force

It is essential that all PCASP have a complete understanding of the rules for the use of force as agreed between shipowner, PMSC and Master and fully comply with them. PCASP should be fully aware that their primary function is the prevention of boarding using the minimal force necessary to do so. The PMSC should provide a detailed graduated response plan to a pirate attack as part of its teams' operational procedures.

PMSC should require their personnel to take all reasonable steps to avoid the use of force. If force is used, it should be in a manner consistent with applicable law. In no case should the use of force exceed what is strictly necessary, and in all cases should be proportionate to the threat and appropriate to the situation.

PMSC should require that their personnel not use firearms against persons except in self-defence or defence of others against the imminent threat of death or serious injury, or to prevent the perpetration of a particularly serious crime involving grave threat to life.

3.6 Reporting and Record Keeping

The Master should maintain a log of every circumstance in which firearms are discharged, whether accidental or deliberate. Such actions should be fully documented in sufficient detail in order to produce a formal written record of the incident.

The requirements of a formal written report may be considered to include the following:

.1 time and location of the incident;

.2 details of events leading up to the incident;

.3 written statements by all witnesses and those involved from the vessel crew and security team in the incident;

.4 the identity and details of personnel involved in the incident;

.5 details of the incident;

.6 injuries and/or material damage sustained during the incident; and

.7 lessons learned from the incident and, where applicable, recommended procedures to prevent a recurrence of the incident.

In the event that the PCASP uses force, PCASP team leaders should be advised to photograph (if appropriate), log, report and collate contemporaneous written statements from all persons present at the incident in anticipation of legal proceedings.

In addition to incident reporting it is suggested that following a tour of duty the PCASP team should submit a full report to the shipowner / ship operator, via their employers if required, giving full details of the deployment, operational matters, any training and/or ship hardening conducted, and offering advice as to any further enhancements to security that may be considered.

3.7 Categorization of PCASP

Ship owners/operators should refer to any applicable national legislation of the flag State in relation to the categorization of PCASP on board their ships.

3.8 Reporting within the High Risk Area

The Master should report to the appropriate military authorities when a ship intending to transit, or transiting the High Risk Area is carrying PCASP, firearms and security-related equipment on board.

3.9 Familiarization for Master and the crew

Shipowners and ship operators should ensure that the Master and the crew receive familiarization in relation to this guidance.

Guidance for private maritime security companies agreed by IMO's Maritime Safety Committee

Maritime Safety Committee (MSC), 90th session, 16 to 25 May 2012

Briefing: 17, May 25, 2012

Interim guidance to private maritime security companies (PMSCs) was agreed by IMO's Maritime Safety Committee (MSC), when it met at the Organization's London Headquarters for its 90th session from 16 to 25 May 2012.

A special high-level segment of the MSC saw an intense debate, over the first day and a half of the Committee's session (See Briefing 16/2012* below), on how the international community should deal with issues related to the deployment of privately contracted armed security personnel (PCASP) on board ships and the carriage of arms on board.

Following further debate during a working group, the MSC agreed Interim Guidance to private maritime security companies (PMSC) providing contracted armed security personnel on board ships in the High Risk Area.

The guidance covers:

• PMSC Professional Certification, including the recommendation that PMSC should seek certification with relevant national and international private maritime security service standards when these are established;

• PMSC Company requirements, including the recommendation that PMSC should establish procedures to provide maritime security services to ship owners and ship operators and comply with all relevant legal requirements;

• Management, including recommendations on selection, vetting and training of personnel for a PCASP team;

• Deployment considerations, addressing the specific aspects of PCASP deployment and the role of the PMSC in ensuring efficient and successful deployments, including communications with the ship owner or operator, and including recommendations relating to management of firearms and ammunition from embarkation to disembarkation and use of force. (The PMSC should recognize that laws governing the use of force may differ over time and according to location. The applicable national law, including any criminal laws, for an incident on a ship from which PCASP will be operating will be principally that of the flag State. It may also include the laws and regulations of coastal, port and other States.)

The MSC agreed that the International Organization for Standardization (ISO) would be best placed to develop international standards for PMSCs based on the IMO-developed guidance and with relevant IMO liaison and participation in the ISO process for standards' development.

The MSC also agreed to consequential revisions to the interim guidance for shipowners, ship operators and shipmasters; flag States; and port and coastal States on the use of PCASP on board ships to counter Somali-based piracy, to reflect the new guidance to PMSCs.

The MSC also approved interim guidance for flag States on measures to prevent and mitigate Somalia-based piracy, which lists recommended practices that flag States are encouraged to apply, taking into account their own circumstances and subject to their national law, in order to maximize their efforts to implement counter-piracy measures.

The MSC noted that, globally, the number of acts of piracy and armed robbery against ships reported to IMO and which occurred in 2011 was 544, an increase of 55 (11.3%), compared with the 489 reported for 2010.

The areas most affected in 2011, as in 2010, were East Africa and the Far East, in particular the South China Sea, followed by the Indian Ocean, West Africa, South America and the Caribbean. The majority of incidents occurred off East Africa and increased to 223 in 2011, from 172 in 2010. The deployment of motherships by Somali pirates and the increased range of their operation contributed to the rise in the number of incidents occurring in the Arabian Sea increased to 28 in 2011, up from 16 in 2010. However, the number of incidents in the Indian Ocean decreased from 77 to 63 in 2011. Despite the high number of Somalia-based piracy attacks, the pirates' success rate has been significantly reduced. In 2011, out of 286 attacks, 33 resulted in the ship being hijacked (11.5%), while in 2010 Somali pirates attacked 172 ships in 2010 and hijacked 50 of them (29%).

Worldwide, seven crewmembers were killed in 2011, up from two in 2010, while 569 crewmembers were reportedly taken hostage/kidnapped, in 2011, down from 1,027 in 2010.

The Committee urged, once again, all Governments and the industry to intensify and coordinate their efforts to eradicate piracy and armed robbery against ships.

Guidance for private maritime security companies to be developed by IMO's Maritime Safety Committee

Maritime Safety Committee (MSC), 90th session, 16 to 25 May 2012

Briefing: 16* 18th May 2012

A special high-level segment of IMO's Maritime Safety Committee (MSC), convened by IMO Secretary-General Koji Sekimizu to discuss policy matters related to arms on board ships in the piracy high risk area, has requested a working group of the MSC to develop interim guidance for private maritime security companies (PMSCs).

The MSC is meeting for its 90th session at IMO Headquarters from 16 to 25 May, with some 900 delegates registered from IMO member States and observers from international and non-governmental organizations.

The instruction to the working group to develop the guidance for PMSCs followed an intense debate on arms on board ships during the high-level segment, held over the first day and a half of the Committee's session, which saw interventions from a number of Ministers, Secretaries of State and other senior Government representatives as well as the UN Assistant Secretary-General for Legal Affairs.

In his address to the high-level segment Mr. Sekmizu said:

"The carriage of firearms on board merchant ships is a complex legal issue with Member States taking diverse positions. The Committee has determined that the carriage of armed personnel is a matter for flag States to authorize, however it has also accepted that their carriage has legal implications for coastal and port States, particularly with respect to the carriage, embarkation and disembarkation of firearms and security equipment in areas under the jurisdiction of such port or coastal States."

He went on to emphasize that carriage of arms was a high-priority issue for the shipping industry, and said: "While recognizing the reality of the situation in which private security guards are employed and the diverse positions of Governments, there is a need to consider how the international community should deal with the issue of private security guards and, in particular, the need to arrive at practical solutions to the issue."

The high-level segment agreed that the use of PMSC on board ships was an exceptional measure to be used only in exceptional circumstances in the high risk area, and should not become institutionalized. However, guidance was needed to assist policy development at the national level and facilitate greater harmonization of policies in international shipping related to the issue of arms on board. Such guidance would not constitute a recommendation or an endorsement of the general use of privately contracted armed security personnel.

The high-level segment endorsed the view that the carriage of armed personnel aboard ships for enhancing their protection in the high risk area should be left to flag States to decide, once a thorough risk-assessment exercise had been carried out and following consultations with the shipowners concerned.

I:\CIRC\MSC\01\1406-Rev-1.doc
E
MSC.1/Circ.1406/Rev.1
16 September 2011

REVISED INTERIM RECOMMENDATIONS FOR FLAG STATES REGARDING THE USE OF PRIVATELY CONTRACTED ARMED SECURITY PERSONNEL ON BOARD SHIPS IN THE HIGH RISK AREA[1]

1 The Maritime Safety Committee, at its eighty-ninth session (11 to 20 May 2011), approved Interim recommendations for flag States regarding the use of privately contracted armed security personnel on board ships in the High Risk Area.

2 Given the importance and urgent nature of this issue, and the need to further develop and promulgate detailed guidance and recommendations as soon as possible, the Committee approved and the Council authorized the convening of an intersessional meeting of the Maritime Security and Piracy Working Group (13 to 15 September 2011) to update the recommendations.

3 The Revised interim recommendations for flag States regarding the use of privately contracted armed security personnel on board ships in the High Risk Area is set out in the annex.

4 The attached revised interim recommendations should be read in conjunction with the interim guidance set out in MSC.1/Circ.1405/Rev.1 on Revised interim guidance to shipowners, ship operators, and shipmasters on the use of privately contracted armed security personnel on board ships in the High Risk Area, the interim recommendations set out in MSC.1/Circ.1408 on Interim recommendations for port and coastal States regarding the use of privately contracted armed security personnel on board ships in the High Risk Area, and the information provided in MSC-FAL.1/Circ.2 on the Questionnaire on information on port and coastal State requirements related to privately contracted armed security personnel on board ships, as well as the other recommendations and guidance developed by the Organization for preventing and suppressing piracy and armed robbery against ships.

5 Member Governments are urged to bring this circular to the attention of all national agencies concerned with anti-piracy activities, shipowners, ship operators, shipping companies, shipmasters and crews.

6 Member Governments are also urged to take any necessary action to implement, as appropriate, the revised interim recommendations given in the annex.

---

[1] High Risk Area: an area as defined in the Best Management Practices for Protection against Somalia Based Piracy (MSC.1/Circ.1339) unless otherwise defined by the flag State.

7 Member Governments, international organizations and non-governmental organizations with consultative status are invited to bring to the attention of the Committee, at the earliest opportunity, the results of the experience gained from the use of the revised interim recommendations so as to assist the Committee in deciding on any action to be taken.

8 MSC.1/Circ.1406 is hereby revoked.

ANNEX

REVISED INTERIM RECOMMENDATIONS FOR FLAG STATES REGARDING THE USE OF PRIVATELY CONTRACTED ARMED SECURITY PERSONNEL ON BOARD SHIPS IN THE HIGH RISK AREA[1]

1 These interim recommendations provide considerations on the use of privately contracted armed security personnel (PCASP) if and when a flag State determines that such a measure would be appropriate and lawful. They are not intended to endorse or institutionalize their use. The recommendations do not address all the legal issues that might be associated with the use of PCASP on board ships.

2 In an increasing number of cases, shipowners are considering the use of PCASP to augment shipboard security arrangements when transiting the High Risk Area. The carriage of such personnel and their firearms and security-related equipment[2] is subject to flag State legislation and policies and it is a matter for flag States to determine if and under which conditions this will be authorized.

3 Flag States should take into account the possible escalation of violence which could result from the use of firearms and carriage of armed personnel on board ships when deciding on their policy. Flag States should provide clarity to Masters, seafarers, shipowners, operators and companies with respect to the national policy on carriage of armed security personnel.

4 Flag States should require the parties concerned to comply with all relevant requirements of flag, port and coastal States.

5 Flag States should have in place a policy on whether or not the use of PCASP will be authorized and, if so, under which conditions. In developing such a policy, flag States are encouraged to take into account the following recommendations:

.1 As a first step, consider whether the use of PCASP:

.1 would be permitted under the national legislation of the flag State;

.2 would be an appropriate measure under some circumstances to augment the security arrangements put in place, in accordance with related instruments and guidelines developed and promulgated by the Organization including the industry-developed best management practices, on ships flying its flag when operating in the High Risk Area; and

.3 As a second step, if the use of PCASP is determined to be an appropriate and lawful measure, establish a policy which may include, inter alia:

---

[1] High Risk Area: an area as defined in the Best Management Practices for Protection against Somalia Based Piracy (MSC.1/Circ.1339) unless otherwise defined by the flag State.

[2] In the present recommendations, all references to firearms include the associated ammunition, consumables, spare parts and maintenance equipment for use by PCASP, and all references to security-related equipment include protective and communication equipment for use by PCASP.

.1 the minimum criteria or minimum requirements with which PCASP should comply, taking into account the relevant aspects of the guidance set out in MSC.1/Circ.1405/Rev.1 on Revised interim guidance to shipowners, ship operators, and shipmasters on the use of privately contracted armed security personnel on board ships in the High Risk Area;

.2 a process for authorizing the use of PCASP which have been found to meet minimum requirements for ships flying its flag;

.3 a process by which shipowners, ship operators or shipping companies may be authorized to use PCASP;

.4 the terms and conditions under which the authorization is granted and the accountability for compliance associated with that authorization;

.5 references to any directly applicable national legislation pertaining to the carriage and use of firearms by PCASP, the category assigned to PCASP, and the relationship of PCASP with the Master while on board; and

.6 reporting and record-keeping requirements; and

.7 Provide information to the Organization on the use of PCASP for circulation to Member States.

I:\CIRC\MSC\01\1408.doc
E
MSC.1/Circ.1408
16 September 2011

INTERIM RECOMMENDATIONS FOR PORT AND COASTAL STATES REGARDING THE USE OF PRIVATELY CONTRACTED ARMED SECURITY PERSONNELON BOARD SHIPS IN THE HIGH RISK AREA[1]

1 The Maritime Safety Committee (the Committee), at its eighty-ninth session (11 to 20 May 2011), having approved:

(1) MSC.1/Circ.1405 on Interim guidance to shipowners, ship operators, and shipmasters on the use of privately contracted armed security personnel on board ships in the High Risk Area[2]; and

(2) MSC.1/Circ.1406 on Interim recommendations for flag States regarding the use of privately contracted armed security personnel on board ships in the High Risk Area[3],

agreed that there was an urgent need to develop further recommendations to Governments and, in particular, for coastal and port States, on aspects related to the embarkation, disembarkation and carriage of privately contracted armed security personnel (PCASP) and of firearms and security-related equipment for use by PCASP[4].

2 In this respect the Committee recognized that the facilitation of the movement of PCASP and of the firearms and security-related equipment for use by PCASP was affected by the national legislation and policies of port and coastal States and in this connection there was also a need to address the concerns of port and coastal States with respect to the presence of PCASP and of firearms and security-related equipment for use by PCASP on ships entering, transiting or leaving their territorial sea(s).

3 Given the importance and urgent nature of the issue, and the need to develop and promulgate detailed guidance and recommendations as soon as possible, the Committee approved and the Council authorized the convening of an intersessional meeting of the Maritime Security and Piracy Working Group (13 to 15 September 2011) to update and expand upon the guidance previously issued.

---

[1] High Risk Area: an area as defined in the Best Management Practices for Protection against Somalia Based Piracy (MSC.1/Circ.1339) unless otherwise defined by the flag State.

2 Revoked and replaced by MSC.1/Circ.1405/Rev.1.

3 Revoked and replaced by MSC.1/Circ.1406/Rev.1.

[4] In the present recommendations, all references to firearms include the associated ammunition, consumables, spare parts and maintenance equipment for use by PCASP, and all references to security-related equipment include protective and communication equipment for use by PCASP.

4 The interim recommendations for port and coastal States regarding the use of privately contracted armed security personnel on board ships in the High Risk Area are set out in the annex.

5 The interim recommendations should be read in conjunction with the interim guidance and recommendations set out in MSC.1/Circs.1405/Rev.1 and 1406/Rev.1, the information provided in MSC-FAL.1/Circ.2 on Questionnaire on information on port and coastal State requirements related to PCASP on board ships, as well as the other recommendations and guidance developed by the Organization for preventing and suppressing piracy and armed robbery against ships.

6 Member Governments are urged to bring this circular to the attention of all national authorities concerned with anti-piracy activities and/or border control issues, shipowners, ship operators, shipping companies, shipmasters and crews.

7 Member Governments, international organizations and non-governmental organizations with consultative status are invited to bring to the attention of the Committee, at the earliest opportunity, the results of the experience gained from the use of the interim recommendations so as to assist the Committee in deciding on any action to be taken.

ANNEX

INTERIM RECOMMENDATIONS FOR PORT AND COASTAL STATES REGARDING THE USE OF PRIVATELY CONTRACTED ARMED SECURITY PERSONNEL ON BOARD SHIPS IN THE HIGH RISK AREA[1]

1 These interim recommendations have been developed to address the growing use of privately contracted armed security personnel (PCASP) in the High Risk Area to counter Somali-based piracy, and specifically to provide further recommendations on aspects related to the embarkation, disembarkation and carriage of PCASP and of firearms and security-related equipment for use by PCASP. These recommendations do not address all the legal issues that might be associated with the movement of PCASP or of the firearms or equipment intended for use by them.

2 The recommendations contained in this document are not intended in any manner to override or otherwise interfere with the implementation and enforcement of the national legislation of a State or to interfere with that State's rights under international law. However, at the same time, they recognize the concerns and interests of the owners and operators of ships navigating in or through the High Risk Area to provide means for enhancing the security of their ships so as to protect the seafarers working on board, the passengers and cargo being carried and their assets from being hijacked.

3 In the present recommendations, all references to firearms include the associated ammunition, consumables, spare parts and maintenance equipment for use by PCASP, and all references to security-related equipment include protective and communication equipment for use by PCASP.

4 In view of the growing use of PCASP in the High Risk Area and the need to enhance the protection of ships navigating there, flag States, the shipping industry and the private maritime security companies (PMSC) who provide PCASP need to know whether and under what conditions the embarkation and disembarkation of PCASP and/or of firearms and security-related equipment for use by PCASP is allowed. In addition, the shipping industry, masters of ships and the PCASP service providers need to know what requirements have to be complied with when, during its voyage, a ship carrying PCASP is arriving in, staying at and departing from ports, offshore terminals, anchorage or roadstead located areas within the territory or under the jurisdiction of a port or a coastal State.

5 As a result Member Governments, and, in particular, those of the coastal States bordering the Indian Ocean, Arabian Sea, Gulf of Aden and Red Sea, should have in place relevant policies and related procedures. Such policies and procedures, whilst addressing the concerns of the State which has promulgated them, should facilitate the movement of PCASP and of their firearms and security-related equipment and be made known to the shipping industry and to the PCASP service providers. In addition, they should be communicated to the Organization for the information of all Member Governments, in order to enable flag States to act accordingly.

6 The use of PCASP for enhancing the security of ships navigating in or through the High Risk Area is a very recent and still evolving development. Hence, it is recognized that existing national legislation, policies and procedures may not have been developed taking into account or to cater for the various scenarios related to the embarkation or disembarkation of PCASP or of their firearms or security-related equipment or for the arrival, stay or departure of ships carrying PCASP or their firearms or security-related equipment, during their voyage. Thus, when developing their policies and procedures on the issue, Governments, aside from ensuring internal coordination and coherence amongst the approaches of the different ministries, departments, authorities or
High Risk Area: an area as defined in the Best Management Practices for Protection against Somalia-based Piracy (MSC.1/Circ.1339), unless otherwise defined by the flag State.

---

[1] High Risk Area: an area as defined in the Best Management Practices for Protection against Somalia Based Piracy (MSC.1/Circ.1339) unless otherwise defined by the flag State.

Agencies within whose competency the various matters may fall, should not establish policies and procedures which hinder or may hinder the continuation of maritime trade or interfere with the navigation of ships and should ensure that all are consistent with international law.

7 In developing such policies and related procedures, Governments are encouraged to take into account the following considerations:

Embarkation

- requirements regarding notification of firearms and security-related equipment proposed for embarkation;
- arrangements and requirements relating to firearms in transit, including pre-embarkation storage and security;
- requirements regarding identification and notification of PCASP;
- requirements regarding documentation of flag State authorization of PCASP, firearms and security-related equipment, as applicable; and
- requirements regarding arrangements for storage, security and control of firearms and security-related equipment on board the ship prior to departure, and within the territorial sea.

Disembarkation

- requirements relating to pre-arrival notification of ships carrying PCASP, firearms and security-related equipment;
- requirements relating to notification of intention to disembark firearms and security-related equipment;
- requirements regarding identification and notification of PCASP;
- requirements regarding documentation of flag State authorization of PCASP, firearms and security-related equipment, as applicable; and
- requirements relating to post-disembarkation storage, security and control of firearms and security-related equipment.

Vessel calling

- requirements regarding notification of PCASP, firearms and security-related equipment retained on board;
- requirements regarding storage, security and control of firearms and security-related equipment retained on board; and
- requirements regarding documentation of flag State authorization of PCASP, firearms and security-related equipment, as applicable.

BIMCO

Guidance on Rules for the Use of Force (RUF) by Privately Contracted Armed Security Personnel (PCASP) in Defence of a Merchant Vessel (MV) (Sample from the BIMCO website)

References:
A. GUARDCON
B. IMO MSC Circular 1405 Rev1.

1. Introduction

This Paper provides guidance to ship owners (and their Masters) and Private Maritime Security Companies (PMSC) in areas and in those exceptional circumstances where the use of armed guards are permitted by the Flag State.
This guidance is written to assist ship owners and PMSC meet the requirements listed in the References and agree RUF in support of the above References. It sets out guidelines for a graduated response by armed security guards to any actual, perceived or threatened act of piracy and/or violent robbery and/or capture/seizure by third parties in order to protect the crew and defend a vessel from being hijacked.
In providing this Guidance it is assumed that no armed guards shall be deployed without a detailed risk assessment by the Ship owners and that the deployment of armed guards shall not be an alternative to the implementation of the current Best Management Practices (BMP) and other protective measures.

2. Aim of the Guidance

The aim of the this Guidance is to assist Ship owners and PMSC to review RUF, pertaining to the type, carriage and use of firearms and equipment, in order to provide an accurate and graduated level of response for employment by PCASP that is reasonable and proportionate.

3. Scope

The general requirements of any RUF should be that they are:
(a) In accordance with Flag state law;

(b) In accordance with regulations of any port and any Port and Coastal state laws which govern the storage and use by PCASP of their weapons and Security Equipment;

(c) Consistent with the aim of protecting and defending the crew and vessel;

(d) Consistent with the use of force only being used when essential and then using the minimum level necessary;

(e) Part of a detailed and graduated response plan which is reasonable and proportionate;

(f) Clear in setting out the roles of the Master and the Team Leader of the PCASP;

(g) Documented, agreed and signed by the Owners and the Contractors as an Annex to any contract/agreement for the provision of security services on board a ship; and

(h) Recommended to be submitted by the Owners to the Flag State prior to embarkation of the PCASP.

4. PMSC and PCASP Obligations

The RUF should reflect the obligations imposed and agreed under any contract/agreement and should ensure that the PMSC Team Leader (TL) and the PCASP confirm that they understand these obligations. The RUF should contain guidance that PCASP:
(a) Are trained and qualified to relevant documented PMSC standards in the appropriate use of force in accordance with Flag state law;

(b) If they use force it is in a manner consistent with applicable law;

(c) If they use force it does not exceed what is strictly necessary;

(d) Use of force is proportionate and appropriate to the situation;

(e) Have clear and unambiguous instructions and training on when and how force may be used; and

(f) Take all reasonable steps to avoid the use of lethal force.

5. Self-Defence and the inherent right to exercise it

The RUF should reflect that each of the Security Personnel shall always have the sole responsibility for any decision taken by him for the use of lethal force, including targeting and weapon discharge, always in accordance with the Rules for the Use of Force and applicable national law. Under most national laws individuals have a right to use reasonable force to prevent a serious crime and the right to use force in their own personal self-defence, and the RUF should reflect these rights as appropriate.

6. Chain of Command

The RUF should reflect the regime set out in Clause 8 (Master's Authority and Division of Responsibilities) of GUARDCON and Reference B, namely that the Master has overall control of the vessel and that any decisions made by the Master shall be binding.
It is envisaged that once the Team Leader has decided that there is an actual, perceived or threatened attack he will advise the Master or the Officer of the Watch that he intends to invoke the RUF. It is recognised that consultation with the Master may not always be possible, but there is always a responsible officer on the bridge of the vessel with whom the TL should be able to communicate.
The RUF should reflect that once the RUF has been invoked the TL is responsible for all decisions on the use of force, save that the Master maintains the right to order a ceasefire.

7. Graduated and Proportional Defence

The RUF should reflect the following guidance on graduated and proportional use of force:
(a) Principles

(i) To enable the graduated approach and command and control of the situation defined above the force used must be necessary and proportional;

(ii) Respect for human dignity and the human rights of all persons should prevail; and

(iii) Attempts at non-violent means should be applied first.

(b) Non-violent measures

Examples of non-violent means for consideration are:

(i) Presence – being visible on the upper deck and bridge wings to potential attackers;

(ii) Visual – the use of flares or lasers initially aimed over a potential attackers head and then at them;

(iii) Sound – the use of long range acoustic signalling devices (LRAD) giving warnings or any other means such as loud hailers or even written banners; and

(iv) Show Intent – the use of passive measures such as hoses, releasing objects to hinder approaches of skiffs (nets, logs etc), showing PCASP weapons and raising them to indicate intent to use.

(c) Weapon states

Firearms are to be stowed in a firearms' container when not required. The keys to the container should be under the control of the TL as guided by the Master.
(d) The RUF should consider "states of readiness" for the PCASP. It is suggested that there should be three states for consideration:

(i) Normal: Firearms are stowed in the container/locker with PCASP maintaining normal watchkeeping;

(ii) Heightened: Firearms out of the container/locker with PCASP on watches with crew and weapons loaded but made safe; and

(iii) Stand To: PCASP prepares stand to positions with weapons made ready with safety catches applied and under orders of the TL.

(e) The following actions should then be considered:

(i) The TL assesses the precise level of risk and decides on action to be taken;

(ii) The TL issues fire control orders to the PCASP team clearly identifying the intended target/s and type of fire;

(iii) PCASP open fire as directed by the TL.

(f) Types of Fire

(i) The decision to open fire having been taken by the TL, the type of fire should be defined in the RUF taking into account the distance and behaviour of the suspect craft.

(ii) First, warning shots should be:

(1) fired into the air a safe distance above the skiff/over the pirates' heads or, to the side of the skiff, to display clearly the armed capability of the PCASP;

(2) fired into the water ahead of the skiff for the same purpose;

(3) utilised to assess the accurate range, speed and angle of approach of the target skiff.

(iii) Second, disabling fire should be used against the skiff engine or hull in order to stop the attack but without intentionally using lethal force.

(iv) Third, deliberate direct fire should be used against the attackers when all other methods have failed.

(g) Use of Lethal Force and Opening Fire at a Person

(i) Lethal force should be used only as a last resort and in accordance with the principles referred to in Paragraph 5 above. The circumstances where lethal force in self-defence can be used will vary. Such circumstances may include an armed attack of an MV where the attackers are, for example:

(1) Firing directly at the MV or persons on board in circumstances where the attackers have failed to heed warning shots or other deterrent measures (assuming there was sufficient time for such measures).

(2) Preparing to fire or firing at the vessel whilst clearly demonstrating an intention to close with vessel in an attempt to board, by positioning very close or alongside and preparing climbing ladders for that purpose.

(3) Aiming, launching, rocket propelled grenade or equivalent.

(h) If a PCASP opens fire the RUF should explain that only:

(i) Aimed shots should be fired to stop the attack;

(ii) No more rounds than are necessary should be fired in order to stop the attack; and

(iii) All precautions should be taken not to injure anyone other than the targeted person.

8. Post Incident Action

The RUF should provide that any attack should be reported immediately to UKMTO (the UK Maritime Trade Operations office in Dubai) and other authorities, as appropriate; furthermore that the use of firearms needs to be reported to the Flag State. The RUF should also consider the necessary reporting responsibilities which may involve their personnel having to give statements.

Courtesy to the author Mr. Jakob P. Larsen and BIMCO.

19. SAFE HAVENS, CITADELS AND SECURE AREAS [1]

Definition of a Citadel: A citadel is a fortress for protecting a town, sometimes incorporating a castle. The term derives from the same Latin root as the word "city," civis, meaning citizen.

In a fortification with bastions, the citadel is the strongest part of the system; sometimes well inside the outer walls and bastions, but often forming part of the outer wall for the sake of economy. It is positioned to be the last line of defence should the enemy breach the other components of the fortification system. A citadel is also a term of the third part of a medieval castle, with higher walls than the rest. It was to be the last line of defence before the keep itself.

Safe Rooms Modern day homes and buildings may contain a safe room if the client or threat requires it. On many an occasion, they have been successfully used and have save lives.

Safe Room Features Safe rooms may contain communications equipment, such as a mobile telephone, land-line telephone or an amateur radio transceiver, so that law enforcement authorities can be contacted. There may also be a monitor for external security cameras and an alarm system. In basic safe rooms, a peephole in the door may be used for a similar purpose. Safe rooms are typically stocked with basic emergency and survival items such as a flashlight, blankets, a first-aid kit, water, packaged food, self-defence tools, firearms, a gas mask, and a simple portable toilet. In Naval terms, a safe room on a vessel is called a citadel.

Citadel on ships

Safe rooms on ships are often called "citadels" and are increasingly being installed as a countermeasure against piracy. When attacked, the crew can retreat into the citadel and call for help (which in the case of ships of some countries may include the intervention of military forces). Because of the nature of ship construction, citadel is typically constructed in a concealed location within a void within the ship, to resist efforts by the pirates to find the crew before help arrives.

Citadels should have facilities to allow the crew to remotely disable the ship's engines and electronic systems, making it impossible for the pirates to sail the ship to a location they control. A copy of this book should be available in the citadel as well as the bridge. During an attack, the bridge book will probably be forgotten, so a second book should be with your citadel stores.

---

[1] Due to the fact that pirates and criminals will read this book, some of the sensitive information has been removed; that key information should be obtained from IMAAG or by your security company provider.

The citadel is also typically armoured against direct physical attack, to allow the crew to remain safe for a few days, even if located by the pirates, and to allow rescuing forces full scope for the use of armed force to re-take the ship without risk to the crew.
The effect of the citadel is thus to deny the pirates access to the crew for hostage-taking, to remove the capability to move the ship to a location favourable for the pirates, and to facilitate retaking the ship by armed force without risk to the crew. **The retreat of the crew to a citadel could encourage the pirates to leave the ship of their own accord.**

The reason for having a citadel is to protect the crew until assistance arrives whilst the ship is shut down. When moving through high-risk areas frequented by thieves and pirates, forward planning and preparation will prevent a poor performance, should an attack occur. With the exception of the GoA, most thieves and pirates want to steal as much as possible and make a rapid departure. It is wise to expose as few persons to that threat as possible; the best way to do this is to nominate a safe area; the citadel, safe haven, strong room or secure area, where persons can remain safely and quietly without having to physically encounter the illegal boarders. A citadel will only work if all persons are securely locked away; if one person is captured then the citadel will fail.
Some Company Security Officers CSOs will say whether or not their fleet of vessels will adopt citadels or not. As all vessels are different, it should be the Captain, Mate or engineer who nominates the safe area. Not all citadels have kept the crew safe, on occasion; the citadel door has been breached by varying methods before the coalition forces have arrived (8th April 2011). On more than one occasion the galley or dining area has been chosen as a citadel. This was so that the crew had access to tea and toast whilst waiting in comfort- definitely not the main criteria for choosing a safe area. Normally the ship's crew would muster in a muster station; this could be the galley/dining area, but once the Captain has decided to make the citadel call, everyone should make their way down to the nominated area. It could be that if the security measures that are in place fail and that the remaining persons would have to join the others in there. All the crew must know which alarm or command tells them to go to the citadel. The principal purpose of a safe area, citadel or strong room, is so that crewmembers can lock themselves in behind secure doors. It should therefore be somewhere on board with strong doors that an attacker cannot easily kick down – not a flimsy plywood galley door! In addition, the citadel should be located low down, ideally below the waterline, so that, if bullets start flying around, the chances of the vessel's keel or structure being penetrated and people being hit, are minimised. On some vessels the engine room is the only suitable option, on other vessels there are areas that can be modified to make a semi-comfortable and safe waiting area.
Pirates know ships use citadels, so make it as hard as possible for them to find, ensure as many doors and bulkheads are shut and locked between you and them. The use of CCTV cameras or one way peep holes can make life much easier as it's reassuring to know the whereabouts of the pirates and whether they are even still on the ship. Safety is paramount, comfort is a luxury. During training drills people often complain that their designated safe haven is hot, noisy and smelly. It has to be remembered that being in such a position for the duration of a raid is far better than being raped, beaten or kidnapped by a lawless gang and held for months.
The citadel should have the following: ease of access, it shouldn't be too far away from the accommodation, such as the rope locker in the bow. A secure door (ideally an escape hatch as well), communications with the bridge and spare VHF handset/satellite phone for emergency use only (a charger should be located there too); enough water and rations to sustain the crew for up to four to five days; toilet facilities (ideally three sealable dustbins for liquid, solids and vomit, with toilet paper); breathing apparatus, cutting equipment and fire extinguishers. An electrical supply should be available to recharge Sat-phones and other emergency radios. An external antenna needs to be pre-fitted for these phones/radios to ensure clear communication with the outside world during a 'lockdown' situation. Pirates are now aware of citadels in use; they also have Internet access and copies of BMP4.

On at least three occasions citadels have been attacked by pirates, so make your citadel very difficult to locate or access to in the first place. Even consider marking a dummy citadel signs to throw their trail, extra time is required to allow friendly forces to come to your aid.

If you are concerned over entrapment etc, then keep an orbital steel cutter within should you need to cut yourselves out in a worst-case scenario. Don't ever leave cutting torches or discs in areas where pirates can use them to their advantage.
Training exercises held prior to sailing should allow the crew to experience how it will feel down in the citadel; small creature comforts such as a sweat rag, pillow, playing cards or ear protectors can make all the difference.

Sustainability within the citadel

It is recommended that a safe haven should be able to sustain all the ship's personnel for a period of up to 4-5 days. Therefore the S.H should have water, long lasting food, 3x toilets, First Aid radios, and chargers, EPIRB & Sat-phone..

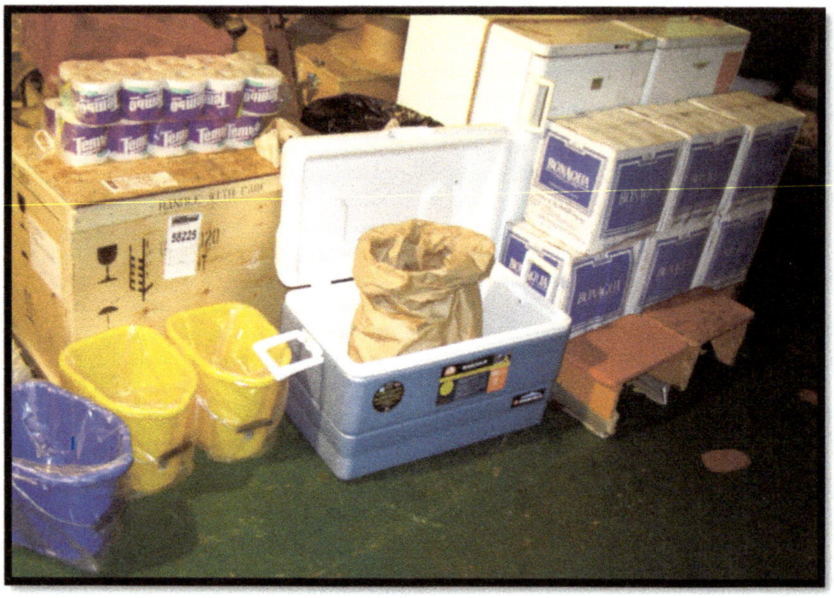

There should be a citadel commander who has a register of the vessel's crew, particularly important on larger vessels, so that everyone can be accounted for and the captain informed on numbers, as it may be that not all crewmembers get to the citadel in time. Any crewmember locked out of the citadel should lock themselves in a safe place, remain quiet and if possible inform the citadel of their situation. Never volunteer yourself to the pirates; they will use you to open the citadel by ANY means.

The crew locked inside the citadel should remain calm and make themselves as comfortable as possible, taking time to reassure other members during what is for many a very worrying experience. Any crew who require medicine should either store a supply in the citadel or take it in with them (easier said than done in the panic of the situation). A good idea that has been recommended before is that playing cards are part of the kit list. Waiting nervously and bored in a hot, noisy cramped space will be unpleasant for all, but by playing cards it will create social interaction, raise morale and make the time pass quicker. Holders of winning hands must not shout for joy however! Crew must remain silent throughout the ordeal and not make any transmissions on communication devices; they should let the Captain or Mate speak first.

Thieves v pirates.

Thieves usually want high-value goods, money, food or alcohol. In this situation, give them what they want) and not put up a fight (prior to transit, leave only a percentage of the ship's money in the safe, in small denominations so it looks like a large wad of cash. The aim is to hand over the goods and get the thieves off the vessel as soon as possible. Once all intruders are off the vessel, the Captain or Mate can instruct the crew to leave the safe area.

Pirates such as those from Somalia or Nigeria are interested in the crew, with live hostages they can wait offshore for the hefty ransom to be delivered, so depending upon where your vessel is depends upon how you react to the raiding party. You definitely should not try to negotiate with intruders in the GoA HRA, in this area you should be safely locked in the citadel awaiting for naval forces to come to your aid.

Point to note: coalition warships require that ALL crew are secured in a citadel prior to military intervention, If they are not, the naval forces will not help.

Below, Citadel guidance as found on the GoA anti-piracy planning chart.

CITADEL GUIDANCE

When considering the installation and implementation of a CITADEL as part of a ship security plan, in keeping with the definition set out in BMP3, please be aware of the following risks that must be evaluated before the ship security plan is finalised.

- Using a citadel when outside the Gulf of Aden is NOT recommended because any opposed boarding that could be executed is highly unlikely to occur because of the scarcity of naval assets;
- In the event of all the crew being mustered safely and contained inside a secured citadel an opposed boarding by counter-piracy forces MIGHT NOT take place despite the close presence of a counter-piracy warship;
- In the event that an opposed boarding does NOT result, the pirates' frustration in being denied entry to the citadel may significantly increase the risk of harm to the crew;
- In the event that an opposed boarding does NOT take place, there is a significant risk of pirates exacting excessive damage to the ship, including but not limited to, setting fire to the bridge. This situation has occurred already in the Somali Basin;
- Intelligence collected by debriefing teams from Counter Piracy Task Forces of pirated released ships, indicate that pirate attack capabilities are evolving and include steel cutting equipment which may render a secured citadel unprotected;
- If citadels are to be installed, it is strongly recommended that they must be seen as complementary to, rather than a replacement for, all other self-protection measures set out on this chart and in BMF 4

It says above not to use citadels outside of the GoA and explains why. However this choice is down to the shipping company, CSO or Captain. Even if a warship does not come to your assistance, after a few hours or days of waiting, the pirates may well give up and leave, surely this is better than no citadel and going directly to Somalia for six months as hostages? Recently Somali pirates have become more aggressive in their actions, such as in January 2012 when the cut off the right arm of Capt. Chao-I Wu after negotiations to pay a $3million ransom for his fishing ship, the FV Shiuh Fu-1, broke down.

Citadel doors:

This galley access door is not suitable and is above the waterline

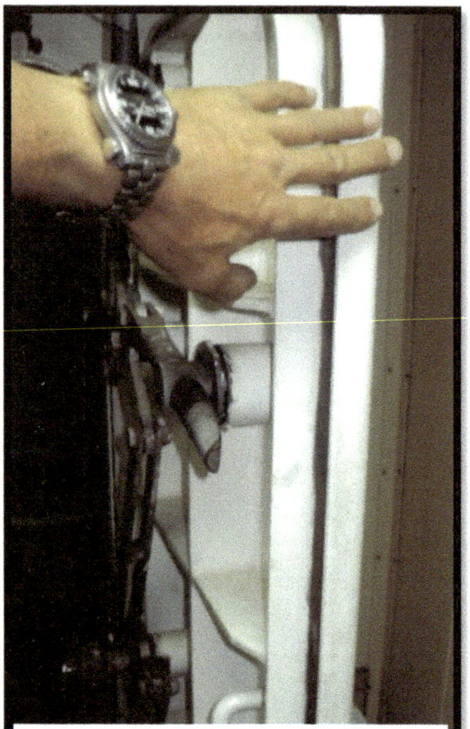

Chose your citadel carefully. This type of door is perfect.

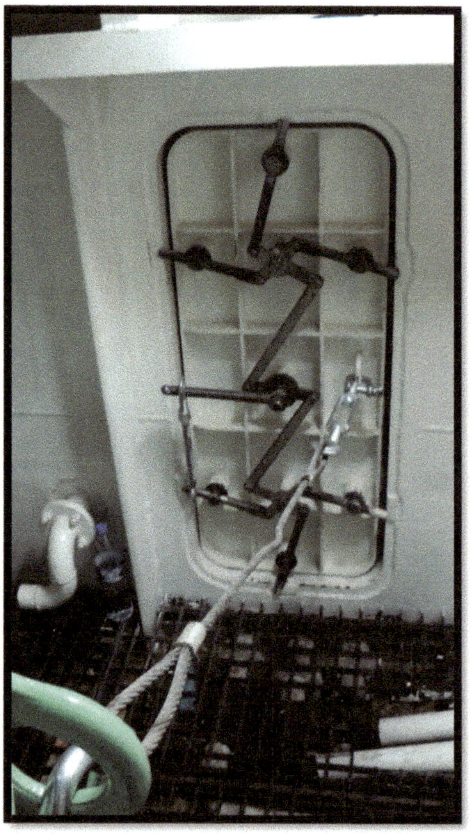

Watertight doors are perfect, but don't make it obvious. Any number of ways can be used to lock the door and keep it closed.

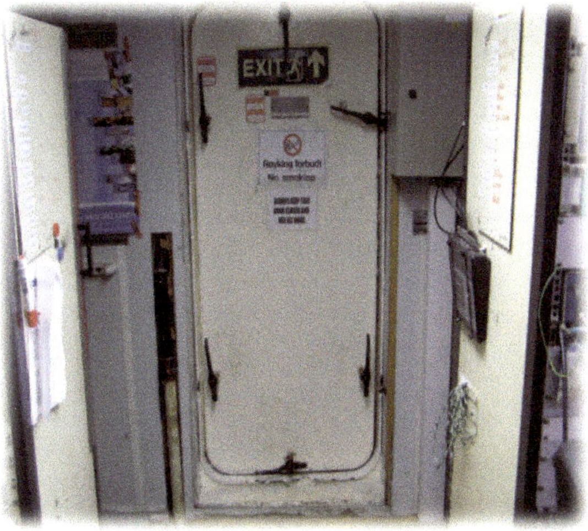

The Citadel:

Changes Made.

The dining area was the ship's old, nominated safe haven for a piracy drill/situation. The hollow wooden doors were not sufficient to withstand physical abuse. The most secure area that offered the highest security and a degree of comfort was the Forward Hold. This had 2x steel doors and 2x steel escape hatches and was below the waterline. Considerations include amenities, such as access to water, electrical supply and comfort factors such as temperature and what materials/machinery is within the citadel.

Safe Haven Old Locking Mechanism

Originally there were security bolts fitted to the steel doors of the forward hold. These were welded on the wrong side. The retaining nuts for the 6 "dogs" (the closing mechanism) could be undone from the outer side, thus insecure. A new system was required

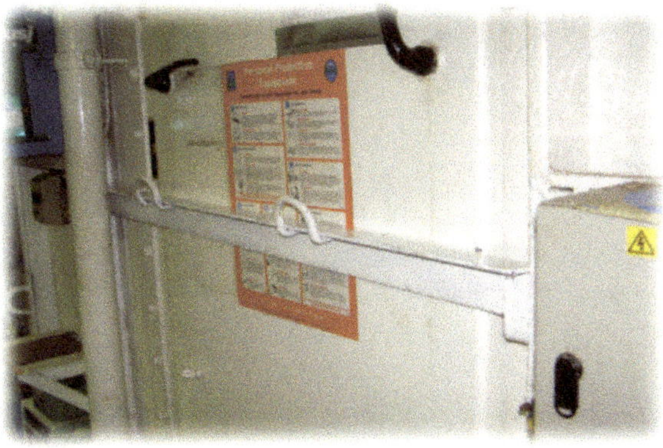

Safe Haven New Locking Mechanism

A pair of steel brackets were welded either side of the door to ensure that the doors could not be opened from the outside. The steel bar was cut and fitted to slide easily into the recesses.

Safe Haven New Locking Mechanism

The heavy duty steel brackets were welded either side of both the doors.

	**Escape Hatches** The forward hold has 2x steel escape hatches. These were originally tied down with old ropes (seen left). As these ropes were not under tension, it would have been possible to open the hatch from the outside enough to slide a blade underneath and cut through the rope. The rope was replaced with heavy-duty cargo ratchets that are under taunt tension, are extremely strong and can be released very quickly in an emergency.
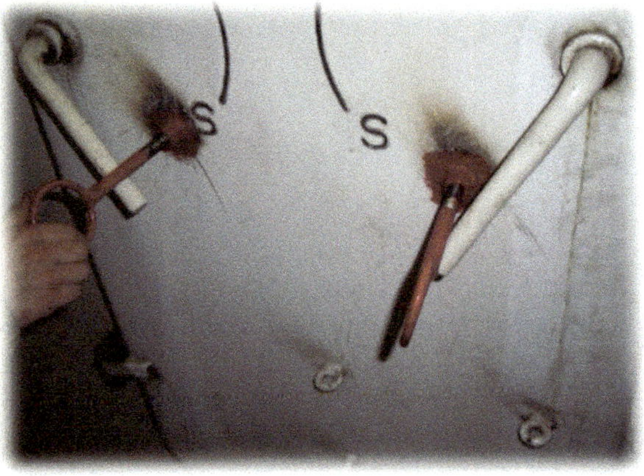	**Pre-citadel doors** Heavy-duty nuts were welded to the outer door. These retaining bolts could be hand tightened easily, thus blocking the pirates' access to the citadel door. The more physical barriers the better.
	**Locking bolts** These simple but strong locking bolts are set up ready to go. The user just needs to drop the bolt in the sleeve, in addition nuts were also welded to the door to prevent the opening of the 'dogs' (metal closing levers).

Pre-citadel doors

Every door and hatch that leads to the citadel should be locked and secured, so it makes it as difficult as possible to access the real citadel door This watertight door that was closed by cross-bar and retaining bolts.

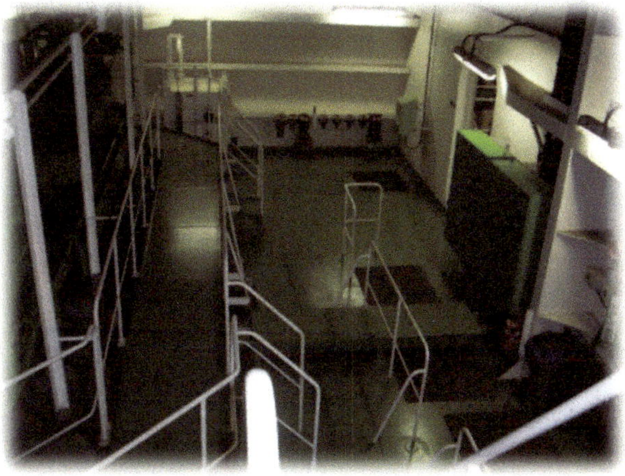

Citadel location

On larger commercial ships, there are so many options to house a secure citadel. Don't make yours an obvious one, use dummy signage to throw the pirates and consider your escape plan should you need one, or you are locked in there by the pirates.

Hopefully you will never have to use a citadel, but if you are going to have one, make it as perfect as possible. Ensure there is an emergency exit, that is easy to open from within, but not obvious or accessible from the outside.

Actual event: In November 2009 a commercial vessel was transitting through the GoA. /The security team leader (Leeds) had fully briefed the ship's crew about all the necessary drills required to make the transit as safe as possible. Exercises had been run prior to entering the ever-increasing high-risk area. The vessel was attacked by Somali skiffs armed with RPG 7s and AK47s. Everyone was placed in the nominated citadel in the depths of the ship. Warning shots were fired but the ship did not slow down or stop. An RPG was fired at the ship; it hit the bulkhead and exploded, causing considerable destruction in the galley and dining areas. If it hadn't had been for the prior training and rehearsals by the team leader and the safety of the citadel, many crewmembers may have lost their lives during that attack. Citadels do work and should be considered. As of April 2011, four citadels have been breached by pirates. The standard of those citadels is not known.

Ensure that like all safety drills, the citadel drill is done frequently,
Here the citadel commander counts the crew in the muster point, informing the Capt. on the bridge.

Citadel locations

In larger commercial vessels it would be possible to hold the Hide and Seek World Championships: There are a great many places in which to place a secure citadel, so chose well.

Training and reassurances are important to the morale of the crew during the HRA transit The vessel protection team should ensure that professional and realistic training and helpful advice is given to the crew.   Photo courtesy of Neptune Maritime Security

When moving into the citadel, the last man in, usually the Capt. should ensure that every single door leading to the citadel area has been locked, chocked and secured in some way. This includes access to the funnel stack at all levels.

The need for maximum protection (such as below the waterline) is that the Somali Pirates fire RPG 7s at ships to persuade them to stop

The damage sustained to the New York Star is obvious.

This is exactly why a Captain/CSO should ensure his ship has adequate protection against such an attack. Simple items can effectively stop RPG warheads from doing this level of damage.

The chain-mail fencing seen in BMP4, water filled drums, sandbags or pallets will all provide varying forms of anti-RPG protection.

Below: RPG Warhead embedded into a ship's side, GoA.

Below: An RPG 7 impact

Below, the damage sustained from RPG and AK47 fire.

Citadel check

Citadel check list		
#	Item	Tick
001	Close proximately to the accommodation, easy to get to?	
002	Below the water line?	
003	Secure access doors? Should be completely reinforced.	
004	Escape hatch? As above.	
005	Fresh water supply?	
006	Communications; internal, VHF and Sat phone (with tested, not obvious external antennas)	
007	Toilet facilities: 3x dustbins or similar, solids, liquid, vomit. Toilet paper, screening for privacy?	
008	Medical kit and medicine for occupants. Sea sick tablets.	
009	Cutting equipment should be stored in the citadel	
010	Fire extinguishers	
011	Breathing apparatus	
012	Ship's nominal (crew list) and list of authorities to contact UKMTO, MSCHOA etc	
013	Bottled water 3litres per man per day minimum, if there is no fresh water supply	
014	Food supplies, tinned meats, fish, baked beans, tinned vegetables, peanut butter, biscuits, cereals and UHT milk cartons. Utensils to eat food with?	
015	Dustbin sacks for rubbish and toilets	
016	CCTV to observe what is happening on the ship, are the pirates still onboard?	
017	Personal creature comforts	
018	Small generator. If the ship is disabled, there will be no power, no lights, no charging facility for the radios etc, if a small generator is fitted the fumes need to be securely vented externally ensuring the poisonous gases go out, an air inlet should also be fitted. The very small generators are very quiet, larger models are noisy and will make the citadel's location obvious to all. Fuel will be required too.	
019	Pop – in ear protection.	
020	A second copy of this guidebook.	
Food	Food is generally overlooked and under stocked. The entire crew in the citadel for up to 5 days. That's a lot of food and water going into the body and leaving. Make considerations for both!	
Food	Food types: Tinned Tuna and other fish. Tinned meat, such as ham, spam, corned beef, stew, sausages, meatballs. Tinned food in general, vegetables, fruits, beans and pulses. Cereals such as Mueslis, not Rice Krispies types. Dried food such as fish, meat, chocolate, fruit and Nuts. High protein foods such as red meat, fish and peanut butter are great, but do required more water to digest, so 3L per man per day is the minimum amount. Long life bread and biscuits can be used but not as a main source of sustenance. Many ships place 3 boxes of biscuits and Corn flakes in there; this is completely wrong!	

When the alarm or code word has been given to move to the muster point, the citadel commander should have a crew list and hand held radio with him. He should ensure that all crew are mustered except for those nominated to remain out (bridge/engine control room & security). He should inform the Capt. That all are mustered and that the ship is locked down, this is vitally important! Many will argue that if the security team are as good as they say, there should be no need for a citadel, or even 'other defences'. This is not the attitude, like it states in the definition, the citadel is the last secure area to fall back to should all else fail. The ship should have maximum hardening and security measures when in HRAs, regardless of the security team.

Imagine if the ammunition is all faulty and security cannot fire warning shots, the pirates will soon realise and board the vessel, the chance of such an incident is very slim, but it could and contingency plans have to be made.

When the Capt. Deems it, the second notification should order the crew to proceed to the citadel from the muster station, members must go quickly, with the right equipment, as once inside, the citadel commander cannot open the door to allow an A.B to go back inside his cabin to collect his medicine (insulin for example). Once inside the citadel commander should notify the bridge that they are all inside and the door should be closed and secured.

It may be that the remaining members may have to join the citadel later on, this has happened in the past when and unarmed private security team failed to stop the pirates from boarding, unarmed security teams cannot stop pirates from boarding compared to an armed team (unless in conjunction they use the very best anti-climb systems such as electric fences, vapour, steam etc). Once in the citadel, the commander needs to take charge, ensure that morale is kept high with reassuring words. Responsibilities should be nominated and the rations should be controlled. Whilst waiting, the crew should make themselves as comfortable as possible.

Do not cut corners and use minimalistic defences. This barricade was quickly smashed open by adrenaline fuelled pirates: they successfully hijacked this ship.

The citadel drill must be a simple and clear drill that is practiced thoroughly and frequently.

Below are photographs of different closing systems used for securing doors leading to, and in the citadel.

A piece of wood stops the door handle being opened, again very poor security. If this is used, rather than a groove in the top, a hole should be drilled through the wood, this prevents it from falling over, as does happen.

In conjunction with the door lock, a rope tied to the door handle, a poor example indeed, but better than nothing.

This escape hatch has been locked using shackles and threaded bar

Here the bosun welded 20mm nuts to the door, the easy to fix bolts prevent the 'dogs' from being opened

18mm steel bar passes through the opening wheel and is secured by the 2 welded retainers

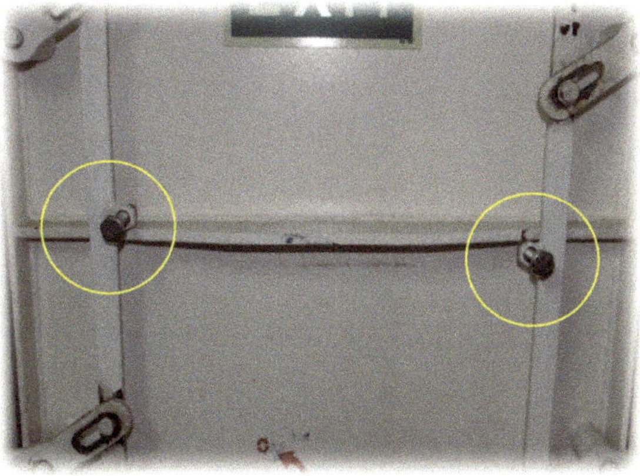

14mm Stainless steel bolts can be hand screwed into the welded nuts preventing opening

35mm steel bar secures this water tight door Solid, simple and very effective.

If padlocks are used, then used heavy duty types, not like this pathetic example! Abloy or Ingersoll are very good.

This emergency escape hatch leads to a citadel. It needs to be locked shut from the inside, but easily and quickly opened should it be required. In order for the communications to work effectively, external antennas were fitted, but their obvious location could lead the pirates into the safe area. When external antennas are fitted, use guile and fit them covertly, it's much better to run the cables up the funnel stack and use an antenna on the bridge roof where the other antennas are fitted.

The obvious antenna giving a clear tell-tale sign. Avoid this.

Post citadel procedure:

The CCTV will allow you to know if the pirates have left the ship, if the citadel doesn't have CCTV or a peep-hole then someone needs to check and confirm an empty ship. Normally skiffs will be seen alongside or intruders will be seen heard in key areas, such as the galley, officer's cabin or bridge.

If the ship is still occupied then the Capt. needs to make a decision as to how long the crew need to remain in the citadel, hence the need for life supporting items; water, food, toilets, medicine. Once the Captain deems it safe to exit the citadel, the ship should be searched for stowaways/remaining pirates. The Capt. needs to inform all agencies of his situation and hope that help is close to hand, after such a frightening ordeal, the escorting of a warship will be greatly appreciated by the crew.

A muster needs to be done of ships and personal equipment taken, damage sustained and incident report clearly written with key timings etc. The ship should be underway as soon as possible; the destination may have changed or may be the same depending upon the advice/orders from the shipping company or coalition warship.

It's important that a thorough debrief takes place and that everyone from the Capt. down are reassured etc, some people are prone to stress more than others and may suffer post-traumatic stress disorder, those who are clearly and genuinely suffering should be carefully handled, reassured, rested and observed. Some may pretend to suffer, only to avoid work for the next few days. If crewmembers are suffering badly from their ordeal then a rotation may be required at the next available safe port.

As soon as the ship is underway and still in the HRA, the A.Bs need to clean up and restock the citadel, as the pirates could be waiting close by and re-attack. A citadel without food, water charged batteries and overflowing toilets will not suffice for very long.

The below pictures were taken after the pirates left the ship; not a pretty sight.

20. KIDNAP AND RANSOM

The BMP 4, websites, blogs and magazine articles give great advice to commercial shipping, on how to avoid capture by pirates in the GoA HRA including ship's hardening and the use of citadels. However, there are not many guides as what to do if pirates do board and take control the vessel. This chapter will cover some of those points.

The scenario being, your ship has left the IRTC and is now steaming south to Durban. Some 200 miles east of Socotra Island you saw two white skiffs closing towards your stern. The hoses are turned on, the ship increases her speed and steadily zigzags as the distress calls are made and the SSAS button is pressed. You have no response on Ch16, you see pirates onboard and inform the crew to move from their muster station to the citadel, an hour later the pirates have breached the citadel using the ship's tools.

The pirates at this point will be very aggressive and assertive; the shock of capture for the crew will be overwhelming. Every crewmember will be shocked and frightened, normally with very negative thoughts running through their heads. This is normal, but one must remain calm and stay optimistic. Do what the pirates say, be polite, calm and abiding, do no shout, question, threaten or take photos. Move slowly, no sudden movements, avoid eye contact, think about the situation; capture, move to Somali location, held for a period of time, payment, release, normality back in the safe environment of your own work place and home with your loved ones. This mental picture will help put you at ease, rather than dwelling upon negativity. A knowing wink and a covert thumbs-up to your fellow crewmember will make him feel much better and silently reassured.

The first few hours will be the worst part, the pirate leader will want to know who the Captain is and how many crew there are, who is the cook etc. You will be taken to a place to be held, such as the mess room, bridge or other large area. They will check for weapons/security onboard and tell you to turn off distress signals, beacons etc. If you are being called by coalition forces, as with what happened to the Chandlers, the military were told to go away or the hostages will be shot. This is not an idle threat or bluff, the pirates that boarded the sailing yacht SY Quest executed the 4 American hostages when they panicked under the pressure. The author went to see the yacht in Djibouti Harbour, but was not allowed inside. The entire yacht and rigging was peppered with bullet holes; it was a very sad sight indeed. The whole purpose of this book is to try to prevent this from happening.

Bullet holes

Once the pirate commander feels he has control of the vessel and crew, that the crew are not a threat, he will order the Captain to set sail, normally on a course to Somalia, however don't be surprised if he decides to use the ship as a mother ship before going home, this has happened in the past. The skiffs will normally be towed at the stern or alongside, or even craned aboard by the crew.

The thought to overwhelm the pirates may be great; this is something that is seen in Hollywood movies, but in reality will not be successful, it will only lead to fatalities.

To remain passive and polite is the main thing, the pirates may make demands that just aren't acceptable; the Captain should try to justify why a particular demand cannot be made. On some ships, there are female crew, it should be imperative that the ladies are kept with the men for safety in numbers and moral support, to separate them would be an extremely traumatic experience for the obvious reasons.

On the journey to Somali the pirates will shower, feed, chew Khat and ransack every cabin, room, store, drawer looking for 'shiny' items such as mp3 players, cameras, for better clothing and footwear. Don't get upset when you see an unsavoury pirate dressed in your best 'going ashore' clothes, wearing your watch your wife bought you last Christmas and your new RayBans you just purchased in the last port. All of these things can be replaced, life and limbs cannot.

The quicker that you mentally adjust to captivity, the easier it will be. It will be boring, maybe hot, uncomfortable, you maybe thirsty, hungry and suffering from insomnia, but that's the way it's going to be until the ransom is paid, an average period of captivity is around 4 months, that's a long time of waiting and thinking. To help stay positive, fantasize about being home after the ordeal, about how you will spend your time with you family and what you will spend your wages on.

Seafarers normally get paid 'HRA danger pay ' for being in the HRA, often it is paid for each day in captivity, so after a long period of captivity, at least you have the pleasure of spending lots of money on the better things in life.

The chef will usually be allowed to cook for all in the galley, under the guard's watchful eye. If your captivity is long and decent rations start to run out, then a simple diet of rice, fish, goat can be expected. The pirates will have this delivered from ashore.

Certain items will be used up quickly; such as sugar loaded drinks like 7 Up or other soft drinks, Sprite, Coca-Cola etc, these are usually drank with Khat chewing sessions, cigarettes too will be in demand.

Do not expect the pirates to keep the area tidy, in their eyes; litter bins don't exist, once full the rubbish will be thrown onto the floor. Your rooms will be trashed completely, the contents of your drawers and lockers strewn about the floor, with rubbish piling up on top. Again, if you are allowed to go to your cabin to collect something important, such as personal medicine, keep control of your temper as a heated argument or explosive outburst could lead to a nervous pirate using his weapon without thinking.

Somalis, like many Africans have a different attitude towards life, and to them, life is cheap. They have probably seen civil war, have fought in civil wars, have killed people in the past, they think it normal and acceptable to stone a criminal to death, to drag a victim through the streets behind a vehicle until he has no more skin or tissue left, so having a foreign seaman shouting and screaming at him in close confines will not go down well at all. Far better is to work out who are the friendlier pirates and try to befriend them regardless of what you feel. However, there is also 'Stockholm Syndrome' where upon the victim eventually becomes almost brainwashed by the captor and will side with him, doing what he is told to do, thinking that it is correct.

As we see almost weekly, Somali pirates are attacking vessels, unfortunately some ships and their crews are taken to Somalia, where negotiations are made, eventually large ransoms paid and the ship/crew is released.. As a result, many vessels choose to sail around the Cape, or choose alternative routes.

The business of maritime kidnap and ransom in the GoA is a successful and lucrative one, and very well organised. The mother craft deploy to their area of operations, launch their skiffs and vessels are attacked, some taken. It is said that they are paid for each part of the operation. The pirates in the skiffs being paid approximately $120,000 each, depending upon the size of the ransom. These pirates will try to take a ship with western crews or tankers with high value cargoes such as carried by the VLCCs, or ships that belong to the larger shipping companies such as MSC, Maersk and Hapag Lloyd.

The 'guarding team' then takes over once the captured vessel arrives close to the Somalia coast; the crew are taken to a place of holding where they are kept until the negotiators settle for a payment. The payment, in cash is usually air dropped by fixed wing plane and parachute, or by helicopter. Deadly fights have erupted of the 'dash for cash' in the past, Somalis shooting each other over the bundle of money. Once payment is made, the pirates normally throw away their mobile phones, go to land and covertly go to their home areas.

This is a dangerous and vulnerable time for the pirates as they are alone now and susceptible to robbery themselves. It was at this point of the piracy operation where the French soldiers ambushed the home going pirate party after the release of a French vessel, some pirates were shot and half the money was re-taken by the military.

The Somali pirates do, or used to follow a code of conduct, whereby the hostages are looked after to quite a reasonable degree. Before 2010, there were not been many reports of rape, beatings, torture and death, as experienced by unfortunate victims of armed groups that can be found in areas of conflict such as Iraq or Afghanistan.

Pirates holding the crew of the Chinese fishing vessel Tian Yu No. 8 GoA 2009

Armed pirates and their hostages are seen aboard the French yacht Tanit off the coast of Somalia.

How should victims behave when captured? Basically, they should remain calm, optimistic and positive, do as the hostage takers say (within reason) and be passive, this applies initially and long term.. Victims should not give away personal information about themselves or their family. If a lie is necessary, it should be based on true facts, which are easier to remember than elaborate lies.

There may be the chance of escape, but there is uncertainty about where to go and how long freedom would last? We are not talking about escaping soldiers here, but seaman, many of whom will be very unfit in a cardio-vascular way, not the type ready to 'go on the run' through rural Somalia at night, hoping to reach Djibouti without any kind of helpful equipment. Escaping can also make life worse for those who remain behind; the best advice is to stay put and await the payment to be made. The only time this should be considered would be when on the ship, to overpower the pirates and sail to a rendezvous with a coalition warship would be your only chance. Recommended? Definitely not! Stay put, stay calm and be very patient.

The Chandlers held by Somali Pirates from Oct 2009 – Oct 2010

Captured on from their sailing yacht SY Lynn Rival. An incredibly high ransom. was originally asked for their release

President Sheikh Sharif Sheikh Ahmed of Somalia, talks with David Miliband

President Sheikh Sharif Sheikh Ahmed of Somalia visited the UK from 8-11 March 2010, meeting the then Prime Minister Gordon Brown and other government ministers to discuss a range of issues. The PM thanked the president for his government's assistance in trying to secure the safe release of Paul and Rachel Chandler, held by pirates in Somalia.

People who have endured the ordeal of kidnap may suffer Post-Traumatic Stress Disorder (PTSD). Captains and shipping managers should be aware of this fact and seek advice. The signs and symptoms of post-traumatic stress disorder typically begin within three months of a traumatic event. In a small number of cases, though, PTSD symptoms may not occur until years after the event. Post-traumatic stress disorder symptoms are commonly grouped into three types: intrusive memories, avoidance and numbing, and increased anxiety or emotional arousal (hyperarousal). Those who have experienced the above should consider counselling, or at least let their doctor know of the situation.

Crew Action during Kidnap – What to Expect

Situation Awareness:

- A person will lose almost all control of their ability to decide and act

- They could suffer a varying period of physical discomfort, sensory deprivation, deception and physical and psychological abuse including mock executions and rape

- The motivation and capability of the captors (the pirates' motivation is the exchange for you and the crew for x amount of US Dollars, bodies are worthless. Capability; as we know, Somali pirates are very capable of 'pulling this off'). A person may be at greater peril by staying (such as the Ken Bigley case in Iraq) and have nothing to lose by attempting a planned or opportune escape rather than imminent execution. There is no such thing as 100% security, which means there could always be the potential for escape. However, this must be measured carefully against a number of factors, including the person's physical and mental condition. If a person has not been heavily beaten and is in reasonable shape, they should always be looking for weaknesses and failures in security that may allow escape opportunities.

- The circumstances and conditions a person is being held in: Where a captive is held, how they are restrained, the effectiveness and ability of the guards, their routines and procedures, the prevailing weather conditions, the ground.

- Communications. If a captive is able to communicate with other hostages, together they may be able to construct an escape strategy.

Crew Action during Kidnap – Actions

- Immediate action on attack: the immediate action should be to take control oneself and read the developing situation – beware of 'denial'
- Control the natural 'fight or flight' response and thoughts of fear and anxiety: These emotions could cloud a person's judgement at this critical time
- Conduct a dynamic risk assessment of the situation: Consider if it is possible to break away
- Avoid antagonising the abductors; this may put a person's own life or that of the crew in severe danger, or the abductors may issue out severe punishment
- Avoid rapid movements: Abductors may also be nervous and any rapid movement may cause them to discharge a weapon
- Psychologically prepare oneself: For physical and mental hardship, to lessen 'shock of capture'
- Do not look the abductors directly in the eye
- Adopt a positive mental attitude from the outset:

Somali pirates holding the ship's crew hostage

For advice on kidnap and ransom, reputed companies such as AKE Group or Control Risks should be contacted. See www.akegroup.com or www.control-risks.com.

Pirate attacks sink insurance premiums. August 2010

Kidnap and ransom premiums paid to insure against Somali piracy have slumped since the BBC Trinidad was hijacked in the Gulf of Aden in August 2008 as escalating attacks spurred more companies to offer coverage.
Buying US$5 million of coverage now costs as little as US$15,000 per voyage, half the peak rate in 2008, said William Miller, divisional director of Willis Group Holding Plc's Kidnap and Ransom, or K&R, unit in London.

"Piracy is a peak risk with a relatively low probability of happening, but with an immensely high damage potential," said Niels Stolberg, head of Bremen, Germany-based Beluga Shipping GmbH, the Trinidad's owner. The company now buys kidnap and ransom coverage for every ship crossing "this dangerous passage," after paying a US$1.1 million ransom to release the vessel and its 13 crew from the pirate haven of Eyl, he said.
Kidnap and ransom premiums climbed to US$100 million last year as pirate attacks on the 25,000 ships passing through the Gulf of Aden rose 70 percent. That prompted more insurers, including Aspen Insurance Holdings Ltd., Ascot Underwriting Ltd. and Chubb Corp., to offer marine K&R coverage, a policy first developed to address kidnapping in South America.

The insurance covers the ransom of the ship and its crew, including negotiations with pirates and hiring ex-special forces teams to deliver the money. With Somali pirates usually returning hijacked vessels undamaged, kidnap and ransom plugs a gap in war-risk insurance that only covers damage to a ship and its cargo, said Stolberg.

Ransoms increase
The average ransom has almost doubled to between US$3.5 million and US$4 million since Chubb entered the market 22 months ago, said K&R Manager Greg Bangs, adding that the company expects to expand its piracy business further.
"At first the rates were a little higher than they should have been and then over time insurers realized they could reduce their rates and still make money," said Bangs.
The decline in rates has deterred Ascot from writing any policies since being authorized to offer kidnap and ransom coverage last November, said Andrew Moulton, a marine underwriter at the Lloyd's of London arm of American International Group Inc.
"Traditional carriers have been cutting each other so much to get the premium in that the price has fallen off the end of a cliff," said Moulton, adding that in the current economic climate, most ship owners won't buy kidnap and ransom insurance as they view it as "icing on the cake" rather than core coverage.

Big problem
Pirates are currently holding 18 ships and 379 hostages, up from 11 ships and 261 hostages at the beginning of the year, according to the International Maritime Bureau. When the summer monsoon in the Indian Ocean ends this month, attacks may rise as pirates venture from lairs such as Garacad, Hobyo and Harardhere on the Somali coast, said bureau Director Pottengal Mukundan.
"It's a big problem," said Per Gullestrup, chief executive officer of Clipper Ferries. He arranged for a US$1.7 million cash ransom to be parachuted to pirates that used AK-47s and rocket-propelled grenades to hijack the CEC Future in November 2008. "The Somali pirates have shown they are quite good at adapting to the situation." Pirates are being encouraged by the ransoms and the ease with which they capture ships, said Sven Gerhard, global product leader of marine hull & liabilities at Allianz SE's corporate and specialty unit. Ship owners must also pay as much as US$2.5 million to negotiators and security firms that fly the ransom to a drop-off point, he said.

Premiums depend on the ship's speed, height of its deck above sea level and measures taken to protect the vessel, said Sean Woollerson, a partner at Jardine Lloyd Thompson Group Plc, the U.K.'s biggest publicly traded insurance broker. While most insurers advise ship owners to deploy razor wire and train sailors how to legally fend off attacks, Woollerson also aims to raise funds for a fleet of escort ships to shepherd vessels through the Gulf of Aden. That may push rates down further, he said.

Private navy
"We are working on a unique concept to create a legitimate private navy for the shipping industry to complement the existing naval forces to stop this kind of piracy escalating," said Woollerson, who estimates start-up costs of US$15 million. "This is the only way we're ever going to stem these attacks."
For the moment, Beluga Shipping deploys high-pressure hoses and cardboard dummies called "soldiers" to deter boarders, after the Trinidad was captured by nine pirates using two speedboats, said Stolberg.
"Sending armed teams aboard is a last resort," said Mark Hankey, a spokesman for Maritime & Underwater Security Consultants, which gives shipping lines transit advice from its basement control centre opposite London's Royal Courts of Justice. Using arms involves the risk of "massive escalation," he said.
When the company does employ guards on cargo vessels it stations three to four former British Royal Marines or Royal Navy personnel to escort ships through pirate waters, said Hankey.

No guarantees
The naval task force is no longer effective after the pirates expanded the scope of their operations, said Jan-Thiess Heitmann, head of the legal department at the German Ship Owners' Association. While the association is against arming crewmembers or hiring armed security guards, it's in talks with the German government on installing soldiers on merchant ships. "The number of forces is never going to be enough to guarantee protection," a spokesman for the 24-nation Combined Maritime Forces said in an e-mailed statement. "Pirates are opportunists who will seek the easiest target available."

The naval force deploys as many as 25 vessels in counter-piracy operations along a recommended transit corridor that runs from close to the Bab-el-Mandeb at the southern end of the Red Sea through the Gulf of Aden to a point north of the Yemeni island of Socotra. The corridor carries about a fifth of the world's trade.
Gullestrup says a set of best practices, introduced by the naval task force, have helped keep the rest of Clipper's fleet safe. Still, he says the only long-term solution to piracy is to help Somalia, a country that has lacked a central government since the overthrow of former dictator Mohamed Siad Barre in 1991, develop its own security and coastguard infrastructure.

"All the money would be much better spent in assisting the Somalis in capacity building," he said. The author strongly disagrees with the above and previous arguments stating that armed security should be avoided or a last option and that it will lead to an escalation of force and blood loss. The only way to guarantee to stop pirates illegally boarding your vessel is to use professional armed security, whether it is private or military. If every vessel had 4 UN soldiers onboard with night vision equipment and weapons, piracy would cease, end of story! The answer does lie in stabilising Somalia, helping them re-establish law and order, peace and commerce, but this will take years, and as America witnessed in 1994, hard-line militant Somalis will fight bitterly using guerrilla tactics making another long drawn out war or jihad, as seen now in Afghanistan. That will lead to a huge spillage of blood and loss of lives on both sides. It is questionable if some so called "Maritime Security Experts" really know what is happening 'out on the ground' as some comments over the years sound like they have come from the mouth of General Melchett from the Black Adder series! They should venture out of their ivory towers and speak with the directors of leading security companies such as PVI, Solace and Neptune for real time facts.
Thankfully 'shipping' is realising this as of 2011 and people at last changing their attitudes.

In June 2012, a South African and Italian couple held hostage for 20 months after being kidnapped by Somali pirates have been freed, Somalia's defense minister said Thursday. The couple was among the longest-held by Somali pirates. South African Deborah Calitz and Italian Bruno Pelizzari smiled but appeared exhausted at a news conference at the presidential palace in Mogadishu.

"We are very happy to get our freedom again," Calitz said, speaking haltingly. "We are so happy today and to join our families again." The two were kidnapped in October 2010 from a yacht off the southeastern coast of Africa. Their pirate captors originally demanded a ransom of $10 million. Kerri-Ann Cross, Calitz's 21-year-old daughter, said: "All I know is that she is safe. I am so happy." Cross, speaking by phone from Pretoria, South Africa, said she hadn't yet spoken to her mother by mid-day Thursday and didn't have any additional information. The couple's 20-month captivity is among the longest periods hostages have been held by pirates. When Somali pirates first began attacking ships off East Africa in about 2005, they attacked large container ships.

But as those vessels improved their on-board defenses, pirates began attacking more vulnerable private yachts. An international flotilla of warships patrols waters off Somalia, leading to a decrease in pirate attacks over the last year.

Somali Defense Minister Hussein Arab Isse credited Somali security forces with helping with the couple's release, but he did not say that the pair had been rescued. He also declined to say if a ransom was paid. Most pirate hostage cases end with payment of multi-million dollar ransoms. South Africa's government said it is gratified at the couple's release and expressed its gratitude to Somalia's government for helping with the release. South Africa also thanked the government of Italy for its role. "Arrangements are being made for the return of the couple to South Africa," the South African statement said.

The European Union Naval Force says Somali pirates currently hold seven ships and 213 hostages. The EU force says 25 ships were hijacked last year, down from 47 in 2010. Only five ships have been hijacked in 2012, an indication that on-board defenses and the international patrols are succeeding against pirate attacks. The EU Naval Force saw its mandate expand earlier this year and is now allowed to carry out attacks on the Somali coast against suspected pirates.

Photo; Solace Global Maritime Solutions

Just the sight of armed security is enough to stop most attacks.
The firing of flares and nearby warning shots has made the most daring Somali pirates cease the attack.

First hand account of what happened to Nigel Watson Clark when he was captured by MEND in 2006.

Nigel Watson Clark

Consultant Anti-piracy operations.

The FPSO Sea Eagle

Background: *A quick outline of my roll for SNEPCo (Shell) in the EA Field, a brief history of the field and my role on M.V Liberty Service as the dedicated Field Security Vessel.*

I'd held the position of SLO (Security Liaison Officer) for over 3 years and my job was to implement the 24 hour security cover that was required to protect all of SNEPCO assists and personnel in the EA Field positioned 8 nm offshore by the DoDo River. The Floating Platform Storage Offshore Facility (FPSO) Sea Eagle had upwards of 60 personnel on board her was of course the main asset and we were to enforce the integrity of a 2.5 nm MEZ (Maritime Exclusion Zone) around all of our EA installations. There were also up to 4 service and supply vessels in the field. Liberty Service had a Nigeria Naval Detachment of 12 ratings and an IOC with a crew of up to 16. We had two 7.5meter RIBs deployed to patrol the area daily and with an independent intercept capability.

So my job was to Liaise with Shell's shore based security, the FPSO Marine Superintendent, the Naval Base Command in Warri and the vessel operators: Tidex, to make sure to tasks were carried out. There were also other duties including briefing support and supply vessels, the Capt and crew, maintaining the RIBs, and admin and Logistics.

History.

We patrolled 24/7, never went into port and only anchored while bunkering fuel and water. We'd had a colourful history of incursions, invasions, kidnapping and hostage taking ever since the development stage, the most serious in April 2002 when the FPSO support vessel Maersk Shipper was overrun by youths from the local community and threatened with grounding it on the beach. I was involved in that incident as well and witnessed some seriously intimidating behaviour and at times, more violent and intense than the MEND action.

On the lead up to the incident we'd had a number of community invasions over Christmas and beyond, and the region was experiencing a coordinated series of attacks in many oil and gas fields; we were one of only two still operating normally (at ISPS Level II). However, the bar was raised on the afternoon January 11th. 2006.

Twenty days in January 2006.

Nigeria is a difficult environment to work in. A toxic mix of fabulous natural resources, wealth, corruption, ethnic division and abject poverty. Over the years working in the region, I'd listened and sympathised with many Nigerians who had worked hard but witnessed the imbalance and lack of distribution of that wealth. The thread of corruption reached into every level of Nigerian society and sooner or later, it was almost inevitable it would spill over into some sort of movement. We'd been tested at sea many times but in the swamps of the Niger Delta, a group of disenfranchised, disillusioned, well trained, well-armed, organised and violent men planned their first operation.

They were powerfully backed, these were not merely common criminals, and the bar was about to be raised. The Movement for the Emancipation of the Niger Delta (MEND) was about the launch their ideology on the world.

The first time I saw the three 'fast movers' (fast boats) approaching our 'field' is burnt in my memory. There was something very different in the silhouettes I was watching through binoculars from the bridge wing of M.V Liberty Service, there was no time to dwell or spend time analysing. Our Emergency Security Procedures were well rehearsed, I'd trained up a new Naval Detachment and while they bordered the intercept RIBs my job was to coordinate the field evacuation of the field support vessels and instruct the 'lock-down' of the Sea Eagle; ***a big call!*** *Echo Alpha 1 left the side, 6 fully armed navy ratings and our two coxswains were on their way to intercept the invaders and I felt 'chuffed' the operation had got off to a good start. I was never totally confident that the Navy upon being asked the step up, that they would deliver, but today they were on the ball.*

One of the fast patrol RIBs

We'd seen the 'fast movers' early. Red and White streamers and flags adorned their boats. They were quicker, larger than previous and moved as a body across our bow about 2 nautical miles ahead of us heading directly to the huge FPSO. The startled support vessel's Captain reported back they were heading to deep water, the Sea Eagle Marine Superintendent confirmed lock-down. Echo Alpha 1, our intercept craft, were closing and with all our immediate actions going well, I felt a real sense of confidence that we were on top of it. I didn't see Echo Alpha 1 turn 180 degrees and but shear panic in my coxswain's voice over the radio net drew my attention. Instead of intercepting and stopping the invasion, they were now being chased and under automatic fire. I never saw them again. With all the support vessels now out of the area, Liberty Service was one of only two targets and two of the fast movers turned directly towards us. Our remaining Navy were positioned at action stations and looking down from my position on a rear facing bridge, I caught the eye of one young rating, gave him a wink, the thumbs up and he gave a nervous but reassuring nod in reply. We'd drilled this many times. We'd talked through all scenarios on a Saturday morning 'clear lower deck' a weekly meeting with the detachment and drilled, exercised emergency SOP's...... this vessel would be secured. With belt fed GPMG's we had the advantage and I felt an illogical sense of calm that we were still in charge. As the two boats took up positions closing to our port and starboard quarters and as the Sea Eagle Marine Supervisor screamed down the radio that they were under fire from RPG's that sense of calm was interrupted with a burst of automatic fire. Our bridge erupted as incoming 7.62mm high velocity rounds smashed through the windows and ricochet inside hitting the bridge equipment, the radio bank, radars and computers. The noise of the rounds hitting the steel superstructure drowned out any radio traffic from the Sea Eagle, all I heard then from Mark was "good luck Nige'". We were in our own fire fight now and taking a staggering amount of rounds.

I took a moment to look down on the carnage, I witnessed the terrifying sight of 20 militants, six with GPMG's, slung from the shoulders, at hip level, their barrels now glowing red still aimed and firing at us. I'd been showered by the glass of the bridge windows shattering on the first volley and my face was cut by the broken glass. The bridge crew screamed as they scattered down the stairwell taking cover, fear etched on black faces seeing my own covered in blood but it was the sight of the militants, dressed in 'battle dress', their faces painted for war that struck me most. In this frenzied atmosphere in the centre of a firefight, I was momentarily the rabbit caught in the headlights.

The Navy had gone. There was no more return fire from them and I looked down onto the prepared firing positions and saw only discarded weapons, still with belts of ammunition attached, the Navy had fled. For about 5 more minutes the bridge continued to be the focus point until gradually the impacts slowed. Pat, the Captain, still on the wheel was the only company I had and we had to try and prevent them now getting on and taking Liberty Service.

Locked down, I didn't have access to the Navy Detachments weapons on the deck below, EA1 had fled and was heading for the horizon and we were now defenceless. "Hard to port Pat!" Pat was a small, grey haired 60 year old uncompromising American from Louisiana, a seasoned 'hard nut' and he wasn't going to surrender his vessel easily. As I watched one of the militants boat approach closer to board on the starboard side Pat swung the wheel to port and knocked off their approach. There was another burst of automatic fire but I had cover and the approach had failed. Another approach on the port side and I barked "Hard to Starboard Pat... hard to starboard!".

We were now in a kind of dance and as the wake from the stern of Liberty Service knocked each approach, the militants became more animated, we looked into each others eyes, I saw determination, anger and they let off another burst. The Zig Zag manoeuvring kept the militants off Liberty Service for a few exhilarating minutes but as she struggled to recover on each turn her speed slowed, there could be only one outcome. Then the inevitable final command from me to the Captain " they're on board .... we have to surrender the vessel Pat!"

As soon as one got on the rest quickly followed. They appeared in no time on the bridge wings; terrifying, dressed and equipped for war. One guy, 'Peter' (who I got to know well later on in the ordeal, fired through the side windows that remained intact I gestured to his white painted face that I would unlock the watertight doors of the bridge. As fired up, animated young men streamed onto the bridge, the Captain got a smack across the back of his head with an AK47. Chaos, more weapons being fired, some in victorious celebration, some in anger. I shouted something at 'Peter' who I identified as some sort of leader and he barked instructions in Ijew and the mood calmed. They'd dispatched more than 500 rounds at us; I rather hoped that was the end of it.

The vessel had been taken, the remainder of the crew were assembled on the deck and now the interrogation began. "Where's the Navy?"...Where's the Navy!?" I had no doubt in my mind that if they were found, hiding somewhere within the superstructure of the Liberty Service, that they would be lined up and executed there, on the spot. All the shouting was directed at me but I didn't know where they were. 'Peter' pulled out one of the crew from the line and calmly instructed me to tell him where the Navy were hiding or our crane operator would be executed. A weapon nozzle pressed firmly against his forehead, his knees buckled and froze in silence. I pleaded with Peter not to shoot him and he eventually lowered his weapon, pushed the terrified young Nigerian back into the ranks and spat. The Navy were never found on board by the militants.

Four of us, two Chief engineers, the Captain, and myself were taken by the three militant boats deep into the Niger Delta swamps. I still retain the images of us at speed in formation weaving our way through the river systems that make up this unique and beautiful landscape, they were mesmerising and I have to admit I found it exhilarating, adrenaline-charged and I marvelled at the skill of the coxswains handling these powerful wooden boats through the tight tributaries.

Safe in their own environment we would occasionally stop and 'raft alongside, so they could discuss, smoke a cigarette, take a piss, intimidate, take the piss. Villagers would gather on the banks as we passed through communities waving flags and cheering at the sight of these victorious boats heading deeper into the delta and after 4 hours as the light faded and the full moon rose we reached the isolated militant camp that we would remain for the following 20 days.

It was grim. We witnessed erratic young men celebrating the murder of 17 civilian and Navy Nigerians in one operation to destroy an oil facility; there were others. They danced, staggered engaged in a diatribe of violence and chanting fuelled by African Hemp and alcohol. I toiled with the impossible option of trying to escape as I felt a self-imposed burden and responsibility to pick the right moment. I hovered on a number of occasions of an opportune moment to over-power the armed guards and make a selfish attempt of escape only to finally accept I was incapable of doing it. There was no peace, no real attempt between us to lift moral having tried and failed with storytelling and occasional joke in the first couple of days of our ordeal.

Having scrutinised our situation the only collective sense of how to approach our relationship with those personalities in the group and the varying degrees of command was to be submissive and not to antagonise anyone. They were volatile, had proved themselves as capable of cold blooded murder, of carrying out execution and they would keep us only as long as we were of any use to them. I feared a Nigerian 'Special Forces or military' rescue attempt. As an ex-military guy I couldn't help but analyse how such an operation would unfold and came up with only one outcome and not a happy one, but prepared for one and briefed the other three on what to do when the Mi-24 Hind attack helicopters appeared above the tree tops. A ransom demand of $1.5 Billion for our release was requested along with some totally unattainable demands aimed at the Nigerian Government.

We were fed once a day with a watermelon supplemented by one tin of corn-beef or sardines and four slices of bread between us... but rarely did we feel hungry. I knew my family would be hurting, worried and praying for an end to our ordeal. My kids were never far from my thoughts. I spoke and had 'thought conversations' with each one and was able to escape, for a few moments from the hot, dusty and oppressive reality of an isolated militant camp. As the days slipped by we did make an attempt to 'humanise' ourselves with some of our captors, a deliberate attempt to build a kind of relationship with guys who stood over us with AK47's and SLRs as we dug a hole and took a dump.

Guys who took pleasure in watching us wash down naked with half a tea towel and a bucket of filthy river water and who threatened to take me out on their next operation as a human shield. We slept on foam on a stone floor and for the thirteen hours of daylight and made to sit on those white plastic chairs. Harry and I would sow the water melon seeds in neat lines and if a coconut fell from the palms he would harvest it and we shared a momentary treat. Yet these were young men, who occasionally went home at weekends to their own families. Young men who could articulate their plight...." Mr Nigel, do you think I want to sleep with an AK47 as my pillow.... I studied to be a lawyer, now I'm forced to take up arms and fight for what I believe!?"

Our release came quickly and un-expectedly. After one botched attempt and returning back to the camp, we were finally dropped off at a predetermined R.V and civilian clothed State Security Service (SSS) personnel drove us the short distance to Goodluck Jonathan's (now Nigerian President) residence near Yenagoa. I have no contact these days with the three other guys I shared those 20 days with, but I am immensely proud of how we conducted ourselves collectively under such intense pressure. I do feel privileged to have seen the staggering beauty of this inaccessible place for Westerners and listened opened mouthed to the mass chanting of the Ijew nation. If they could bring that to the West End of London, to a theatre, people would cue around the block to buy tickets to see the show. Experiencing and coming into contact with an aboriginal, indigenous tribe who had never seen or heard of white people was fascinating. I'm humbled by the Hostage release team sent out from the U.K to help in securing our release yet rarely think of those militants that went on the kidnap and subject many others to what we endured, and far worse.

Many, including Peter, will have grounded their weapons and returned to their families, a few I suspect will still carry arms, others will have perished. Our incident was the first MEND operation and plunged Nigeria and worldwide oil supplies from the region into chaos, cost billions of dollars and hundreds of lives. We were four of the fortunate ones, although I very much doubt we reached the $1.5 billion demanded for our freedom, I'm very pleased to have it back.
~ NWC Nov' 2012

Shortly the following press release was issued:

Four foreign oil workers held hostage in Nigeria for nearly three weeks have been freed.

BBC.com, January 30 2006

The four men - an American, Briton, Bulgarian and Honduran - have now left the oil-producing Niger Delta region and met Nigeria's president in Abuja. "They are as well as could be hoped," a British diplomat said. Officials have denied that any ransom demand was paid. The four were seized in an armed raid by militants demanding more control over oil resources for local residents. The Movement for the Emancipation of the Niger Delta had also been demanding the release of two ethnic Ijaw leaders currently in detention and $1Billion in compensation for local communities affected by oil spills. It has also carried out several attacks on oil interests in the region.

One of the patrol craft pictured with the FSPO in the background.

The hijacking of MV .... by Somali pirates

November 5th 2009

Information is from the former Chief Officer of the MV ....: now Capt. .... of whom the author had the pleasure of sailing with in the HRA mid 2012.

In November 2009, the bulk carrier MV .... was delivering wheat from the Ukraine to Mombasa, Kenya. Her course would take her within close vicinity of the Seychelles island group.

The crew made up of 7 Ukrainians and 14 Filipinos were aware of the dangers within the high-risk area. They prepared the ship for the transit, but only had fire hoses to be fixed as an anti-piracy deterrent.

On the morning of the 5th November 2009, not far away were the beautiful islands of Mahe and Praslin, in flat calm seas, the first skiff was seen 5 nm ahead of the bow on the radar. The fire hoses were turned on and the ship started to zigzag through the flat sea. Due to the aggressive steering the ships speed decreased down to 7 knots as expected, however the wash did very little to prevent the skiffs from coming alongside. A mayday message was sent, the SSAS button pressed as well as the GMDSS unit.

The first pirate skiff is alongside on the forward Stbd side, the 2nd approaches from in front of the bow

The first skiff approached on its attack run from the aft, the second approached from the starboard quarter. The freeboard was only 6m and with the calm seas and low speed it was easy for the pirates to establish their aluminum ladder and climb aboard.

Very quickly the pirates were up the ladder and assaulting the bridge.

Within seconds they were all onboard, it was terrifying to see armed pirates running towards the bridge firing their deadly AK47 rifles at the bridge. Then an RPG7 was fired, this impacted between the crane and the accommodation deck, bullets impacted into the bridge smashing the bridge windows with a terrifying noise.

Just one of the many bullet holes

There were only 2 skiffs which were launched from a nearby mother ship, the term mothership should be used lightly as it was merely an oversized open whaler, full of fuel, water and rations, hardly an open ocean craft by any means. In each skiff were 5 pirates, all armed and very aggressive. It took the 10 pirates no time to get to the bridge where the Captain and Chief Engineer remained. In the Engine Control Room (ECR) 2 crewmembers remained, the rest of the crew was mustered in the mess room. As soon as the pirates burst into the bridge, the crew was ordered to the bridge.

The pirate leader asked in perfect English "who is the Captain?" and wanted to know nationalities, they were worried that the crew may be French, Korean or Spanish due to those nations being famed for hostage rescue. The pirate leader used to be an English teacher in Somalia before he took up arms; he was clearly in charge but treated the crew fairly in a menacing way.

The tiny mothervessel craned onboard

The skiffs and mothervessel were craned aboard as well as their other possessions including the 7m ladders. Now there were a total of 12 Somalis onboard, the new course was given to the Captain to the area of Raas Cusbad, Somalia.

The ship arrived at Raas Cusbad on the 8th November and dropped anchor 1.5nm from the shore, 2 pirates stayed onboard the other 10 went home with a salary of $10 000 each. Also in the anchorage were other hijacked vessels including a Spanish and Russian fishing boat, the container ship MV Kota Wajar and bulk carrier MV Al Kaliq.

The new Somali guards arrived along with their own chef and their own food supplies. The sentries were well posted, all the bridge doors were 'locked down' except for the port door. The armed guards were permanently stationed on the port and starboard bridge wings, another at the aft of the bridge and one on the Monkey Island. The ship had enough food onboard to last 2 months. The crew, the hostages were all kept on the bridge, on the port side, they were fed 3 times per day, the ship's cook would cook with the Somali cook, albeit different meals. The Somalis would not eat the western food, but did eat and drink and smoke everything from the bonded store.

There were goats brought onboard to be used as fresh rations as well as Kenyan cigarettes and plenty of Khat. The leaves from the Khat were fed to the goats.

On the first day the crew were allowed to shower, after that they had one every 3 days. The Captain had a satellite phone in his cabin and would make a call to his family and office every time he showered.

He would also press the SSAS button daily to inform the ship's office all was well, if he didn't press it, it meant that things were not good onboard. This secret messaging system worked very well and helped keep the crew's families informed and lessened the anxiety.

On the first day that the pirates had control of the ship, they naturally ransacked it, systematically from cabin to cabin and then through the stores. The crew initially lied about the ship's safe, but the doubting pirates grabbed a crewmember and threatened to kill him there and then, this ended as a mock execution (which can have a huge mental impact later on in life).

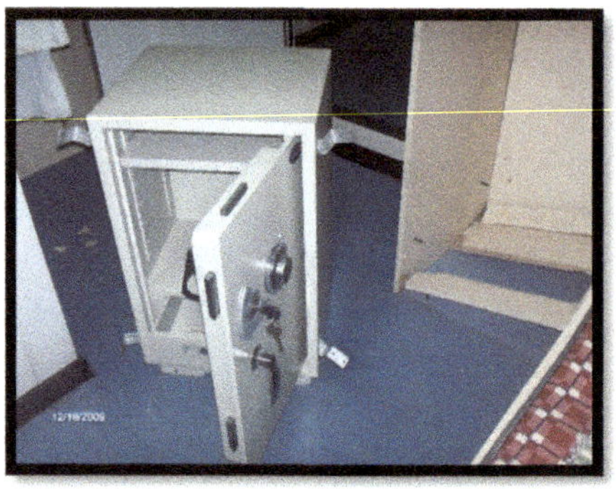

Lying about the safe almost cost the life of a crew member

After that the pirates were told almost everything, the personal affects, the money and stores were all looted despite pirates stating they don't do this. They also stole the ship's computers that control the ship's ballast, they were however returned and the pirates helped to reconnect them in the bridge.

The Captain was allowed to make a call using the satellite phone, he called the company office and his family, the next call was made after 10 days. The crew was very happy with the way the Greek owned shipping company Medway, dealt with the situation. It was on the 17th December that the Captain liaised with Medway about the transfer of the ransom
The 6 weeks of being held as hostage on the cramped bridge passed slowly, the crew tried to befriend the pirates and the Captain would play cards with his captors as a way to bond and fake trust. For the crew they considered every day to be their last. At last a ransom was negotiated and it was arranged that a small fixed wing aircraft would drop the money. The small plane, a Cessna, flying low level circled the ship 3 times before dropping the sacks into the sea. The pirates cleared the area ensuring there were no other boats nearby and collected the sacks, the pirate leader and Captain counted the contents a total of $3.3 million USD.
Once the pirate leader was happy, he wrote a letter ordering safe passage (port clearance) to Mombasa, then their boats were lowered into the sea and they were gone, leaving an emaciated goat as a present.

The German Navy lowers soldiers onto the ship. The warship is seen behind. Below a soldier examines the debris left behind by the Khat chewing pirates.

The German Navy arrived in the warship 'Bremen' on the 17th December and lowered a liaison team onto the freed ship by Lynx helicopter using a fast rope system. The crew had a party on the night of the 17th to celebrate their release and return to normality. The Navy ensured everyone was OK and escorted the ship to Mombasa that arrived on the 21st December. She stayed there until 30th December with an entire crew change on the 28th. The crew flew home from Mombasa to Odessa via London and Kiev, (in Kiev, the Ukrainians threw a party for them) when they arrived the crew were asked if they needed counseling, they declined as it was the 31st December and wanted to see their families and friends as well as celebrate the end of year festivities.
Soon afterwards they were on the local TV station being asked about their ordeal, it would only be 6 weeks before they returned to the high-risk area of the Somali pirates.

The German warship escorts the released ship back to Mombasa, Kenya

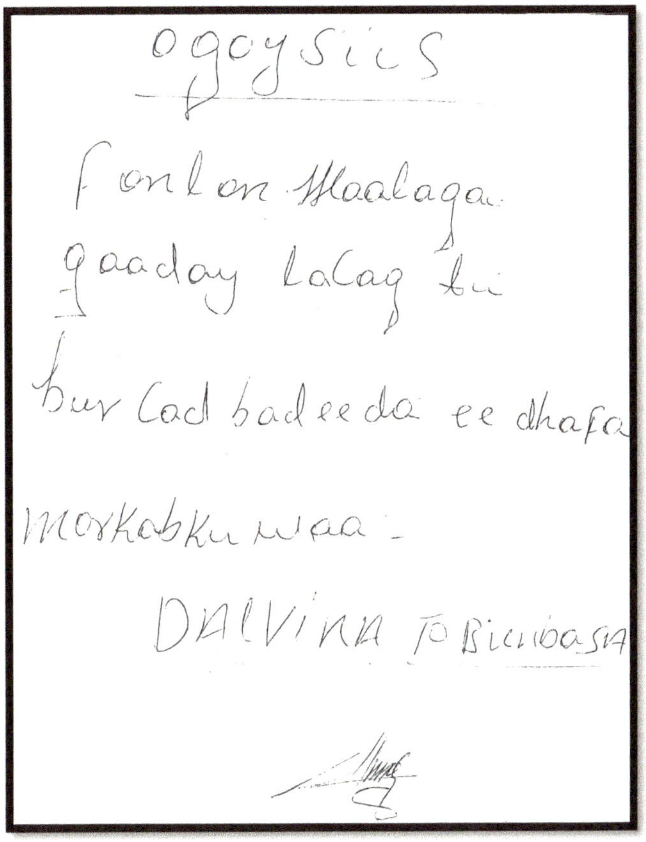

Left is the 'port clearance' note the pirate leader wrote ensuring that the ship would be left alone if it were to be boarded again by other Somali pirates after her release.

Above is the Khat and Kenyan cigarettes favoured by the pirates

Below the 2 photos show the crew living in the bridge for 7 weeks, the officers had mattresses, the crew had cardboard. This should never happen, it is up to the CSO and Capt. To ensure the ship is a safe as possible when it is going to be in a high risk area.

Below is the letter of instruction as how to execute the exchange of the ransom.

TELiX MSG: DB87D-00 13/12/09 10:08 Page 1 of 2

TO: Mr. Ali - Chief Negotiator

TO: Captain

FROM: Captain

DATE: 13 December 2009

The Company will deliver USD$3.5M to the vessel on Thursday 17th December to release the crew, vessel and cargo.

The delivery will be made by a civilian aircraft that will drop 3 packages into the sea on small parachutes close to the vessel. The packages will be dropped one at a time. The EXPECTED time of the delivery is in the early afternoon. The time may have to change dependent upon circumstances and the weather conditions.

Please read these instructions and carry them out EXACTLY. Please confirm that you have read, understood and agree to all the instructions and conditions in this e-mail.

A confirmation must be sent from Mr. Ali and that he understands and agrees to these instructions.

Instructions

1. For security and identification you are to move the vessel on Thursday morning to a position 5nm AWAY from any other vessel or craft. You should be in your new position by 1100hrs on Thursday. We will call you at 1130 to take your new position. On arrival at the new position the vessel must be against the wind (pointing into the wind). The aircraft will arrive between 1200 and 1600. We will call you when we have spoken to the pilot and we know the time. DO NOT BE LATE. The aircraft has limited fuel and cannot wait around for long.

2. 15 minutes before the aircraft arrives you must have one small boat in the water on the starboard side of the vessel. The boat must have three people on board. There should be at least 3 flares on board. The crew of the boat must understand how to use the flares. There should be a second boat in the water at the stern of the vessel in case there are any problems.

3. If the pilot sees any weapons pointed at the aircraft he will NOT drop the money. If the pilot feels threatened at any time he will NOT drop the money. Please make sure ALL the pirate guards understand this very clearly. No Khat, no alcohol, no drugs on Thursday. Mr. Ali must order this or there will be NO drop.

4. When the crew of the small boat see the aircraft and when THEY ARE READY to accept the air drop they should light and hold up a flare. The boat should travel in a circle of no larger than 100 meters in diameter. The aircraft will identify the vessel first and will then do a PRACTICE pass. If the aircraft is unable to make the drop on the second pass it will circle and try again.

5. There are THREE packages to be dropped. The pirates should collect and hold up the first package for the pilot to see. When the aircraft confirms the pirates have the first package the aircraft will make another pass to drop the second package. The pirates should hold up the second package for the pilot to see, then the third package. When the pilot confirms all three packages have been collected the aircraft will leave.

packages and inform the Company by e-mail. The Captain and First Officer must witness the counting of all the money. The Captain must be on the bridge all day so we can speak to him.

7. When the money has been counted and distributed the pirates agree to leave the vessel as soon as possible.

8. The pirates agree not to harm any member of the crew, not to take any of the crew's private possessions, not to take or damage any if the vessel's equipment or cargo.

Signed:

Mr. Ali - Chief Negotiator..

The Pirate Leader..

Witnessed:

Captain ....

Date: 13 December 2009

20. FIRST AID

All vessels carry some sort of first-aid equipment, from the most basic to a full trauma unit. When a vessel is planning to transit or work in an area where it may encounter piracy and armed robbery, it is essential to have not only first-aid equipment, but also to ensure that the items are suitable to treat trauma, and that the nominated medic knows this kit inside out and knows how to use it. Prior to entering high-risk areas, the crew should carry out realistic drills to rehearse the treatment and recovery of a crew member. Crews don't like such drills and tend to regard them as an inconvenience, but like man overboard and fire drills they are necessary and may save lives.

Photo MedAire Yacht lifeline

Most boats have comprehensive medical equipment on board, but in a crisis it can take the first aider valuable time to make up a trauma 'crash-pack' from many different medical packs stowed under seats or in the keel compartments. If a crew member does sustain a serious injury like a torrential bleed or gunshot wound, there simply isn't the time to go hunting for the appropriate kit.

Some companies offer a service whereby the on-call doctor can be called 24 hours a day to give immediate advice. This must not be relied upon to replace an on-board medic though. A very good company that provides training, equipment and the 24/7 doctor's service is www.lifeline.com Other leading UK-based medical companies are ERS www.ers999.com or Ex-med, www.exmed.co.uk both are ex-UK Special Forces combat medic instructors and have an excellent service history of life-saving situations in war-torn countries. Both companies have excellent reputations and can provide training and medical equipment.

ex+med UK Ltd

1. **EX-MED**

Global leaders of medical equipment supply, medical support and training, Ex-med, an ISO 9001/2000 registered company, is an independent provider of specialist medical support and training for companies, media, and international humanitarian organisations operating in remote and hostile environments.

Led by doctors, clinicians, military medics and occupational health specialists, the company offers on-the-ground support, training and specialised equipment tailor-made to meet the medical and operational needs of clients.

Exmed UK ltd,
Pengethley Manor Hotel
Pengethley Park,
Ross on Wye
Herefordshire, HR9 6LL

- **Tel: 01432 355964**
- **Email: info@exmed.co.uk**

2. **ERS INTERNATIONAL GROUP LIMITED**

ERS Medical
SRCL Group Company

On call manager (for urgent communications)
01484 500001 (24/7)
19-27 Thistle Street
Huddersfield
HD1 6PU

ERS INTERNATIONAL GROUP LIMITED

Tel: +44 (0) 8455 202999

Fax: +44 (0) 8455 203999

contact@ersgroup.co.uk

3. MEDAIRE LIFELINE: www.medaire.com/yachtlifeline
   info@yatchlifeline.com

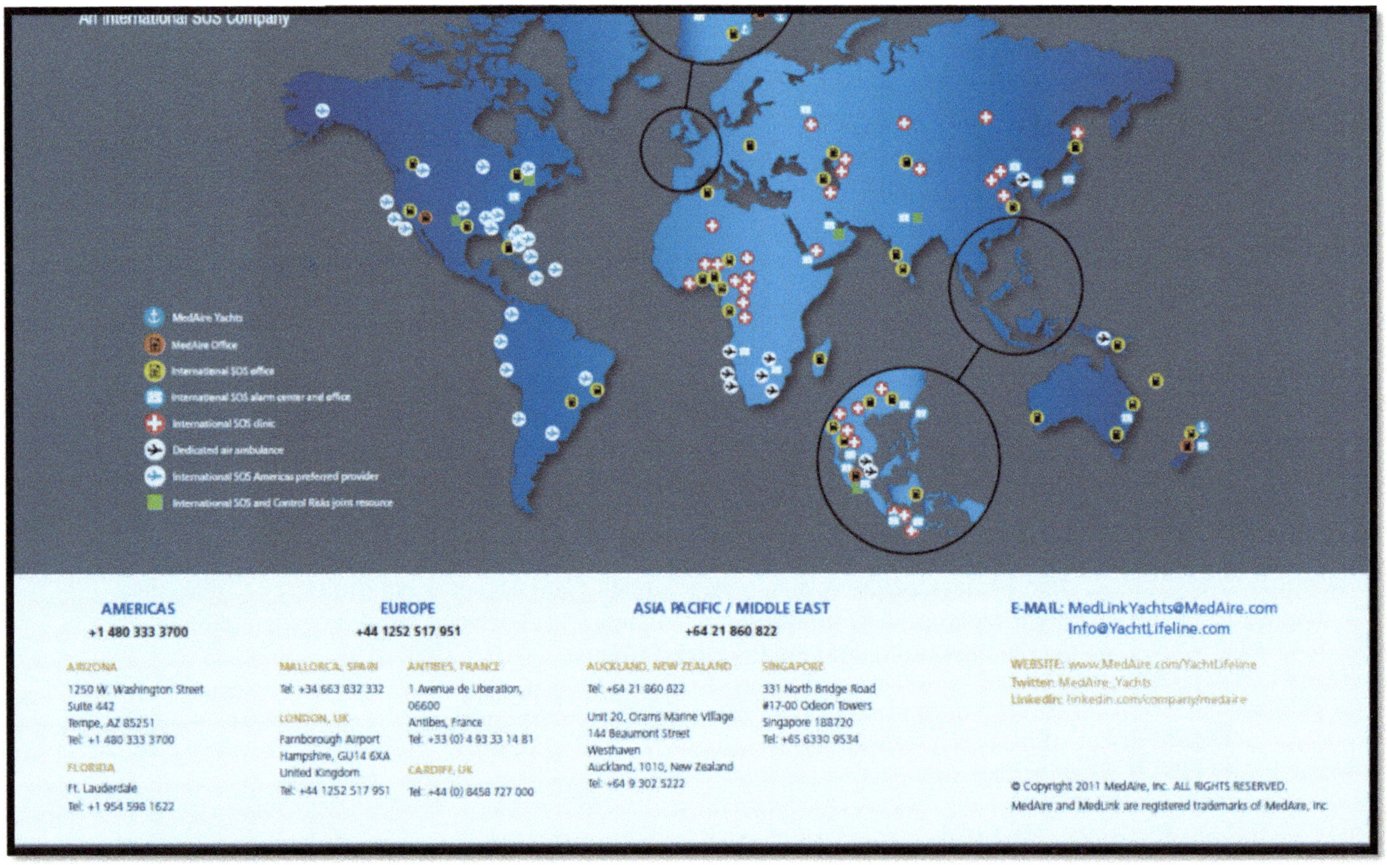

Contact details for London, UK
Tel: +44 1252 517 951
Farnborough Airport
Hampshire,
GU14 6XA
Fax: +44 1252 373 299

First Aid for High Risk Waters

Next is a aide memoire of the correct treatment for the types of injury that may be sustained when in high-risk areas. Somali pirates normally fire their AK47 type rifles and RPGs at the bridge. The types of injuries that could be expected are gun shot wounds caused by the high velocity bullet, a blast injury caused by the RPG warhead detonating upon the bridge, arterial bleeding (also known as torrential or massive bleeding) and burns. All of these are life threatening and those persons designated to remain in the bridge during an attack plus the ship's medical officer and VPT must know these basic life saving techniques.

The following information derives from Mr. John Butterfield, Steve Barrans and ERS999

Introduction

Blast and Gunshot wounds

Permanent cavitation is the hole made by the missile as it moves through the body (Like the hole made when you stick your finger in butter). This hole remains after the missile has passed.

Temporary cavitation is caused by the force behind the missile, which pushes it along. This wave is larger than the missile itself and crushes tissues in its way. This leaves a mass of damaged tissues around the permanent cavity and causes the large exit wounds.

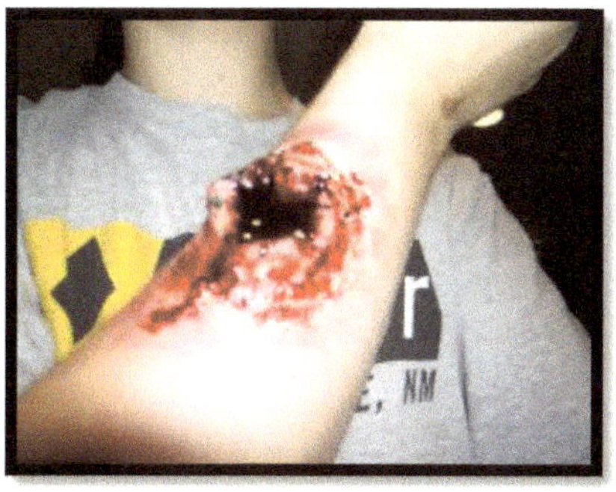

Low energy weapons are normally hand held such a knives and only cause a permanent cavity. Medium and high-energy weapons cause both temporary and permanent cavities.

Blast injuries

Blast injuries are categorized into four stages

- Primary - Shockwave. This damages organs which contain air such as the ears, lungs and sinuses
- Secondary – Fragments of the bomb or from the ship hit the body causing bleeding and fractures
- Tertiary – Blast wind throws body causing fractures and wounds
- Quaternary – Burns, Nightmares

Fragment injuries

Fragment injuries can cause penetrating or blunt trauma. Any casualty who has suffered a fragment injury from a blast must also be treated for a neck injury if possible.

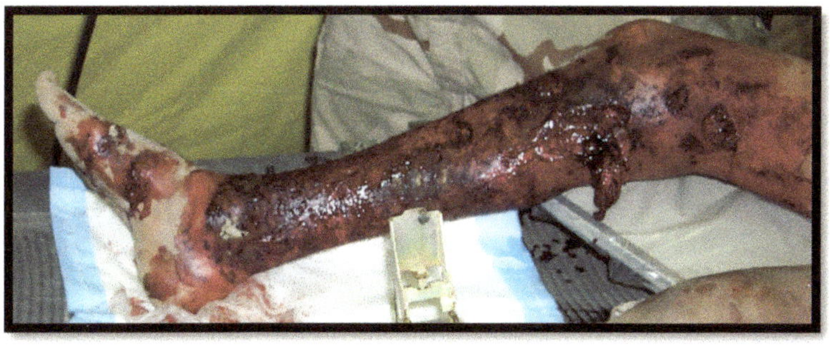

TREATMENTS

Check the casualty for injury using this order

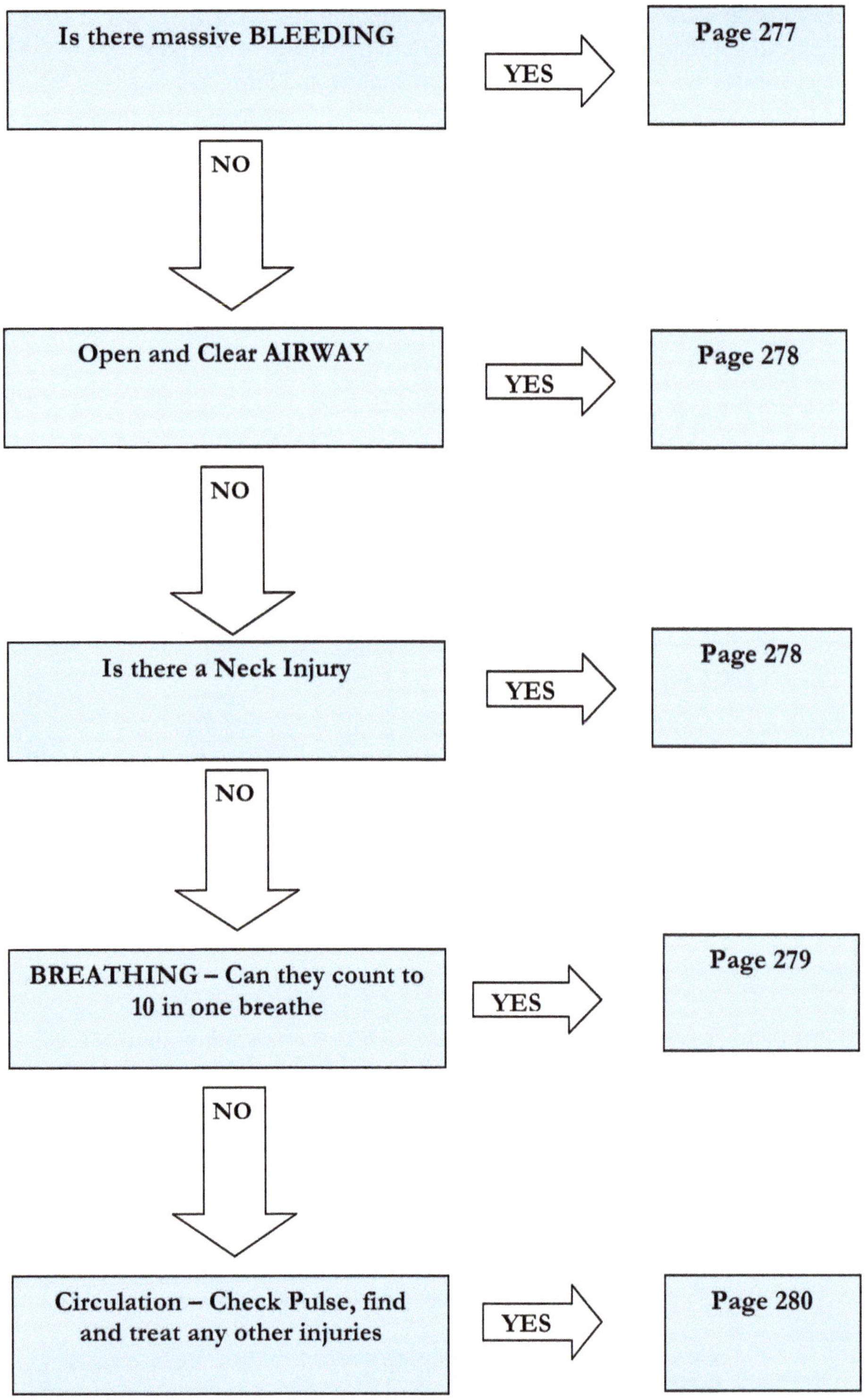

Massive Bleeding

The first priority in major injury is to stop massive bleeding. Depending on medical equipment available there may be a need to improvise.

Where is the Massive Bleed

Body (torso), neck, head

Apply pressure to the wound

If available insert celox, quikclot or hemcon into wound

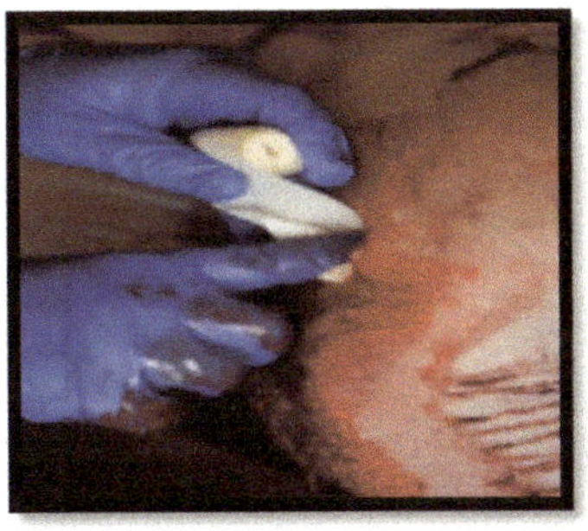

Limbs (arms/ legs)

Apply pressure to above the wound

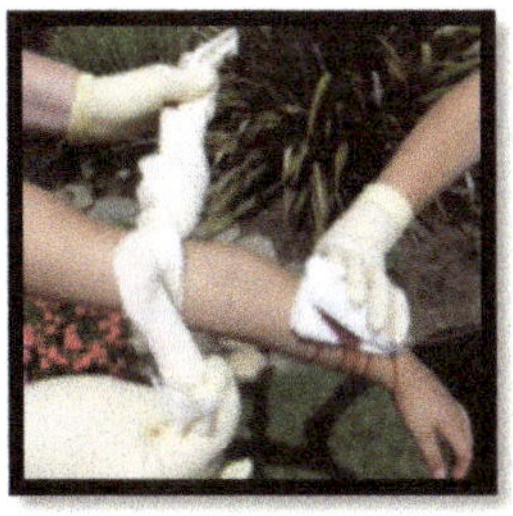

Apply a tourniquet

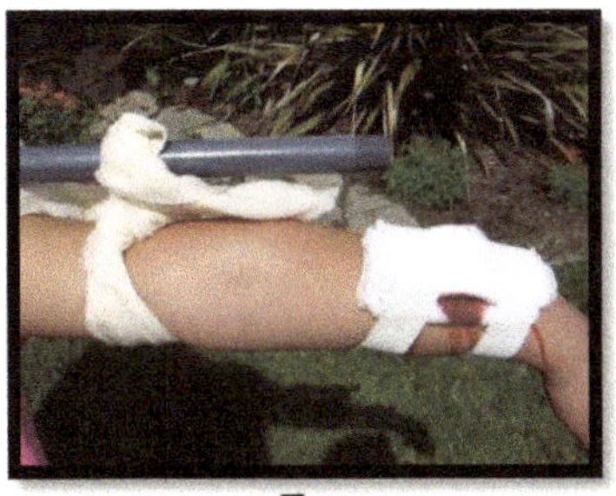

Put on a tight dressing. Apply more if needed

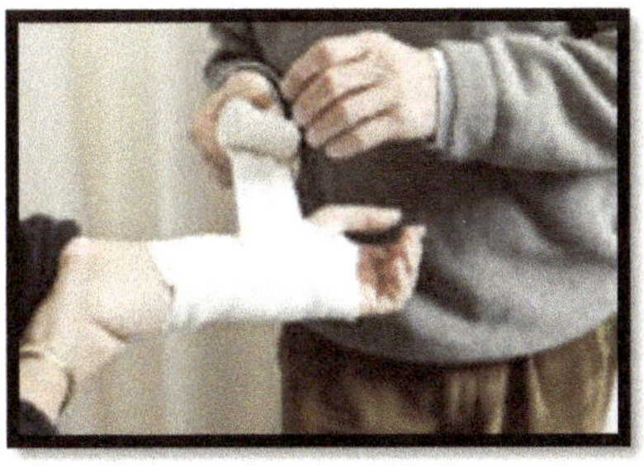

If the injury is amputation and the limb is intact

1. Clean limb and put in plastic bag or plastic
2. Put bag into ice but do NOT let any part of the limb touch the ice

Airway

Once all massive bleeding has been stopped, the next step is to open the airway.

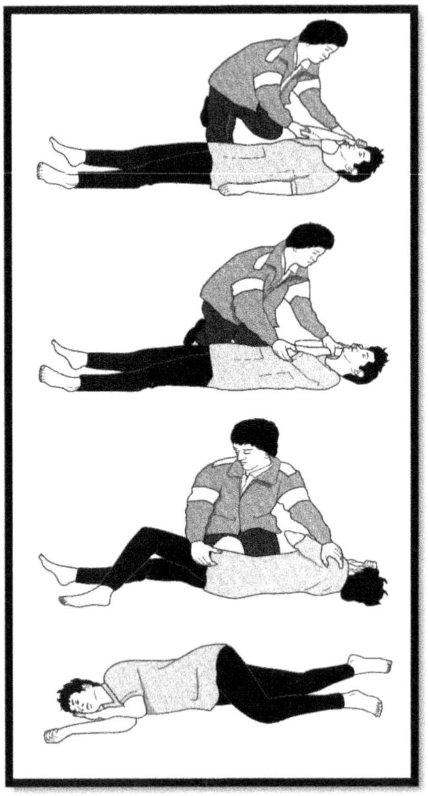

Look inside the mouth and remove any obstructions

Place the casualties hand on the side of their face and hold with your hand

Role the casualty towards you, onto their side

Put their head slightly down so any blood or vomit pours out the mouth.

Neck Injury

Suspect if the casualty has been hit above the shoulder, been thrown by the blast, fallen from height or complains of pain in their neck and/or pins and needles in their body.

If there is a possible neck injury and it is possible at the time, the head should be held still.

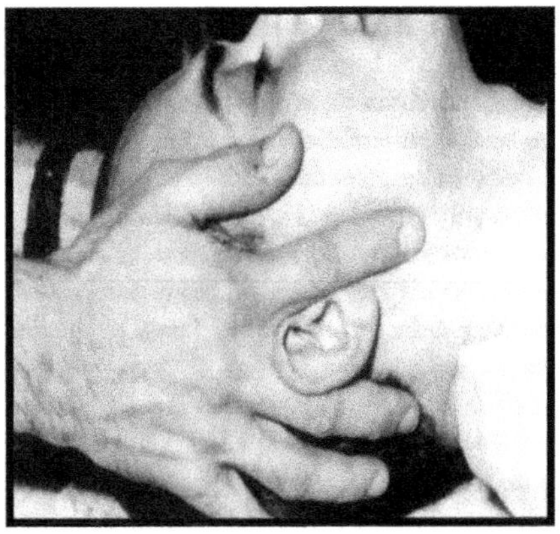

Breathing

If the casualty cannot count to 10 in one breath they may have a chest injury. Common chest injuries from blasts or gunshots are sucking chest wounds or multiple broken ribs (Flail segments)

Sucking Chest Injury (Open pneumothorax)

If there is a hole in the chest, air moves through the hole instead of going into the lung

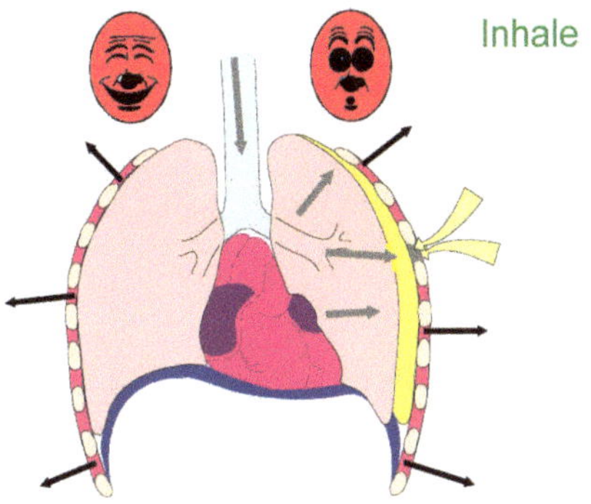

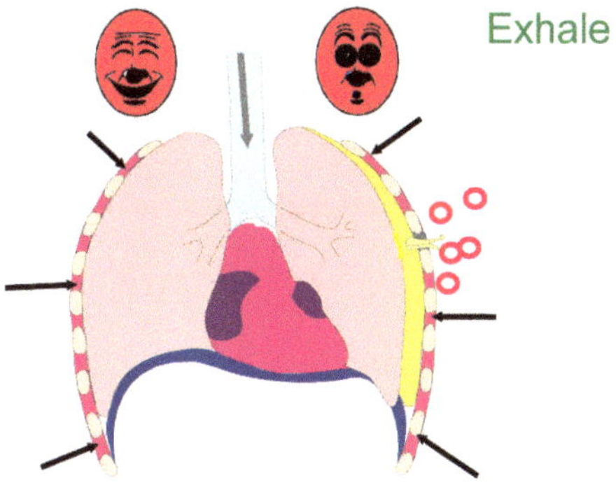

1. Place hand over hole
2. Clean area
3. Apply chest seal over wound or improvise. Cut a piece of plastic bag (a wrapper from a bandage, a piece of waterproof map) just larger than the chest injury. Put it over wound and secure with tape on 3 sides. The open side should be on the side closest to the arm
4. Check for exit wound on chest/back. If found treat as a massive bleed.
5. If the casualty is awake sit them up leaning towards the injured side of the body.
6. If the casualty is not awake, roll onto injured side (see Airway) but make sure the open side of the plastic does not get blocked.

Broken ribs (Flail segment)

Broken ribs are very painful and this may be why the casualty is having breathing problems. If more than 2 ribs are broken in 2 or more places, and the ribs are next to each other this will make it very difficult to breathe.

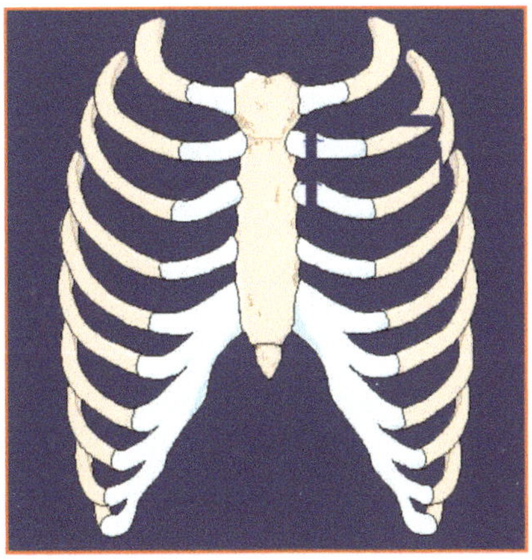

Treatment - Splint

1. Place a solid item, the same size as injury eg. Folded up cardboard
2. Tape this to the chest ensuring that you do not go all the way around the chest

Circulation

1. Check the Radial pulse.

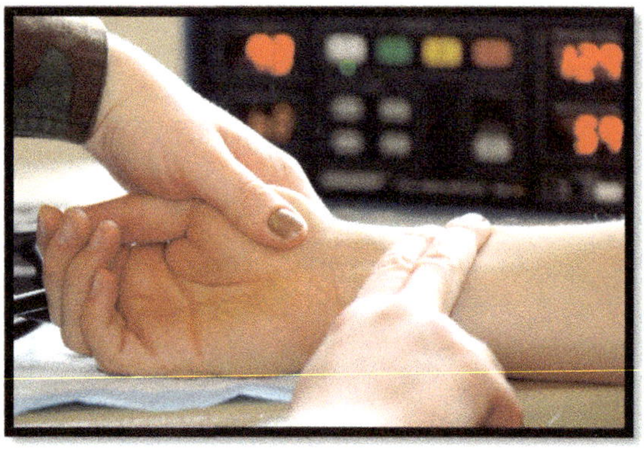

If you can not find it take a carotid pulse

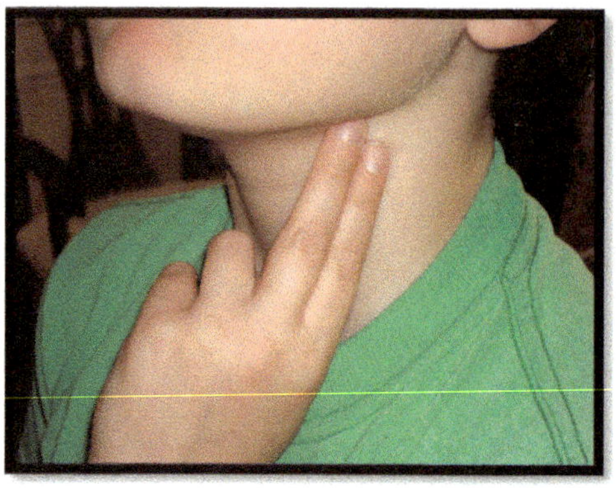

2. Check the whole body for any other injuries such as broken bones or burns.

Broken Bones (Fractures)

1. Ask the casualty if anywhere else hurts and feel the whole body for any bones that look or feel out of place or do not feel straight.
2. Support in the position found by using slings or improvising using cardboard and tape

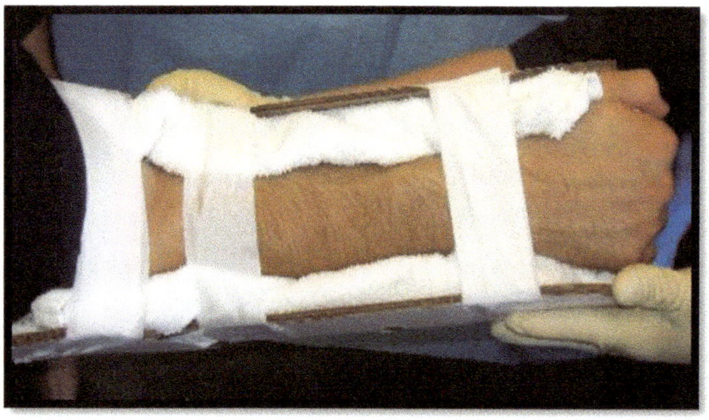

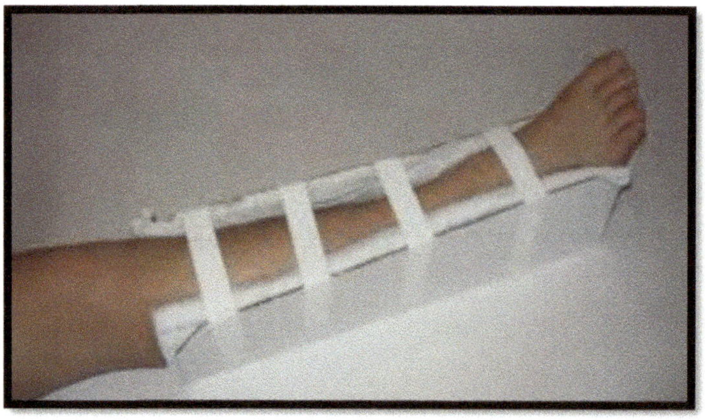

Burns

There are three layers of burns

- Superficial – red swollen and tender
- Partial thickness – raw and blisters
- Full thickness – involve all layers of skin

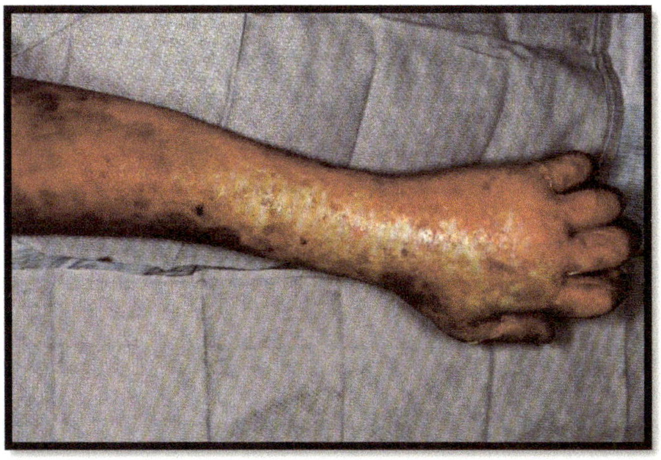

Left is a second-degree, superficial burn

Treatment

- Cool with water for min of 10 minutes
- Remove rings/watches and hot or wet clothing not stuck to skin
- Cover burn with sheets of Clingfilm or dressing. The opening of freezer type, food bags also works well due to them being sterilised on the inside. Never wrap plastic around the burn tightly, it should always be done in strips to allow swelling.

With all types of injuries at sea, there is always a way to request medical assistance such as 'Radio Medical Assistance' whereupon a landstation or nearby vessel may have someone who is qualified in such. Also use the satellite phone, the shipping company will have a point of contact for a medical emergency. If in doubt, seek help as there have been cases whereupon a casualty at sea has died due to illness or infection.

21. REPORTS AND REPORTING

Prevention is better than cure, so before transitting through a high-risk area, previous and current reports should be read from as many sources as possible. The use of public source information from the internet would be a first recommendation for sailors in remote parts of the world that are deemed high-risk, also there are excellent sailing guides and local information in pilots regarding anchorages and possible hazards/problems.

As we all kwon, there are some very professional agencies such as the IMO, UKMTO, MARLO and MSCHOA, which give excellent advice and have reports of activity in areas all over the world. The International Maritime Bureau (IMB), based in London and the Piracy Reporting Centre in Kuala Lumpur (PRC) are also very good sources of reliable information. For GoA commercial transits, there is the downloadable Best Management Practices 4 (BMP4) available from www.marisec.org; some facts agree and disagree with facts in this book, but most are along similar lines.

UKMTO

MERCHANT VESSEL VOLUNTARY REPORTING SCHEME

The UK Royal Navy's Maritime Trade Organisation (MTO) has been established in the Middle East since late 2001 as an extension of Royal Navy operations in the region. Although the MTO team focus is in support of UK flag and UK interest shipping in the area it is available to provide support across the entire maritime industry including shipping of all flag registry and ownership. The team will remain in the region for the foreseeable future.

In November 2002 the voluntary reporting scheme for UK interest shipping was extended to cover the Red Sea, Indian Ocean north of 10S as well as the Arabian Gulf. On a voluntary basis only, ships (of any flag or ownership) are invited to report to the Maritime Trade Operations team on passing the following reference points:

a. Suez for vessels entering or leaving the Region via the Red Sea
b. 10S for ships entering or leaving the Region via the Indian Ocean (SOUTH)
c. 78E for ships entering or leaving the Region via the Indian Ocean (EAST)

The initial report should contain the following;

Ship Name
IRCS (International Radio Call Sign)
Flag
IMO number
MMSI
Inmarsat telephone number including satellite prefix
Telex and fax number
Email address
Name of Company having day-to-day management
Type of Ship
Date/time of current position course and speed
Itinerary in the region with route way points and destination port(s)
British personnel onboard (if any)

Subsequently, ships are requested to report their noon positions and speed, actual departure times and estimated arrival times at ports and destination when outward bound from the defined area. All timings are requested in UTC and the preferred method of communication is e-mail.

Contact numbers/details for UKMTO as follows:

E-mail ukmto@eim.ae
Telephone CO +971 50 552 3215
2IC +971 50 552 6007
Fax +971 4 306 5710
Telex (51) 210473

The information provided is treated in strict commercial confidence and is only used within coalition military circles. Royal Navy assets in the region and Northwood Headquarters in UK are kept advised. If further advice or guidance is required please do not hesitate to contact the UKMTO Team.

There are websites that deal only with these subjects and have links to other sources too (see 'Moonsite'). Sailors and sea goers often write articles or blogs about such subjects, and many contain good advice. Readers should be aware that information of this type may not be completely correct, and may even be incorrect. Quality boat and sailing magazines often have articles about piracy, theft, and recommendations; these can be ordered as back copies and are sometimes available in larger libraries.
Probably two of the best private companies for up-to-date information reporting are Dryad Maritime Intelligence Service, based in Portsmouth, and Ironside Associates Ltd (IAL), based in Norwich. IAL is also one of the leading maritime security companies and deals with a broad range of security needs including equipment and manpower. Both offer all kinds of information about anywhere in the world and have very comprehensive information about piracy including coalition warship activity, weather, and tides. These reports can be sent out on a daily basis to any vessel.

Contact Details:

Ironside Associates Limited

PO Box 3239
Norwich
Norfolk
NR7 7BF

Ironside Associates Ltd
Specialist Security Consultancy Services

Phone: +44 (0) 1603 702930
Email: info@ironsideassociates.co.uk
www.ironsideassociates.co.uk

Dryad Maritime Intelligence Service

DRYAD MARITIME

E-mail: enquiries@dryadmaritime.com
www.dryad-maritime.com

USA Telephone: 1-888-316-3260
UK General & Sales Enquiries: +44 (0) 845 060 0072
Operations: +44 (0) 845 060 0071
Address: *Dryad Maritime Intelligence Service PO Box 947 Portsmouth PO1 9LY United Kingdom*

Another very professional company to consider is RiskIntelligence.
http://www.riskintelligence.eu/

Risk Intelligence ApS

Marievej 23
2950 Vedbaek
Denmark
Tel: +45 70 26 62 30
Fax: +45 70 26 62 40

SPOT: All Captains and crewmembers know how to send distress calls using VHF CH16. As well as a Mayday call, all other means should be used to call for help and inform authorities of what is happening or what has happened. On pages 289-290 there are simple report forms that can be filled in during an incident, with headings prompting the writer to note all the correct information.

When sailing through the GoA IRTC, ensure that the ship's co-ords are sent to the UKMTO (copied to MSCHOA) every 6 hours and every 24 hours when in the HRA. Information from the ship is usually sent back to the shipping company and security company on a frequent basis whilst in high-risk areas, with this information either can warn the ship as to where the pirate PAGs are and which areas to avoid.

There is a piece of equipment called 'SPOT', which is a programmable GPS tracking device. This system works very well for any vessel or individual as it can send its location coordinates every time it is activated. The receiving end can see its position in conjunction with Google Earth. It has an emergency button that when activated will show up on the receiver's computer as an emergency, a mobile phone number can be added to the alert, so a text will be sent immediately to the phone informing that person that 'Spot" number x has sent an emergency signal. Each 'Spot' has its own unique ID, so for companies with multiple trackers, they know which ship has which tracker. Well-recommended and cheap to buy at less than £200 & a small annual contract.

IMB Piracy Reporting Centre

Before 1992, shipmasters and ship operators had nowhere to turn to when their ships were attacked, robbed or hijacked either in port or out at sea. Local law enforcement either turned a deaf ear, or chose to ignore that there was a serious problem in their waters.

The International Maritime Bureau was aware of the escalating level of piracy and wanted to provide a free service to the seafarer and established the 24-hour IMB Piracy Reporting Centre (PRC) in Kuala Lumpur, Malaysia. The main objective of the PRC is to be the first point of contact for the shipmaster to report an actual or attempted attack or even suspicious movements, thus initiating the process of response.

Supported by financial contributions from the shipping industry, its services are free and are available to all ships, irrespective of flag.

The main aim of the PRC is to raise awareness within the shipping industry, which includes the shipmaster, ship owner, insurance companies and traders, of the areas of high risk associated with piratical attacks or specific ports and anchorages associated with armed robberies on board ships.

The PRC works closely with various governments and law enforcement agencies and is involved in information sharing in an attempt to reduce and ultimately eradicate this crime.

The key services provided by the Centre are:

- Receiving reports from ships of suspicious or unexplained craft movements and actual boarding and armed robbery, and alerting other ships and law enforcement agencies in the region
- Issuing regular status reports of piracy and armed robbery via routine broadcasts on INMARSAT-C through its Safety NET service. Ships can also obtain these status reports by contacting the IMB Centre
- Collation and analysis of all information received, as well as the issuing of consolidated reports to interested bodies, including IMO

Reporting of incidents
Ships are advised to maintain strict anti-piracy watches and report all piratical attacks and suspicious movements of crafts to the IMB Piracy Reporting Centre, Kuala Lumpur, Malaysia.

IMB Maritime Security Hotline

The International Maritime Bureau (IMB) has also launched a dedicated hotline for seafarers, port workers, shipping agents, shipyard personnel, brokers, stevedores, and all concerned parties, to report any information that they may have seen or heard relating to maritime crime and security, including terrorism, piracy and other illegal activities.

All information received is treated in strict confidence and passed on to relevant authorities for further action. Maritime crime and security concerns everyone, and it is everyone's responsibility to try to minimise the risks and help save lives and property.

IBM International Maritime Bureau

International Piracy Reporting Centre, Kuala Lumpur (PRC)
ICC INTERNATIONAL MARITIME BUREAU
P.O. BOX 12559
50782 Kuala Lumpur
MALAYSIA.
Website: http://www.icc-ccs.org/imb/overview.php
Anti-Piracy Helpline Numbers:
Tel.: +603 2031 0014
Fax: +603 2078 5769
E-mail: imbkl@icc-ccs.org

Piracy Reporting Centre: The IMB Piracy Reporting Centre is funded by voluntary contribution. Without this contribution the PRC could not function. If you would like to make a donation or contribution towards the funding of the centre please contact IMB.
The services of the Centre are available to the shipping industry 24 hours a day, 365 days a year.
Website: http://www.icc-ccs.org/prc/overview.php

IMO International Maritime Organisation

The convention establishing the International Maritime Organisation (IMO) was adopted in Geneva in 1948 and IMO first met in 1959. IMO's main task has been to develop and maintain a comprehensive regulatory framework for shipping and its remit today includes safety, environmental concerns, legal matters, technical co-operation, maritime security and the efficiency of shipping.
A specialised agency of the United Nations with 169 member states and three associate members, IMO is based in the United Kingdom with around 300 international staff.

International Maritime Organization
4, Albert Embankment
London
SE1 7SR
United Kingdom

Tel +44 (0)20 7735 7611
Fax +44 (0)20 7587 3210
Email: info@imo.org

Also consider the Piracy Analysis and Warning Weekly (PAWW) Report:

UNCLASSIFIED

Maritime OPINTEL Report

(U) SOMALIA: Piracy Analysis and Warning Weekly (PAWW) Report (Horn of Africa) for *23 Sep –29 Sep 2010*

29 September 2010

Maritime Crime/Piracy, Commercial (301) 669-4448

1. (U) Scope

(U) The Piracy Analysis and Warning Weekly (PAWW) Report provides a review of incidents and an outlook on the threat to merchant shipping in or near the Gulf of Aden and off the East coast of Somalia from piracy and associated maritime crime. This report is produced primarily to inform merchant mariners and naval forces operating in and near the Horn of Africa of recent pirate activity.

Voluntary reporting requirements as found on the GoA Anti-piracy planning chart:

VOLUNTARY REPORTING REQUIREMENTS

Merchant vessel voluntary reporting schemes are established to increase security, provide anti-piracy support and to maintain the freedom of navigation to all vessels in the Indian Ocean, Arabian Sea, Gulf of Aden and the Red Sea.

Merchant vessels operating in these areas are strongly encouraged to liaise, as detailed below, with the authorities. Any vessel, owner, operator or manager choosing not to report may delay any military assistance in the event of an incident as military assets will not be expecting the ship and valuable information may not be available.

The schemes are free to participate in and vessels of any flag or ownership are invited to participate.
All information is treated in strict commercial confidence and only used within military circles.

REPORTING

Upon entering the UKMTO voluntary reporting area (bounded by Suez in the north, to 10°S and 78°E), or when leaving a port within the area:

(a) Send an Initial Report to UKMTO (by email to ukmto@eim.ae). See "UKMTO STANDARD MESSAGE FORMAT" on this chart and BMP3 Annex B for report details;

(b) Register Vessel Movement with MSC-HOA (on-line at www.mschoa.org, by email to postmaster@mschoa.org, or by fax +44 1923 958520). See www.mschoa.org for report details:

(c) After transmitting the initial reports above, vessels are asked to report daily to UKMTO (with a copy to MSC-HOA) giving their position, course, speed and ETA. In addition, when calling at ports within the reporting area, the date/time of arrival and the ETD should be reported;

(d) If planning to transit the Gulf of Aden, vessels are requested to add the ETA at the IRTC entry point ("Point A" or "Point B") to the daily reports to UKMTO and MSC-HOA;

(e) vessels are also encouraged to increase the frequency of such reports to 6 hourly intervals within 6 hours of entering or navigating within the Internationally Recommended Transit Corridor (IRTC);

(f) When making reports all times should be in "UTC";

(g) Reports may be made by either the vessel or by the owner/operator.

REPORTS AND REPORT FORMATS

Initial Quick Message

Piracy/Armed Robbery Attack Alert

ICC-INTERNATIONAL MARITIME BUREAU

Ship's name and call sign, IMO number, INSMART ID'S (Plus ocean region code) and MMSI	______________________
MAYDAY/DISTRESS ALERT	______________________
URGENCY SIGNAL	______________________
PIRACY/ ARMED ROBBERY ATTACK	______________________
Ship's position (and time of position UTC)	Lat__________ Long__________
Latitude /longitude	Time__________ Knots__________
Course speed (Knots)	

Nature of event

____

____

____

____

____

____

UKMTO Piracy Attack Report

If you have been approached or attacked by pirates, please send UKMTO a piracy attack report including the following information:

Ships particulars/details:

1. Name of Ship:
2. IMO No:
3. Flag:
4. Call Sign:
5. Type of Ship:
6. Last Port/Next Port:

Details of Incident:

7. Date & Time of Incident: Lt/Utc
8. Position: Lat: (N/S) Long: (E/W)
9. Own Ship's Speed:
10. Ship's Freeboard During Attack:
11. Weather During Attack (Rain/Fog/Mist/Clear/etc, Wind (Speed and Direction), Sea/Swell Height):
12. Types of Attack (Boarded/Attempted):
13. Consequences for Crew, Ship and Cargo:
14. Any Crew Injured/Killed:
15. Items/Cash Stolen:
16. Area of the Ship being Attacked:
17. Last Observed Movements of Pirates/Suspect Craft:

Details of Raiding Party:

18. Number of Pirates/Robbers:
19. Dress/Physical Appearance:
20. Language Spoken:
21. Weapons Used:
22. Distinctive Details:
23. Craft Used:
24. Method of Approach:
25. Duration of Attack:
26. Aggressive/Violent:

Further Details:

27. Action Taken by Master and Crew and its effectiveness:
28. Was Incident Reported to the Coastal Authority? If so to whom?
29. Preferred Communications with Reporting Ship:
30. Action Taken by the Authorities:
31. Number of Crew/Nationality:
32. Please Attach with this Report – A Brief Description/Full Report/Master – Crew Statement of the Attack/Photographs taken if any.
33. Details of Self Protection Measures.

22. The ISPS Code

The International Ship and Port Facility Code (ISPS)

- Implemented through SOLAS Chapter XI-2 - special measures to enhance maritime security
- Developed in the wake of the 9/11 attacks in the US
- Adopted in 2002, under the auspices of the International Maritime Organisation (IMO), became mandatory 1 July 2004
- Compliance is mandatory for the 148 contracting parties to SOLAS

  Purpose:

- To detect and deter acts that threaten security
- Establish roles and responsibilities regarding maritime security
- Collate and promulgate security related information
- Provide methodology for security assessments, plans and procedures to react to changing security levels

The ISPS Code

As of the 1 July 2004, internationally trading ships above 500gt will be required, under the ISPS code and SOLAS amendments, to carry on board a Ship Security Plan (SSP) approved by or on behalf of the flag state. This plan will identify measures adopted by the ship to protect it from the risks of a security incident. The code contains specific, mandatory areas of the Plan, which should receive particular focus when operating in high-risk areas. By concentrating on these provisions and the main actions for securing operations in dangerous waters (see Preventative Measures), a ship may be able to reduce the threat of attack:

- Identification of restricted areas
- Measures for the prevention of unauthorised access to the ship
- Procedures for responding to security threats or breaches of security, including provisions for maintaining critical operations of the ship or the interface with the port
- Procedures for evacuation in case of security threats or breaches of security
- Duties of shipboard personnel assigned security responsibilities and of other shipboard personnel on security aspects
- Procedures for training, drills and exercises associated with the plan
- Procedures for reporting security incidents
- Identification of the Company Security Officer, including 24-hour contact details
- Use of the Ship Security Alert System

Contracting governments to SOLAS are recommended to establish 24-hour contact points from which ships may request security advice, and communicate information regarding threats to security to ships flying their flag, or operating in their territorial waters.

Similarly, they should offer advice to ships entering, or intending to enter, their territorial waters and should also provide the contact details of government officers to whom Ship Security Officers (SSOs) can report security concerns. It is recommended that masters and SSOs make use of these facilities when entering known hazardous areas.

It is the responsibility of governments to establish security levels for ships flying their flag, and inform vessels intending to enter their territorial waters or ports of the relevant security levels pertaining to them.
Flag states should provide specific advice on action to be taken in accordance with the three maritime security (MARSEC) levels defined by the ISPS code if there is a change in the security level, a security incident or threat of such and should establish the best methods and procedures for these purposes. In the event of an imminent incident, the ship should seek to establish direct communication with those responsible in the flag state for responding to security incidents.

Where an incident occurs and these recommendations have not been adhered to by the contracting government of the relevant sea area or the flag state, the master should note this fully in his report (see Part E: After an attack).

The master has overriding authority and responsibility to make decisions with respect to the safety and security of the ship and within his rights to implement measures, which he feels, are in his interest. Therefore, although it is normally the duty of the flag state to inform the vessel when to change its security level, as laid out in the Ship Security Plan, the master may operate at – or implement certain measures that would normally come into force when operating at – a higher level, when he feels it is necessary.

General Advice

The following industry guidance incorporates relevant sections from Part B of the ISPS Code. It is intended that the guidance, in conjunction with the specific Ship Security Plan (SSP), will help significantly to reduce the risk of attack when operating in dangerous sea-lanes, ports or anchorages.

Be vigilant

The majority of attacks will be deterred if robbers are aware that they have been observed, and that the crew has been alerted and is prepared to resist attempts to board. Ensure that crewmembers are constantly seen to be moving around the vessels, making random rather than predictable patrols.

Avoid high-risk areas

Wherever possible, avoid high-risk areas and route ships away from areas where attacks have frequently and recently occurred. Attempt to avoid remaining in anchorages in high-risk areas, where ships are most vulnerable to attack, and either steam or drift (with engines on standby) at least20andup to 40 miles offshore at night only returning within VHF range at intervals for orders or news from agents.

Access control

Reduce unauthorised access. Wherever possible, access should be restricted to a single controlled point on the ship. Failing this, the access points specified as such in the SSP should be secured.
Check and record the identities of all persons trying to gain access to the ship and check their reason for doing so – it is the right of the master to refuse access to anyone who, in his opinion, has not provided sufficient proof to warrant boarding.
All persons intending to board should be liable for searching, and in high-risk areas the frequency of such searches should be increased.
Photographing those who board can act as a deterrent or assist the identification of attackers.

In liaison with the port authorities, a secure area should be provided where the monitoring of persons requesting access should be carried out.
In high-risk areas visitors to the ship should be accompanied by a crew member at all times.
Trading between crew and locals on board ship should be prohibited.
When in port, access to the ship should be restricted to one point. All persons who are admitted should be identified and have their names recorded.
Crewmembers should be advised not to discuss the voyage or cargo, increasing the likelihood of an attack.
Caution should be exercised when transmitting information about cargo or valuables on board by radio.

Seal off means of access to the ship

Waterside access to the ship should be prevented. Hawse pipe plates should be fitted, doors, hatches and other openings locked. Ensure that ropes or wires do not hang unnecessarily over the sides of the ship.
Whilst taking due account of the need to escape in the event of fire or other emergency, so far as possible all means of access to the accommodation should be sealed off and windows and doors of crews' quarters should be kept locked at all times. The fitting of internally operated 'quick-release' mechanisms on external accommodation doors might be considered.
All unattended areas adjoining those to which visitors and crew have access should be locked and secured.
All restricted areas should be clearly marked, indicating that unauthorised presence within the area constitutes a breach of security. During heightened security levels, additional restricted areas may be established according to the provisions of the SSP.

Reduce opportunities for theft

Remove all portable equipment from the deck. So far as possible stow containers containing valuables door-to-door and in tiers. Seal off access to the accommodation. Avoid carrying large amounts of cash on board (the ship's safe is often the prime target).

Provide water hoses and any other equipment

Equipment which may be used to repel potential boarders should be readily available.
Keep hoses ready to use at all times and the fire-main pressurised. Spray water over the stern deck where it is easier for attackers to board (although care must be taken to avoid spraying unprotected lighting and electrical equipment).
Maintain a constant supply of water to the hawse pipes.

Establish a secure area or areas

If large numbers of armed robbers succeed in boarding the ship, it is essential that crewmembers retreat to a secure area or areas.

Depending upon the construction of the accommodation and the extent to which areas can be effectively sealed off, the secure area may be established in the accommodation as a whole, or in more restricted parts around the bridge and inside the engine room. Provision should be made, however, for escape during a fire or other emergency.
Consider special procedures so that crewmembers do not open their cabin doors unless they are certain that it is safe to do so.
Thoroughly check compartments before leaving port.

Watches and patrols

Maintain a 24-hour visual and security watch. Increase the frequency and detail of security patrols. Keep a special lookout for approaching small craft and fishing boats which are difficult to observe on radar. In piracy blackspots, discourage the crew from trading with locals using small craft which may approach the ship.
Maintain a constant visual and radar watch for small craft.
Maintain a constant deck watch and exhibit clear signs of alertness, switching deck lights on and off, sweeping surrounding waters with searchlights periodically, testing water hoses etc.
The gangway watch should be fit and capable. In certain ports it is not wise to rely solely on private security guards. Ensure the gangway watch is linked by a two-way radio to the security patrol and/or other watchkeepers.
Where threats have been identified, additional specific security briefings should be provided to all personnel, emphasising the procedures for reporting suspicious persons, objects or activities and stressing the need for increasing vigilance.

Strengthen night watches

Strengthen watches, especially around the rear of the vessel and particularly between the hours of 0100 and 0600 when most attacks occur, with continuous patrols linked by hand-held two-way radios to the bridge.
If possible, an additional officer should assist the normal bridge watchkeepers at night, in order to provide a dedicated radar and visual watch for small craft which might attempt to manoeuvre alongside, and to allow the watchkeepers to concentrate on normal navigational duties.

Provide maximum lighting available consistent with safe navigation

Deck and over-side lights, particularly at the bow and stern, can be used to good effect to illuminate the deck and the waters beyond and dazzle potential boarders. Ideally searchlights should be available on the bridge wings, and torches carried by the security patrols to identify suspicious craft. Such additional lighting should not, however, be so bright as to obscure navigation lights or to interfere with the safe navigation of other vessels.
When in port or a designated anchorage, the ship's personnel should be able to detect activities beyond the ship. Full lighting should be provided both on deck and over the side, particularly at the bow and stern where raiders may attempt to board unseen. Where necessary, additional lighting may be provided in co-ordination with the port facility.

Establish radio (VHF) contact

Agree emergency signals specifically for pirate attacks with:

- Crew (using hand-held radios)
- Ships in the vicinity
- Shore authorities

Drills and training

Inform Crew of the Ship Security Plan (SSP)

Hold training exercises, particularly when about to enter potential danger areas, and ensure that all crewmembers are fully briefed on the actions to take in the event of an attack by armed robbers. Crews should be proficient in all assigned duties at all security levels, and able to identify any security-related deficiencies that need to be addressed.

There are many guidelines available now, especially for commercial ships in the GoA/IO. Below is another example:

Advice to Masters

General advice to Masters transiting thru / calling at ports of piratical / armed robbery:
The best form of defence is to ensure that a threat of an attack is detected at an early stage - hence a proper all round lookouts using all available means is of vital importance.
In most of the incidents as soon as the pirates / armed robbers know that they have been spotted they will abandon the attack

- Follow company and ship specific procedures
- Follow advice in IMO circular MSC.1/Circ.1334 (23 June 2009)

In Addition:

- Be aware of the sea areas / and ports affected by piracy and armed robbery (the PRC broadcasts regularly to ships in the IOR and AOR regions. See Live Piracy Map)
- Brief crew: Inform them to be vigilant and inform bridge / duty officer of anything suspicious / not normal
- The attitude "this will not happen to me" should be strongly discouraged
- Conduct a drill prior to entering a high risk area. This will ensure emergency communication procedures are tested and contact information is readily available
- Ensure all crew are fully aware of alarm procedures and muster stations
- Keeping in mind multinational crews - all internal communications should be carried out in the working language of the ship
- Master to adjust ship routines prior to entering high risk area to ensure well rested and additional crew on watch at all times
- Ensure blind spots and dark areas are lit up (ensure lighting does not hamper safe navigation and lookout duties)
- Ensure the deck watch work in pairs at all times
- Ensure rounds on deck are taken at irregular intervals
- Reporting from deck to bridge at regular intervals (if reporting not done it is the first indication that there is something wrong)
- Be especially vigilant during watch change over times
- Keeping in mind watchkeepers on deck - access into the accommodation, bridge, steering gear room and engine room to be secured.
- Rig and pressurise fire hoses prior to entry into high risk areas
- Depending on ship type - engine room to be manned
- Keep security / urgency messages ready to transmit while transiting high-risk areas
- Keep important telephone numbers ready at hand especially those of CSO, Flag State and PRC
- Have a designated communications officer (this will ensure the master is able to concentrate and deal with the situation rather than being distracted by communication procedures)
- If applicable keep emergency checklist ready at hand
- Test the SSAS as required by manufacturer
- It is vital that all incidents are reported to the PRC (actual, attempted, suspicious)
- Masters should evaluate the situation and report the incident as soon as it develops, this will ensure that there is time for assistance to be made available. In the event of attack:

1. Raise Alarm, Muster Crew
2. Increase Speed
3. Commence evasive manoeuvres and use bow wave and stern wash to prevent the small boats approaching close to the ship
4. Identify the mother vessel and move away from it (if there is one)
5. Steam away from land
6. Head into the sea and swell: this makes it more difficult for boats to come alongside

In the event of pirates boarding and gaining control of the bridge it is essential to try to keep calm and follow the instructions of the pirates in order to avoid physical confrontation. The master should at all times endeavour to keep the vessel in command to prevent collision / grounding etc.

23. CHANGES AND UPDATES WITHIN MARITIME SAFETY AND SECURITY 2011-12

In late 2010 and the early quarter of 2011, it became apparent that despite the best efforts of all these involved with anti-piracy, especially in and around the Horn of Africa, the Somali pirates are not slowing in their efforts but accelerating. The amount of attacks in early 2011 showed that if they had kept up their tempo, it would have been a record year. Alarmingly, seven seafarers had already been murdered and the pirates were becoming more aggressive and clever with their modus operandi. Hostages have been tortured in recent times; when the US Navy SEALs boarded the sailing yacht SY Quest they found that the American citizens had been shot by the Somali pirates, all of which died. Despite attacks increasing, success rates fell due to ships hardening themselves, employing private security guards and the efforts of the coalition forces.

The days of poor, ex-fishermen robbing the occasional vessel off the Island of Socotra have gone. The Somali pirates will now take a commercial vessel and force the crew to use it as a mother craft to spread to the far reaches of the Indian Ocean/Red Sea to attack other vessels in waters thought to be safer. The hostages are used as human shields; pirates have vowed to execute them all if Coalition Forces try to stop them. The razor wire and high freeboard of a recent attack stopped the pirates from gaining access from their skiffs. Normally, that would have prevented a boarding. The skiffs returned to the mothership, a captured ship of larger size. The pirates sailed their mothership alongside the target ship, the pirates leapt from one ship to the other, over the razor wire and successfully took control of that vessel. Times and tactics are changing, the pirates are becoming more advanced, the authorities recognise this and are now changing their views and recommendations to seafarers.

One of the biggest U-turns is the fact that firearms on ships were not recommended, even now, many companies and authorities are not happy or agreeing, but sure enough the realisation of this successful anti-piracy method is being slowly actioned. The author would suggest that by 2014, BMP will recommend the arming of ships in high-risk areas as the default solution, as will the P&I companies. This may come from the use of UN soldiers, but if private security guards are to be used then the industry needs to be regulated by way of formal training, backgrounds checks on the guard's mental health, criminal record check on so on.

The source of piracy problems come from within Somalia, the fact that there is the complete lack of command and control by regulating authorities. This instability is fuelling terrorism, piracy and the proliferation of weapons. The G8 members recently held a meeting to discuss which ways Somalia could be assisted to prevent and stop these illegal activities, which are clearly a threat to global security. International nations are pleading for help and a solution to stop the fastest ever increase in maritime piracy; in New York, March 2011, the UN held a meeting attended by some 60 nations in ways to stop piracy. UK government (William Hague) has pledged £6 million to help with anti-piracy operations. Tactics are changing; during the same month the Indonesian ship MV Sinar Kudus was captured and immediately used as a mother ship using the crew to assist and to be used as human shields. Since the four US sailors were killed, pirates have sworn to kill all hostages should military action be taken. Somali pirate tactics are changing; previously, small groups of pirates would attack a vessel; now similar to the tactics as used by MEND (Nigeria), large groups of pirates are swarming the vessel to take it. Hostages continue to be badly treated and tortured; captives complained of being fed only once every 3 days and never washing for the duration of x amount of months.

Armed security companies continue to provide more and more cover by placing armed men on ships or provide armed gunboats to escort the vessel. It is said that a UK group of insurers have decided to spend £7 million on the use of a private security company and escorting vessels.
Despite the coalition warships provided from 21 international navies, a record number of attacks are taking place in 2011; there are around 30 vessels being held by pirates (who are demanding larger and larger ransoms) and some 600 +/- hostages either held on land or on ships.

Human rights violations and torture are increasing; the code of conduct for hostages is being ignored more and more. The Indian Navy have had great success in their operations; they recently handed over 61 pirates and 13 hostages.

ICS: target pirate mother ships 22 Mar 2011

SHIPPING is pushing a plan to disable Somali mother ships at sea and slash piracy's operational range.

Recently the International Chamber of Shipping chairman Spyros Polemis has outlined the latest proposed strategy at the Connecticut Shipping Association conference, but the provided specifics in an interview with Fairplay. He said that naval forces could disable hijacked mother ships with nets that foul propellers. This counter-offensive strategy could conceivably move ahead this year, it would "have to be very comprehensive and all-encompassing" and not just target certain mother ships piecemeal.

Naval forces have yet to receive "the political OK" for the plan, which would inevitably put crew aboard multiple mother ships at risk. Navies have already obtained political approval to disable potential mother ships at anchorage in Somali waters, but that could lead to removing the hostages and putting them ashore. Shipping instead favours disabling pirate mother ships at sea because then pirates would be compelled to leave crew unharmed on immobilised mother ships in return for their lives. "If they harm the crew, naval forces would board the ships and kill the pirates. Therefore, I think the likelihood is that the pirates will leave," If mother ships can be disabled en masse this year (2011), then capacity-limited naval forces could more effectively patrol the reduced hijacking range near the Somali coast, Polemis asserted

Mr. Polemis underscored that the piracy crisis has degenerated to a point "where there's no way it can continue without taking steps".

The Norwegians have suggested boycotting the Suez Canal completely to pressurize action to be taken against Somalia. Private security firm Saracen were supposed to train an anti-piracy force of some 1050 men, but that contract has been postponed at present. The Tanzanian government has asked South Africa for help with this local piracy problem.

Below are relevant articles that show the changes that are coming about.

Shipping Industry Changes Stance on Armed Guards (see page 184)

UN launches new anti-piracy plan calling for greater global naval support

3 February 2011 – The United Nations today launched an action plan to combat piracy off the Somali coast, calling for greater support from national navies to fight a "global menace" that threatens not only international trade but the world body's delivery of vital food aid to millions of hungry people. "We are neither proud of, nor content with, the results achieved so far," the (ex) Secretary-General of the UN International Maritime Organization (IMO), Efthimios Mitropoulos, said at the official launch at his agency's London headquarters on World Maritime Day. He added that the past year alone saw 286 piracy -related incidents off the coast of Somalia, resulting in 67 hijacked ships, with 1,130 seafarers on board; while a recent study estimated the cost to the world economy from disruptions to international trade at between $7 billion and $12 billion.

One of the prime objectives of the new plan is "to promote greater levels of support from, and coordination with, navies" off Somalia, where patrols by the European Union, the North Atlantic Treaty Organization and UN member states already provide "vital protection" for UN vessels delivering logistical support to the African Union force in Mogadishu, which seeks to help stabilize the war-torn country, and for UN food shipments to the 2.4 million Somalis who urgently need it.

"We were appalled by yesterday's news that pirates had executed, apparently in cold blood, a seafarer on the Beluga Nomination, a ship which had been attacked and hijacked last month, 390 miles off the Seychelles," Mr. Mitropoulos said. "This year, we are resolved to redouble our efforts and, in so doing, generate and galvanize a broader, global response to modern-day piracy
The IMO chief added that more needs to be done, including the tracing of money and the imposition of sanctions on the proceeds derived from hijacked ships, if the ultimate goal of "consigning piracy to the realms of history" is to be achieved.

Formally launching the plan, Secretary-General Ban Ki-moon called for a long-term strategy of deterrence, security, rule of law and development to fight the scourge. Somalia has not had a functioning central government for the past 20 years during which it has been torn apart by factional warfare, most recently involving Al Shabaab and other Islamist militias. "Although piracy manifests itself at sea, the roots of the problem are to be found ashore," Mr. Ban said. "In essence, piracy is a criminal offence that is driven by economic hardship, and that flourishes in the absence of effective law enforcement."
Ransom payments add up to hundreds of millions of dollars, creating a "pirate economy" in areas of Somalia that make them more resistant to efforts to develop alternative livelihoods, the Secretary-General added, noting that despite the deployment of significant naval assets to the region, the number of hijackings and victims has risen significantly.

"More needs to be done. We need to move beyond the impressive deterrence efforts, and to make sure that they are carried out in concert with the other elements of the strategy on land. We need to support alternative livelihoods and the rehabilitation of coastal fisheries," Mr. Ban said.
The crucial humanitarian element in piracy was underlined by the presence at the launch of the Executive Director of the UN World Food Programme (WFP), Josette Sheeran, whose chartered ships of vital food aid for Somalia were hijacked prior to the deployment of international naval forces in surrounding sea-lanes.
The Executive Director of the UN Office on Drugs and Crime (UNODC), Yuryedotov, also attended. In partnership with UNODC, IMO is helping countries in the region develop the legal framework needed to prosecute pirates. The anti-crime agency's Counter-piracy Programme, based in Nairobi, Kenya, is aiding efforts to help deal with suspected pirates who have been caught in the region, with an approach centred on three main objectives: fair and efficient trials and imprisonment in regional centres; humane and secure imprisonment in Somalia; and fair and efficient trials in Somalia.

Noting that IMO has been dealing with piracy issues for the last 30 years, Mr. Mitropoulos said earlier strategies used in the Gulf of Guinea in the 1980s and the South China Sea, the Straits of Malacca and Singapore in the late 1990s and earlier this century, could be used "to good effect in the current arena as well, but to do so requires a well-orchestrated response."
Beyond promoting greater support from navies, the plan's priorities include boosting anti-piracy coordination and co-operation among countries, regions, organizations and industry, through information-sharing and military and civil efforts; and helping countries to build capacity in piracy - infested regions in order "to deter, interdict and bring to justice" the perpetrators.

IMB supports global campaign vs piracy
March 22, 2011

MANILA, Philippines – The ICC International Maritime Bureau (IMB) has come out in support of a joint campaign launched by the International Chamber of Shipping (ICS), Intertanko, Intercargo, BIMCO and the International Transport Workers Federation (ITF) that urges governments to take firm action on the issue of maritime piracy off the coast of Somalia.

The campaign, aimed at raising awareness of the human and economic costs of maritime piracy, urges governments around the world to prioritise six key actions:

1. Reducing the effectiveness of easily identifiable motherships.
2. Authorizing naval forces to hold pirates and deliver them for prosecution and punishment.
3. Fully criminalizing all acts of piracy and intent to commit piracy under national laws, in accordance with their mandatory duty to co-operate to suppress piracy under international conventions.
4. Increasing naval assets available in the affected areas.
5. Providing greater protection and support for seafarers.
6. Tracing and criminalizing the organisers and financiers behind the criminal networks.

Up until March 2011, 13 vessels have been hijacked by suspected Somali pirates, with a total of 243 crewmembers taken hostage.

In addition, six crew were kidnapped from a vessel that was hijacked and then left adrift in the Indian Ocean. Of most concern, however, are the seven murders committed by Somali pirates- three of which were crew on board the hijacked Beluga Nomination. (EHL)

Global piracy as of November 2012

Map data © 2007 - 2012 Google

European Union Updates.

Brussels, 21 March 2011 The Council adopted the following conclusions:

"1. The EU expresses its continued deep concern about the political, security, development and humanitarian situation in Somalia, including the resulting increase in the number of displaced people. Instability in Somalia is posing a growing challenge not only to the security of people in Somalia, but also to the region and the rest of the world, through terrorism, piracy and the proliferation of weapons.

2. The EU confirms its continued support for the Djibouti peace process, which remains the framework for peace building and stability in Somalia. It is imperative that the Transitional Federal Institutions (TFIs) demonstrate unity, common purpose and determination to advance in this incremental and all-inclusive process.

3. The EU deeply regrets the recent unilateral decision by the Somali Transitional Federal Parliament (TFP) to extend its mandate. It urges the TFIs to focus on implementing the reforms that are necessary to build their legitimacy, representativeness and credibility and without which there can be no extension. Any bridging period between the current and the reformed institutional set up should be as short as possible.

The EU expects the TFIs to use any such period to advance reconciliation, security and justice and to develop minimum levels of governance to allow a more transparent management of state revenues and the provision of basic services to the people of Somalia. The EU agrees that future support to the TFIs including stipends for parliamentarians should be contingent on progress on reform and delivery of the transitional tasks.

4. The EU stands ready to contribute, together with regional and international partners, to the implementation of an agreed reform agenda for the TFIs on the basis of clear agreed benchmarks with a timeline for implementation.

5. The EU emphasises the importance of re-energising the constitutional process, in order to conclude the transitional period. If it is to have legitimacy, this process should be based on broad participation by the Somali people. The EU supports the role of the UN in facilitating a Somali-led process.

6. The EU calls on the Somali leadership to engage more actively with all stakeholders, including regional administrations and parties to agreements with the TFIs, clan elders, religious leaders, businesspeople, women and the diaspora, in order to develop a credible and inclusive Somali-owned political process for the benefit of all Somali people.

The EU encourages regional entities to actively and constructively participate in this process. It also calls on all armed groups to urgently lay down their weapons and join in a genuine broad based peaceful dialogue with the Transitional Federal Government (TFG).

7. The EU confirms its full support to the UN and the Special Representative of the UN Secretary General (UNSRSG), Mr Mahiga. It calls for more effective use of the current mechanisms of coordination between the Somali authorities and the international community, to ensure a common position favourable and conducive to reform and stability. The EU calls on the Somali authorities to continue their co-operation with the UNSRSG and to use his good offices as well as his leadership within the International Contact Group (ICG) on Somalia, as a means for more effective consultation.

8. The EU notes the conclusions of the last ICG on Somalia held in Madrid on 27-28 September 2010, and confirms its willingness to increase its political support to Somalia which will aim at supporting partnership with federal, regional and local authorities.

9. The EU recalls that there can be no purely military solution to the crisis in Somalia. The EU reaffirms its support for AMISOM and praises the commitment and bravery of the AMISOM peacekeeping troops who, together with the security forces of the TFG, have paid a heavy toll to help build security for the Somali people. The EU underlines that such support must be matched by complementary political efforts by the TFG, including initiatives to demonstrate peace dividends to people in safe areas. Considerations on future engagement in the framework of the EU Common Security and Defence Policy (CSDP), including the EU Training Mission (EUTM) in Uganda, will depend on the political context, satisfactory progress on a command and control structure, and on the evaluation of the reintegration of the first batch of trainees.

10. The EU reiterates the need to strengthen initiatives to fight piracy. The EU commends the contribution of the EU counter-piracy operation, EU NAVFOR Atalanta, to this end. EU NAVFOR will continue to adapt to the changing tactics of pirates and seek to implement agreed measures pro-actively where possible.

The EU expresses its grave concern over the growing number of people, including seafarers, held hostage. Prosecution and detention of pirates are key components of counter-piracy: the EU agrees on the need for strong support for continued capacity-building in the rule of law and penal detention sectors in Somalia and the wider region, which would also facilitate the conclusion of transfer agreements.

The EU considers that work needs to be taken forward on contributing towards making progress on implementing lasting solutions for the prosecution of pirates, building on the work already done last year by the EU, and taking into account on-going work in the UN context. In this regard, the EU welcomes the report of the Special Advisor to the UN Secretary General on Legal Issues related to Piracy off the Coast of Somalia, and looks forward to the further debate in the UN on the implementation of its recommendations. The EU also welcomes the agreement on post-trial transfer between the Seychelles Government and the Somali TFG. The EU emphasizes the need for work on disrupting the financial flows linked to piracy and addressing the situation of hostages.

11. The EU is committed to supporting the counter-piracy "Kampala Process", bringing together the TFG and the regions Puntland and Somaliland, the Djibouti Code of Conduct and the implementation of the Regional Plan of Action agreed by ministers from the region in October 2010. The EU recognises the need to target its technical and financial support in this sector most effectively, working closely alongside the UN-mandated Contact Group on Piracy off the Coast of Somalia, which plays an international coordinating role.

12. Containment at sea will be further strengthened by efforts to tackle the root causes of piracy, focussed on improving livelihoods, economic opportunities and the rule of law. The EU will continue to support regional initiatives to this end and will take an active role in co-ordinating international efforts in those regions of Somalia most affected, including in Puntland.

13. The EU expresses particular concern about the increasing tension and evidence of military build-up in Sool Region and Buhoodle District, and calls on the regional authorities to contain the confrontation, exert restraint and foster dialogue to resolve differences.

14. The EU is actively considering increasing its financial assistance to support central, regional and local level administrations in consolidating stable and accountable governance and improving livelihood opportunities and the provision of basic services. The EU aim is to enhance its support to regions of Somalia, such as Somaliland and Puntland, committed to peace, stability and democracy.

15. Given the scale of the humanitarian crisis facing Somalia, the EU will continue to provide humanitarian assistance to the most vulnerable populations in accordance with the humanitarian principles of independence, neutrality, impartiality and humanity.

The EU is deeply concerned by the continuing contraction of humanitarian space and access in Somalia, and calls on all actors to ensure free and unhindered access for the delivery of humanitarian assistance."

Pirates: The Economic Costs of Maritime Crime.[18]

Piracy cost $6.9 billion. Two recent studies shed light on the negative and positive effects of piracy.

MOMBASA, Kenya — Tugs ply the oily waters, leading immense cargo ships down the narrow channel towards the towering cranes of one of Africa's busiest ports. Yet despite the bustle, Mombasa is feeling the pinch from the piracy flourishing around it in the Indian Ocean. The cargo held in the long, low-slung container ships that dot the horizon is more expensive. There are no cruise liners to be seen. These changes are a direct result of Somali piracy. Since the US-flagged Maersk Alabama was attacked by pirates in 2009 on its way to Mombasa, the dangers of approaching the port are widely known. Officials at the port have warned of losing trade to other regional competitors, like Tanzania's Dar es Salaam. The cruise industry was damaged by the hijacking of the French luxury yacht Le Ponant in 2008. "We used to get around 40 cruise liners every season, this season there was only one and I think it was there by mistake," said Bernard Osero, a spokesman for the Mombasa Port Authority.

Osero said Mombasa port is working hard to maintain its share of the cargo market. He said cargo volumes and container numbers are both increasing steadily, with close to 20 million tons processed last year. But higher insurance and other costs means goods are more expensive. "The consumer pays," said Osero. The economic cost of the piracy reaches far beyond Mombasa's cargo-clogged port to Kenya and deep into central Africa to the Democratic Republic of Congo and the new nation of South Sudan. The impact of Somalia's piracy has been felt both further away and closer to home as two recent studies have shown.

The Colorado-based research and advocacy group One Earth Future Foundation estimated that the total cost of piracy in 2011 was as high as $6.9 billion, according to the annual "Economic Cost of Somali Piracy" report published by its Oceans Beyond Piracy program. Ransom payments are the most obvious cost created by piracy. The magnitude of these reportedly reached a new record in April 2011 when Greek owners paid $13.5 million for the release of the Irene, an oil tanker.

Two kidnapped in pirate attack off Nigerian coast

While ransoms increased during 2011 to average $5 million per vessel, the $160 million in ransoms paid for 31 ships last year were only about 2 percent of the total cost of piracy, wrote Anna Bowden, the report's author. The cost of attempting to prevent and protect against piracy far outweighs the ransom payments themselves. The largest share — roughly 80.5 percent — is borne by the shipping industry, mostly in the form of extra fuel consumed while steaming through dangerous waters at faster than usual speeds. To avoid pirates riskier parts of the high seas ships take longer routes along India's west coast. Firms must now give danger pay for seafarers. In case their vessels and crews are seized, ship owners have paid “war risk” and “kidnap and ransom” insurance worth $635 million.

No ship travelling at more than 18 knots (21 mph; compared to a ‘normal’ speed of 12 knots) has been successfully hijacked, but the fuel costs of increased speed came to $2.7 billion for container ships alone, Bowden calculated.

---

18 **from GlobalPost**

Governments that provide warships and sailors to the anti-piracy navies patrolling the Gulf of Aden, Indian Ocean, Red Sea and Gulf of Oman where most pirate attacks now take place account for the other 19.5 percent of the total costs. They spent $1.27 billion on "administrative and headquarter operations, military vessels, aircraft and unmanned aerial vehicles."

More than 30 countries that provided warships either unilaterally or as part of the three naval coalitions headed by the European Union (EUNAVFOR), NATO (Operation Ocean Shield) and the US (Combined Task Force-151).

Bowden found that only $38 million was spent on prosecuting arrested pirates, and on refurbishing jails and court rooms in Somalia and elsewhere in the region. While the $6.9 billion that Somali piracy cost the world economy last year is a staggering amount, it is, of course, not a cost to everyone. Insurance and oil companies, as well as private security contractors, have all profited from the dangers of piracy.

Recent USCG Counter-Piracy Documents [19]

February 16, 2012

So far this year the US Coast Guard has issued two revised documents material to the struggle against maritime piracy. One is the latest version of the applicable Maritime Security Directive; the other provides updated information regarding the policies of various countries concerning self-defense weapons onboard merchant ships visiting their ports.

Maritime Security Directive 104-6 (Rev 6)

On January 30th, the Coast Guard announced the release of the sixth revision to Maritime Security (MARSEC) Directive 104-6, "Guidelines for U.S. Vessels Operating in High Risk Waters," in a Notice of Availability in the Federal Register. According to this Notice, Revision 6 had been available since December 30, 2011 and Revision 5 was no longer valid as of that date. Interesting legal question: How can you be bound to comply with a Directive for a month before you are given legal notice that the Directive exists?

The Notice states that Revisions 6 provides "a revised and updated list of designated high risk waters and areas," but does not indicate any other substantive change to the MARSEC Directive. The Directive applies only to US-flag vessels and is designated Sensitive Security Information (SSI). Accordingly, owners and operators of U.S.-flag vessels that travel on international voyages have to contact the USCG (the local Captain of the Port, cognizant District Commander, or the Office of Vessel Activities at USCG Headquarters) to obtain a copy. Although the Notice says that a non-SSI version of the Directive "is available," the USCG Homeport website, as of this writing, offers only a sanitized version of Revision 5. If in fact, Revision 6 only changes the list of designated High Risk Waters, the sanitized version of Revision 6, when eventually posted, will differ only as to date and version number. The list of High Risk Waters was not included in previous non-SSI renditions, and presumably won't be this time either. What might the changes be?

Presumably coverage of more of West Africa's Gulf of Guinea, to account for expansion of piracy outwards from Nigerian shores, as well as possibly some adjustments in the Indian Ocean reflecting changes in the operations of Somali pirates. But that is rampant speculation by someone who hasn't seen the document.

---

[19] **With thanks to: John C. W. Bennett Maritime Transportation Security News and Views**

To view the sanitized version of MARSEC Directive 104-6, open Homeport and click on Counter Piracy in the "featured Homeport Links" menu on the left. Then click on PSA 2-09 under "Port Security Advisories" in the middle of the page. This will take to a link for the PDF document (at the moment, still the older version).

Updated Port Information Matrix

Dennis Bryant reported in his preeminent Bryant's Maritime Blog that the Coast Guard had posted an updated Port Information Matrix on Homeport. This Matrix presents information on countries' policies regarding the carriage of weapons by merchant ships in their ports and by private security team members while transiting the country to or from ships in their ports.

The Matrix summarizes countries' responses to a US State Department demarche on the subject sent out in May 2009 and to follow-up inquiries.

The Coast Guard began reporting on the responses in October 2009 with Port Security Advisory (PSA) 8-09, "Port State Response to Request for Information Regarding Carriage and Transport of Self-Defense Weapons Aboard U.S. Commercial Vessels." Updates have been issued by replacing the Port Information Matrix accompanying PSA 8-09. This is the first update since the August 2010 edition.

There are now 47 countries covered by the Matrix, although many are listed without information. Substantive information (defined subjectively by me to mean information providing or changing policies regarding either weapons on ships or carried on land by teams to or from ships) is presented for nine new countries (Australia, France, Gabon, Malta, Panama, Senegal, Spain, Turkey, Venezuela). New substantive information is given for nine countries that were already on the list (Brazil, Cameroon, China [for Hong Kong only], Egypt, Iraq, Peru, Saudi Arabia, UAE, Yemen). Notably, Egypt, formerly listed as "NO" for each of the two policies, is now "in flux." The entry for Fujairah, UAE, which previously stated: "Persons or vessels entering with arms will be arrested," now credits the port with having a slightly positive policy towards ships arriving with weapons, with the caveat that "Fujairah policy is a bit confused and post recommends prudence." On the other hand, Abu Dhabi, UAE, formerly not listed, is now on unambiguous yes on that subject. (Neither permits arms to transit through the country to or from ships.)

Minor information changes are presented for 12 countries (Djibouti, Guinea, India, Israel, Kenya, Kuwait, Mauritius, Mexico, Nicaragua, Singapore, South Africa, Tanzania). Sudan and Oman have information that has not changed, while 15 countries (Bahrain, Bangladesh, Indonesia, Ivory Coast, Lebanon, Malaysia, Mozambique, Nigeria, Pakistan, Qatar, Seychelles, Sierra Leone, Somalia, Sri Lanka, Thailand) remain on the list without information.

One interesting change in the Matrix since the last version is that countries or ports are no longer marked as HPP ("Highest Priority Ports Provided by Industry") and/or HRW ("High Risk Waters Defined by U.S. Coast Guard"). Evidently someone realized that the latter marking was inconsistent with treating the list of High Risk Waters in MARSEC Directive 104-6 as SSI.

Although the country-by-country information is summarized at a very general level, the Matrix, taken as a whole, does provide a useful starting point for planning when the carriage of armed security is being considered. It is clear that some countries will not allow it. Where countries are shown as permitting the practice, further inquiries are called for to ferret out the details. The main problem is that a number of nations in key locations have not furnished any information at all, but that's not the Coast Guard's fault.

To access the new Port Information Matrix, or PSA 8-09, go to Homeport, click on "Counter Piracy" under "Featured Homeport Links" menu at the top of the right side of the page. On the Counter Piracy page, scroll down to the link to PSA 8-09. Clicking on that will give you a choice of PDFs-the PSA or the Matrix.

When tanker master Miro Alibasic takes one of his company's vast ships across the Indian Ocean, he likes to have all the firepower he can get on board.
Having seen last year how Somali pirates treat their captives, the 61-year-old is in no hurry to experience it again. "It was hell on earth," he told Reuters by telephone from his home in the Croatian port of Dubrovnik.
The number of ships seized in the region by Somali pirates fell last year, industry data shows, but the overall number of attempted attacks continues to rise and the raids have become increasingly violent.
Breaking the piracy "business model" and tackling Somalia's onshore problems will be among the aims of a major international conference on Somalia in London on Thursday. But few are optimistic of a solution any time soon, and shippers say they must take matters into their own hands.

Greater use of private armed security guards on ships and a much tougher approach by international navies is beginning to work, some mariners, officials, contractors and military officers say. But others worry they may simply fuelling a growing arms race, ramping up the conflict and producing a rising human and financial cost.
In March last year, Alibasic was transporting a cargo of crude oil from Sudan to Asia when his tanker - the 100,000 ton United Arab Emirates-registered Zirku - came under attack. For 90 minutes, the pirates poured heavy machine gun and rocket propelled grenade fire into the vessel. Then they were aboard, swarming over the two levels of barbed wire that surrounded the decks. The ferocity of the initial onslaught, he says, was matched by much of the treatment suffered by him and his 28 crew during their 75 days in captivity.
As the shipowners negotiated the payment of an unspecified but reportedly "massive" ransom, he did everything he could to keep the multinational crew - including Jordanians, Egyptians, Ukrainians and Pakistanis - safe from sometimes drugged and bored captors.
"I read them poetry and played them opera to try to calm them down," he said, adding that he also played chess with the pirate leader "Abdallah" to win his respect. "But they nearly hanged my second mate."
The unlucky second officer's only offence, he said, was to have demanded the right to have a shower after spending hours working in the tanker's sweltering engine room. By the time Alibasic persuaded the pirates to let him go, the rope was already around his neck.
Seafarers' organisations say the treatment of prisoners has worsened over time. Other sailors have been suspended hung upside down for hours, dumped overboard or even keelhauled - dragged under the ship from one side to the other on a rope, a traditional punishment of the age of sail barely reported since the 17th or early 18th centuries. Estimates suggest at least 60 seafarers have died.

TOUGHER NAVAL APPROACH

When the pirates forced Alibasic to sail back out into the Indian Ocean to rescue some of their stranded colleagues, he found himself on the receiving end of a new set of naval rules of engagement.
On one of his trips, his tanker came under fire from the U.S. Navy.
"I got on the radio and said: "What are you doing? They (the pirates) will kill us all ... They were using us as human shields," he said.
About 25 warships from various nations now patrol the Indian Ocean at any given time.
Some states - such as Russia - have always adopted an aggressive approach when their ships were hijacked, storming them with force and either killing the pirates or leaving them to die in open boats.
The United States has also launched Special Forces missions to rescue its nationals.
Other Western states - particularly the Europeans who make up the bulk of EU and NATO-led task forces - were initially more cautious. But even they have started to take a tougher stance, engaging pirate "motherships" and retaking captured vessels.

Many commanders have welcomed the new approach, saying it is behind the slump in successful pirate attacks in the second half of 2011. Only 25 ships were seized in 2011, the European Union Naval Force Somalia (EU NAVFOR) says, compared to 47 the year earlier.
Pirates now hold six ships and roughly 176 hostages, the EU says, again well down from last year. But average ransoms continue to rise - now about $5 million compared to $4 million last year. Estimates of the cost to the global economy are also up - one report put it at $7 billion in 2011.
The fastest growing component of that, the US-based Oceans Beyond Piracy report said, was the cost of the rising number of armed private security guards. At the beginning of 2011, they estimated perhaps a quarter of ships carried such guards, rising to an estimated half now. Shipping companies spent roughly $1 billion on private guards alone in 2011, the report said - much more than the estimated $160 million earned by the pirates themselves in ransoms.

SECURITY COSTS, WORRIES [20]

Many piracy experts - including serving naval officers - believe it was the private guards who made the real difference against piracy in 2011.
But the unregulated industry raises a host of new worries.
A 2011 UN report details one incident, in which naval forces rescued a damaged skiff containing one dead Somali and six survivors, who said two other compatriots had also been killed and had fallen overboard.
Naval observers concluded gunfire had come from illegally-held weapons on a ship recently attacked by the skiff, but were unable to provide definitive proof.
"It's very likely people are being killed out in the Indian Ocean by private guards and it's not being reported," says Rory Lamrock, piracy analyst at UK-based risk consultancy AKE.
A former military officer himself, tanker captain Alibasic worries over the moral and legal implications of dispensing lethal force from the deck of a civilian merchant ship.
But he also has a more immediate concern - will the guards he now carries on his voyages through the region have enough arms and ammunition to fight off the kind of concerted assault he faced last March?
As to solving the wider problem of Somali piracy, he says that is something that will only happen when the world gets seriously involved onshore in the pirate havens of Puntland and elsewhere.
"When we had a war in Croatia, we did not become pirates," he says, referring to the Balkan wars of the 1990s. "The international community and the UN came and things were sorted out in only a few years. That's what needs to happen in Somalia."

---

[20] With thanks to Peter Apps & Andrew Heavens

Human Cost of Somali Piracy (Updated Report Released)

Friday, June 22, 2012

The joint report is an update of the first report on the Human Cost of Piracy for 2010, launched in London by Oceans Beyond Piracy in June last year. This report includes a statistical analysis of the threats of violence caused by acts of piracy as well as the first published findings collected as a result of the Declaration Condemning Acts of Violence Against Seafarers. The Declaration, signed initially in Washington in August last year by Liberia, the Marshall Islands, and Panama, and by the Bahamas in March 2012, commits signatory states to submit reports to the IMB on the treatment of seafarers held hostage. "Thousands are attacked for financial gain without regard for the human cost to attain a ransom," says Kaija Hurlburt, Project Manager with Oceans Beyond Piracy. "In 2011, at least 3,863 seafarers were fired upon by Somali pirates armed with assault rifles and rocket propelled grenades. While the number of hostages has gone down over the past year, the violence faced by seafarers has remained high and attacks are often carried out with a determined ferocity – even against vessels protected by private security teams." Of that number, 968 seafarers faced armed pirates who managed to board their vessels. 413 of these seafarers were rescued from citadels (secured rooms) on their vessels by naval forces after waiting, terrified, for hours or even days while pirates tried to break into the citadels.

A total of at least 1,206 hostages were held captive by Somali pirates in 2011. These included 555 seafarers who were attacked and taken hostage during the year, 645 hostages captured in 2010 who remained in pirate hands during 2011, and 6 tourists and aid workers kidnapped on land. The average length of captivity has also increased by 50% over last year, up to an average length of over 8 months. Often these hostages face systematic and daily psychological and physical abuse and were even used as human shields: "One day pirates drew us out to the open deck, told us to turn back and stand still facing the sea side. Then we heard how they reloaded their machine guns. We understood nothing. We saw US Navy not far out and we were standing and waiting for about two hours . . ." (Report of released seafarer) Some 35 hostages died during 2011: 8 were killed by pirates during an initial attack or after being taken captive; 8 died from disease or malnutrition while being held; and 19 died in crossfire while being used as human shields and during hostage rescue attempts. The International Maritime Bureau (IMB) notes in the report the experiences of the seafarers from 23 of the 77 vessels hijacked in 2010 and 2011based on reports submitted by the Flag States of Liberia, the Marshall Islands, Panama and the Bahamas, various ship owners and operators, former hostages, and by the Maritime Piracy Humanitarian Response Programme. "Various analyses of the Somali piracy problem have so far ignored a meaningful study into the human cost upon the seafarers and their families," says Captain Pottengal Mukundan, Director of the IMB. "This report aims to fill this gap and highlight some of the shocking consequences of this crime upon merchant seafarers, who are in the main, silent, involuntary victims. As other initiatives to counter piracy at sea off Somalia have become established, this important area of support to the victim seafarers and their families remains unaddressed. The challenge of any report of this kind is in getting the victims to recall their painful experiences and report them to help victims in the future."

The report shows that all of the captive crews were subject to treatments in violation of basic human rights and psychological abuse. At least half experienced physical abuse. In addition to those reported to have died in captivity, it says that three of the hostages died following release because of the abuse they experienced at pirate hands. According to Marcel Arsenault, Chairman of the One Earth Future Foundation and sponsor of the report, piracy is a systemic problem that proliferates from a failed state. "While the report rightfully focuses on violence faced by innocent seafarers, increased violence has also exacted a huge cost on Somali society. The desperate situation in Somalia continues to breed piracy. Piracy will ultimately be solved only by a new global initiative to create jobs and improve governance."

INTERNATIONAL MARITIME ORGANIZATION

MSC-FAL.1/Circ.2
22 September 2011

QUESTIONNAIRE ON INFORMATION ON PORT AND COASTAL STATE REQUIREMENTS RELATED TO PRIVATELY CONTRACTED ARMED SECURITY PERSONNEL ON BOARD SHIPS

1 The Maritime Safety Committee, at its eighty-ninth session (11 to 20 May 2011) (MSC 89), having noted the increasing use of armed personnel on board ships operating in the High Risk Area (1) decided, on the understanding that the carriage of armed personnel was a matter to be decided by the shipowner within the framework of the national legislation and policies of the flag State concerned, that there was an urgent need for a consistent approach to the issue and the avoidance of an escalation of violence due to the inappropriate use of force. In this respect MSC 89 approved MSC.1/Circ.1405[2] on Interim Guidance to shipowners, ship operators, and shipmasters on the use of privately contracted armed security personnel on board ships in the High Risk Area, and MSC.1/Circ.1406[3] on Interim Recommendations for Flag States regarding the use of privately contracted armed security personnel on board ships in the High Risk Area.

2 Given the importance and urgent nature of these issues, MSC 89 agreed also that there was an urgent need to develop further recommendations to Governments and, in particular for coastal and port States, on aspects related to the embarkation, disembarkation and carriage of privately contracted armed security personnel (PCASP) and of firearms and security-related equipment[4] for use by PCASP. In this respect MSC 89, inter alia:

(1) requested the Facilitation Committee at its thirty-seventh session (5 to 9 September 2011) (FAL 37) to consider the above-mentioned issues; and

(2) approved, subject to authorization by the Council, the convening of an intersessional meeting of the Maritime Security and Piracy Working Group (the Group).

3 FAL 37 considered the above-mentioned issues and, inter alia, decided that both Committees should liaise with the various national authorities responsible for regulating the embarkation, disembarkation and carriage of firearms and security-related equipment through their territory and the movement of PCASP, and should collect and disseminate information on the relevant national legislation, policies and procedures. In this respect and with a view to collecting the relevant information in a systematic manner FAL 37 developed a draft questionnaire for consideration and completion by Member Governments.

1 High Risk Area: an area as defined in the Best Management Practices for Protection against Somalia Based Piracy (MSC.1/Circ.1339) unless otherwise defined by the flag State.

2 Revoked and replaced by MSC.1/Circ.1405/Rev.1.

3 Revoked and replaced by MSC.1/Circ.1406/Rev.1.

In this questionnaire, all references to firearms include the associated ammunition, consumables, spare parts and maintenance equipment for use by PCASP, and all references to security-related equipment includes protective and communication equipment for use by PCASP.

4 The Group, which met from 13 to 15 September 2011, taking into account the discussions during MSC 89 and FAL 37, the draft questionnaire developed by FAL 37 and the result of its deliberation, finalized and decided to circulate the Questionnaire on information on port and coastal State requirements related to privately contracted armed security personnel on board ships set out in the annex.

5 In the present circular and on the attached questionnaire, all references to firearms include the associated ammunition, consumables, spare parts and maintenance equipment for use by PCASP, and all references to security-related equipment includes protective and communication equip' for use by PCASP.

6 In view of the growing use of PCASP in the High Risk Area and the need to enhance the protection of ships navigating in the High Risk Area, flag States, the shipping industry and the private maritime security companies (PMSC) who provide PCASP need to know whether and under what conditions the embarkation and disembarkation of PCASP and/or of firearms and security-related equipment for use by PCASP is allowed. In addition, the shipping industry, masters of ships and the PCASP service providers need to know what requirements they have to comply with when, during its voyage, a ship carrying a PCASP is arriving in, staying at and departing from ports, offshore terminals, anchorage or roadstead located areas within the territory or under the jurisdiction of a port or a coastal State.

7 As a result Member Governments, and, in particular, those of the coastal States bordering the Indian Ocean, Arabian Sea, Gulf of Aden and Red Sea either as SOLAS Contracting Governments or as FAL Contracting Governments, or both, should raise awareness of their relevant national legislation, policies and procedures relating to the carriage, embarkation and disembarkation of firearms and security-related equipment through their territory and the movement of PCASP.

8 Member Governments are urged to complete the attached questionnaire and submit it to the Organization at their earliest convenience and preferably not later than 30 November 2011, if possible with a copy of their related national legislation, policies and procedures. The responses to the questionnaire and any related national legislation, policies and procedures provided will be posted by the Secretariat, in the language received[5], on IMO's public website. In view of the importance of the issue, Member Governments are also urged to provide to the Organization follow-up information in case of changes in their national legislation, policies and procedures on the issue, as and when such changes occur.

[5] If the information provided by Member States is not in one of the official languages of the Organization, Member States are encouraged to provide a summary of the legislation in English.

ANNEX

QUESTIONNAIRE ON INFORMATION ON PORT AND COASTAL STATE REQUIREMENTS RELATED TO PRIVATELY CONTRACTED ARMED SECURITY PERSONNEL ON BOARD SHIPS

(The present questionnaire should be read in conjunction with MSC.1/Circ.1408 on the Interim Recommendations for port and coastal States regarding the use of privately contracted armed security personnel on board ships in the High Risk Area[1])

1 Requirements regarding ships intending to enter in or depart from your ports, anchorages, roadstead or offshore terminals when carrying firearms and/or security-related equipment and/or PCASP[2].

1.1 Do you require specific notification from ships intending to enter in or depart from your ports, anchorages, roadstead or offshore terminals?

.1 If yes,

- What information do you require?
- When do you require it?
- To whom is it required to be sent?

Note: FAL Standard 2.2, establishes the principle that the "General Declaration" (IMO FAL Form 1) shall be the document providing data required by public authorities relating to the ship.

1.2 Do you require information regarding flag State authorization for use of PCASP and/or the firearms and/or the security-related equipment for use by the PCASP from ships intending to enter in or depart from your ports, anchorages, roadstead or offshore terminals?

.1 If yes,

- What information do you require?
- When do you require it?
- To whom is it required to be sent?

Note: MSC.1/Circ.1406/Rev.1 establishes the principle that "Flag States should have in place a policy on whether or not the use of PCASP will be authorized and, if so, under which conditions." This policy "may include a process for authorizing the use of PCASP which have been found to meet minimum requirements for ships flying its flag."

---

1 High Risk Area: an area as defined in the Best Management Practices for Protection against Somalia Based Piracy (MSC.1/Circ.1339) unless otherwise defined by the flag State.

2 All references to firearms include the associated ammunition, consumables, spare parts and maintenance equipment for use by PCASP, and all references to security-related equipment includes protective and communication equipment for use by PCASP.

1.3 Do you require specific notification regarding firearms for use by the PCASP carried on board ships intending to enter in or depart from your ports, anchorages, roadstead or offshore terminals?

.1 If yes,

- What information do you require?
- When do you require it?
- To whom is it required to be sent?

Note: FAL Standard 2.4 establishes the principle that the "Ship's Stores Declaration" (IMO FAL Form 3) shall be the document providing data required by public authorities.

1.4 Do you require specific notification regarding security-related equipment for use by the PCASP carried on board ships intending to enter in or depart from your ports, anchorages, roadstead or offshore terminals?

.1 If yes,

- What information do you require?
- When do you require it?

- To whom is it required to be sent?

Note: FAL Standard 2.4, establishes the principle that the "Ship's Stores Declaration" (IMO FAL Form 3) shall be the document providing data required by public authorities.

1.5 Do you require specific notification regarding PCASP carried on board ships intending to enter in or depart from your ports, anchorages, roadstead or offshore terminals?

.1 If yes,

- What information do you require?
- When do you require it?
- To whom is it required to be sent?

Note: FAL Standard 2.6 establishes the principle that the "Crew List" (FAL Form 5) shall be the document providing data required by public authorities.

1.6 What requirements, if any, do you have in place for ships carrying firearms and/or the security-related equipment for use by the PCASP or PCASP when transiting through your territorial seas and/or contiguous zones before arrival in or after departure from your ports, anchorages, roadstead or offshore terminals?

2 Requirements regarding ships intending to enter in or depart from your ports, anchorages, roadstead or offshore terminals for the purpose of embarking or disembarking firearms and/or security-related equipment and/or PCASP.

2.1 Do you allow the embarkation or disembarkation of firearms and/or the security-related equipment for use by the PCASP or of PCASP in your ports, anchorages, roadstead or offshore terminals or elsewhere in your territorial sea(s)?

.1 If yes,

- What information do you require?
- When do you require it?
- To whom is it required to be sent?

2.2 Do you require information regarding flag State authorization for use of PCASP and/or the firearms and/or the security-related equipment for use by the PCASP from ships intending to enter in or depart from your ports for the purpose of embarking or disembarking firearms and/or the security-related equipment for use by the PCASP or PCASP?

.1 If yes,

- What information do you require?
- When do you require it?
- To whom is it required to be sent?

Note: MSC.1/Circ.1406/Rev.1 establishes the principle that "Flag States should have in place a policy on whether or not the use of PCASP will be authorized and, if so, under which conditions." This policy "may include a process for authorizing the use of PCASP which have been found to meet minimum requirements for ships flying its flag."

2.3 What requirements, if any, do you have in place in connection with the import or arrival in and/or export or departure from your territory of firearms and/or security-related equipment for use by PCASP?

2.4 What requirements, if any, do you have in place in connection with the storage, security or control of the firearms and/or security-related equipment for use by the PCASP prior to their embarkation or after their disembarkation?

2.5 What requirements, if any, do you have in place in connection with the storage, security or control of the firearms and/or security-related equipment carried on board for use by the PCASP after their embarkation or prior to their disembarkation, when the ship is in your port, anchorage, roadstead or territorial waters?

2.6 What requirements, if any, do you have in place for ships carrying firearms and/or the security-related equipment for use by the PCASP or of PCASP (which they have embarked your anchorages, roadstead or offshore terminals) when transiting through your territorial seas and/or contiguous zones after departure from your ports, anchorages, roadstead or offshore terminals?

3 Reporting of security-related incidents in territorial seas.

3.1 What do you consider to constitute a security incident in your territorial sea(s)?

3.2 Do you require information regarding security-related incidents occurring in your territorial sea(s)?

.1 If yes,

- What information do you require?
- When do you require it?
- To whom is it required to be sent?

In the latter months of 2012, shipping awaits new documentation regarding to the regulating of PMSCs and PCASPs.

PRESENTATION AT ISO 28007 PAS INFORMATIVE MEETING

INTERPOL HEADQUARTERS – LYON 26 Jul 2012

By James Rapp (Managing Partner 3rg Security) – representative of the UK's Security in Complex Environments Group

3rg Excellence In Security

Introduction

- Remarkable to be here today at Interpol discussing a future ISO PAS for Maritime Private Security Companies - or Private Maritime Security Companies in the language of the IMO. And we are all very aware that the IMO is eagerly awaiting the results of ISO's work in just a few months' time.

- The UK is playing a leading role in the international community's efforts to improve the situation in Somalia. This was demonstrated by the International Conference on Somalia hosted by the Prime Minister, David Cameron, in London earlier this year. As we all know the situation within Somalia cannot be changed overnight and the threat from pirates will remain in the High Risk Area for the foreseeable future. The final communiqué after the London Conference 'welcomed current work on international guidance on the use of private armed security companies, and reiterated a determination to eradicate piracy, noting that the problem requires a comprehensive approach on land as well as at sea.'

- I am here as a representative of the UK's 'Security in Complex Environments Group' and sit on its Executive Committee. I'm also the Managing Partner of 3rg Security. I will start by explaining where the SCEG is positioned and then say a little about what the SCEG is doing in support of international efforts to create internationally recognised Standards - both on land and at sea. I'll finish with some thoughts about areas that I believe need to be addressed in the preparation of this PAS.

The SCEG

- The SCEG arose from the UK government's involvement with the International Code of Conduct for Private Security Service Providers - ICOC for short. The ICOC was driven by the Swiss government and signed in Geneva in November 2010 by 58 private security companies, including two well established British maritime companies. The number of signatories had grown to 404 last month with a high proportion operating in the maritime sector.

- While some might wish to decouple maritime security companies from their land brethren, work on an international code of conduct and Standard started in the land environment. And the processes developed for land companies are one of the drivers for maritime companies.

- Para 7 of the Code calls for objective and measurable standards to be established with the objective of realising common and internationally recognised operational and business practices. But we do need to remember that the Code was not designed to apply to the provision of maritime security services and this has been recognised by the IMO MSC.

- As the ICOC was being finalised, the UK Government ran a competition to identify a partner to create a process for the regulation of PSCs. ADS – the premier international trade association for the UK's Aerospace, Defence, Security and Space industries - won the competition. ADS then set up the SCEG and the SCEG became the FCO's industry partner last year.

Through SCEG there is a very healthy engagement between different government departments and industry and SCEG has been working since then on the creation of standards and the sharing of best practice.

- The initial focus was on the ICOC and creating a Land Standard. But attention quickly turned to the maritime sector. This was driven by concern about the large number of companies springing up to offer counter piracy services without any form of regulation and also by David Cameron's announcement last autumn that armed guards were to be permitted onboard UK Flagged ships.

- Although ADS and SCEG represent UK-based industry, our industry works for multinational clients around globe – our interest is therefore also international and SCEG members have played and are continuing to play a key role in all international initiatives on standards for PSCs/MPSCs in both the land and maritime environments.

- On land, there is now an internationally negotiated text (ANSI/ASIS PSC1) that sets out best practice and processes for land companies. The SCEG has recommended PSC1 to the UK Government as the land standard.

- Because of expertise built up in developing standards for land companies, a small group of SCEG members – within its Maritime Security Working Group – then drafted a full management standard for maritime companies. This was completed in May.

- We felt the best way to proceed was to draft a Quality Assurance Security Management System of a kind that clients and industry could easily recognise, and which would help identify the companies applying best practice – in other words, doing things properly and legally and not cutting corners.

- We chose to include the management elements of a future standard. But we now recognise that these will be covered in a different manner within ISO28007, with companies being certified under ISO 28000. However, the relationship between various other key ISOs, particularly 9001 is important and does need to be kept under review. Companies already 9001 certified will want to see that the effort and cost of completing ISO28007 adds tangible value to their operations and business. And so, we need to ensure that ISO28007 becomes recognised as the international benchmark for assessing PMSCs and also that certification against 28007/28000 complements existing quality management systems.

- In SCEG, we drew on the extensive guidance in IMO MSC circulars, Best Management Practice 4 and more recently GUARDCON. We also drew on relevant aspects of land operations, not least the increasingly demanding and complex contractual requirements of clients on land, be it the US Department of Defence or larger corporations requiring private security services. We also drew on the expertise gained in developing PSC1 and the matching conformity assessment. Many elements of operations are common to both the land and maritime environments such as:

- Leadership, and the internal and external processes to be followed by a company;
- Selection, screening and vetting of personnel and sub-contractors
- Identification of security staff personnel to distinguish them from others
- The importance of training, and keeping records of the training
- Procurement, licensing and management of firearms - the main principles apply both on land and at sea;
- The need to comply with international and national law and the need to comply with laws in a multitude of jurisdictions;
- Reporting and documenting of incidents, (and for that matter the detailed paper trail for all aspects of operations)

Areas addressed in the PAS

- Turning now to ISO 28007, and the need for a common maritime standard the SCEG is delighted that we are able to contribute to the work being undertaken by ISO to establish this PAS for maritime security companies.

- The maritime security industry has a very real stake in establishing and improving standards. We need an internationally recognised Standard:

- To reassure the many interested parties – such as international organisations, governments, insurers, ship owners, the media ... the list is large – that the industry is responsible, professional and effective
- To improve accountability – across every aspect of operations
- To assist our Clients to differentiate the good Companies from the poor ones and most importantly
- To raise standards internationally

- To finish, here are some critical issues that we may wish to debate over the next 2 days:

1. How do we deliver a transparent and effective process that provides assurance to clients as to the quality of a company but also provides a standard to which all responsible companies can aspire? The Standard will be handicapped from the start if it is so onerous and/or costly that only the large companies can meet it.
2. How do we best encourage independent internationally recognised certification bodies to play their part in this process? The IMO has told ISO it does not support self-certification or self-regulation.
3. How do we ensure that the Standard demands accountability for acts contrary to the Standard and especially contrary to international law, and helps establish a regime where all incidents are reported? There have been relatively few reported major incidents but stories continue to be told of incidents involving loss of life that are never reported.
4. To be effective internationally, we need common international standards and performance levels for vetting, training and competency - including the safe and proficient use of firearms, and accountability as regards their procurement, licensing, storage, use and disposal.
5. And we need to achieve wide ranging buy-in to this International Standard - with an appropriate balance of liability between the MPSC and the Client. And so we will need to engage widely with clients, plus State and non-State actors.

- To conclude, I hope the SCEG's work and experience will contribute to an effective PAS. The SCEG has already committed to having a maritime standard in place by the end of 2012. And so we are fully committed to supporting ISO in developing this PAS for presentation to the MSC at IMO at the end of November.

Courtesy to Mr. James Rapp

24. USEFUL INFORMATION AND WEBSITES

To help save time finding contact details or trying to establish which product or company provides the best equipment or services the following list has been compiled.

KEY AGENCIES

International Maritime Bureau

The ICC International Maritime Bureau (IMB) is a specialised division of the International Chamber Of Commerce (ICC). The IMB is a non-profit making organisation, established in 1981 to act as a focal point in the fight against all types of maritime crime and malpractice. The International Maritime Organisation (IMO) in its resolution A 504 (XII) (5) and (9) adopted on 20 November 1981, has inter alia, urged governments, all interests and organisations to co-operate and exchange information with each other and the IMB with a view to maintaining and developing a co-ordinated action in combating maritime fraud. The IMB has a MOU with the World Customs Organisation (WCO) and has observer status with Interpol (ICPO).

IMB's main task is to protect the integrity of international trade by seeking out fraud and malpractice. For over 25 years, it has used industry knowledge, experience and access to a large number of well-placed contacts around the world to do this: identifying and investigating frauds, spotting new criminal methods and trends, and highlighting other threats to trade.

The information gathered from sources and during investigations is provided to members in the form of timely advice via a number of different communication routes. It lists the threats and explains how members can reduce their vulnerability to them. Over the years, this approach has thwarted many attempted frauds and saved the shipping and trading industry many millions of dollars.

The IMB provides an authentication service for trade finance documentation. It also investigates and reports on a number of other topics, notably documentary credit fraud, charter party fraud, cargo theft, ship deviation and ship finance fraud.

As well as helping to prevent crime, the IMB also has a duty to educate both the shipping community and a wider audience that comprises just about every entity engaged in trade. To this end, the IMB runs a regular series of courses and training programmes that have a wide-ranging syllabus and many proven benefits. It also offers bespoke consultancy services in areas such as ship and port security.

One of the IMB's principal areas of expertise is in the suppression of piracy. Concerned at the alarming growth in the phenomenon, this led to the creation of the IMB Piracy Reporting Centre in 1992. The Centre is based in Kuala Lumpur, Malaysia. It maintains a round-the-clock watch on the world's shipping lanes, reporting pirate attacks to local law enforcement and issuing warnings about piracy hotspots to shipping.

With its multi-lingual and multi-disciplined staff, experience, unique structure, industry support and well-placed contacts, the IMB can rightly claim to be the world's premier independent crime-fighting watchdog for international trade.

If you wish to report an piratical incident or armed robbery please contact the 24-hour Piracy Reporting Centre:

Tel: + 60 3 2078 5763
Fax: + 60 3 2078 5769
Telex: MA34199 IMBPCI E-mail: imbkl@icc-ccs.org/ piracy@icc-ccs.org
24-hour Anti-Piracy helpline, Tel: + 60 3 2031 0014

Maritime Liaison Office (MARLO) Bahrain

Core Working Hours: Sunday - Thursday 0800-1700
Daytime Tel: +973-17-85-3925, Fax: +973-17-85-3930 E-mail:marlo.bahrain@me.navy.mil
MARLO EMERGENCY NUMBER - 24 HOURS DAY:
+9733940-1395
Address: Maritime Liaison Office, Box 116, Manama, Bahrain

Counter-piracy guidance summary

- REVIEW FULL COUNTER-PIRACY GUIDANCE
- For ships transiting high-risk piracy areas
- Contact MARLO or register at MSCHOA at http://www.mschoa.org to receive the Gulf of Aden Group Transits (GOA GT) times.
    - All ships are strongly urged to use the IRTC and follow the GOA GT if their speed is below 18 knots but greater than 10 knots.
    - Vessels faster than 18 knots should transit between 47°E and 49 °E during the hours of darkness.
    - Vessels less than 10 knots should contact UKMTO for routing guidance.
- All vessels should establish contact with UKMTO, MSCHOA or MARLO for additional guidance.

Maritime Administration

The Maritime Administration is the agency within the U.S. Department of Transportation dealing with waterborne transportation. Its programs promote the use of waterborne transportation and its seamless integration with other segments of the transportation system, and the viability of the U.S. merchant marine.

The Maritime Administration works in many areas involving ships and shipping, shipbuilding, port operations, vessel operations, national security, environment, and safety. The Maritime Administration is also charged with maintaining the health of the merchant marine, since commercial mariners, vessels, and intermodal facilities are vital for supporting national security, and so the agency provides support and information for current mariners, extensive support for educating future mariners, and programs to educate America's young people about the vital role the maritime industry plays in the lives of all Americans.

The Maritime Administration also maintains a fleet of cargo ships in reserve to provide surge sealift during war and national emergencies, and is responsible for disposing of ships in that fleet, as well as other non-combatant Government ships, as they become obsolete.

The Maritime Administration recently realigned many of its functions, to revitalize its role as an industry facilitator, and to bring greater focus to the areas of environment and safety.

Contact Information

Mailing Address
U.S. Department of Transportation
Maritime Administration
West Building
1200 New Jersey Avenue, SE
Washington, DC 20590

Email

- Office of Congressional & Public Affairs: pao.marad@dot.gov
- Questions about this web site: webmaster.marad@dot.gov

Telephone

- General Information
  1-800-99-MARAD
  1-800-996-2723
- Personnel Locator
  202-366-4000
- Office of Congressional and
  Public Affairs
  202-366-5807

Also see:

The IMB urges governments to heighten security patrols in their waters and ships to remain vigilant against attacks. Unfortunately for the operating navies, their hands are tied: under the current rules of engagement they can only engage if they are fired upon – pirates have soon become aware of this law, or flaw as seen by frustrated naval forces and seaman alike.

The following illustrations are to show how the scourge of piracy, both from Somalia and globally has spread over the last 5 years. These IMB images paint a clear picture of piracy increases and hotspots

The following information is courtesy of Capt. P Mukundan and the ICC IMB/PRC.

Below: Gulf of Aden, 2007

Map data © 2007 Google

As seen here, there are very few attacks and well spread out, all within reach of the Somali coast

7

Kidnap and ransom (K&R)	
AKE **Control Risks**	www.akegroup.com www.akegroup.com/contingencies/k&r-threat-extortion.php www.controlrisks.com
Specialist equipment	
International Maritime Anti-piracy Advisory Group (IMAAG)	www.imaag.co.uk
Weapons	
Imperial Defence Systems	www.imperialdefence.co.uk
Water cannon system	www.nemesis5000.com www.mpsint.com
Medical Training and Equipment	
Exmed	www.exmed.com
ERS999	www.ers999.com
MedAire Lifeline:	www.medaire.com/yachtlifeline
Maritime Agencies	
International Maritime Bureau	www.icc-ccs.org
International Maritime Organisation	www.imo.org
DEA	www.justice.gov/dea
RYA Royal Yachting Association	www.rya.org.uk
Nato Shipping Centre	Website www.shipping.nato.int Email: info@shipping.nato.int Telephone (24hrs): +44(0)1923 956574 Fax: +44(0)1923 956575
Interpol	Website www.interpol.int Email: os-ccc@interpol.int Telephone (24hrs): +33(0) 4 72 44 76 76
MARLO	Website www.cusnc.navy.mil/marlo/ Email: marlo.bahrain@me.navy.mil Office: +9785 3925 Duty (24hrs): +973 3940 1395 Fax : +973 1785 3930

MSCHOA	www.mschoa.org Telephone: +44 (0) 1923 958545 Fax: +44 (0) 1923 958520 Email: postmaster@mschoa.org
UKMTO	Email: UKMTO@eim.ae Telephone (24hrs): +971 50 552 3215
Intelligence Briefings, Weather, and Updates	
Ironside Associates	www.ironsideassociates.com
Dryad Maritime	www.dryadmaritime.com
Maritime and Seafarers' Websites	
Noonsite	www.noonsite.com
MarineBuzz	www.marinebuzz.com

Equipment Manufacturers	
Fast RIBs	www.buzzi-design.com
Fast RIBs	www.halmatic.com
Flares And Sea Safety Equipment	www.painswessex.com
Long Range Acoustic Device LRAD	www.lradx.com
Weapons	www.imperialdefencesupplies.com
Search Lamps	www.peakbeam.com
Hand-Held Torches	www.surefire.com
Polarised Sunglasses Maui Jim	www.mauijim.com
Revo	www.revo.com
Oakley	www.oakley-sunglasses.com
S6 Radar Enhancer	www.imaag.co.uk
Night Vision	www.bushnell.com
ITT	www.nightvision.com/
Litton	www.night-vision-scopes-outpost.com/litton-night-vision.html

Image Stabilising (I.S) Binoculars **Canon**	www.canon.co.uk/For_Home/Product_Finder/Binoculars/Optical_Image_Stabilisation/index.asp
Non I.S Binoculars	www.swarovskioptik.com
Leica	www.uk.leica-camera.com/sport_optics
Zeiss	www.zeiss.com/sports
Steiner	www.steiner-binoculars.com
IS Camcorder Sony	www.sony.com

LIST OF MOST MARITIME SECURITY COMPANIES AS OF MAY 2012

1	Advanced Security Protection
2	AKE Group
3	Ambrey Risk
4	Anti Piracy Maritime Security Services
5	Antipirates.Org
6	Anubis Associates Limited Security Training and Services
7	APPDS Ltd - Personal Protection & Defence Systems - Intro
8	AQUATIC MARINE LTD
9	Aspida Maritime Security · Maritime Security Services
10	Associated Risk Maritime Risk Management
11	Bancroft Maritime Security Solutions
12	Barantas Security Group "where standards are set not sought"
13	Bechtel Corporation: Home
14	Black Pearl Maritime Security
15	Blackstone Consultancy
16	Blue Hackle
17	Blue Mountain Group - Security, Maritime, Adventure and Driver Training
18	Blue Sky Group International
19	Blue Water Partners Global
20	blueskysc.org
21	BP Global | BP
22	Britam Defence - A Special Force in Security
23	British Maritime Solutions
24	BW Offshore
25	Calibre International Security
26	Canine (K9) Disciplines, Consultancy and Training Services
27	Centurion Risk Assessment Services
28	Cerberus International
29	Chilport:

30	Chiron Resources
31	Clearwater Special Projects :
32	Contact Orchid Family
33	Control Risks
34	Dascam Consulting
35	Decatur Maritime Security
36	Decaturms - Home
37	Drum Cussac
38	Dryad Maritime Intelligence Services
39	DynCorp International
40	Edinburgh International
41	Elite Maritime Protection Services
42	EOS Risk Management Limited
43	Erus Maritime
44	Espada
45	Ex Military Recruitment
46	Exploration Logistics Group
47	FrontierMEDEX
48	G4S Maritime
49	Genesis Security Group
50	Global Executive Outreach
51	Global Integrity
52	Global Risk Management - by Olchon Ltd
53	Global Risk Security
54	Global Solace
55	Global Strategies Group
56	Grail Security
57	Halliburton:
58	Halogen Security Company Limited
59	Hart Maritime
60	Hill & Associates
61	The Risk Advisory Group
62	Drum Cussac,
63	HP TerraMarine International
64	http://britishmaritimesolutions.com
65	http://macgregorprotectionservices.com
66	http://maritimecareers.com.
67	http://oceanprotectionservices.com
68	http://www.ambreyrisk.com
69	http://www.aquaticmarineltd.com
70	http://www.associated-risks.com
71	http://www.blackstoneconsultancy.com;
72	http://www.calibre-international.com

73	http://www.chironresources.com
74	http://www.control-risks.com
75	http://www.elitemaritimeprotection.com
75a	http://www.erusrisk.com
76	http://www.espadaservices.com
77	http://www.g4s.uk.com
78	http://www.geo-ops.com/
79	http://www.globalrisksecurity.co.uk/
80	http://www.grail.co.za
81	http://www.hartsecurity.com
82	http://www.hillassoc.com
83	http://www.hpterramarine.com/
84	http://www.iernetwork.com
85	http://www.intmarsec.co.uk
86	http://www.isn.eu.com
87	http://www.longmoor-security.com
88	http://www.lotusmaritime.com
89	http://www.lpyemen.com
90	http://www.maritimesecuritysolutions.co.uk
91	http://www.marsec.eu.com
92	http://www.mast-commercial.com
93	http://www.mss-uk.com
94	http://www.navalguards.com
95	http://www.nemesisgroup.org
96	http://www.northbridgeservices.com/
97	http://www.nyainternational.com
98	http://www.oceanmarshalls.com
99	http://www.oxberryrisk.com/maritime_services
100	http://www.pilgrimsgroup.com
101	http://www.pilgrimsgroup.com
102	http://www.ravenspecialprojects.com
103	http://www.redcellsecurity.co.uk
104	http://www.redfour-group.com
105	http://www.salamancarm.com
106	http://www.seamarshals.com
107	http://www.securoquest.co.za
108	http://www.sps-global.com
109	http://www.sps-global.com
110	http://www.tacticalintel.com
111	http://www.torcuss.co.za/
112	http://www.triskelservices.com
113	http://www.tritoninternationalltd.com
114	http://www.trojansecurities.com

115	https://www.exmil.co.uk
116	https://www.nnkcorporation.com
117	Neptune Risk
155	Neptune Maritime Security
156	NNK Group
157	North Bridge Services
158	NYA International
159	Ocean Marshalls
160	Ocean Protective Services
161	Oceaneering International
162	Oilfield Services | Halliburton - Solving Challenges. - Halliburton
163	Olchon
164	Olive Group :: Creating a Secure Environment
165	Orchid Security
166	Over Watch
167	Oxberry Risk Strategies
168	Pilgrim Group
169	Pilgrim Security
170	Pistris:
171	Protect Asia
172	Protect Asia Group
173	PVI | Protection Vessels International Ltd
174	Raven Special Projects Ltd
175	Red Cell Security
176	Redfour-MSS
177	Saladin Security Group
178	Saladin Security, LTD
179	saladinsecurity.com
180	Salama Fikira
181	Salamanca Risk Management
182	Sea Marshalls Ltd UK
183	SEAL Security - Home
184	SECOPEX : Socit spcialise dans la formation, les contractors, la protection et garde rapproche - Accueil
185	Security Networking Events Ltd. | Private Security Services, SNE Special Projects, SNE Recruitment
186	www.specialistmarineservices.com
187	TOR International -
188	Trojan Securities International
189	
	This list is growing every week, please email us to add your company here.

26. About the Author

Peter King, the director of the International Maritime Anti-piracy Advisory Group (IMAAG), started life as a gamekeeper, and then joined the Royal Marines at the age of 19; he excelled in his basic training, particularly with weapons and field craft, but hated the drill square and the long hours it wasted. Within his first five years of Commando service he saw action in Europe and Iraq during the first Gulf War. He spent much time on and off ships as well as 18 months as part of a 15-man, quick reaction security team on board HMS Invincible. Little did he know that this would be his grounding for the start of a long and dangerous road in the world of maritime security and anti-piracy?
At 24 years old he joined the Special Forces. For the rest of his colourful career he worked with other international maritime agencies both on and off the seas, spanning from South America, through North Africa to the sleepy creeks of Falmouth Harbour. Whether pursuing drug dealers, terrorists or teaching young soldiers their boating skills, all would be invaluable experience for the commercial world.

Now working as a subject matter expert in maritime security, Peter has spent the last six years focusing on anti-piracy, helping clients to protect their people and assets in high-risk areas around the world. Other aspects of his work include surveillance, investigation, training, close protection and explosive demolition.

It was in 2007 when Peter explosively sunk the New Zealand warship HMNZS Canterbury to create an underwater marine reserve and dive site whilst working with Cadre One.
Photo: Keith Simpson / Andrew Lumley CadreOne. Ltd

In 2008, it was apparent that there was need for an up-to-date, detailed guidebook to help fellow mariners when faced with security concerns such as armed pirates and robbers. This book has been produced using his knowledge and experience, guidance from friends, Captains within the industry and agencies such as the IMB.

Please note that a percentage of any profit made from the sales of this book will go to the Help for Heroes and the Special Boat Service Association charities.

SPECIAL BOAT SERVICE ASSOCIATION

HELP *for* HEROES
Support for our Wounded

Contact information for Peter King:
www.imaag.co.uk

Email: info@imaag.co.uk

DISCLAIMER

It is hoped that the contents of this book, with or without the pre-deployment brief, will be of considerable use to fellow mariners around the world, regardless of their vessel or experience. However, the author cannot accept any responsibility should a vessel be either attacked or successfully boarded: that cannot be guaranteed, but by using the methods mentioned a seafarer will certainly have a much better chance of preventing this from happening.

Fair winds and following seas.

Peter King

International Maritime Anti-piracy Advisory Group (IMAAG)

2012

Photo courtesy of yachting legend; Captain Ben Marshall

ANNEX A

PRE-DEPLOYMENT CHECKLIST FOR SAILING/MOTOR VESSELS, SUPERYACHTS AND LARGER COMMERCIAL SHIPS

Unfortunately, most attention is drawn towards the commercial market and people and agencies bear little attention to the private market. For example, why is there not a military naval convoy designed to escort small, slower vessels through the GoA at 6 knots? If this were the case, even if it were only monthly, then skippers could plan their trips to be at the start point, along with a whole flotilla of similar, slower vessels to ensure their safety. Below are some recommendations (not all*) to make your passage safer.

PRE-DEPLOYMENT GENERIC CHECKLIST FOR ALL VESSELS.

1. Read BMP4 twice and adhere to it, this should be your very minimum protection.
2. Plan your route well; decide where you will sail at what speed and with whom.
3. Consider weather and sea states; piracy attacks are less in the monsoon period.
4. Is your crew capable of handling the stresses of such a passage? Consider removing females and less experienced members and replace with a more robust delivery crew.
5. Carry out training drills prior to entering high-risk areas.
6. Photocopy report formats and keep close to hand in the bridge.
7. Ensure all are familiar with the vessel's fire fighting equipment, pumps, hoses, etc.
8. Never stop in the GoA or other high-risk areas, people are regularly tricked into helping 'stranded fishermen' with dire results.
9. Black out all lights at night; if you must use nav. lights, use low-power bulbs, ensure all hatches and windows are blacked out and someone checks them externally every night.
10. Avoid sailing through the GoA HRA under a full moon; the darker, the better.
11. Adopt radio silence. If you must use the radio, think before you speak and use only low power unless calling for help. If travelling with others, use code words. Rather than telling the world you are 20 miles south of Aden and heading towards Salalah at 9 knots, use waypoints and speech that won't compromise your location.
12. Avoid the use of your vessel's name, use call sign or IMO number, even if talking to a coalition warship, unless absolutely necessary. They should understand and be happy that you are 'a friendly vessel'.
13. Take plenty of items that may prevent an illegal boarding, such as old ropes, nets, smoke, powerful flares to attract the attention of other vessels or helicopters.
14. Consider a professional brief prior to departure and daily situation reports (Sitreps).
15. Do you need security men on board, or enhanced counter measures?
16. How low is your freeboard and stern, how can you modify it to prevent easy access?
17. Is your medic up to date, are your supplies sufficient?

18. Have a comprehensive first-aid kit to hand, with trauma kit as an accessible bundle. Imagine what you will need for a bullet wound, put all those items together within the first-aid grab bag - vital seconds may save lives.
19. Do you need a medical refresher course or a bespoke trauma course?
20. Stay well away from the coastline; use recommended routes such as the IRTC, sail around the HRA.
21. AIS on 'receive' only, or edit the information that is being broadcast, such as "Armed Security Onboard."
22. Have a pre-deployment brief and training prior to departure.
23. Make changes to improve the security of your nominated citadel or safe haven.
24. Check all available post attack reports in the area you are sailing though.
25. Contact the MSCHOA/UKMTO if you are sailing through the GoA and surrounding areas

***Some key information has been removed as criminals may also read this book.**

Be fully prepared in every way before entering a high risk area

PRE-DEPLOYMENT CHECKLIST FOR LARGER COMMERCIAL SHIPS

1. Ensure you do all of the points on the previous "Generic' page.
2. All OOWs to read BMP4 prior to the HRA passage.
3. Ship's speed is vital. Ships travelling at less than 18 knots should travel in group transits in the IRTC or consider an escort with a convoy.
4. Ships with low freeboards should consider extra preventative measures, such as professionally installed razor wire, electric fences, steam curtains, and high-pressure water systems.
5. Consider an armed security team; on large vessels a minimum of three good men, ideally four!
6. If using the above, don't save money by employing cheap labour.
7. If using point four, remember that employing armed, professional guards is the only sure way to stop illegal boarding.
8. If armed personnel aren't possible, consider other passive devices such as Nemesis 5000, P-Trap etc.
9. Keep your generators and pumps running and fire hoses charged for immediate use.
10. Consider having fire hoses on permanently, washing down the sides on vulnerable areas. Can ballast pumps be switched on if the ship's tanks are empty?
11. Keep Jacob's Ladders, wire hawsers, pilot's ladders, and gangplanks high or stowed on deck.
12. Employ darkened ship at night, only use nav. lights. (Consider no nav' lights if safe).
13. Use a sentry port and starboard on the bridge wings as lookouts, keep shifts under 4 hours.
14. Ensure the OOW is constantly observing the radar systems.
15. Consider radar enhancers such as the Sigma S6 for identifying small targets in choppy seas.
16. When at anchor use a high-pressure anchor wash to prevent climbing.
17. Are the captain and SSO fully conversant with the ISPS requirements and have they 'hardened' their vessel as much as possible to minimise any threat, as recommended in BMP4?
18. Keep contact information and blank reports close to hand in the bridge.
19. Adhere to the CSO's recommendations; make sure the CSO's plans and passage mesh in with the BMP4's recommendations to make your passage as smooth and safe as possible.
20. Ensure the ship is locked down, only vital work to be done externally with the Chief Offr's permission, inform the bridge before and after the work has been done.
21. All windows and port holes are blacked out, at last light the duty sentry should check to ensure this has happened.
22. All external access doors need to have locking enhancements to prevent internal access by pirates and thieves.

23. Coalition warships to be called on VHF Ch. 16 in case of emergency or Ch 8 if Ch16 is being blocked or jammed, Music on channel 16 or jamming of Ch16 are to be viewed as signs of suspicious activity in the area as is very much the case. In the event of the vessel being pursued or suspected as being pursued raise the alarm, the Priority is VHF and DSC alerting.
24. Keep flares close to hand for firing at approaching skiffs if ladders or weapons have been seen.
25. Consider methods such as trailing lines to foul the pirates' propellers or swinging 45 gallon drums at points most likely to be climbed (poop deck).

PHOTO FROM ROB FAULKNER,
MARITIME SECURITY CONSULTANT

PRE-DEPLOYMENT CHECKLIST FOR SAILING AND MOTOR YACHTS

1. Never deploy sails in the GoA unless absolutely necessary. A mast is difficult to spot over a distance, as sail or sails can be seen over the horizon even when the deck is out of sight.
2. Consider making your vessel 'armoured', fenders full of water will slow down and deflect high velocity bullets, as will lockers tightly packed with Dynema and Kevlar type ropes. Never leave storage bins around the cockpit empty, presuming that you have nothing to protect yourselves with. Anything is better than nothing.
3. Sailing vessels need to calculate time, distance and speed to ensure they have enough fuel to get them through the area of high risk. Ensure you have all the necessary rations; water, spares, and that your vessel is 100% ship shape. (Some are beautiful, but old and need maintenance).
4. Try to travel in a convoy or group transit with other vessels travelling at the same speed.
5. Read post-transit reports from reliable websites for your area of passage.
6. Private and superyachts always look very attractive; many have open sterns. Try to make this area impossible to board using electric fencing or steam/irritant systems, concertina wire is not feasible.
7. If you feel especially vulnerable, don't take the risk by going to those areas. Have the vessel transported or employ a reputable, armed security team or have it delivered to your nearest safe harbour. Don't ever think that because your vessel is old and low value that the pirates will ignore it, they don't want your vessel; it's your lives that will be spared for a high ransom.
8. Consider informing your last port of a false destination.
9. Have a rehearsed cover story that all the crew know when talking to people ashore.
10. Have 3-4 trailing lines on your stern, 150m is ideal of 8mm polypropylene line, ensure there is a weak point before attaching it to the cleats.

ANNEX B
ADVERTISEMENT AND DETAILED INFORMATION ON KEY PRODUCTS:

LASERSEC SYSTEMS

Home | Company | Applications | Products | Technology | Contact |

Maritime applications

Lasersec Systems **SeaLase** is ideally suited for a number of applications in the maritime sector including:

Superyachts

Commercial Shipping

Offshore Oil and Gas

Naval Security

Port Security

LASERSEC SYSTEMS

Home | Company | Applications | Products | Technology | Contact |

SeaLase - Marine Laser Threat Deterrent

SeaLase is a revolutionary high power laser light source to warn, deter, and prevent the approach of potential threats. Fiber optic beam delivery allows remote positioning of the transmitter, up to 50 meters away from the base unit. The transmitter can be mounted with visible, night vision, or thermal infrared cameras for targeting.

Specifications

Effective range	>4000 meters
Laser power	>5 Watts
Fiber length	2-50 meters
Size, base unit	4U rack, 460 mm depth
Base unit op. temp.	-10 - +55 C
Transmitter op. temp.	-20 - +70 C
Input power	85 - 240 VAC
Power consumption	< 200 Watts

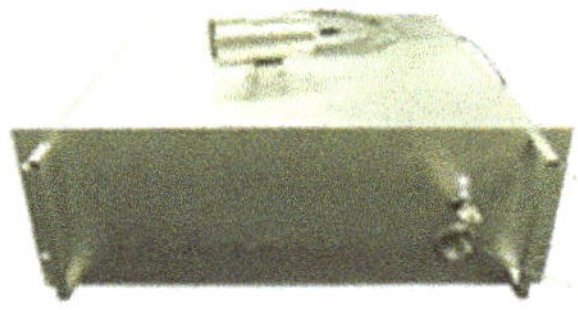

Please contact sales for additional information

LRAD / LRAD FACT SHEET

LRAD for Public Safety Applications Fact
Sheet
The Long Range Acoustic Device™ (LRAD®), innovated and distributed by LRAD Corporation, is a powerful communications tool that is highly effective in a broad variety of public safety situations for government, commercial, and law enforcement organizations.

LRAD has been successfully deployed in support of:

- Large crowd communications
- Search and rescue operations
- Infrastructure and perimeter protection
- Enforcing security zones from secure remote locations
- SWAT operations
- Emergency responder situations
- Crowd/riot control
- Mass notification
- CBRN incident response
- Hostage negotiation from a safe location
- Serving warrants
- Fire/HAZMAT evacuation and communication

LRAD Corporation maintains a strict policy of selling LRAD systems only to qualified government agencies and commercial entities that are fully trained in the device's operation and use.

LRAD provides the acoustic performance, flexibility and reliability needed for operation at distances from 10 to 3,000 meters. LRAD's beam width, frequency range and maximum continuous output ensures 100% intelligible communication over distance and loud background noise. Each LRAD model presents the loudest and most intelligible product in its size and weight category. LRAD's performance record coupled with military construction and survivability standards has made each model the communication tool of choice for police departments and military units around the world. Additionally LRADs provide a portable capability in a rugged lightweight waterproof casing, as well as the option to operate the device remotely across an IP-accessible network. LRAD can provide communication solutions to meet any operational requirement.

LRAD provides a critical part of the layered defence/escalation of force strategy for law enforcement and government agencies. LRAD's warning tone is similar to police and fire sirens broadcasting at the range of human hearing that ensures maximum effectiveness in gaining attention and compliance. Contrary to some reports, LRAD does not generate the ultra-low frequency tones that are needed to cause nausea and disorientation.

The following steps are taken when deploying LRAD for communications.

- Step 1 – Operator broadcasts directions/instructions in a loud, clear voice
    - The focused directional audio broadcast is an effective tool for communicating clearly over distance or loud background noise to individuals, small groups and large crowds.
    - Pre-recorded messages can be broadcast in multiple languages providing law enforcement with pre-planned responses that address a variety of populations clearly and effectively.
    - Hailing and warning in a clear, authoritative voice to provide undeniable instructions and direction.

- Step 2 – If direction is not taken, operator then broadcasts with a more authoritative message
    - Deployment of LRAD at increased volume levels can influence behaviour and create safety zones for law enforcement personnel while preventing the need for additional escalation of force.
    - Stand-down or move to more aggressive stance.
- Step 3 – If directions/instructions are not taken, operator employs the LRAD deterrent tone towards people/persons creating the threatening situation
    - LRAD creates increased standoff and safety zones, supports resolution of uncertain situations, and potentially prevents the use of harmful or deadly force
    - LRAD is equipped with a volume control knob. Unlike tear gas, tasers, rubber bullets, pepper spray and other non-lethal and lethal responses, LRAD can be modulated in response to actions of the target threat
- Step 4 - Law enforcement utilizes higher levels of force such as tear gas, smoke, FN 303 or Tasers

Advantages of deploying LRAD include:

1. Performance – longest range, clearest communication, reliable and demonstrated safe operation.
2. Flexibility – scalable, portable and available in a number of mounting configurations, including an IP addressable option.
3. Design - overcomes background noise to further increase the audible range in almost any environment.
4. Controls – simple to operate, allowing immediate response and process initiation. Single operator use reduces required manpower while improving law enforcement coordination efforts and increasing security coverage.
5. Escalation of Force - safe alternative to non-lethal deterrent options such as pepper spray or rubber bullets.
6. Officer Safety - Increased standoff distance enhances officer safety by keeping personnel at extended ranges which gives additional time to assess the situation and respond appropriately.

LRAD® directed sound systems communicate clearly and effectively over distance, have the capability to resolve uncertain situations peacefully, and the potential to prevent injuries and even save lives on both sides of the device without resorting to the use of non-lethal or lethal weapons. The proven effectiveness of LRAD makes it a 'must have' solution for a variety of public safety, law enforcement and emergency responder situations.

Commercial Maritime

L-3 Harbor Guard

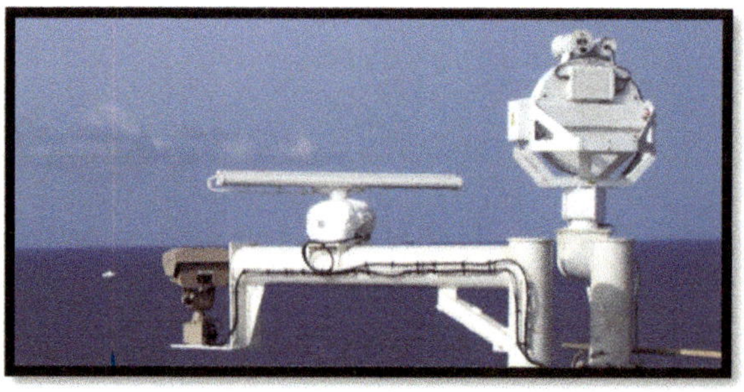

International Statistics

According to the International Maritime Bureau, during the first six months of 2010 alone there were 196 confirmed pirate incidents globally. Of those incidents, 31 resulted in completed hijackings with 544 crew taken hostage. There still remains 360 crewmembers being held hostage as of June 30, 2010.LRAD enables vessels to hail, notify and warn approaching vessels at significant ranges with clear voice or pre-recorded messages in any language.

Seabourn Spirit

In November 2005, the luxury cruise liner Seabourn Spirit employed LRAD to repel a pirate attack off the coast of Somalia. The pirates did not succeed in boarding the vessel and eventually fled.

M/V Resolve & Sunshine Sky

Repelled Pirate Attack at 1100 Meters."aimed her (LRAD) using the sight, went to maximum power and volume and activated. The first time the boat seemed to fall off course momentarily, then come back. I activated the unit a second time, this time holding it for a longer period and "waving" it across the target to make sure I "hit". The boat instantly went dead in the water and broke off its attack. The range was estimated at .6 to .8 km. The crew all saw it and they were cheering. I now have a ship full of believers. Lessons learned: It works."
- Captain M/V Resolve

Green Ridge

Repelled Swarming Pirate Attack at 250 yards. "There was a group of 5 small speed boats disguised as fisherman. Then two of them took off towards us. The captain called the mate on the radio to get the LRAD over to the port side. Once the boats got within 1 mile of the ship we turned on the LRAD. The speed boats got within 500 to 250 yards of the ship before stopping." - Mechanic M/V Green Ridge

Cable Laying Vessels

"By the way our ship ... has had to use her LRAD's 4 times in the last week to warn fishing vessels to remain clear of our cable track. Each time the fishing vessels responded immediately. We are using a warning we had translate into Egyptian when we hail them."

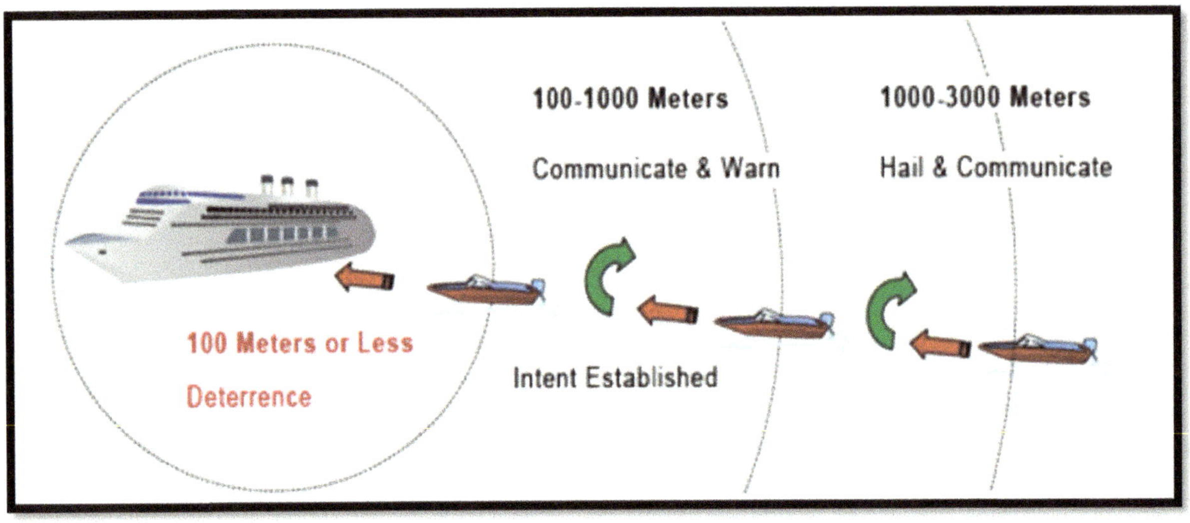

LRAD provides vessel/platform operators the ability to determine the intent of a potential threat at the earliest possible moment and at the greatest distance.

Personal Vessel Security

Protecting high-value assets against piracy threats requires a military-tested shipboard protection device. The Long Range Acoustic Device® (LRAD®) has been successfully used against piracy threats since the Seabourn Spirit incident off the coast of Somalia in November 2005.

LRAD is an easily transportable communication tool that overcomes background noise to clearly transmit critical information, instructions and warnings up to 3000 meters away. Optimized driver and wave-guide design ensures clear, loud voice communication so every syllable is understood. Through the use of voice commands and powerful deterrent tones, LRAD can clearly communicate over long distances, create large safety zones and potentially resolve uncertain situations.
LRAD's unmatched acoustic performance comes in a rugged package that can be operated in the most harsh maritime conditions. Interfaces include a standard microphone as well as a rugged mp3 player designed for easy operation.

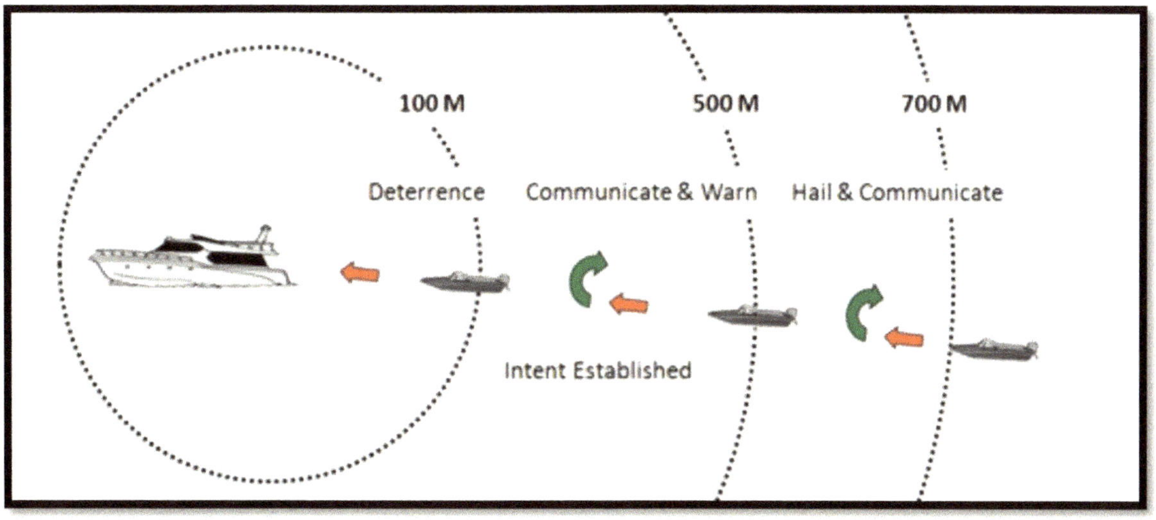

LRAD provides vessel operators the ability to determine the intent of a potential threat at the earliest possible moment and at the greatest distance

Contact LRAD Corporation for more information.
Whether used for short or long term pleasure cruising, LRAD is a cost effective way to extend a yacht's security perimeter and enable ship and crew to determine intent and demonstrate their preparedness at safe distance. When properly deployed, in most confrontations LRAD causes attackers to abort their assault and seek out less prepared vessels.

LRAD Systems Enable:

- Create longer stand-off distances and increased protection for ship and crew
- Determine the intent of unidentified threats from extended distances
- Enforce and extend yacht safety zones

LRAD Corporation

15378 Avenue of Science, Suite 100
San Diego, CA 92128 USA

Phone: 858.676.1112
Fax: 858.676.1120

United States /Europe/Africa/Middle East
Scott Stuckey
Vice President Business Development
207.522.2439
sstuckey@lradx.com

South/Central America Asia Pacific
Ryk Williams
Director, Business Development
858.395.2979
rwilliams@lradx.com

LRAD Regional Sales Commercial/Government/Military Products

General Sales Inquiries	858.676.1112	Sales@lradx.com
Technical Support Inquiries	858.676.0574	technical@lradx.com

HSS Products

David Pratt - Director, Business Development	858.676.0551	dpratt@lradx.com

Investor Relations	858.676.0519	info@lradx.com
Media Relations: Marketing	858.676.1112	marketing@lradx.com
General Inquiries	858.676.1112	

Nemesis 5000 Maritime Anti-Piracy

nemesis 5000

Dasic Marine Anti-Piracy

- Nemesis 5000 is a non lethal, unmanned, high pressure, water deterrent designed from proven tank cleaning technology.
- It takes water from the fire/ballast system to both drive the machines and create the high pressure jets.
- Mounted at set intervals (approx 20m) around the vessel on handrails or gunwhales.
- Fully portable system which is installed as part of the ships hardening procedure.
- Multiple machines create a continuous moving water jet curtain around the vessel.
- Adaptable mounting brackets to fit any size and freeboard of vessel.
- Water jets only in a downward arc to ensure full utilization of available water.

Supply Pressure Bar	Typical Nozzle Data			
	14mm Nozzle		16mm Nozzle	
	Flow M3/HR	Jet Length M	Flow M3/HR	Jet Length M
8 Bar	41	20	55	23
10 Bar	49	24	59	25
12 Bar	55	26	63	27

Approximate Number of Machines per Vessel							
Ship Type	ULCC	VLCC	Suezmax	Aframax	Panamax	Handymax	Handysize
Length	380m	335m	274m	253m	228m	183m	176m
DWT	440K	175K	150K	120K	65K	50K	35k
No of Machines	38	34	28	26	24	20	18
All dimensions and details are typical only.							

NEMESIS 5000 IN OPERATION SHOWING JET OVERLAP

nemesis 5000

nemesis 5000

nemesis 5000 — Dasic® Marine Anti-Piracy

Typical Machine Data	
Operating Pressure	8 to 14 bar
Operating Flows	35 to 60m3/hr
Nozzle Sizes	14 to 20mm
Number of Nozzles	6
Materials	316 stst / PTFE / PEAK
Water Connection	To fit Fire/Ballast Systems
Dimensions	350mm x 220mm
Weight	20kg

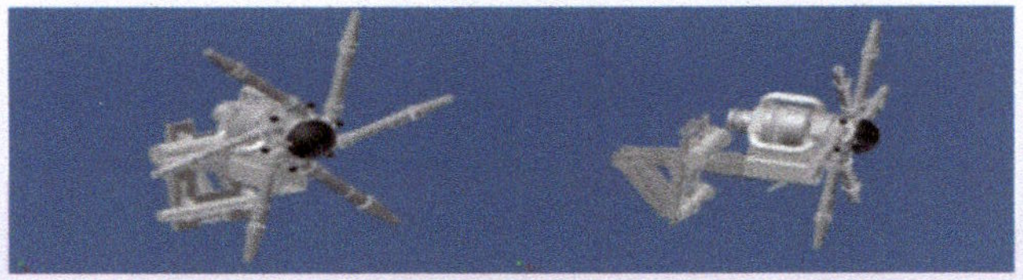

Contact Details

James Murray	Nemesis 5000 Ltd	jmurray@mpsint.com	+44(0)7733 363876 +44(0)1202 684686
Simon Robinson	Dasic Marine Ltd	simon.robinson@dasic-marine.co.uk	+44(0)7768 357729 +44(0)2380 252264

Nemesis 5000 is partnered with MPS (Maritime Protective Services Inc) at:

Purbeck House
New Harbour Road
Continental Ferry Terminal
Poole
Dorset

MPS
MARITIME PROTECTIVE SERVICES (UK) Ltd

nemesis 5000

nemesis 5000 — Dasic® Marine Anti-Piracy

nemesis 5000

NON LETHAL

BOARDING DETERRENT

ANTI-PIRACY SYSTEM

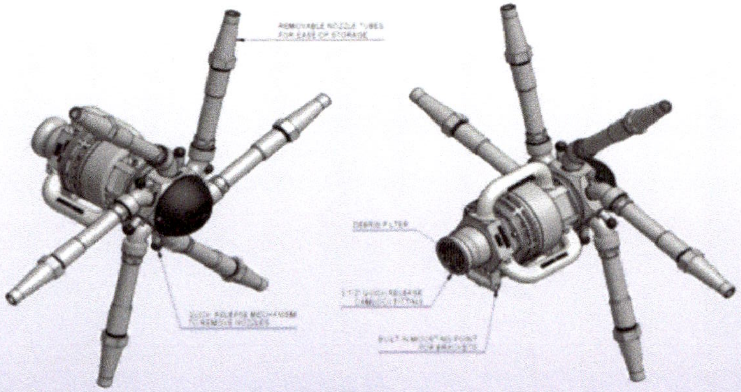

PATENT PENDING; 0908306.4.

nemesis 5000

SF
Salama Fikira
RISK CONSULTANCY
SALAMA FIKIRA INTERNATIONAL LIMITED
Offices in Kenya | Mauritius
Direct +254 20 260 3670 | Office +254 20 259 2879 | Email enquiries@salamafikira.com
www.salamafikira.com
MARITIME | OFFSHORE | LAND | AVIATION | PROJECTS

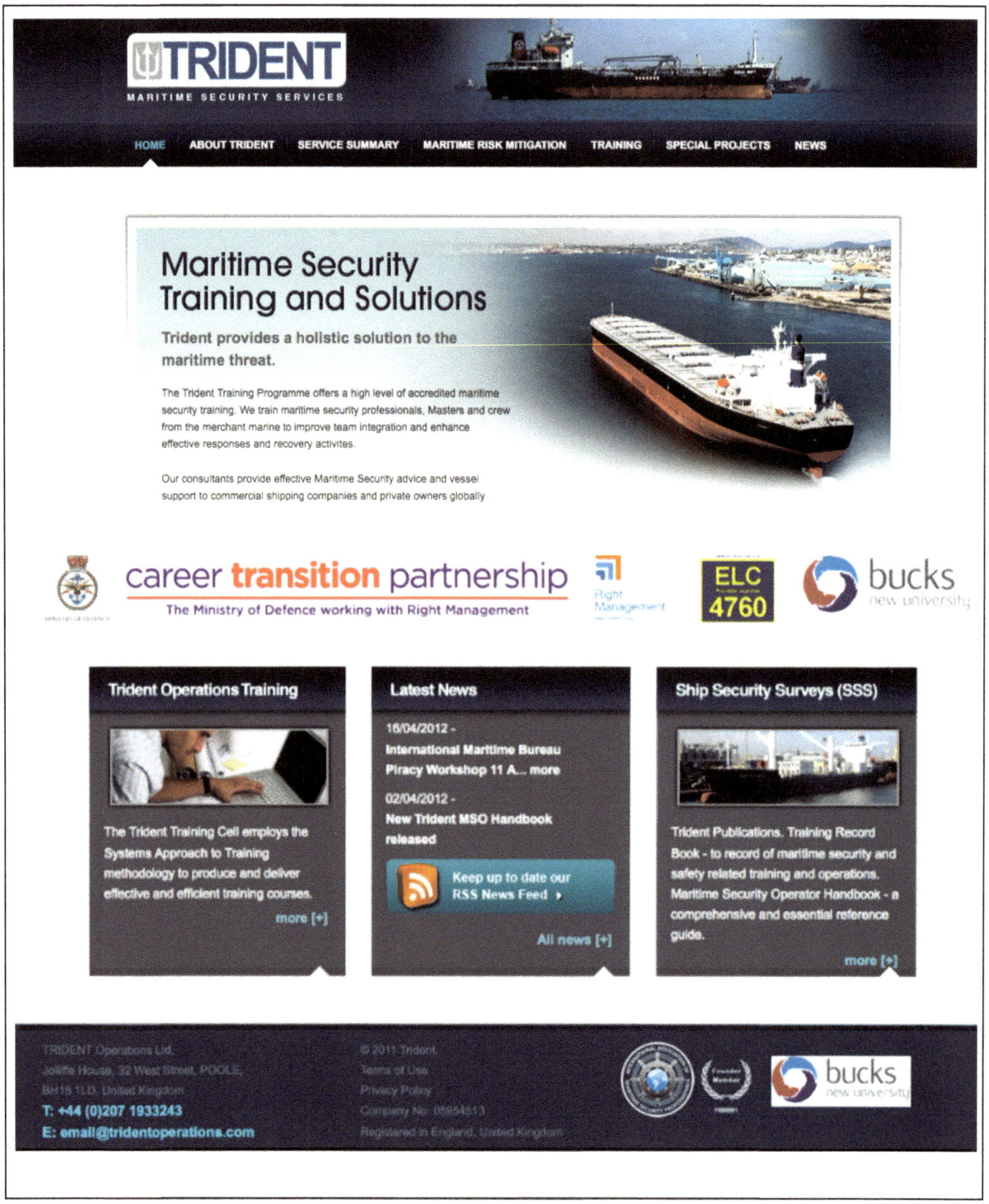

TRIDENT
MARITIME SECURITY SERVICES
HOME
ABOUT TRIDENT
SERVICE SUMMARY
MARITIME RISK MITIGATION
TRAINING
SPECIAL PROJECTS
NEWS
Maritime Security Training and Solutions
Trident provides a holistic solution to the maritime threat.
The Trident Training Programme offers a high level of accredited maritime security training. We train maritime security professionals, Masters and crew from the merchant marine to improve team integration and enhance effective responses and recovery activites.
Our consultants provide effective Maritime Security advice and vessel support to commercial shipping companies and private owners globally
career transition partnership
The Ministry of Defence working with Right Management
Right Management
ELC
4760
bucks
new university
Trident Operations Training
The Trident Training Cell employs the Systems Approach to Training methodology to produce and deliver effective and efficient training courses.
more [+]
Latest News
16/04/2012 -
International Maritime Bureau Piracy Workshop 11 A... more
02/04/2012 -
New Trident MSO Handbook released
Keep up to date our RSS News Feed
All news [+]
Ship Security Surveys (SSS)
Trident Publications. Training Record Book - to record of maritime security and safety related training and operations. Maritime Security Operator Handbook - a comprehensive and essential reference guide.
more [+]
TRIDENT Operations Ltd.
Joliffe House, 32 West Street, POOLE,
BH15 1LD, United Kingdom
T: +44 (0)207 1933243
E: email@tridentoperations.com
© 2011 Trident.
Terms of Use
Privacy Policy
Company No:
Registered in England, United Kingdom
bucks
new university

The Sigma S6 Radar enhancer, perfect for identifying fast moving, low lying skiffs.

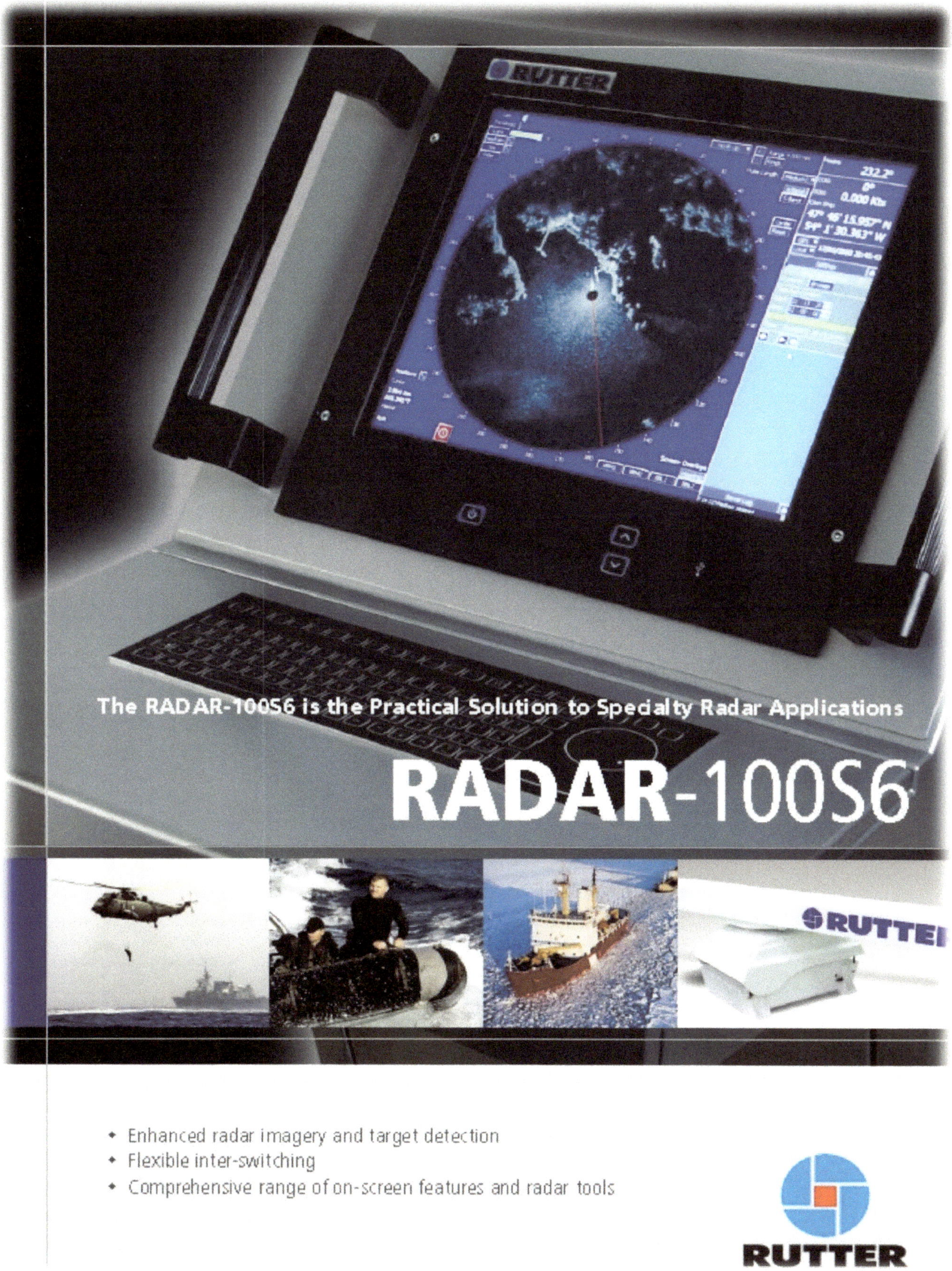

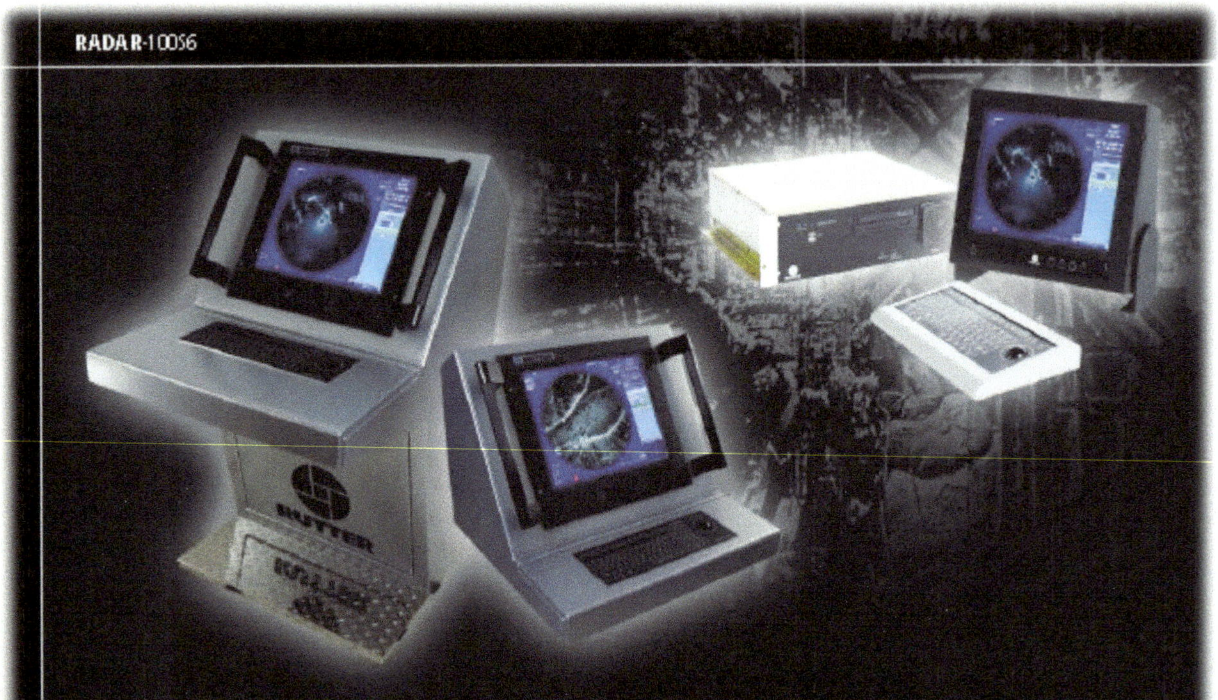

RADAR-100S6

The RADAR-100S6 leverages proven Sigma S6 radar processing technology to provide superior radar imagery and enhanced target detection that leads to improved situational analysis and superior decision making. The RADAR-100S6 is the practical solution to specialty radar applications such as Ice Detection, Search and Rescue, Coastal Surveillance, Port Security, and Vessel Traffic Systems.

- Proven Sigma S6 Radar Processing Technology
- Pulse-to-pulse processing for superior noise reduction and target detection
- Unique scan average processing optimized for detection and tracking of slow-moving targets

CAPABILITIES

The RADAR-100S6 is differentiated from more conventional radars by its unique mix of processing capabilities layered together to provide superior radar imagery, noise and clutter reduction and target tracking.

Flexibility for Optimal Performance

The RADAR-100S6 can use a wired or wireless link to provide remote access and enable radar images to be viewed and manipulated by operators and technicians at different locations. Through its flexible design, multiple RADAR-100S6 radars and multiple radar displays can be connected via Ethernet to allow any display to view any radar on the network. This provides a truly flexible approach to radar configuration.

Multiple Target Tracking

With a tracking capability of up to 1000 targets, the Sigma S6 Dual-Mode Tracker can simultaneously detect and track very small slow-speed targets and high-speed targets by optimizing plot extraction signal processing on separate channels, thereby providing uncompromised target detection and tracking.

AIS Overlay

The optional AIS Overlay module provides AIS targets overlayed on the radar image and provides a full AIS informational display. The AIS Overlay module provides radar track and AIS target association for a clearer operational picture.

Advanced Radar Recording

The optional Sigma S6 radar recording provides for full dynamic range and full-resolution recording capability. The Sigma S6 digital recorder may be used to capture real incidents and isolate best practices for training and simulation exercises or post incident investigation analysis.

Radar Fusion

The optional SeaBridge software module allows the fusion of radar data from multiple radars to be displayed in a single radar image. This allows the use of multiple radars to fill the 360° coverage area that may otherwise be blocked by ship's or platform's superstructure. Target tracking is also calculated from this fused radar image and is also available on the radar network and viewable at any RADAR-100S6 radar display station.

The Sigma S6 provides superior technology and flexibility and meets customer needs in the most challenging situations. The Sigma S6 is increasingly the choice for marine monitoring needs.

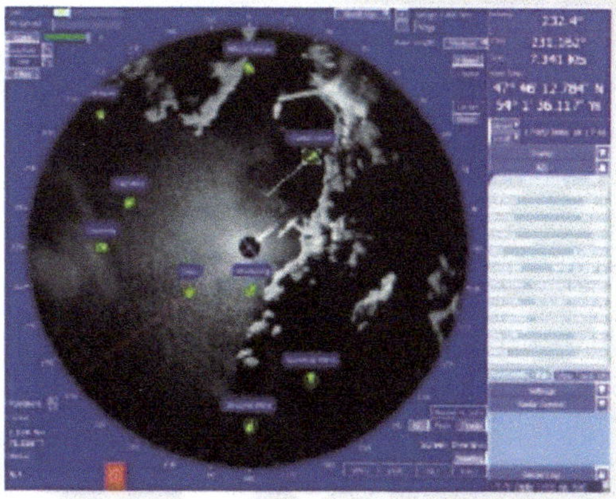

Radar image with both AIS targets and associated AIS and radar targets

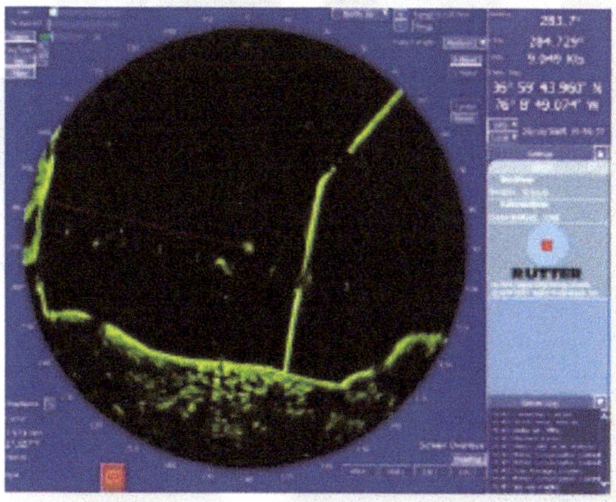

Radar image of vessel in Chesapeake Bay

- Adjustable Scan Average Processor averages up to 64 consecutive radar scans for unsurpassed clutter removal and target detection
- Adjustable Sea and Rain clutter processor enhances detection of near-range targets in high-clutter environments

RUTTER

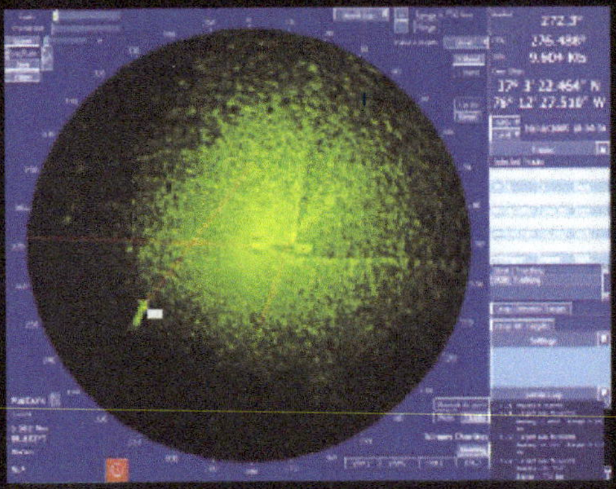

Radar Image with tracked targets

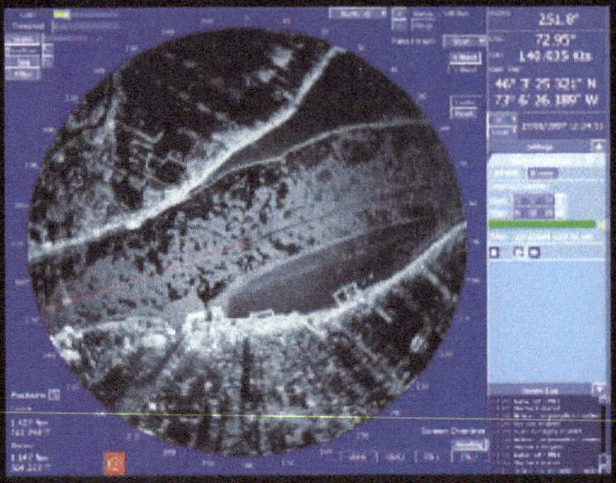

Radar Image of vessel traveling in ice in the St. Lawrence Seaway

RUTTER 3CM SCANNER (COMPRISING ANTENNA AND TURNING UNIT)

- 2535mm (8ft) Scanner
  - Weight 55kg max.
- 1920mm (6ft) Scanner
  - Weight 52kg max.
- 1310mm (4ft) Scanner
  - Weight 50kg max.

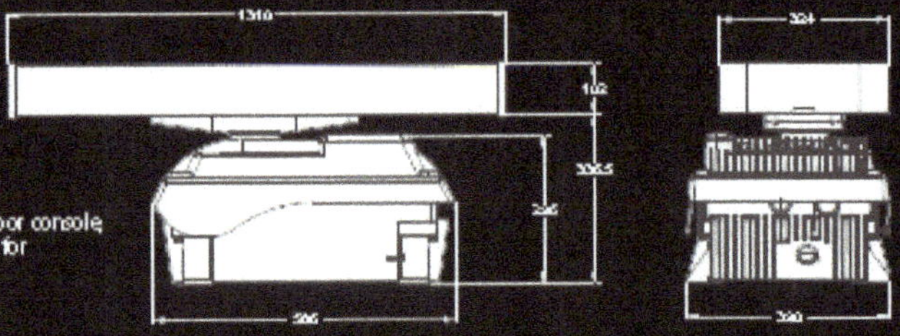

Rutter offers its RADAR-10056 system as a floor console, desktop console and as a component system for integration into existing bridges.

SYSTEM CONFIGURATIONS

OPTIONS	X Band (3cm)	S Band (10cm)
ANTENNA SIZE	1.2, 1.8 or 2.4m	2.7 or 3.6m
TRANSCEIVER CONFIGURATION	bulkhead or masthead	bulkhead or masthead
POWER	10kW or 25kW	30kW

Sweden
Tel: + 46 706 386 396
Fax: + 46 706 143 143
sweden@ruttertech.com

Italy
Tel: + 39 0571 945099
Fax: + 39 0571 945406
italy@ruttertech.com

Germany
Tel: + 49 421 34 99 538
Fax: + 49 721 151 329 560
germany@ruttertech.com

Greece
Tel: + 30 210 3236935
Fax: + 30 210 3220643
greece@ruttertech.com

Head Office
70 Brookfield Road
St. John's, NL
Canada A1E 3T9
Tel: + 1 709 368 4213
Fax: + 1 709 368 1337
sales@ruttertech.com

www.ruttertech.com

RUTTER

Annex C

Best management practices and advice to sailors from various international authorities.

All vessels operating in high-risk areas should have a copy of the latest BMP, as of November 2012, this is BMP4. The contents should be memorised by Captains and OOWs prior to sailing.

FOR SAILING YACHTS

INTERNATIONAL SAILING FEDERATION

Danger of Piracy - Guidelines for yachts considering a passage through the Gulf of Aden, Yemeni and Somali waters including the NW Indian Ocean north of 15o south and west of 78o east

These notes are published in co-operation with the MSCHOA (Maritime Security Centre – Horn of Africa) set up by EU NAVFOR ATALANTA and UKMTO. The notes are for guidance only and a final decision on whether to enter the Gulf of Aden or any waters where pirates operate and how to conduct a vessel in those waters remains entirely the responsibility of the master of each vessel. All vessels entering the area do so at their own risk.

1 The danger of piracy and consequent loss of life and property in the GoA (Gulf of Aden), Yemeni and the Somali waters (up to 750 miles offshore), is high. Yachts are strongly recommended to avoid the area. See advice from the UK FCO (Foreign and Commonwealth Office) athttp://www.fco.gov.uk/ and the Noonsite web site http://www.noonsite.com/General/Piracy. Piracy has also occurred in the adjoining areas of the Indian Ocean north of 10o south and west of 78o east and you should take appropriate self protections when in this area.

2 MSCHOA liaises with anti-piracy patrols being conducted by warships from several nations in the area and UKMTO Dubai coordinates the management of all merchant ship and yachts in the area. The patrols operate mainly in the Gulf of Aden and the Somali Basin but may operate anywhere within the area and will provide surveillance and support as far as possible to yachts however no guarantee whatever can be offered as to the safe transit of any yacht through these waters, and no dedicated escort can be expected.

3 A yacht which, despite the risks described decides to make a passage should advise her plans with as much notice as possible* to UKMTO Dubai and provide the information set out in the attached Yacht Vessel Movement Form, preferably by email but alternatively by telephone:- UKMTO (UK Maritime Trade Organization) (RN) Dubai ukmto@eim.ae+971 50 552 3215; Telex (51) 210473 (24 hour watch)
US-flagged vessels may wish to contact MARLO (Maritime Liaison Office) (USN) Bahrain marlo.bahrain@me.navy.mil +973 3940 1395 (24 hour watch)
A vessel considering entering the area is recommended to carry UK Admiralty Anti-Piracy Planning Chart – Red Sea, Gulf of Aden and Arabian Sea – Q6099.
March 2010 v 2.3 Page 2 of 7

3.1 If under attack a 'mayday' call should be made using VHF or HF DSC, VHF 16 or VHF 8, Sat-C or any other means, please contact UKMTO by telephone and pass your last known position. *Yachts are urged to register at least two weeks before entering a high risk area. Yachts coming south through the Red Sea should report well before reaching Bab al Mandeb and should register before reaching Safaga/Jeddah.

1.2.1 When a yacht registers its movements UKMTO will pass details to patrolling warships and will regularly send to the yacht piracy alerts by email.

3.3 During her passage a yacht should monitor VHF 16 and VHF 8 and report by the means and at the intervals advised by UKMTO, or by a patrolling warship.

4 Merchant ships transiting the GoA are being advised to use an Internationally Recognised Transit Corridor (IRTC) in order for warship patrols to be effective. UKMTO advises yachts to remain close to or within the IRTC as follows:

4.1 The IRTC has two lanes, each 5NM wide and a separation zone between them 2NM wide. To all intents and purposes it operates as a Traffic Separation Scheme (TSS) although formally it does not have that status. The co-ordinates of the IRTC lanes are:
Westbound lane, northern boundary: 12 00N 45 00E 14 30N 53 00E southern boundary: 11 55N 45 00E 14 25N 53 00E
Eastbound lane, northern boundary: 11 53N 45 00E 14 23N 53 00E southern boundary: 11 48N 45 00E 14 18N 5300E
The course eastbound is 072°T and westbound 252°T.

4.2 A yacht which has registered her intention to transit the GoA is invited to sail EITHER in the 2-mile-wide buffer zone between the two lanes OR close to the outer limit of the appropriate lane. These options give the best chance of a yacht's transmission on VHF16 or VHF 8 being received by a patrolling warship, or being relayed by a merchant vessel. However VHF contact is not guaranteed.

4.3 A yacht coming from for example Aden eastbound or Salalah westbound may join the IRTC some way from its start point. The area of the IRTC between 47E and 49E is considered the most dangerous and a yacht should ensure she has joined well before the "high risk area" to enjoy the maximum possible protection. The yacht should plan to conduct as much of this part of the passage as possible at night. In the interests of navigation safety, on joining the IRTC mid way along its length a yacht should act as if joining a Traffic Separation Scheme.
March 2010 v 2.3 Page 3 of 7

5 It has long been common practice for yachts intending to transit the GoA to form small informal convoys in either Djibouti, Aden or Salalah. It is emphasized that this is a decision for individual skippers but the military forces support this concept. If the convoy approach is to be followed it is suggested that there is a limit of no more than five vessels in any one convoy. This is because vessels will need to keep close to one another if they are to offer any protection through numbers, and close station-keeping for the duration of the voyage through the GoA may prove a strain particularly if short-handed.

6 Carriage of arms is not advised. There is a serious risk of escalation of the levels of violence.

7 AIS, Communications, Radar, EPIRBs etc.
Current advice to ships (which are required to carry AIS class A) is to have it transmitting limited information whilst transiting the Gulf of Aden, restricted to ship's identity, position, course, speed, navigational status and safety related information.
Most AIS class B transponders (commonly carried by yachts) can only transmit limited information and are not configurable by the user. Current naval advice to yachts is to leave it switched on in the Gulf of Aden so that the warships know where they are. Navigation lights are to be illuminated at night or periods of low visibility and should not be turned off because of a perceived threat.

In the Somali Basin or further afield where there are fewer warships an AIS transponder should be switched off unless the yacht is either aware of military forces in their vicinity, or is under attack. Use of AIS should be verified when possible through contact with MSCHOA for the latest advice. A 406 EPIRB or PLB will quickly draw attention to you but remember these are emergency devices intended specifically for saving life. An SART will show a signal on any nearby marine radar which may include that of pirates.
It is legitimate to call "mayday" if under attack (VHF or HF DSC, VHF 16 or 8, Sat-C or any other means). For an early warning call discreet use of a satellite phone to one of the numbers in para 3 above may be the best option. When in transit a radar transceiver should be used in the normal way. A radar target enhancer (RTE) provides an apparently large echo and should be switched off unless there is danger of collision. The possibility of an HF communications facility for yachts in the region is under discussion.

8 Preparations. Ensure that all systems (in particular the engine) are in good shape, radios and satphones are working properly, that you have plenty of fuel and the ship's batteries are in good shape. Be prepared to motor or motor-sail at your maximum speed for the entire transit of the IRTC. Carry additional supplies (particularly water purification, medical supplies and vitamin supplements) in the event that you are unfortunate enough to be pirated.

8.1 Split up money into different caches keep electronic copies of your passport etc. on Yahoo- or Google-type accounts with spurious names - if your original papers are lost you can access the copies from any police station or internet café consider carrying only copies (not originals) of essential documents on the boat, consider having two passports (a legitimate exercise for e.g. business travellers), wear a cheap watch, have an old mobile phone, keep only old (out of date) credit cards in your wallet (if ashore) wear only such clothing that you can afford to lose before entering a dangerous area study FCO advice on conduct if you are taken hostage advise your next of kin if you are going into a dangerous area so they are prepared to deal with matters if the worst happens – they should know in advance which authorities to talk to, etc.

9 Pirates operate from very small craft, which limits their operation to moderate weather conditions. While no statistics exist, it is likely to be difficult to operate these small craft in sea states 3 and above though operation in higher sea states cannot be ruled out. Pirates are less likely to launch attacks in the dark and merchant ships try to pass through the area between 47E and 49E in the IRTC during the hours of darkness for this reason. Even during the day, the typical pirate's visual horizon is less than five miles; he will see a merchantman long before he sees a yacht.

10.1 In a typical pirate attack small high speed (up to 25knot) open boats deploy from a mother ship, often a pirated fishing vessel or dhow. Commonly two or more of these small high speed open boats are used in attacks, often approaching from either quarter of the intended target. Be aware that perfectly legitimate tuna fishermen often employ similar tactics when chasing fish.
It can be very hard to differentiate between a genuine fisherman and a prospective pirate; in general, the crew of a fishing boat will have 'all eyes' trained on their elusive target; in a pirate boat, the 'gunmen' may remain hidden.

11 Despite the odds being uneven, it is worth making a risk assessment in advance of a transit and making sure everyone on board (including new crew) has thought through and agreed how they will respond. Guidance on what to do in the event of an attack is at para 13.

Thorough mental preparation is essential – think through all the scenarios. Continuous vigilance and an early call to the authorities if in doubt, is recommended as the arrival of military units (by sea or air) or a VHF call to a warship (even if you cannot see a warship) may cause an impending attack to be called off.
If you can delay the pirates from boarding by even 15 minutes, it may give the warships time to react. The time between first sighting a pirate and the commencement of an attack could be as little as 5 minutes.
When making a routine call on VHF, do not give your Posn in Lat and Long, unless you are absolutely certain that the warship is close enough to be able to assist you, or you are making a May Day call. The risk is that in reporting what turns out to be a false alarm, you could alert other skiffs of your position and excite their interest in you.

12 Under Attack. A vessel is recommended to: make a mayday call report immediately to UKMTO Dubai by telephone if possible on +971 50552 3215 – please make sure you know your position. If possible, the call to UKMTO Dubai should be followed by a call to MSCHOA, and MARLO Bahrain (who focus on US-flagged vessels).

13 Pirates on Board
Stay calm - attackers are likely to be excitable and nervous - you will think more clearly and your conduct may also calm them – do not make sudden movements Stay together as far as it is practicable to do so Offer no resistance,
Cooperate with the pirates
Do not use firearms, even if available – the risk of escalation is significant.
Do not use flash photography, which may be mistaken for muzzle flashes by the pirates or by any military force sent to assist
Do not use flares or other pyrotechnics as weapons against pirates.
In the event that military personnel take action on board the vessel, unless otherwise directed all crewmembers should keep low to the deck, cover their head with both hands (always ensuring that both hands are empty and visible). Be prepared to answer questions on identity and status as military personnel will need to differentiate quickly between crew and pirates.

14 Follow-up Reports should be sent to MSCHOA who will advise on information needed.

ISAF acknowledges with appreciation assistance in preparing these guidelines, from MSCHOA, UKMTO

Yachting Guidance

In view of the recent escalation in piratical attacks in the area of the Southern Red Sea, Gulf o Aden and Indian Ocean, and the consequent very high risk, the essential advice is not to ente this area. However a yacht which, despite this advice, decides on such a passage is recommended to make contact in advance with the naval authorities and to rend the ISAF Warning Notice. The Warning Notice is a joint production of MSC(HOA) and ISAF under the auspices of the **ISAF International Regulations Commission.**

The International Regulations Commission has been established and appointed by the ISAF Executive Committee in accordance with Regulation 41 to provide advice on matters related to the regulation of recreational boats or craft by government actions or otherwise.

One of the aims of the International Regulations Commission is to "monitor any legislation or actions by international or national institutions and national Governments or other similar bodies which affect the navigation, manning, construction, equipment, safety and use of recreational craft or the environment and take (in conjunction with National Authorities and other bodies representative of the users of all types of recreational craft) appropriate action in regard thereto".

MSC(HOA) aims to provide a service to mariners in the Gulf of Aden, the Somali Basin and off the Horn of Africa. It is a Coordination Centre dedicated to safeguarding legitimate freedom of navigation in the light of increasing risks of pirate attack against merchant shipping in the region, in support of the UN Security Council's Resolutions (UNSCR) 1814, 1816 and 1838.

Click here to download a copy of the ISAF Warning Notice.
Click here to download a one page ISAF flyer.

If you are due to travel the area of high threat, please inform MSC(HOA) by emailing **postmaster@mschoa.org**, with the subject lin 'Yacht Vessel Movement'.

ISAF Cruising microsite - **www.sailing.org/cruising**

Also, **Grail Solutions** has a very good guide called Grail Guide to Anti-Piracy available at www.grail.co.za

GRAIL

From the IMB website: Advice to Masters

General advice to Masters transiting thru / calling at ports of piratical / armed robbery:
The best form of defence is to ensure that a threat of an attack is detected at an early stage - hence a proper all round lookout using all available means is of vital importance.
In most of the incidents as soon as the pirates / armed robbers know that they have been spotted they will abandon the attack

- Follow company and ship specific procedures
- Follow advice in IMO circular MSC.1/Circ.1334 (23 June 2009)

  In Addition:
- Be aware of the sea areas / and ports affected by piracy and armed robbery (the PRC broadcasts regularly to ships in the IOR and AOR regions. See Live Piracy Map)
- Brief crew: Inform them to be vigilant and inform bridge / duty officer of anything suspicious / not normal
- The attitude "this will not happen to me" should be strongly discouraged
- Conduct a drill prior to entering a high risk area. This will ensure emergency communication procedures are tested and contact information is readily available
- Ensure all crew are fully aware of alarm procedures and muster stations
- Keeping in mind multinational crews - all internal communications should be carried out in the working language of the ship
- Master to adjust ship routines prior to entering high risk area to ensure well rested and additional crew on watch at all times
- Ensure blind spots and dark areas are lit up (ensure lighting does not hamper safe navigation and lookout duties)
- Ensure the deck watch work in pairs at all times
- Ensure rounds on deck are taken at irregular intervals
- Reporting from deck to bridge at regular intervals (if reporting not done it is the first indication that there is something wrong)
- Be especially vigilant during watch change over times
- Keeping in mind watchkeepers on deck - access into the accommodation, bridge, steering gear room and engine room to be secured.
- Rig and pressurise fire hoses prior to entry into high risk areas
- Depending on ship type - engine room to be manned
- Keep security / urgency messages ready to transmit while transiting high-risk areas
- Keep important telephone numbers ready at hand especially those of CSO, Flag State and PRC
- Have a designated communications officer (this will ensure the master is able to concentrate and deal with the situation rather than being distracted by communication procedures)
- If applicable keep emergency checklist ready at hand
- Test the SSAS as required by manufacturer
- It is vital that all incidents are reported to the PRC (actual, attempted, suspicious)
- Masters should evaluate the situation and report the incident as soon as it develops, this will ensure that there is time for assistance to be made available. In the event of attack:

1. Raise Alarm, Muster Crew
2. Increase Speed
3. Commence evasive manoeuvres and use bow wave and stern wash to prevent the small boats approaching close to the ship
4. Identify the mother vessel and move away from it (if there is one)
5. Steam away from land
6. Head into the sea and swell: this makes it more difficult for boats to come alongside
7. In the event of pirates boarding and gaining control of the bridge it is essential to try to keep calm and follow the instructions of the pirates in order to avoid physical confrontation. The master should at all times endeavour to keep the vessel in command to prevent collision / grounding etc.

Another publication is the OCIMF guide below, albeit super seceded by BMP4:

ANNEX D

A chronological list of most ships and vessels that have been taken by Somali pirates since 2008.

With help from Ironsides Associates, one of Great Britain's leading security companies.
Every care has been taken to use photographs that are not copyrighted or require permission to print.

	Vessel Hijacked	Name	Date	Location	Crew	Release date and Ransom Paid	Remarks
1		Yemeni Fishing Trawler hijacked and used as Mother Ship for Le PONANT attack	28th March	50nm off the coast of Yemen	28	The pirates spotted the Le PONANT on the 4th April and deserted the Yemeni trawler for greater rewards.	9 Pirates attacked. They commandeered the trawler and sailed towards Somalia. A further 7 pirates boarded the trawler and headed back out to sea to act as Mothership.
2		French cruise yacht Le PONANT	4th April		30	Crew released 11th April. Reported $2 Million ransom paid by yacht owner.	10 Pirates. French Special forces launched raid to capture pirates on Somali territory. Six alleged pirates captured and are currently under arrest in France.
3		Spanish Fishing Boat Playa de Bakio	20th April		28	Crew released on 26th April.$1.2 Million ransom demand was paid.	Various reports on numbers of pirates range from 4 to 10.
4		Dubai -flagged ship Al-Khaleech entering Bossaso Port.	21st April	approx 11 Nm from Bossaso	16	Somali rescue mission launched 22nd April 08.	Reports state 7 pirates were arrested. 3 pirates and a Somali soldier were wounded in the assault. The captured pirates were transported out of Bossaso.
5		MV Amiya Scan Cargo dismantled oil platform	25th May		9	Released on 25 June 08. $1.1 million ransom paid	Held for 31 days.
6		MV Arean	28th May			Crew released 24th June 08. $1 Million ransom paid.	
7		MV Lehmann Timber	28th May		15	$750,000 ransom paid.	Crew held for 41 days,

8		Yacht Rockall	23rd June		2	Freed on 8th Aug 08. $1.4 Million ransom paid.	German couple freed after 46 days in captivity.
9		MV Stellis Maris Panama flag. Cargo of Lead-zinc ore.	20th July		20	$2 Million paid. Released 26th Sept	
10		Tug Yenagoa Ocean	4th Aug 08		9	Ransom paid $43,000 Released 6th June 09	Was being used as a "Mother ship" Original ransom demand $1 Million. Held hostage for 10 months
11		Thor Star Thailand flag Cargo Timber	12th Aug		28	Ransom paid $?? Released in Oct 08	
12		MISC Bunga Metali Dua Malaysian Flag Cargo Palm Oil	19th Aug		39	Released 30th Sept $2 Million Ransom paid.	Reports that a Filipino crew member was killed during the assault by a ricochet bullet.
13		BBC Trinidad Antigua flag	21st Aug		13	Released 12th Sept $1.1 million ransom paid.	
14		MV Iran Deyanat	21st Aug		29	$2 Million ransom demanded.	Iranian vessel with strange chemicals aboard. Reports of pirates dying aboard.
15		Irene Panama Flag	21st Aug		25	Released on 10th Oct 08 $1.6 Million ransom paid	
16		Bunga Melati 5 Cargo Petrochemical s	29th Aug		41	Released on 27th Sept 08 $2 Million ransom paid	

25		MT Action	10th Oct	20	Released on ??th Nov 08 $ ransom paid no details	Details that 3 crew members were killed emerged but no details how the deaths happened.
26		MV African Sanderling Panama Flag	14th Oct	21	Released on 11th Jan 09 $ ransom paid no details	
27		MV Yasa Nesliahan Turkish	29th Oct	20	Released on 6th Jan 09 $ ransom paid no details	
28		MV CEC Future	7th Nov		Released on 15th Jan 09 $ ransom paid no details	
29		MT Stolt Strength	10th Nov	21	Released on 15th Mar 09 $2.2 ransom potentially paid. not confirmed	Attacked once again on 31 May 09 in the Bab al Mendeb Straits.
30		MV Karagol Turkish Flag	12th Nov	14	Released on 13th Jan 09 $ ransom paid no details	Hijacked 16Nm off the coast of Yemen
31		MT Sirius Star Liberian Flag	15th Nov	25	Released on 9th Jan 09 $3.5 ransom was reported to be paid	Ransom demand started at $25 Million, ship taked 450Nm offshore. Ransom money parachuted to the Pirates.
32		FV Tianyu No.8 Chineese Trawler	15th Nov	24	Released on 8th Feb 09 $1.7 ransom was reported to be paid	Hijacked in Kenyan Waters
33		MV Chemstar Venus Panama Flag	15th Nov	23	Released on 12th Feb 09 $?? ransom was reported to be paid	Hijacked 96Nm East of the GOA.

34		MV Delight Hong Kong Flag	18th Nov		25	Released on 9th Jan 09 $ ransom paid no details	
35		FV Ekawatnava 5	18th Nov		14		Sunk by the INS Tabar. Only 1 crew member survived.
36		MT Biscaglia Liberian Flag	28th Nov		27	Released on 23rd Jan 09 ransom thought to be $1 Million	3 Security guards jumped overboard.
37		Yemeni Fishing Vessel, Fallujah	10th Dec	Mait Area near the Port of Aden	12	Released on ??th Jan 09 no details of ransom	reported that 7 men escaped in a small craft
38		Yemeni Fishing Vessel, Kana	10th Dec	Mait Area near the Port of Aden	10	Released on ??th Jan 09 no details of ransom	
39	No Image Available	Masindra 7, Tug and barge	16th Dec		11	Released on 01st Aug 09 no details of ransom	Malaysian owned. Held captive for 8 months
40	No Image Available	Yacht	16th Dec		2		
41		Bosphorus Prodigy	16th Dec		11	Released on 3rd Feb 09 no details of ransom	

42		MV Blue Star St Kitts-Nevis Flag	1st Jan 09	50nm off the coast of Yemen, Al Mukala	28	Released on 6th Feb 09 $1 Million ransom paid	Cargo - 6000 tons of fertiliser
43		MV Sea Princess II Panama Flag	2nd Jan 09		15	Released on 26th Apr 09 $?? ransom paid	
44		MV Longchamp Bahamas Flag	29th Jan 09		13	Released on 28th Mar 09 no details of ransom paid	German LPG tanker. Ranson demands had been for $6.25 million
45		MV Saldanha Maltese Flag	22nd Feb 09		22		Coal as cargo
46		MV Titan St Vincent & Grenadines Flag	19th Mar 09	GOA	24	Released on 15th Apr 09 no details of ransom	Cargo of Steel. Vessel belongs to Albamare City Shipping company.
47	No Image Available	Yacht Serenity	15-Mar-09	Indian Ocean	3	Released on 13th Sep 09 no ransom paid- Prisoner exchange instead	Delivery crew from Seychelles. Left Mahe on 28th Feb heading to Madagascar. Crew swapped for 23 Pirates held captive in the Seychelles.
48		MT Bow Asir Bahamas Flag	?? Mar 09	Indian Ocean	27	Released on 11th Apr 09 ransom paid $2.4 million	Norwegian owned, operated by Salhus shipping
49		MT Napayiya Panama Flag	25-Mar-09	Indian Ocean	19		Greek owned Lotus shipping

50		Indian Ocean Explorer Seychelle Flag	28-Mar-09	Indian Ocean	7	Released on 22nd June 09 ransom paid $450,000	Crew flown home, vessel reportedly set on fire as the ransom was insufficient (TBC)
51		MV Hansa Stavanger	04-Apr-09	Indian Ocean	19	Released on 04th Aug 09 ransom paid $2.7 Million	German container vessel. Captured 400Nm off Somalia between the Seychelles and Kenya
52		Yacht Tanit	04-Apr-09	Indian Ocean	5	Rescued by French Commandos.	French yacht with two couples and a 3 year old boy. French commandos free yacht but father of child killed in assult.
53		Malaspina Castle	06-Apr-09	Indian Ocean	24	Released on 9th May 09 $2 million ransom paid	British owned ship.
54		MV Win Far 161 Taiwan fishing trawler	06-Apr-09	Indian Ocean	30	Released on 11th Feb 10 $?? ransom paid	Reported to being used as a Mother ship? Aug 09. 3 crew members reported to be killed during captivity.
55		Maersk Alabama	08-Apr-09	Indian Ocean	21	Crew overpowered pirates but the Captain was taken into a liferaft by the pirates for 5 days.	1 pirate captured and 3 killed by US snipers.
56		Momtaz 1 & Ahmad Samra Egyptian fishing vessels	01-Apr-09	Gulf of Aden	34	Escaped 13 Aug 09. Managed to break free killing 2 Pirates and capturing 8 more.	The crews sailed the vessels back to Egypt to a heros reception with 8 Pirates locked in a compartment onboard to face trial in Egypt.
57		MV Buccaneer Tug	11-Apr-09	Gulf of Aden	16	Released on 09th Aug 09 ransom paid $4 Million????	Italian owned Tug towing 2 barges. Belongs to Micoperi Marine Contractors
58		MV Irene EM St Vincent and Grenadines Flag	13-Apr-09	Gulf of Aden	22	Released on 13th Sep 09 $2 million ransom paid	Greek owned

59		MV Sea Horse Togo Flag	14-Apr-09			Released on 17th Apr 09 no details of ransom	
60		MV Pompei Belgium Flag	14-Apr-09	Near Seychelles	10	Released on 28 Jun 09 $3.5 million ransom paid	Only 93 miles North of the Seychelles
61		MV Ariana Maltese Flag	02-May-09	Near Seychelles	24	Released on 10 Dec 09 $2.8 million ransom	Greek owned by All Oceans shipping
62		MV Victoria Antigua & Barbuda Flag	05-May-09		11	Released 18th July 09 $1.8 million ransom paid	German owned
63		MV Marathon	07-May-09			Released on ?? June 09 $1.3 million ransom paid	One crew member killed and one wounded. Details immerged after the vessel was released.
64		MV Charelle	12-Jun-09	Gulf of Oman	10	Released on 4th Dec 09 $?? million ransom paid	Vessel owned by Tarmstedt International
65		MV Horizon 1 Turkish Flag	08-Jul-09	BAM	23	Released on 6th Oct 09 $1.5 million ransom paid	Hijacked at 05.30hrs. Female Officer onboard
66		Spanish Fishing Boat Alakrana	02-Oct-09	Indian Ocean	36	Released on 16th Nov 09 $3.5 million ransom paid	
67		MV Kota Wajar	15-Oct-09	Indian Ocean	21	Released on 28th Dec 09 $4 million ransom paid	Singapore container ship

50		Indian Ocean Explorer Seychelle Flag	28-Mar-09	Indian Ocean	7	Released on 22nd June 09 ransom paid $450,000	Crew flown home, vessel reportedly set on fire as the ransom was insufficient (TBC)
51		MV Hansa Stavanger	04-Apr-09	Indian Ocean	19	Released on 04th Aug 09 ransom paid $2.7 Million	German container vessel. Captured 400Nm off Somalia between the Seychelles and Kenya
52		Yacht Tanit	04-Apr-09	Indian Ocean	5	Rescued by French Commandos.	French yacht with two couples and a 3 year old boy. French commandos free yacht but father of child killed in assult.
53		Malaspina Castle	06-Apr-09	Indian Ocean	24	Released on 9th May 09 $2 million ransom paid	British owned ship.
54		MV Win Far 161 Taiwan fishing trawler	06-Apr-09	Indian Ocean	30	Released on 11th Feb 10 $?? ransom paid	Reported to being used as a Mother ship? Aug 09. 3 crew members reported to be killed during captivity.
55		Maersk Alabama	08-Apr-09	Indian Ocean	21	Crew overpowered pirates but the Captain was taken into a liferaft by the pirates for 5 days.	1 pirate captured and 3 killed by US snipers.
56		Momtaz 1 & Ahmad Samra Egyptian fishing vessels	01-Apr-09	Gulf of Aden	34	Escaped 13 Aug 09. Managed to break free killing 2 Pirates and capturing 8 more.	The crews sailed the vessels back to Egypt to a heros reception with 8 Pirates locked in a compartment onboard to face trial in Egypt.
57		MV Buccaneer Tug	11-Apr-09	Gulf of Aden	16	Released on 09th Aug 09 ransom paid $4 Million????	Italian owned Tug towing 2 barges. Belongs to Micoperi Marine Contractors
58		MV Irene EM St Vincent and Grenadines Flag	13-Apr-09	Gulf of Aden	22	Released on 13th Sep 09 $2 million ransom paid	Greek owned

76		MT Maran Centaurus Greek Tanker	29-Nov-09	Indian Ocean	28	Released on 17th Jan 10 $7 million ransom paid	Maran Tankers Management run the tanker
77	No Image Available	Indian Dhow	12-Dec-09	Indian Ocean		Released on 1st Feb 10 No ransom paid	Pirates set the dhow free.
78		St James Park UK Flagged Tanker	29-Dec-09	GOA	26	Released on ???? 10 Ransom paid ??	Zodiac Maritime Agencies owned
79		MV Navios Apollon Panama Flag	29-Dec-09	240Nm off the Seychelles	19	Released on 1st Mar 10 Ransom paid ??	Cargo of Fertilizer - Greek owned
80		MV Asian Glory British Flag	01-Jan-10	Somali Basin	25	Released on 11 June 10 Ransom paid ??	Zodiac Maritime Agencies owned
81		MT Pramoni Singapore Flag	01-Jan-10	GOA	24	Released on 26 Feb 10 Ransom paid ??	GBLT Shipmanagment Pte. Owned
82		MV Rim North Korean Flag	03-Feb-10	GOA	17	Escaped	Lybian Company
83		MT Al Nisr Al Saudi Saudi Arabia Flag	02-Mar-10	GOA	14	Released on 8th December 10 Ransom paid ??	
84		MT UBT Ocean Marshall Islands Flag	05-Mar-10	Off Madagascar	21	Released on 20 July 10 Ransom paid ??	Norweigan owned by Brovigtank

85	No Image Available	FV Scoba	05-Mar-10		16	Released on 20 July 10 Ransom paid ??	Spanish owned Fishing vessel
86		MV Friga Malta Flagged	23-Mar-10	Off Indian Coast	21	Released on 28 July 10 Ransom paid ??	Furthest hijack so far
87		MV Iceberg UAE Flag	29-Mar-10	Gulf of Aden	24		10Nm outside Aden Port - 1 x crew member died during captivety
88		7 Indian Fishing Dhows	30-Mar-10	Somali Basin	100		Believed to be used as Mother ships
89		VLCC Samho Dream Marshall Islands Flag	04-Apr-10	Indian Ocean	24	Released on 06 Nov 10 $9.6 Million Ransom paid	South Korean owned carrying $170 million worth of crude oil. Hijacked 970 NM East of the Somali Coastline
90		MV RAK Africana St Vincent & Grenadines Flag	11-Apr-10	280Nm West of the Seycheles	15	Released on 9 Mar 11 $3 million Ransom paid	Owned by Seychelles RAK Africana Shipping Ltd
91		3 Thai Fishing Vessels Prantalay 11,12 & 14	17-Apr-10		77	Prantalay 14 sunk by Indian Navy while being used as a mothership. Prantalay 11 captured by Indian Navy whilst being used as a mothership. Jan 11	FV Prantalay 11 - crew 26 FV Prantalay 12 - crew 25 FV Prantalay 14 - crew 26
92		MV Voc Daisy Panama Flag	21-Apr-10		21	Released on Ransom paid	Hijacked 190 Nm South East of Salalah, Oman
93		MT Marida Marguerite	08-May-10	Gulf of Aden	22	Released on 28 Dec 10 $5.5million Ransom paid	German operated

94		MV Panega	11-May-10	Gulf of Aden	15		100 Nm East of Aden
95		MV Eleni P Liberia Flag	12-May-10	Gulf of Aden	24		Greek Owned
96		QSM Dubai	02-Jun-10	Gulf of Aden	24		Inside the IRTC
97		MV Gloden Blessing Singapore Flag	28-Jun-10	Gulf of Aden	19	Released on 06 Nov 10 Ransom paid ??	
98		MT Motivator Marshall Islands Flag	04-Jul-10	Red Sea - Bab Al Mandeb		Released on 16 Jan 11 Ransom paid $4.5 million	
99		MV Suez Panama Flag	02-Aug-10	GOA-IRTC	23	Released on 12 Jun 11 Ransom paid $2.1 million	
100		MV Syria Star St Vincent & Grenadines Flag	04-Aug-10	GOA-IRTC	24	Released on 06 Aug 10 No Ransom paid ??	Released after 24 hours. A couple of crew members required medical attention.
101		MV Lugela Panama Flag	25-Sep-10	900Nm East of Eyl	12	Released on 26 Sept 10 No Ransom paid.	Crew held up in Citidel. Pirates gave up and left the ship after 24 hours.

102		MV Olib G Malta Flag	08-Sep-10		15		
103		MT Asphalt Venture Panama Flag	28-Sep-10		15	Released on 15 Apr 11 Ransom paid $3.5 million	
104		FV Golden Wave Korean Flag	10-Oct-10		43	Released on 9 Feb 11 No Ransom paid.	
105		MV IZUMI Panama Flag	10-Oct-10		20	Released on 25 Feb 11 Ransom paid $4.5 million	Japanese owned
106		MT York Singapore Flag	23-Oct-10	98Nm East of Mombassa	17	Released on 10 Mar 11 Ransom paid $4.5 million	
107		MT POLAR Panama Flag	30-Oct-10	East of Scotra	24	Released on 26 Aug 11 Ransom paid $7.7 million	9 crew on board with 20 passengers
108		SY Choizil	31-Oct-10	Off Island of Lamu	3		2 crew taken hostage but the Captain Peter Eldridge escaped by refusing to leave with the pirates.
109		MV ALY ZOULFECAR Comorian Flag	03-Nov-10	Between Comoros and Dar es Salam	29		9 crew on board with 20 passengers
110		Yuan Xiang Panama Flag	11-Nov-10		29	Released on 8 Jun 11 Ransom paid $2.1 million	Chinese owned

111		MV Hannibal II Panama Flag	11-Nov-10	Somali Basin	31	Released on 17 Mar 11 Ransom paid $2 million	Used as a Mothership while held captive
112		MV Albedo Malaysian Flag	26-Nov-10	900 East of Mogadishu	23		
113		MV Jahan Moni Bangladesh Flag	05-Dec-10		16	Released on 13 Mar 11 Ransom paid $4 million	
114		MV Panama Liberia Flag	10-Dec-10	80Nm East of Tanzania - Mozambique border	23	Released on 6 Sep 11 Ransom paid $7 million	
115		MV Renuar Panama Flag	11-Dec-10		24	Released on 23 Apr 11 Ransom paid $6 million	
116		MV Orna Panama Flag	20-Dec-10		19		
117		MV Thor Nexus Thailand Flag	25-Dec-10	Gulf of Oman	22	Released on 12 Apr 11 Ransom paid $5 million	
118		MV EMS River Antigua & Barbuda Flag	27-Dec-10	175Nm from Salalah	8	Released on 1 Mar 11 Ransom paid $3 million	German owned
119		MV Blida Algerian Flag	01-Jan-11	150Nm SE from Salalah	27	Released on 3 Nov 11 Ransom paid $2.6 million	
120		MV Leopard Danish Flag	12-Jan-11		6		Vessel hijacked but crew removed to a mothership and Leopard disguarded.

121		MV Samho Jewelry Panama Flag	15-Jan-11		21	Released by South Korean SF Troops.	8 Pirates killed and ?? Captured alive. Captain shot but survived.
122		MV Eagle Cyprus Flag	17-Jan-11		24	Released on 24 Sep 11 Ransom paid $6 million	
123		MV Hoang Son Sun Mongolian Flag	19-Jan-11		24	Released on 16 Sep 11 Ransom paid $4.5 million	
124		MV Khalled Muhieddine	20-Jan-11		25	Released on 26 May 11 Ransom paid $2.5 million	
125		MV Blida. Algerian Flag	01-Jan-11	Off the Omani Coast in the Aranbian Sea 15:45N - 055:52E	17	03/11/2011	Cargo Cement
126		Al Musa, Indian Flag	09-Jan-11	hijacked in position 17:42N - 057:17E, around 152nm ENE of Salalah, Oman at approximately 0400	14	24/01/2011	Dhow
127		Denmark MV Leopard (Cargo ship)	12-Jan-2011	Leopard was attacked evening 12 JAN in Arabian Sea off Oman	?	Abandoned 13 JAN	6 (Carrying Arms & Ammo) Crew hijacked . EUNAVFOR believes Somali pirates transferred all 6 crew to Taiwanese F/V Shiuh Fu No. 1, itself captured by pirates 25 DEC 2010.
128		Malta (South Korea) Samho Jewelry (Tanker)	15-Jan-11	The 11,500-tonne Samho Jewelry had been carrying chemicals from the United Arab Emirates	21	Rescued by Korean Navy 21/01/2011	When South Korean commandos stormed the South Korean Hyundai Samho Heavy Industries ship, eight pirates were killed and none of the captured crew died.
129		Cyprus-flagged bulk carrier, MV Eagle	17-Jan-11	Attacked and hijacked in position 13:17N - 061:42E, around 417nm E of Socotra Isalnd,	24	Vessel released 19-08-2011	Six armed pirates used guns and RPG hijacking the ship and taking 24 crew hostage.

130		(Japan) MV Bunga Laurel (Cargo ship	20-Jan-11	300 miles southeast of the port of Muscat, Oman, near the Gulf of Aden	23	Rescued by Malaysian Navy 20/01/2011	(Lubricating oil & Ethylene dichloride) 2011-01-20 When Malaysian Navy SEALs stormed the Japanese-owned cargo ship, seven pirates were captured and none of the hostages were harmed.
131		Mongolia (Vietnam) MV Hoang Son Sun (Cargo ship)	21-Jan-11	Attacked approximately 520 nautical miles south east of the port of Omani capital Muscat.	24	Released 2011-09-15 US$4.5 million	Carrying cattle feed
132		MV Beluga Nomination German Flag	24-Jan-11		13	Released on 13 Apr 11 Ransom paid $5 million	A hostage release was attempted, one or two pirates died, one crew member was killed by pirates and two escaped in a lifeboat. Pirates breached the citadel using the ship's gas cutting torch.
133		MV New York Star (Tanker) Liberia (Germany)	28-Jan-11	Attacked about 523nm NW of Kavaratti island	?	29-Jan-11	Pirates boarded, but were unable to break into the citadel to seize control of the ship, and had fled by the time naval forces arrived.
134		CMA CGM Verdi	29-Jan-11		?	Attempted attack prevented by the Indian Navy and the Indian Coast Guard 2011-01-29 unknown 2011-01-29	An Indian Coast Guard aircraft while responding to a distress call from the CMA CGM Verdi, located two skiffs attempting a piracy attack near Lakshadweep. . The Indian Navy deployed the INS Cankarso which located and engaged the mothership 100 nautical miles north of the Minicoy island. 10 pirates were killed while 15 were apprehended and 20 Thai and Myanmarese fishermen being held aboard the ship as hostages were rescued.
135		Italy MV Savina Caylyn (Oil Tanker)	08-Feb-11	Savina Caylyn was captured in the Arabian Sea off the coast of Yemen, other reports say 500 miles west of India	22	Somali pirates say a ransom of 11.5 million dollars was paid in 2 installments	The 22 crew members, composed of 17 Indians and five Italians, had spent 11 months in captivity
136		Greece MV Irene SL (VLCC)	09-Feb-11	Irene SL was captured in the Arabian Sea off the coast of Oman.	25	Released 08-Apr-2011 13.5 Million $	The MV IRENE SL has a dead weight of 319,247 tonnes and is Greek flagged and owned. The vessel was on its way to Suez from Fujairah when it was attacked. At present there is no further information on the attack. She has a crew of 25 (7 Greek, 1 Georgian and 17 Filipinos).

137		MV Sinin Malta (Bulk Carrier)	12-Feb-11	MV Sinin was captured in the Arabian Sea off the coast of Oman.	23	Released 2011-08-14 Ransom not known	The Malta flagged ship was confirmed to have been captured at around 350 nautical miles east of Masirah, an island off the Oman's coast. The European Union Naval Force has been monitoring the situation of the vessel since February this year.
138		S/V Quest (Private yacht) United States	18-Feb-11	The private yacht Quest was captured in the Indian Ocean en route from India to Oman.	4	After hearing gunfire early on the morning of February 22, U.S. forces boarded the vessel and discovered that the crew of four had been killed. Pirates engaged the U.S. forces; two pirates were killed and 13 were detained; the bodies of two additional pirates were found	All crewmembers killed, vessel boarded by U.S. forces, pirates killed/detained 22-Feb-2011
139		S/V ING (Private yacht) Denmark	24-Feb-11	600 miles east of the Somali coast	5 passengers: 2 adults, 3 children	Released Aug-2011	A Danish yacht with four adults and three children aged 12 to 16 on board was captured on February 24.They were released after six months in captivity. Government troops tried unsuccessfully to free them on March 10.
140		MV Guanabara (Oil tanker) Bahamas (Japan)	03-Mar-11	Guanabara was captured in the Indian Ocean 328 nautical miles (607 km; 377 mi) southeast of Oman.	24	05/03/2011	The ship was boarded by a team from the USS Bulkeley who detained four pirates. The pirates were tried in Japan.
141		India INS Kalpeni, INS Khukri (P49) (Car Nicobar class fast attack craft, Khukri class corvette)	12-Mar-11	In the Arabian sea about 600 nautical miles west of India	13?	12-Mar-11	While intercepting the captured Spanish-owned vessel, FV Vega 5, two Indian Navy corvettes, INS Kalpeni and INS Khukri were attacked by two pirate skiffs with firearms. During the exchange of fire, crewmembers went overboard while their vessel was being used as an attack base. They found 61 pirates on the captured vessel. Only 13 crewmembers from the FV Vega 5 were rescued.
142		Indonesia MV Sinar Kudus (Cargo ship)	16/03/2011	m.v. Sinar Kudus was pirated approximately 320 nautical miles North East of the island of Socotra in the Somali Basin	20	Released by Indonesian Navy and Indonesian Special force (Secured) unknown 2011-05-01 US$9 million	The Sinar Kudus was carrying 8,300 tons of ferronickel from Aneka Tambang company worth about US$225 million at the current price. a $4.5 million US dollar ransom after the ship had been held for 46 days.The Indonesian government had sent three ships, one aircraft and one helicopter with 800 soldiers deployed including 300 special forces. Although the government chose not to take a military option as it would have put the safety of the hostages in danger, 4 pirates were killed when the last batch of pirates were leaving the ship
143		Italy MV Rosalia D'Amato (bulk carrier)	21/04/2011	In the early morning of April 21, 2011, the 74,500-ton MV Rosalia D' Amato was captured 350NM southeast of Salalah, Oman while on its way from Paranagua, Brazil to Bandar Imam Khomeini, Iran.	21 (6 Italians, 15 Filipinos)	On November 25, 2011, all crew members were released and are reportedly safe and in healthy condition	Ransom unknown

144		Singapore MT Gemini (Oil tanker)	Captured 2011-04-30	The 20,989 tonne, Singapore flagged and owned vessel was on its way to Mombasa (Kenya) from Kuala Tanjung (Malaysia) when it was attacked and hijacked.	25 (4 Korean, 13 Indonesians, 3 Mayanmar, 5 Chinese)	2011-12-03 $10 million	Carrying crude palm oil. On December 2, 2011, the pirates released 21 crewmembers (along with the ship), while keeping 4 Korean crewmembers captive until the South Korean government pays them a ransom of US$ 4 million. The 21 crewmembers and vessel were released after a ransom of US$ 6 million was paid
145		Panama (China) MV Full City (Bulk carrier)	05/05/2011	Chinese Sea Rescue Center revealed that the ship was hijacked in the Arabian Sea, exactly is 800 km off the coast city of Mumbai,India.	24 crew members from China	05/05/2011	The United Kingdom Maritime Trade Organization received a distress call from Full City and passed the information to U.S. Fifth Fleet. An Indian Navy Tu-142 maritime patrol aircraft located the Full City, and while the Turkish frigate Giresun boarded the bulk carrier, the U.S. guided-missile cruiser Bunker Hill intercepted a dhow believed to be the 'mothership' for the pirate attack. Bunker Hill's VBSS boarding party seized weapons and other equipment commonly used in piracy, and the boarding party also sank a small skiff being towed by the dhow. Giresun's boarding party found the Full City's crew safe and in control of their ship.
146		Denmark HDMS Esbern Snare (L17) (Absalon class flexible support ship)	12/05/2011	During a patrol along the Somali coast	16	12/05/2011	During a patrol along the Somali coast on the morning of Thursday May 12, the Esbern Snare was approached by a pirate mother ship. When the Esbern Snare tried to stop the boat using loudspeaker, it opened fire which was immediately returned. Shortly after the exchange of fire, several weapons were thrown overboard and there were signs of surrender. 4 pirates were killed and buried while 10 others were wounded. None of the 16 hostages and no crew members of the Esbern Snare were wounded. The 24 pirates aboard the warship are awaiting trial and the navy has taken control of the mother ship
147		Marshall Islands (India) MT Fairchem Bogey (Oil Tanker) (Oil)	20/08/2011	5 nautical miles from Salalah, Oman	21 Indian	Released 2011-01-12 $8 Million	Fairchem Bogey was in anchorage at the port limit of 5 nautical miles from Salalah, Oman, waiting for berthing instructions when hijacked in the early morning hours of August 20, 2011. This was the first time that a ship was hijacked within the port limits and taken away while the port authorities could do nothing but watch
148		France S/V Tribal Kat (Private yacht)	10/09/2011	...	2 sailors (none) 1 fatality, 1 sailor rescued,	Responding to a Mayday call, the FGS Bayern found the catamaran without crew on September 10. The SPS Galicia later stopped and sank a skiff that was holding one of the sailors; the other one had been killed.	Seven alleged pirates were arrested.
149		Taiwan MV Chin Yi Wen (Fishing vessel)	2011-11-02	The vessel was captured by pirates off the east coast of Africa and took control of the vessel	28 sailors	02/11/2011	Ship recovered by crew: 3 sailors injured, pirates thrown overboard about 2011-11-02 The crew, consisted of several Vietnamese war veterans, was kept hostage but able to fight back throwing the pirates into the ocean and recovering the vessel. (Good effort!!)
150		Iran FV Al-Khaliil (fishing vessel)	2012-01-25	Close to Puntland, engaged in legal fishing	19	Ship and crew released 2012-02-07	An Iranian fishing dhow was captured on 25 January 2012 while a security team on board was asleep. Although Somali sources reported that international maritime forces had eventually freed the dhow and seized the kidnappers, the Operation Atalanta website did not confirm such an action. According to Somalia Report the pirates released ship and crew without ransom on 7 February 2012

151		Panama (United Arab Emirates) MV Leila (RORO)	16/02/2012	in the eastern approach to the Gulf of Aden	24	As of 16 March 2012 a ransom of USD 2 million has been demanded by the pirates but the ship owners reject any payments and have stopped further negotiations. In the maintime the vessel is being used as a pirate mothershi	According to conflicting reports, a Panama-flagged roll-on/roll-off vessel owned by a Dubai-based company was captured either on 16 or 21 February 2012 in the eastern approach to the Gulf of Aden. Initially the Maritime Security Centre – Horn of Africa reported a German tanker to be the victim of this attack.
152		Panama (United Arab Emirates) MT Royal Grace (oil tanker)	Seized, contact lost 2012-03-02 21°27′N 62°37′1″E	East of Oman.	22(India, Pakistan, Nigeria)	....	A Panama-flagged oil tanker owned by a UAE-based company was hijacked on 2 March 2012, east of Oman.
153		Bolivia (Iran) MV Eglantine (Bulk carrier) (Brazilian sugar)	26/03/2012	Somali pirates captured a Bolivian-flagged ship in the Maldives' Exclusive Economical Zone 193 miles off Hoarafushi island.	23	2012-04-02 released by Iranian Navy Commandos	Ship and crew freed by iranian navy commando 2012-03-26 The vessel which was bound for Iran with a cargo of sugar from Brazil is owned by an Iranian company. It was the first such incident to take place directly in Maldive waters

This list will be updated in the second edition

Thank you for purchasing this book. It is hoped that it has been a valuable and collective source of information. It has taken over four years to research and put together; information in this book is not a duplicate of BMP4; it is the author's own knowledge and experience that has created this definitive guide. When we started there were no Best Management Practice guides only the Marisec's guide against robbery and thieves. However, every month the situation changes, new products and situations come along and older products or tactics become obsolete. We at IMAAG have ensured that all the information is as relevant and as up to date as possible at the time of printing. We are aware that by the time you have read this book, some things may have changed; this is inevitable and will be updated in future with newer editions. This guide has been written in order to help mariners to stay as safe as possible.

Products can only be improved by feedback and IMAAG will strive to make this publication as perfect as possible. As time moves on the book must be updated with a new edition. If the reader has any feedback please email info@imaag.co.uk we will address your comments as soon as we can.

Similarly any queries such as bulk orders, change of language or advertisement of products, services or otherwise please contact the office on the above email address.

Notes